D1682888

ASSESSMENT AND ACCESS

SUNY Series, United States Hispanic Studies
Gary D. Keller, Editor

ASSESSMENT AND ACCESS

Hispanics in Higher Education

Edited by
Gary D. Keller,
James R. Deneen,
and Rafael J. Magallán

State University of New York Press

Published by
State University of New York Press, Albany

© 1991 State University of New York

All rights reserved

Printed in the United States of America

No part of this book may be used or reproduced
in any manner whatsoever without written permission
except in the case of brief quotations embodied in
critical articles and reviews.

For information, address State University of New York
Press, State University Plaza, Albany, N.Y., 12246

Production by Diane Ganeles
Marketing by Theresa A. Swierzowski

Library of Congress Cataloging-in-Publication Data

Assessment and access : Hispanics in higher education / edited by Gary
  D. Keller, James R. Deneen, and Rafael J. Magallán.
        p.   cm.—(SUNY series, United States Hispanic studies)
    Includes bibliographical references and index.
    ISBN 0-7914-0779-9 (alk. paper).—ISBN 0-7914-0780-2 (pbk. :
  alk. paper)
       1. Hispanic Americans—Education (Higher)   2. College entrance
    achievement tests—United States.   I. Keller, Gary D.   II. Deneen,
    James R.   III. Magallán, Rafael J., 1945–   .   IV. Series.
    LC2670.6.A87 1991
    378.1'98'298073—dc20   90-48185
                                                                                                              CIP

10 9 8 7 6 5 4 3 2 1

Contents

Foreword   vii

Introduction: Advances in Assessment and the Potential for Increasing the Number of Hispanics in Higher Education
   Gary D. Keller   1

> *Part I: Hispanic Access: The Factors of Culture, Language, Reasoning Skills, and Heuristic Knowledge*

1. Cultural and Linguistic Influences on Latino Testing
   José P. Mestre and James M. Royer   39

2. Diagnostic Testing of Reasoning Skills
   Richard P. Durán   67

3. Assessing Heuristic Knowledge to Enhance College Students' Success
   Raymond V. Padilla   81

> *Part II: Opening New Dimensions and Investigating Advances in Test Construction on Behalf of Hispanics*

4. Time as a Factor in the Cognitive Test Performance of Latino College Students
   María Magdalena Llabre   95

5. Factors Related to Differential Item Functioning for Hispanic Examinees on the Scholastic Aptitude Test
   Alicia P. Schmitt and Neil J. Dorans   105

6. Equating the Scores of the College Board *Prueba de Aptitud Académica* and the College Board *Scholastic Aptitude Test*
   William H. Angoff and Linda L. Cook   133

Part III: Testing and Hispanic Access to the Teaching Profession

7. Competency Testing and Latino Student Access to the Teaching Profession: An Overview of Issues
   Richard R. Valencia and Sofía Aburto   167

8. Research Directions and Practical Strategies in Teacher Testing and Assessment: Implications for Improving Latino Access to Teaching
   Richard R. Valencia and Sofía Aburto   195

Part IV: TestSkills: The First Course of Instruction Directed Specifically to the Improvement of the Test-Taking of Hispanics

9. The Development of *TestSkills:* A Test Familiarization Kit on the PSAT/NMSQT for Hispanic Students
   Lorraine Gaire   235

10. A Preliminary Evaluation of *TestSkills*: A Kit to Prepare Hispanic Students for the PSAT/NMSQT
    María Pennock-Román, Donald E. Powers, and Monte Pérez   243

Notes   265

References   275

Appendix A. The Teacher/Counselor Questionnaire   313

Appendix B. The Student Questionnaire   317

Contributors   321

Index   325

Foreword

~ ~ ~ ~

Gregory R. Anrig and Donald M. Stewart

The underrepresentation of Hispanic students in higher education and the obstacles that continue to hinder their access have been painfully and thoroughly documented, as in an earlier conference and book on Latino college students (Olivas 1986). Thus, we willingly agreed when Gary D. Keller and Rafael J. Magallán proposed that the College Board and Educational Testing Service join with the Hispanic Higher Education Coalition to sponsor a conference to examine solutions as well as ongoing barriers to improving the access of Hispanic students to higher education.

The Conference presenters edited their papers, and this book contains the results of their work. Two papers by Gaire and Pennock-Román deal with the development and evaluation of a program, TestSkills, that directly addresses problems of understanding and motivation that many Hispanic students experience as they approach college admissions tests.

The chapters by Llabre and Angoff and Cook speak to difficulties inherent in assessment instruments taken by students with differing linguistic and cultural backgrounds. Schmitt and Dorans discuss the differential functioning of certain kinds of test items for Hispanics and other students; they also explore implications both for education and assessment practices of differences in test performance. Valencia and Aburto focus on the role of assessment in recruiting and credentialing Hispanic students for the teaching profession. Their chapters show the importance of developing forms of assessment that permit Hispanic students to demonstrate the competencies they can bring to teaching.

In the papers of Durán, Padilla, and Mestre and Royer we see evidence of creative efforts to develop modes of assessment that fairly assess Hispanic students' abilities and positively influence their learning.

Gregory R. Anrig and Donald M. Stewart

We share with the chapter authors the conviction that Hispanic students must be brought into higher education in numbers that far better represent their share of the national population. We have no illusions that the major causes of their current underrepresentation—poverty and inadequate school preparation—will be easily overcome. However, these obstacles are being addressed in projects that the College Board and ETS are sponsoring around the country. One such project, PRIME, in Arizona, has staff and other resources from our organizations that are aiding minority groups in informing parents and students about financial aid for college. In other PRIME projects, we are helping to increase substantially the number of Hispanic high school students who take college level courses and systematically prepare for college admissions examinations.

We at the College Board and ETS share with our colleagues in the Hispanic community a strong desire to make assessment a part of the solution to the underrepresentation of Hispanic students obtaining a college education and to improve educational opportunity for all students. These chapters show some of the current efforts to understand the special difficulties Hispanic students experience as they consider their options, and to link assessment with greater learning and improved access to higher education.

Introduction: Advances in Assessment and the Potential for Increasing the Number of Hispanics in Higher Education

~ ~ ~ ~

Gary D. Keller

Assessment and Access: Hispanics in Higher Education is the first book of its kind. It explores for the purpose of increasing Hispanic access to higher education a variety of developments in educational assessment and test familiarization, both theoretical and practical. At the same time, the book aspires to present a balanced treatment of the relevant issues by a distinguished group of specialists, both within the higher education community and at the Educational Testing Service which is making history in this area.

I have several purposes in writing this introductory essay. First, I would like to make some observations about the value of educational aptitude and achievement tests, including standardized tests for the United States Hispanic community. My view, which is not necessarily shared by everyone, is that tests such as the Scholastic Aptitude Test (SAT), the American College Test (ACT), the Advanced Placement (AP), the Graduate Record Examination (GRE), and others have been moderately helpful in expanding access for U.S. Hispanics to college, and have the potential for being more so in the future. (I limit my affirmation to educational tests; the issues that revolve around other assessments, particularly mental tests, are more complex and the value for Hispanic Americans of these measures is more dubious.[1]) Indeed, part of the rationale of this book is to explore the ways that tests can be better constructed, more effectively implemented, and better prepared for by Hispanic youths so that their aptitudes will be more accurately measured.

A second goal of this essay is to recount, for the first time, some of the historical background that has led to the creation of *Assessment and Access,* focusing particularly on the earlier interactions and subsequent formal partnership between the Hispanic Higher Education Coalition/ Hispanic Association of Colleges and Universities (HHEC/HACU), the College Board, and the Educational Testing Service (ETS). I think readers will find this an interesting story with instructive implications for what can be accomplished on behalf of minority students and parents when minority organizations work in partnership with educational organizations toward common, well-defined goals. In turn this historical background should provide some additional understanding of the papers that constitute this book. Closely related to the purpose of providing background information, I will also review some of the most productive or potentially productive projects in the present or recent past that have utilized assessment instruments as an integral component of their academic initiatives. The projects or products that I have in mind include the Garfield High School initiatives in East Los Angeles; Options for Excellence in San Antonio; the Hispanic Student Success Program (HSSP) in San Antonio, Northern New Mexico, and other sites; Project PRIME (Project to Improve Minority Education) in Arizona; *TestSkills;* and *Sí Se Puede: Information on Academic Planning and Obtaining Financial Aid.*

My final goal is to introduce briefly each of the component chapters of this book, situating them within the context of the ongoing assessment challenges that confront the U.S. Hispanic community that will have been developed earlier in the background section of this essay.

Some Perspectives on the Relative Value of the Tests for Hispanic Access

Let me begin by facing straight on a critical issue: Can tests and other evaluation instruments help Hispanic Americans to enter higher education in greater numbers? Presumably if they can in general, then advances in evaluation, particularly if it is focused on the challenges that confront the accurate testing of Hispanics, will help our community even more effectively.

The answer to the question that is posed is not self-evident, certainly not for the U.S. Hispanic community and probably not for other minorities underrepresented in higher education as well. We all know, of course, that the attitudes of some segments of the U.S. Hispanic community toward published tests, particularly standardized tests, have sometimes not been positive. Many Hispanics have been and continue to be opposed to standardized tests, and most particularly to I.Q. tests, as unfair to Hispanic children. This is not peculiar to the Hispanic community; a similar situation obtains with respect to other minority groups who are underrepresented in education, the professions, or privileged positions in society. Moreover, many teachers, parents, and school administrators find the current tests unsatisfactory as measures of a student's educational progress. In the past, groups such as the National Education Association and others have called for a moratorium of testing. Finally, because the overall record of higher education is not a compelling one for U.S. Hispanics and other underrepresented minorities, by reflection it is not possible to make a compelling argument for the efficacy of aptitude and achievement assessments on behalf of our students. In fact, over the past fifteen years, using our own past level of performance as our standard (even though this performance certainly is modest), while in absolute numbers we have seen very small increases in some academic areas, we have been going in reverse direction when we measure the *percentage* of Hispanics, Blacks, and Native Americans who graduate from high school from the total adolescent cohort eligible to do so and when we measure the *percentage* of high school graduates from these underrepresented minorities who in fact go on to college.

My view is that standardized tests are not the major cause of this retrogression that began about 1975. We should point to much broader problems, particularly the waning of commitments over the last decade among educators and our society at large to equality of educational access, to affirmative action, and to providing effective financial aid for economically disadvantaged students. Nevertheless, in contrast to the post-World War II period, where it can be argued that admissions tests went hand in hand with greatly expanded college attendance, the phenomenon of smaller percentages of underrepresented minorities entering college since the middle 1970s does diminish the argument that can be made in favor of educational admissions tests. Moreover, in various state legislatures of state capitols there have been movements over the past few years, as part of the goal of establishing more rigorous admission standards for public higher education, to overrely on admission test scores for that purpose (Breland, 1985; Goetz and Johnson, 1985). Gregory R. Anrig, president of the ETS, has been one of the first to caution against this overreliance and to call for a balanced use of multiple predictors in determining college admissions. (Anrig, 1985,6). In addition, Anrig has cited a Committee of Ability Testing of the National Academy of Sciences that observed,"a policy decision to base an admissions program strictly on ranking applicants in order of their expected success will tend to screen out minority candidates . . . " (Wigdor and Garner, 1982, 196). The committee judged that the goal of admissions decisions "should be to effect a delicate balance among the principles of selecting applicants who are likely to succeed in the program, of recognizing excellence and of increasing the presence of identifiable underrepresented subpopulations . . . '' (Wigdor and Garner, 1982, 196).

The observations of the Committee on Ability Testing are especially important in light of Richard Durán's subsequent study (1983) which reviewed a considerable amount of data and arrived at the conclusion that both high school grades and admission test scores were not as good predictors of U.S. Hispanics' college grades as they were of White non-Hispanics' college grades. Durán concludes that "admissions officers ought to rely critically on the overall profile of Hispanic students in making admissions decisions. The results of studies reviewed here suggest that admissions personnel need to be provided with a broader range of information on Hispanics' background, language, and culture in weighing admissions decisions" (Durán, 1983, 105).

On the one hand we are faced with the skepticism about some tests and opposition to others by many U.S. Hispanics; the poor record of higher education since 1975 for underrepresented minorities, which in turn impinges against our making a strong argument for tests expanding Hispanic American access during these years; the movements such as those at the state level, to overrely on or use tests inappropriately supposedly to make educational standards more rigorous; and finally, the current conclusion based on the best data available that high school grade point averages and admission test scores do not predict academic aptitudes as accurately for Hispanics as for majority students. What arguments countervail these factors that argue against or at least mitigate the conclusions that tests can help more U.S. Hispanics enter college and that better tests and better test preparation can be even more effective?

I believe that a number of strong arguments can be brought in favor of the use of test for enhancing Hispanic education. Moreover, the potential for improving existing test construction and the technology of test administration, if realized, can further increase Hispanic access. Finally, I believe the pro-tests arguments outweigh the contrary, as substantive as the latter are.

While one sector of the U.S. Hispanic community either is afraid, skeptical about, or opposed to standardized tests, that is not necessarily the most knowledgeable sector. There now exists for the first time a significant group of U.S. Hispanic professionals who are either experts or quite knowledgeable about issues of educational assessment as they impact our community and who have a constructive, critical, but essentially positive outlook, especially in the longer term, about tests for our students. Some among the professional Hispanic community have argued that certain tests such as the SAT, GRE, LSAT, GMAT, and others do in fact significantly underestimate the aptitudes of Hispanic students. We make this argument, however, not with the goal of doing away with tests, but improving them. Moreover, we have begun to use achievement tests such as the AP in distinctive ways both to certify the academic performance of our students and to enhance their college admission possibilities.

Part of the challenge in making standardized tests more accurate predictors of our community's aptitudes and achievements is to address the ignorance and anxiety about tests that affects our community at each level, from the students who take them through parents, teachers, and administrators who have uninformed attitudes about them. Reflexive kinds of anxiety, blanket opposition, and ignorance about the issues do not help us. There is much to be vigilant about with respect to the construction, administration, and interpretation of tests with respect to Hispanic Americans. However, a level of sophisticated knowledge about the tests is necessary to put them to optimal use or to combat their misuse or their faulty construction if they are doing our community a disservice. We have witnessed, for example, in the area of language assessment for the purpose of bilingual education, a relatively sophisticated and positive use of tests that has helped Hispanic students (see Keller, 1982).

While it is true that the percentage of U.S. Hispanics who graduate from high school and go on to college currently is in decline when compared with 1975, and that in some states there are initiatives to overvalue test scores in a way that excludes minorities, it is also documentable that in the history of U.S. higher education, tests have been used more often to open doors rather than close them. The direction—inclusion or exclusion—is determined not by the tests but by the establishment of educational policies for their use. For example, around the turn of the century, the College Board was formed to administer a uniform system of college entrance examinations to address the then chaotic situation where each college had its own subject matter examinations. This development permitted the enrollment of students from secondary schools that were unknown to the colleges which in turn enabled the latter to broaden their student bodies. During the post-World War II period, the use of admissions tests increased most dramatically precisely when quotas were eliminated or at least mitigated at private colleges, including the Ivy League; when public education greatly expanded; and when higher education opened for the first time in a genuine way to racial and ethnic minorities and to all socioeconomic levels. Although the early history of both the College Board and admissions tests was a checkered one, selective admissions to higher education was more a reflection of social class and economic status prior to the use of national admission tests than it has been since. Before the establishment of standardized tests, admissions officers at the elitist colleges of that period relied primarily on grades and recommendations for students from a small group of well-known, elitist, college preparatory schools. The introduction of standardized tests opened opportunities, modest at first, greater in the post-World War II period, for students from high schools without reputations among the selective colleges to provide a demonstration of their academic abilities and to be admitted.[2]

The broadening of opportunities for minorities and lower socioeconomic status students was greatly enhanced by the College Board in its role in advancing and developing, through the College Scholarship Service, the concept of awarding financial aid based on need. This has been an important factor in expanding access to college for low-income students. In recent years both the College Board and the ETS have launched a variety of talent-search, guidance, scholarship, diagnostic, instructional, and other projects or products on behalf of minority and other deserving students. Several of these projects are highlighted later in this essay and elsewhere in this book.

The tendency in some staes toward policies that overrely on tests is not an argument against tests themselves. Tests have been used productively in recent years, projects such as Options for Excellence, Hispanic Student Success Program, Project PRIME and the Garfield High School initiative have in one way or another used tests as an integral part of their educational activities with considerable success both from the perspective of performance and public recognition of the achievements of U.S. Hispanic students. Is it an exaggeration to view Jaime Escalante's and Henry Gradillas' use of the AP as a certifier of academic achievement, especially their decision to retest Hispanic students when their scores were challenged by the ETS, as the most inspiring educational and assessment phenomenon for Hispanics in the United States in recent memory? The developing potential for misuse of standardized tests at the state level requires better preparedness on the issues and political strength on the part of minorities to call into account and change bad policy. It should be noted that past studies (Hilton and Rhett, 1973) have shown that a very large majority of students intending to go to college do so and that in recent decades tests haven't held back students who have taken them and completed their applications. A study conducted for the American Council on Education found that 75% of freshmen were attending their first choice college and nearly 95% were attending their first or second choice college (Astin, King, and Richardson, 1978, 18). The irony should not be lost on the Hispanic and other minority communities that it is at the point when underrepresented minorities have become the majority in many major school systems that state officials have increased their concern about admission standards in public higher education. Minority groups must mobilize at the state levels to resist policies that will consciously or unwittingly reduce the commitment to minority students or reduce their presence on publicly funded college campuses.

That both high school grads and test scores do not measure Hispanics' aptitudes as accurately as they measure majority students' points also, in my mind, to necessary initiatives to improve education for Hispanic students and to improve standardized test measurement of our students. This is a problem *both* in education and its measurement. We know that our students are capable of achieving much more than what is asked for them in most of the schools that they attend. Durán's 1983 study suggests that interpretation. In addition, when we have established creative and distinctive programs for our students, such as some of those described later, the tests administered to those students have confirmed the reality of their high achievement, sometimes to the consternation of would-be nay-sayers. The tests need to be improved to assess more accurately U.S. Hispanics but even in their current state they have certified the achievements of students in East Los Angeles, in Greater San Antonio, and in Arizona.

I have reserved for last what in my mind are the stongest arguments for this book, for optimism, for the improvability of tests, and for their enhanced effectiveness in both measuring Hispanics and helping them go to college in higher numbers. These arguments revolve around the essential fact of assessment, that evaluation abhors a vacuum, around the scientific nature of standardized tests as compared to the alternatives of the past (quota systems, subjective appraisals often conducted by persons hostile to minorities), and by virtue of what the HHEC/HACU, ETS, and the College Board have been able to achieve in partnership thus far.

It is surprising that the arguments against tests by some educators are made in a sort of idealized context, a vacuum if you will. Standardized tests are a relatively new development, but evaluation of one type or another always has been with us. In arguing against tests it is essential to be cognizant of the alternatives. I belong to a group of Hispanic professionals— bilingual educators—who have been exposed to some of the alternatives. We frequently have seen the value of standardized and other "objective" tests (perhaps "machine scorable" is a more appropriate term for what in fact is currently meant by "objective") for bilingual education and the assessment of other than English language skills. During the Vietnam War while some young people were sailing up the Mekong River, I made my journey as a young educator up the Rio Grande or Río Bravo, depending on which side you view the river. To gloss Conrad and Coppola, there is a "heart of darkness" along that river as well. In south Texas and other places, I found egregious misplacements of Spanish-speaking students into classes for the "educable mentally retarded." These students were bright enough but not fluent in English, and teachers misplaced them wholesale on the basis of their own subjective, wrongheaded, and, given the system, unappealable appraisals. These experiences of subjective appraisals will haunt me to my last breath. They are countervailed, if such a thing is possible, by experiences I have had with the positive role of tests such as the Language Assessment Battery which measures fluency and dominance in English and Spanish and which was commissioned by the New York City Board of Education to implement the court-approved ASPIRA consent degree that permitted hundreds of thousands of children to receive bilingual education (Santiago, 1978 and 1986).

The point that needs to be reaffirmed is that in this world evaluation is constant and everpresent. People have been constantly appraising and sizing up each other from prehistory, and there is no likely end to this process. Those who wish to do away with more formal modes of testing in expectation that we will establish an idealized, test-free, and of course, less stressful society, are harboring ill-founded illusions. In a vacuum, evaluation will proceed on the basis of subjective opinions, often by people in power or privilege who harbor either negative stereotypes, or much worse, active, racially motivated hostility toward Hispanics and other minorities. It seems to me highly preferable that we rely on tests, including standardized tests, rather than subject our students to individual, subjective appraisals. Tests, no matter how flawed, at least have the positive features that they are the application of the social sciences, metrics, and education, and that they can be reviewed. Tests can be and usually are, as products of science, open to review, analysis, reasoned criticism, replication, analyses of their effectiveness through measurement of their reliability and validity, and above all, improvement through revision over the decades. In a world where assessment is both essential and unavoidable, I do not believe that the same positive features or levels of openness can be established for any alternatives to tests, including standardized tests.[3] Certainly subjective appraisals by experts or would-be experts can not be monitored or controlled with respect to underlying attitudes toward various minority groups such as U.S. Hispanics. When the Garfield incident attained national recognition many people locally and elsewhere did not believe that so many Hispanic students in a lower socioeconomic status environment and undistinguished school could take AP calculus and excel. It was the genius of Escalante and Gradillas that amidst the tension they took advantage of all that the tests had to offer. The retest procedure was incontrovertible and cast the all too human doubts to the winds.

Standardized tests are a new scientific development. They emerged, particularly at the national level, with the perceived need by the military to test potential recruits during World War I. These robust juveniles in the world of applied science have a long road to travel to maturity, but they are, in the main, improving. Moreover, the tests have built within them their own refining devices. Testmakers have the ability to measure the effective reliability and validity of the instruments that they have created. Because of this, tests improve with revision; over time each version or iteration usually becomes more accurate. Also, as some of the papers in this book suggest, tests can use developments in educational technology to their advantage. Testmakers can incorporate innovations in science, computerization, and educational delivery systems into new and possibly more effective assessment techniques.

An additional argument, as we shall see below, for the value of tests in the effort to increase Hispanic students on college campuses rests in the review of past and ongoing projects that have used them to effective purpose.

Historical Background and Review of Some Important Educational Access and Assessment Projects and Products

The issue of openness in relation to tests and the reporting of their results is not merely general or theoretical, but very germane to the developments that have led to the publishing of this book. This book is timely; actually it's a few decades overdue. It is timely because over the past ten or fifteen years there has accrued a sufficient number of researchers, a sufficient amount of research, and certainly a more than ample number of U.S. Hispanic students for the relevant issues to receive widespread attention. So: overdue, but timely, which is the way things work sometimes in science, but usually less well in less open systems. It has taken and continues to take a great deal of work, some of it adversarial, some cooperative, to convince educators generally and testmakers specifically, of the distinctiveness of the Hispanic American experience and of the reality of educational discrimination, test "error," and other forms of measurement inaccuracy. Part of the problem was that until the 1960s there were few Hispanic specialists in any field, much less psychometrics, statistics, educational assessment, and the like. We were victims with no voice to plead our oppression. Nevertheless, at first very gradually, and lately with vigor, we arrived, we documented, we drew our conclusions, and we promoted them with strength. This book is timely and assuredly not the last of its kind.

Beginning in 1979, as a result of the HHEC's involvement in test improvement issues, the Hispanic professional community began a process of interaction with testmakers, primarily the ETS and the College Board, and less so with the American College Testing Program. The relationship between Hispanic educators and researchers and the testmaking industry can be separated into two phases. The first phase occured between 1979 and 1983 and was of an informal nature. The second phase began in 1984 and continues through the present. In 1984, the HHEC, the College Board, and the ETS agreed to establish a formal partnership. The HHEC polled its organizational members on the priority issues which helped establish an agenda for the three organizations of both practical intervenionist projects and research studies. At the same time the College Board and the ETS established a yearly budget with which to work and the three organizations have been meeting periodically and completing projects ever since. The partnership has worked well and is likely to continue productively for the forseeable future.

Between 1979 and 1983 some of the achievements of the Hispanic community and the testmaking industry included the disclosure of test score distributions by race and ethnicity for most of the major tests; the hiring at the ETS of more U.S. Hispanic researchers and the expansion of research on educational and assessment topics important for U.S. Hispanics; the initiation in 1981 of the very successful Options for Excellence in Greater San Antonio; the publication of Richard Durán's seminal study (1983); and the sponsoring of research conferences, the most productive of which aided the completion of M. Olivas' *Latino College Students* (1986). Independently of other influences until the 1982 challenge by the ETS, it was also the period of academic achievement by increasingly larger numbers of Hispanic high school students at James A. Garfield High School in East Los Angeles.

The period from 1984 through the present has led to the establishment of Project 1000 to increase the number of Hispanic graduate students; the burgeoning influence of the Garfield phenomenon on Hispanic educators and its replication elsewhere; the production of *TestSkills* and *Sí Se Puede: Information on Academic Planning and Obtaining Finanical Aid;* the expansion of promising research in areas such as differential item functioning; the initiation of the Hispanic Student Success Program and Project PRIME; the beginning of the Consortium to Identify and Promote Hispanic Professionals; and the ETS- and College Board-sponsored conference and other forms of support that have led to the publication of this book.

The year 1979 is a critical one because the forces or factors that led to a productive collaboration between the Hispanic community and the testmaking industry coalesced during the heyday of what was then commonly called the "Truth-in-Testing" movement. As a result partially of earlier successes in consumer initiatives such as "truth in advertising" and "truth in lending" and spurred on by considerable dissatisfaction with the general way that such national tests as the SAT and ACT were being used, a vigorous initiative to reform tests or to eliminate them was undertaken in the late 1970s by a number of groups, perhaps the most prominent of which was Ralph Nader and his associates.

In 1979, the HHEC participated in the ongoing debate by providing testimony, which I prepared and delivered with my able colleague Dr. Alvin Rivera, with respect to bills H.R. 3564 and H.R. 4949 (Truth in Testing Act of 1979; The Educational Testing Act of 1979). At the time these bills, which did not pass Congress, were before the Subcommittee on Elementary, Secondary, and Vocational Education of the Committee on Education and Labor of the House of Representatives. The HHEC testimony was constructive: critical of some aspects of testmaking, administering, reporting, and interpreting that were prevalent at that time, but also supportive of the tests and cognizant of their value both generally and for Hispanic Americans. The interaction between the testing industry and the professional Hispanic community dates from that time.

The testimony that the HHEC gave on October 11, 1979, related to a number of issues that are just as relevant today as they were over a decade ago. For example, we pointed out that researchers had demonstrated how "the tests use ambiguities and misleading language in order to make their questions inappropriately difficult," although researchers had not yet reviewed the possible disproportionate effects of such factors on ethnolinguistic minorities including U.S. Hispanics. We called for research "to determine the effect of such artificial test language on minority linguistic and cultural groups." We urged that the testing community or industry consider "a possible interaction effect between artificially created, misleading English test language and the linguistic parameters of the U.S. Hispanic communities." (Keller, 1979, 829). We asked that the testing industry consider our view that a proportion of what standardized test purported to measure in the scholastic aptitudes of Hispanic students was merely "a subterraneous index" of purely linguistic or cultural peculiarites of various hispanic communities. Even the ETS appeared to recognize that issue, although they might have been more inspired by marketing than equity at the time, because they had established ten years earlier a Spanish analog of their GRE, not a translation but a test independently developed for Spanish-speaking students. That test, the Prueba de Aptitud para Estudios Graduatos (PAEG) as well as the Prueba de Aptitud Académica, were and still are used in Puerto Rico and parts of Latin America for measuring aptitudes. The first is used for admission for graduate study and for the study of law and the latter is analogous to the SAT.

The HHEC made another important suggestion: to control for the biases in the testing component by using additional norming procedures. Specifically, we proposed that "scoring be based on the achievement of a student using his or her language and culture groups as the norm or the control." It's a little hard to believe from the vantage point of 1990 (this disbelief in itself is a good index of the progress that can be made in a scientific domain such as testing) but at the time, the College Board, ETS, and ACT had refused to report test distribution scores by race and ethnicity much less to report individual scores by major discernible ethnolinguistic groups. The claim (made verbally but somewhat veiled in writing[4]) was that because minorities did much more poorly on the tests than majority students, that they wanted to "protect" minority students from the allegations of innate inferiority made by some researchers at the time. Some Hispanic educators ventured the opinion that the refusal to provide the data might also have to do with the fact that on the face of it, Hispanic and other minority students were receiving scores about two standard deviations below White students on the average and that this could cast doubt about the accuracy of the tests. In any event, the testmaker's posture was completely counterproductive. Instead of shielding minorities, those who would promote Social Darwinism or other claims for innate racial superiorities or inferiorities were in fact aided by the sense that the testing community had a grisly secret that it couldn't permit to see the light. As for researchers whose work could have benefited from scientific openness, they had to use a roundabout method of correlating test scores with race and ethnicity by estimating them from the relationship of scores and reported levels of income which was published.

The testimony of the HHEC concluded with an expression of support of the testing industry and of objective tests, including standardized tests, although at the same time it fully supported the movement toward more accountability in testing. "It is because the Hispanic educator probably more than any other minority group professional has been privy to the worst, most biased aspects of the testing process, as well as its potential for accurately assessing competencies and determining placement, that these suggestions are entered in the spirit of a thoroughgoing reform of a service that needs to regain public trust in order to continue to be productive and beneficial to society" (Keller, 1979, 837).

In reviewing the testimony and the suggestions that were offered at that time, I am struck by how much in the 1979 document has come to some degree of fruition in the twelve years that have transpired, and as a result finds consideration in *Assessment and Access: Hispanics in Higher Education*. Examples of what I am alluding to follow below. I should observe, however, that much of what has been accomplished reflects a response by the admissions testmakers to the general movement toward test reform on the part of powerful social forces, particularly consumer forces. Thus the HHEC testimony may have framed some of the issues of the time in a way that best described them for the U.S. Hispanic community, but it can not be claimed that the HHEC testimony or any one specific group initiative for that matter, actually caused certain broad test reforms. On the other hand, with the establishment of the informal collaboration beginning in the early 1980s and in 1984 became a formal partnership among the HHEC (which has recently affiliated with HACU), the ETS, and the College Board, some features of the HHEC program have been specifically implemented.

The HHEC had referred to the problem, particularly severe for Hispanic Americans, of the use of ambiguities and misleading language in tests and for the need to determine the effect of such artificial test language on minority linguistic and cultural groups. In December 1979 the ETS proposed and, after considerable review by the broad educational community, its Board of Trustees adopted, in October 1981, *Public Interest Principles for the Design and Use of Admissions Testing Programs.* These principles together with new *ETS Standards for Quality and Fairness* which were adopted at the same time, in my judgment, although some might disagree,[5] have helped considerably in meeting concerns about the design and use of standardized tests in admission to higher education. Among the commitments that were affirmed or, since they were already in effect, reaffirmed were: (1) publication of test content to a degree limited only by reasonable safeguards of efficiency, cost, quality, and the educational impact of the programs; (2) commitment to continue to maintain and strengthen credible procedures for detecting bias and eliminating it from the content of tests, while making such procedures visible to the public; (3) commitment to formulate, maintain, and publish widely principles of appropriate use of scores and other test information derived from testing programs and to be alert to and actively discourage misuse; (4) ensurance that operational forms of the test be independently reviewed before they are given and that the review include the appropriateness of the content of the test and in particular seek to detect and remove potential racial, cultural, or sex bias or other influences extrinsic to the characteristics, skills, or knowledge to be measured.

At the same time the ETS Board of Trustees formalized its support of the principle of openness in admissions testing. Gregory Anrig, who had just arrived at the ETS at the time from his former position as commissioner of education for the Commonwealth of Massachusetts, pointed out in testimony to Congress on November 4, 1981, that the real issue was not "truth" but openness in testing (Anrig, 1981, 3). As I have stated above, I believe openness to be a key advantage of standardized tests, one that when realized helps genuinely to distinguish them as scientific pursuits. The term "truth," taken from earlier consumer initiatives, is much too extravagant a descriptor for what tests currently can provide, whether in terms of correlations between scores and subsequent performances, philosophic explanations of what the tests are actually measuring, or most anything else. The ETS board observed that openness should be construed very broadly and that therefore it involved more than mere test disclosure. Moreover, at the ETS the commitment to reviewing every test in order to eliminate references or language that might be stereotypical or objectionable to any subgroup was reaffirmed and strengthened. The methods have been formalized and currently are described as the "ETS Test Sensitivity Review Process" (Hunter and Slaughter, 1980). Finally, the ETS Board of Trustees committed to developing an industry-wide "Code of Fair Testing" for the development and administration of educational testing nationwide and recommended that this Code be based on the new standards then being developed by the American Psychological Association, the American Educational Research Association, and the National Council on Measurement in Education, and which were completed in 1985.

One strand of research that has emerged since 1979 and which has attained considerable prominence is called "differential analysis" or "differential item functioning." (In this volume, Alicia Pérez Schmitt and Neil J. Dorans review the emergence of this line of research from earlier research conducted since the 1950s.) While differential analysis research is relatively new, it is burgeoning and holds promise for addressing the specific problems of ambiguities, misleading language, cultural or linguistic bias, and the like to which HHEC has referred.

One of the most important developments for the U.S. Hispanic community to date with respect to testing error that may reflect linguistic and/or cultural bias has emerged from the work of Richard P. Durán, who at the time that he published *Hispanics' Education and Background: Predictors of College Achievement* (1983) was a research scientist at the ETS. Michael A. Olivas, who was one of the founding members of HHEC as well as the chairman of its board for several years (and who is currently a member of the board of trustee of the College Board) wrote the foreword to this book in which he observed, "Durán's review found that almost every study conducted showed noticeably lower correlations between standardized admissions tests and first-year college grades for Hispanos, relative to Anglos. Given the extraordinary high school attrition rate for Hispanic children and the likelihood that the very best survivors are taking tests, he is generous towards those who would employ these tests uncritically in admissions decisions" (vii).

In the test world just as in the art world provenance is important. Durán was writing as an ETS scientist and the book was published by the College Board.[6] The best of both worlds because both organizations took seriously the fact that the tests when combined with high school grades were "roughly nine percent less accurate than use of the same procedure to predict Whites' college grades'' (Durán, 1983, 102). As a result of the Durán study, the ETS has attempted to alert the educational community to this state of affairs and to admonish admissions decision-makers to take into account the findings of a less strong association for Hispanics compared to Whites (Anrig, 1985, 1986). The wheels grind very slowly in education, however, in fact much more slowly than in testmaking. It is incumbent on those who are interested in and knowledgeable of U.S. Hispanic academic and test-taking performance to continue to promote the distinctive situation of Hispanic students among the higher education community. This is precisely what Durán has done in his new role as professor and graduate officer at the University of California, Santa Barbara, where he has continued and expanded his research, particularly, as the paper in this volume bears out, to the assessment of cognitive skills.

A second suggestion made by the HHEC was to consider administration of Spanish language tests in addition to (and in a few distinctive cases instead of) their English analogues. The two Spanish language tests that are used very extensively in Puerto Rico and in other Spanish-speaking countries as well for assessment in higher education are the Prueba de Aptitud Académica (PAA), which is analogous to the SAT, and the Prueba de Aptitud para Estudios Graduados (PAEG), which is somewhat akin to the GRE as well as the LSAT. In chapter six, the paper by William H. Angoff and Linda L. Cook review the technical and statistical work that has been accomplished thus far in equating the PAA and the SAT. With respect to the PAEG, initiatives along the lines suggested by the HHEC have been established on an experiemental bases. A number of graduate institutions that are participating in *Project 1000: Recruiting, Admitting, and Graduating Additional U.S. Hispanic Students,* have agreed to accept scores on the PAEG and compare them with scores earned on the GRE, and of course with subsequent performance in graduate school. This experimental study only started in earnest in 1989, but since in a considerable number of cases we have found the PAEG scores to be much higher than the GRE scores, we look forward to deriving interesting and useful conclusions.

In 1979, the HHEC had suggested controlling the innacuracy in measuring Hispanics in the tests by reporting the scores that Hispanic students earn compared to other Hispancis (what we call the ''within ethnic'' score). We believed that this score could serve as an important supplement to the score that Hispanics earn with reference to the entire universe of test takers for a given administration. This is particularly the case since as Robert J. Solomon, then executive vice president at the ETS, pointed out that ''while scores for whites and disadvantaged minority groups overlap, a typical result is to find that only 10–20% of disadvantaged minority groups score above a point that is average for white (i.e., exceeded by 50% of whites)''

(Solomon, 1979, 9). The HHEC suggestion faced some rough sledding for several years. Solomon's posture was indicative of the way the testmaking community explained away this phenomenon, in addition, until 1981–82, to refusing to even publish the test score distributions by race and ethnicity.

> These differences will not surprise anyone familiar with the inequalities in the social, economic, and occupational spheres of American life. Although many special educational programs have been developed at the federal, state, and local levels to repair the effects of educational and social neglect, these programs and other measures cannot change so quickly what years of malpractice have perpetuated. . . . Nevertheless, the argument is made that tests of academic ability are biased because they represent middle class culture. These tests do reflect skills and knowledge considered important in the mainstream culture, in many jobs, and in higher education. But the fact that a test mirrors the common culture is a poor basis for calling the test biased. (Solomon, 1979, 9–10)

Solomon's traditional arguments asserting purely and strictly educational and other forms of "disadvantage" not withstanding, the more recent work of Durán and others who have shown that the tests are less predictive for subsequent Hispanic academic performance in college suggests that there is more (or rather less than mere mirrors of common culture in standardized tests: more error and less accuracy. A good place to review what many Hispanic researchers believe to be a prime source of test measurement error is the work of Mestre (1986a, 1986b, 1988) and Cocking and Mestre (1988). Mestre has shown that even in such supposed relatively culture-free test items involving solving mathematical problems, there are interactions between the language and the problem that can disproportionately affect minority students. Mestre concludes that: "Bilingual Hispanic students possessing the same level of mathematical and computatiuonal sophistication as their monolingual peers often solve word problems incorrectly. The pattern of error suggests the language deficiencies lead to misinterpretations of word problems; the resulting solutions may be incorrect, yet mathematically consistent with the student's interpretation of the problem statement" (Mestre, 1988, 202). Mestre has described this as the "Sorry, you have solved the wrong problem" effect, where a student's mathematics is sound, but his or her understanding of English (e.g., a double negative in Spanish is still a negative) leads to an incorrect setting up of the mathematical variables. It should be noted to the credit of both the ETS and the College Board that, at least to my knowledge, the expertise of researchers like Mestre, who in earlier decades might have seemed threatening to testmakers, is quickly introduced to the industry. Mestre is one of a group of consultants who helped design *Algebridge* and he also serves on the College Board's SAT Committee. Developed jointly by the ETS and the College Board, this is a very promising program of diagnostic testing and instruction that helps all students, but particularly minority students, prepare for high school algebra. Naturally, *Algebridge* takes into account the phenomena that José Mestre has been researching for the past ten years that can take place among Hispanic youth during the mathematics and science educational and assessment processes.

The first break in the posture of the testmaking community as the result of the HHEC's 1979 criticisms and suggestions came with the GRE Board's decision in 1981 to publish its test score distributions by race and ethnicity. The College Board and the American College Testing Program followed suit quickly with respect to the SAT and ACT, providing these data in their 1982 technical reports. It is now possible to determine the three separate "within ethnic" scores for Hispanics, specifically for Chicanos/Mexican-Americans, for Puerto Ricans, and for other Hispanics. For example, the within ethnic score for Chicanos/Mexican-Americans can be used to determine how well a Chicano student did compared to all other Chicano students who took the standardized test in a specific year, and likewise for Puerto Ricans and for other Hispanics. However, these distributions are available in technical reports and are not widely reviewed, except through Project 1000 which makes the distributions available for optional use by the participating graduate institutions. Project 1000 funded, among others, by the Carnegie Corporation, the Pew Charitable Trusts, and the Alfred P. Sloan Foundation is an attempt to recruit an additional 1,000 U.S. Hispanic students into graduate school. The Project uses and is tracking the validity of an extensive number of nontraditional predictors of aptitude for graduate study. These include the within ethnic score, performance on the PAEG or the TOEFL when students have taken these examinations, and a variety of personal qualities and skills. The ETS, the GRE Board, the Graduate and Professional School Financial Aid Service, and the Council of Graduate Schools, as well as dozens of graduate schools and close to 200 primarily undergraduate institutions and other educational organizations are supporting or participating in this project.

It is clear that using the within ethnic score as a supplement to the customary score has great potential as a corrective for test content error (as documented by researchers such as Durán and Mestre) and therefore as a mechanism to enable large increases in the number of Hispanic students who may be admitted into college. One way to appreciate the underrepresentation of U.S. Hispanic students in graduate programs is by reviewing the numbers of Chicanos and Puerto Ricans taking the GRE, which in itself is a necessary precondition in order to be considered for admission to virtually every selective graduate school in the United States. The 1988 ETS summary report indicates that only 2,226 Mexican-Americans/Chicanos and 1,661 Puerto Ricans actually took the GRE during the period in question. This is an exceedingly small number given the large Hispanic American population with baccalaureates who theoretically could take the exam. This figure contrasts mightily with 147,466 Whites who took the test during the same period.

Moreover, when we look at the range of scores that would be competitive for admission to selective graduate schools, the disproportion is accentuated to a deplorable level. Utilizing Table 62 of the 1988 ETS summary report, let us hypothecally consider a 550 on the GRE verbal section to be a competitive, although not outstanding score. A 550 represents approximately the sixty-second percentile for White, and in absolute numbers that represents approximately 56,000 White test-takers in 1988. But for Mexican-Americans and Puerto Ricans, respectively, that score of 550 represents approximately the eighty-fifth and the ninety-second percentile. Seen in absolute numbers, approximately 334 Mexican-Americans and approximately 133 Puerto Ricans competed with approximately 56,000 Whites with test scores of 550 or better in the 1986–87 academic year for the seats available in selective graduate schools. I have used the GRE verbal as a point of comparison for the sake of simplicity. Comparable results are obtained in comparing the GRE Quantitative or analytic. The fact that only about 467 Chicanos and Puerto Ricans obtained a 550 on the verbal (which itself is not an outstanding score, if we were to evaluate 650 or higher the number is reduced to about 130 Chicanos and Puerto Ricans combined) is cause for despair for ever increasing significantly the number of Hispanics who enter selective graduate schools if we are to rely on the usual test score interpretation and if additional measures and forms of evidence for validating the graduate school potential of U.S. Hispanics cannot be identified.

Merely the validation of the within ethnic group test scores has important implications for Hispanic access. If selective institutions were to look at, say, the top 30% of U.S. Hispanics as being within admisssion range, the pool of 1988 GRE test-takers to be so considered would have numbered about 667 Mexican-Americans and 500 Puerto Ricans, for a total potential pool of 1,167 applicants. That is possibly double what the effective pool with genuine admissability was in 1988. Thus, permitting the top 30% of U.S. Hispanics with respect to their within ethnic GRE score to be closely reviewed for possible admission into graduate programs could more than double the Hispanic American cohort.

However, to actually achieve this potential it will be necessary, just as in the case of Durán's finding, to achieve wider understanding among college admission officers of the value of the within ethnic score as well as concrete utilization of it as a supplement in the admissions process.

The most productive of the research conferences before the establishment of the formal partnership between the HHEC, the College Board, and the ETS, was the Latino College Students Conference, jointly sponsored in 1983 by the ETS and the Institute for Higher Education Law and Governance, University of Houston. This conference was valuable in the process of producing the book, *Latino College Students* (Olivas, 1986), another volume that is the first, but hopefully not the last, of its kind. The book, primarily inspired by Olivas' energies and prowess as a researcher, also emerged partially out of the HHEC's involvement with the testing industry. It is a seminal work, establishing the outlines of a theoretical framework for research on Latino college students as well as a detailed treatment through a series of papers on three broad areas: the transition from high school to college; Hispanic student achievement; and economics and stratification. *Latino College Students* is the model on which the present volume is based, although the former is a much broader treatment of issues affecting Hispanic students than the more circumscribed *Assessment and Access*. *Latino College Students* features research studies by several people who have worked at ETS including, Richard P. Durán, Vilma Ortiz, and María Pennock-Román as well as by other important researchers who have worked in the area of assessment: José P. Mestre and Richard R. Verdugo. *Latino College Students* has been influential over the last five years in establishing a better understanding of the Latino college student experience and it has helped inspire additional, at times broad, coverage within the higher education community of topics relevant to our community. A notable example of such coverage was the special issue of *Change: The Magazine of Higher Learning* (1988) that contained a special report on Hispanics in the academy. It is worth noting that the special issue listed in a section entitled "programs that work" several which feature the use of assessment instruments in a key way including Options for Excellence, Project 1000, Hispanic Student Success Program, and the National Hispanic Scholar Award Program.

Books like *Latino College Students* and hopefully the present volume, because they are ground-breaking, have a special historical importance for the U.S. Hispanic community. Arturo Madrid, in his foreword to Olivas' book, expresses this fact most poignantly:

> Our history, or that part of it within the American community, has all too frequently been one of inability to speak up, to speak out, or to speak at all on the issues that concern us. Specifically, our exclusion from the institutional life of American society and from the forums it provides

has kept us from being heard, even when our voices have been loud and our concerns compelling. Denied access to power, especially the power to define, we have had to suffer in silence the denial, distortion, and trivialization of our historical experience. . . . Nowhere have we felt the burden of institutional oppression nor the weight of responsibility more heavily than in education. This supposedly enlightened institution is seemingly also one of the most retrogessive. The educational system continues to blame the victim for its own failures, rather than to adapt its methods and policies to the differing populations and changing circumstances with which it is constantly confronted. Thus, the 1983 Conference on Latino College Students was a signal event, as is this volume of essays issuing therefrom: signal in its focus; signal in its range; signal in its depth. (Madrid, 1986, ix)

And then there was Garfield High School! Jaime Escalante, Henry Gradillas, and Benjamín Jiménez. And Options for Excellence! J. Quentin Jones, Joe Arriaga, George H. Hanford, and Henry G. Cisneros. About Garfield High School, I am reminded of what the character of the French scientist said, played by the late Francois Truffaut in *Close Encounters of the Third Kind* of a no more miraculous event, the apparition of people from around the country to meet with benevolent extraterrestrials: "It is an event sociological!" This extraordinary effort by a charismatic, Bolivian mathematics teacher, combining both advanced instruction and a high payoff for students in the form of evaluation of that instruction through the College Board's Advanced Placement Program (administered by the ETS) has captured the hearts of our society. The events sociological were evoked in a widely viewed film, *Stand and Deliver;* the achievements of Escalante were reflected in the latest presidential debates (Bush referred to Escalante as one of the nation's heroes in a famous moment during the Bush-Dukakis debates); and projects around the country have been set up which seek to replicate some of what teachers, Escalante, Jiménez, and others, together with then-prinicpal Henry Gradillas were able to accomplish at Garfield High School. These projects include two large scale demonstrations: the Hispanic Student Success Program, currently in San Antonio and beginning replication in Northern New Mexico and other sites as well; and Project PRIME (Project to Improve Minority Education) in the State of Arizona.

More than 95% of the Garfield student body is Latino. At least 80% of the students qualify for the federal free or reduced-price lunch program; in order to qualify the annual incomes of their families fall below $15,000 for a family of four (Mathews, 1988, 2). There are several extraordinary elements that need to be pointed out about the Garfield phenomenon in this introduction to a book on promoting Hispanic access through assessment procedures.

First, Garfield is one of the most successful and certainly the most nationally recognized educational events in the United States that combines instruction with assessment. Not too many major films have been made about calculus teachers slaying the dragon of ignorance with the sword of the calculus AP! The essence of Garfield—the stuff apparently that not only dreams are made of but educational movements and events sociological—is the combination of high-level instruction (college level taken during high school) for underrepresented minority students who at first blush and would not seem likely candidates for such instruction, together with the assessment for possible college credit of what was learned by means of the AP test.

Second, Garfield, because of its staying power (at Garfield teachers began offering AP courses in 1973; but things really got started in 1978 with the first Calculus AP course under Escalante), contradicts the notion that U.S. Hispanic students, including students from socioeconomically disadvantaged backgrounds, can not achieve academically along with the very best and the most privileged students. Garfield has increased the number of successful students each year in its AP Courses. The results based on the 1987 AP Calculus examinations show that Garfield gave the test to 129 students and that sixty-six of that group earned a score of three or better (five is the highest score, one the lowest). This was fourth in the nation among public schools, behind Alhambra High School (California) and the Stuyvesant and Bronx High Schools (competitive high schools in New York City where students are selected on the basis of an entrance examination) and ahead of such notable high schools as Evanston, Illinois; Gunn, Palo Alto; Scarsdale, New York; and Hunter College, New York, which also placed among the top fifteen public schools. A recent letter that I have received from Garfield documents that the school is still moving forward at an extraordinary rate. The 1989 AP test results document that 495 Garfield High School AP tests were administered in a variety of disciplines including Calculus AB and BC, Spanish language and literature, Computer Science, English Literature, Biology, American History, and Physics and that 317 test scores were three or above (Mroscak, 1990). Jay Mathews, who has written extensively about the Garfield pheonmenon, points out that this high school's record of performance tells us that educational disadvantages can be overcome. What is needed is to instill drive, high expectations, and the necessary esteem to propel a school and its students, teachers, parents, and community beyond the banal limits that too many of our educational institutions have assumed for themselves.

Finally, we have the events that propelled Garfield to the forefront in the first place: the challenge by the ETS on the grounds of suspicious similarities among tests of the 1982 cohort of Latino students who took the

Calculus AP. The story is well known, at least in the version evoked by *Stand and Deliver.* Mathews, (1988) book has the most detailed, reasoned, and up-to-date account. What is notable for us here, as Henry Gradillas put it during a 1989 AP Institute for Project PRIME, is that the ETS challenge propelled the Garfield initiative to the forefront of public recognition. Once that recognition was achieved, the ETS challenge (successfully resolved, I should note) became incidental to the national recognition and the AP certification of the fact that Garfield has been achieving extraordinary results. This performance was already remarkable in 1982, but it shot forward in the following years to achievement at a level rivaled by only a handful of public schools in the nation. The academic performance of our Hispanic students, certified by a nationally administered achievement test, is indisputable. At the time of the challenge many Hispanic youngsters, teachers, and parents at Garfield felt great pain and anguish. In the intervening years Henry Gradillas has judged the ETS challenge to have been a blessing in disguise. Garfield had been laboring in obscurity before 1982. After 1982 it has become known around the nation, has increased its academic performance manyfold, and has inspired projects of emulation and replication in many other sites. Clearly, what this nation needs, in addition to more Latino astronauts and rocket scientists, more Latino Nobel Laureates and civil rights attorneys, are more Latino or Latino-sympathetic high school teachers and Latino high school students who achieve spectacularly and whose achievement is certified by incontrovertible test results that will refute all those whose inclination is to underestimate or explain away our academic potentials.

But can Garfield-like results be accomplished without charismatic, incredibly committed visionaries such as Jaime Escalante and Henry Gradillas? To answer this all we need do is turn to Options of Excellence which in its own way is an educational and assessment achievement just as powerful as Garfield's, although not as nationally recognized. Designed in 1979–81 by the College Board with considerable involvement by then-president George Hanford at the request of the Minnie Stevens Piper Foundation and receiving considerable support from Henry Cisneros who had just assumed the mayoralty of San Antonio at the time that it was getting off the ground, Options was conducted in 1981–84 with some features similar to Garfield's although the initiatives were developed independently of each other.

Options for Excellence was a large-scale project not dependent on the name recognition of any one teacher or educator. At the heart of the strategy was the administration of two tests: the Preliminary Scholastic Aptitude Test/National Merit Scholarship Qualifying Test (PSAT/NMSQT) and the Advanced Placement Examination. The PSAT/NMSQT was used as a screening device to determine the eligibility of students to take AP courses. All of the schools in Greater San Antonio (Bexar County) participated and approximately 12,000 students, mostly eleventh graders, took the PSAT/NMSQT. This was about 75% of the eligible student body. Based on a liberal review of academic performance on the PSAT/NMSQT, students were permitted into AP high school courses and subsequently encouraged to take the AP examination. Before Options for Excellence, the AP program had relatively little play in Bexar County with its heavily minority student population and a set of modest educational expectations for that population. The total of AP examinations taken in the County in 1981, just before the program was implemented, was 246. In the last year of Options for Excellence as funded by the Piper Foundation, that number had risen to 877 (an increase of 357%). Similarly, at the higher education level in 1981, before the program, San Antonio institutions of higher education received 109 AP candidates. By 1984 the number had more than tripled to 399 AP candidates.

If Options for Excellence had only accomplished the changes described above in advanced placements, this would have been enough to qualify it as a highly successful project on behalf of both majority and minority students. However, these effects were only the tip of an iceberg. Remarkable transformations were obtained in the high schools in order to institutionalize the advanced placement program. There were thirty-seven participating high schools in sixteen school districts or systems, public, private, and parochial. In 1981, before the project, only fifteen of the thirty-seven high schools presented any AP candidates at all and, of those fifteen, the candidates that were presented were clustered in eight high schools. By 1984, of the thirty-seven high schools, thirty-six presented candidates and the mean number of candidates presented by the high schools stood at twenty-four and the median at twenty-five.

In order to present as many candidates as each high school did, major changes were effected in those high schools. These changes had some of the most positive, desirable effects on educational achievement that the HHEC was able to identify in its national search for effective programs, conducted in 1987, which underpinned the design of Project PRIME. Moreover, the use of assessment instruments, particularly the PSAT/NMSQT and the AP, were essential to the project. The AP especially had the effect of supercharging the high schools in a fashion that positively affected many more students and teachers than those only narrowly involved in the program itself. For example, teachers were spurred by the recognition given to winners of stipends through Options for Excellence and voluntarily choose to attend summer school to improve their expertise in their field of certification. While each participating teacher would have only one AP course in his or her complement of classroom preparations, it appears that Options had a strong spillover effect, strengthening the curriculum, the morale, and the achievement of the students and their teachers in *all* of the class periods.

The numbers of students who academically achieved in some of the participating high schools so far outstripped the numbers who were being placed in AP courses that it is no exaggeration to say that the educational profile of those schools had been radically and positively altered. Perhaps the most notable case was Southside High School, which in 1981 had a mere 10% of its graduating seniors attending college, almost exclusively at the local community college. By 1987, three years after the extramural funding of Options for Excellence, this program had been well-institutionalized and was still gathering steam. That year, the college-going rate of graduating seniors had risen to more than 50% and seemed to be on the increase each year. Thus, not only did Southside High School have a 500% increase in the percentage of college-going seniors, but this was accomplished with significant numbers of students attending the University of Texas, and placement, for the first time ever in the school's history, at such institutions as Yale and Princeton.

The Options for Excellence project, because it was large scale, involving thirty-seven high schools, and because it operated with average teachers in their ability and energy levels, documents that what was accomplished at Garfield also can be achieved elsewhere and in numbers. Like Garfield, these schools were heavily minority, in many cases 97% minority. Like Garfield (and for that matter other schools that have gotten involved including Garfield's neighborhood archrival, Roosevelt, Bell High School, Bell, California; Johnston and David Crockett in Austin, Texas, and others[7]), Options for Excellence documents that minority youngsters can achieve and even excel under cirumstances of higher expectations and rigor, but also conditions reflecting the increased morale, enthusiasm, will, persistence, recognition, encouragement, and resources to get the academic job done. Options for Excellence is an extraordinary achievement, and precisely because it contradicts the skeptic's conventional assumptions and the traditional compensatory or remedial sorts of expectations that we associate with programs for minority youth, it is a program that deserves recognition, replication, and expansion in other educational communities.

Two recently established programs that have incorporated the activities at the heart of the Garfield initiative and Options for Excellence into a more comprehensive, multi-grade program, are the HSSP and Project PRIME.

The HSSP, an initiative to increase the number of Hispanic college students, consists of five "Action Components" joined together in a comprehensive, integrated program which begins services at the elementary school level and goes through college attendance. Administered by the Hispanic Association of Colleges and Universities, a membership association of institutions with at least 25% student enrollment, the HSSP enjoyed during its planning phase considerable research on the underlying causes of the Hispanic student dropout problem and of programs throughout the United States that address this problem. The key success characteristics of existing programs have been incorporated into the HSSP.

Each of the five Action Components addresses a different set of problems in order to accomplish the HSSP's goals. The Institutional Change Action Component seeks to bring about substantive changes in federal, state, and local policies and practices that inhibit the participation and success of Hispanic students in higher education. HACU has been very active, for example, at the federal level and is currently working with the Departments of the Interior, Energy, Education, and others toward promoting stronger policies on behalf of Hispanic students. HACU also had major responsibility for the December 5, 1989, memorandum by President Bush establishing a Taskforce on Hispanic Education (Bush, 1989). The Marketing Action Component communicates to large numbers of students and other influential individuals clear and focused messages about the value of higher education. For example, the HSSP has produced professional and effective public service announcements for mass media, including television and radio, that promote the value of attending college. The Training and Technical Assistance Action Component delivers educational and support services to school districts teachers, counselors, and other personnel. The community Organizations/Parental Involvement Action Component serves as a catalyst in fostering meaningful relationships between the parents of Hispanic students and the schools that educate their children through the activities of community-based organizations. The Enrichment Serves Action Component provides academic and academic support services to students through an Elementary Preparation Program, a Leadership Development Summer Program, Evening Enrichment Centers, an Academic Year Enrichment Program, and a Community College Services Program.

Project PRIME is currently operating in about thirty school districts in the State of Arizona. Like the HSSP, this project which begins in the 7th grade and takes students through entrance as college freshmen, provides a combination of both instructional and support programs. PRIME consists of seven components. *Algebridge,* a diagnostic and instructional program that helps 7th, 8th, and 9th grade students learn algebraic thinking through the context of the mathmatics that they have already studied, prepares them to take high school algebra. Mathematics, Engineering, Science Achievement (MESA), which has proven its success in California and elsewhere, provides instruction and educational enrichment in the PRIME version in English, mathematics, and science during both the academic year and the summer to participating high school students. *TestSkills* is a one-semester course of test familiarization and academic review of English and mathematics for students usually in the 10th grade to help enable them to do well on the PSAT/NMSQT and other admissions tests. Options for Excellence, taken from the San Antonio model, provides the necessary support to teachers, students, schools, and communities in order to permit large numbers of high school students, focusing on minorities, to do college-level work and to receive college credit through the AP program while in the 11th or 12th grades. Parents as Partners is a program, loosely modeled on existing initiatives of the National Council of La Raza for elementary school children, which works with parents to have them involved in the academic work and academic progress of their children and to make parents better advocates for their children's educational interests in high schools and other educational settings. Information on Academic Planning and Obtaining Financial Aid provides materials to both youngsters and their parents and to high school guidance counselors that permit them to do appropriate academic and financial planning and be knowledgeable of and obtain financial aid for college. Finally, I Have a Dream is the component that provides the counseling and advice to minority students necessary for them to take the academic track in high school conducive to being admitted into college. Similarly, this component makes the commitment to financially provide for the college education of minority youngsters so that no students who commit to staying in school and applying themselves will be denied a college education because of a lack of funds.

Both the HSSP and PRIME make use of two products that have been developed jointly by the CB, ETS, and the Hispanic community through the construcive efforts of the HHEC. These are *TestSkills* and *Sí Se Puede: Information of Academic Planning and Obtaining Financial Aid*. As the result of a 1984 poll conducted by the HHEC, the Hispanic community identified the issues of test familiarization and academic planning/financial aid information as among the highest priorities for a collaboration among the three organizations. As a result these two products have emerged among the very first concrete results of the partnership. I have briefly described both products earlier and considerable material on *TestSkills* appears in this book. I will dwell briefly on some elements of historical importance for both products. These materials have been produced in accordance with a new and more effective arrangement between the Hispanic community and the testmakers. In contrast to prior efforts by the College Board and the ETS that were on behalf of all minorities lumped together, without taking into account their cultural, language, educational, and other differences,

TestSkills and *Sí Se Puede* really address the distinctive qualities that Hispanic students bring to education and to assessment for the first time. In addition, both of these products as well as others that will be produced, will be the result of all three organizations working in tandem as operational partners, with joint responsibility for conceptualization and execution of each project. As Rafael Magallán, chairman of the board of the HHEC, and I pointed out in the preface to *TestSkills:*

> It is useful for three organizations, such as HHEC, ETS, and the College Board, to work together as partners, collectively identifying needs in the effort to increase the access of U.S. Hispanic students to higher education and cooperatively developing projects to address those needs. . . . Each of the partners has ample opportunity to contribute to the design and development of each cooperative project. That HHEC has an operational, rather than advisory, role gives a distinct advantage to this partnership, permitting the collective development of materials that are closely attuned to the needs of the Hispanic community. . . . The efforts of the three partners are directed toward intervention strategies in promoting the access of Hispanic students to higher education and toward research of the underlying issues. Priority, however, is given to *action*. Our partnership is premised on the notion that with a generous dose of good will and with commitments of energy and time, we can make a tangible difference in the efforts to help more Hispanic students go on to higher education. (Killer and Magallán, 1989, v-vi)

Future Directions

Before turning to the papers that make up this volume, I want to complete this overview by suggesting the development over the near and intermediate term of some of the projects that have been described earlier. My projections of future developments is highly limited. It is not meant to review all of the possibilities for harnessing assessment to the good purpose of increasing Hispanic access to college. Quite to the contrary, I merely wish to evoke the likely development of some of the activities referred to earlier as well as to project into the future some likely developments in assessment.

The precollegiate level probably has more promise than any other. Both the HSSP and Project PRIME are making use of partially or wholly assessment-focused initiatives with documented success such as the use of the AP program both for the purpose of increasing Hispanic and other student achievement and college access, *Algebridge, TestSkills,* and *Sí Se Puede*. These are second generation projects (if we consider Garfield in

1982 and Options for Excellence in the early 1980s as first generation, even as these two continue to develop on their own) with very large scale goals. PRIME aspires to reach 50,000 students in the state of Arizona, double the number of minority students who go to college, and triple the number of students who major in mathematics, science, or engineering-related fields. PRIME currently is serving about 10,000 students (effective fall 1990). The project has helped the State of Arizona to increase the number of AP examinations taken from 3,474 in 1987 to 6,408 in 1990. Similarly, the HSSP has very ambitious goals that involve thousands of students. The Project has completed its first operational year (in 1989–90) in Greater San Antonio and beginning in the fall of 1990 is replicating many of its activities in northern New Mexico. It also is scheduled to implement the project within the next year or two in the Bronx, New York; in Los Angeles, and in Miami. I predict that in the 1990s we will be hearing quite a bit about these two large-scale projects as well as the many others of a smaller dimension that are promoting learning under conditions of high academic expectations for Hispanics and other students.

Another development at the College Board and the ETS, one in which Hispanic educators have been considerably involved, also affects precollege students. With the completion of *Algebridge* and *TestSkills,* both of which seem to be proving their effectiveness, it is likely the College Board and the ETS will become more involved in producing materials that combine both testing (often diagnostic testing rather than evaluation for the purpose of licensure or college admission) with instruction. I predict that minority educators, including Hispanics, will be involved to a substantive degree in the creation of such products.

With respect to the reference points of admission to college, to graduate school, to the teaching profession, and possibly to other professions, there also will be quite a lot brewing in the 1990s. The College Board and the Educational Testing Service are in the process of reviewing many of their major tests. Announcements already have been made (e.g., Educational Testing Service, 1988, October) about the National Teachers Examination (NTE). Although subject to some possible changes, it is likely that beginning in 1991 the NTE will be revised in three phases. The third phase will probably come in 1994 and will likely utilize techniques for "performance assessment" to more effectively evaluate teaching skills. Similarly, in November 1990, the College Board announced that it would revise the PSAT/NMSQT in 1993 and the SAT in 1994. Both of these tests reduce somewhat the amount of reliance on the multiple-choice format. In addition the newly named SAT II, which replaces the Achievement Tests, introduces a writing component in the English test. (The AP and the English achievement test in the December administration already had such features as a free response section and a written essay.) Moreover, the College Board announced it had received a recommendation by a distinguished panel to administer SAT and II through the use of microcomputers rather than paper and pencil by the year 2000. Finally, calculators will now be allowed in the SAT mathematical section. More accurate measurement can only help Hispanic student access or access into the professions; however, there will be an even greater need for Hispanic educators to be knowledgeable about the issues and to be involved as proactors, not reactors. To name one example, the introduction of computers or even hand-held calculators into standardized test-taking could mean a disadvantage for the U.S. Hispanic community. In general, new technology reaches Hispanic student last if at all, and just as the HHEC warned against the possibility of tests unwittingly measuring language peculiarities rather than academic aptitudes, we must be wary of the tests unintentionally measuring familiarity with computers or other forms of technology rather than the target skills.

At the graduate level, I believe that Project 1000 has much potential for improving Hispanic access. In fact, that is being accomplished already with respect to the numbers of students being admitted into graduate school. The Project, which went fully operational two and a half years ago, has achieved about 400 admits thus far. Over the longer term, if such supplemental predictors as the within ethnic score, personal qualities, talents, skills, and the PAEG can be both validated and subsequently used extensively by graduate schools, there is great promise for genuinely increasing the number of Hispanic and other minority graduate students. The ETS is supporting the longitudinal study of Project 1000 graduate students, and ETS researchers Beatriz Chu Clewell and Donald Rock have been helping Project 1000 design its evaluation and manage the data. Because of the time it takes to complete doctorates, however, the validation process may take ten years before substantive judgments can be made about the predictive validity of the supplemental measures.

In addition to large-scale revisions of some of the most important national tests, we are likely to witness positive contributions that will emerge from the important research on sources of evaluation variability or error. The work of researchers such as Pérez Schmitt, Dorans, Mestre, Royer, Durán, Angoff, Llabre, Valencia, Aburto, Pennock-Román, Powers, A. Padilla, R. Padilla, Clewell, Cocking, Manning, García, Olmedo, Ramos, and many others probably will be implemented wherever practical relative to the design of tests and construction of test items, the sensitivity review process, the development of instructional and test familiarization materials, and other areas.

Finally, the partnership that launched some of the activities that have been described earlier is likely to continue its work and possibly, with the participation of the Hispanic Association of Colleges and Universities, even expand this work. Among the projects that are currently scheduled is the revision of *Sí Se Puede* and its possible distribution around the nation, the continued support of the HSSP and PRIME, and the development of the Consortium to Identify and Promote Hispanic Professionals. The Consortium is a cooperative project of Arizona State University, Eastern Michigan University, the ETS (as a supporting but nonoperational partner), Michigan State University, and the University of Michigan. These five institutions are in the process of establishing an extensive data base that will provide research opportunities for scholars interested in U.S. Hispanic studies, facilitate the identification of Hispanic expertise and talent, and permit through its broadly based network, effective communication between Hispanic professionals and interested organizations. The Consortium will maintain a state-of-the-art Hispanic Expert Resources Data Base that makes available, in electronic form through a continuously maintained and updated electronic bulletin board, valuable information for about 20,000 participating Hispanic professionals. Similarly, the Consortium will provide information by facsimile machine and in hard copy, including periodic publication of its data base.

The Component Papers of *Assessment and Access: Hispanics in Higher Education*

Assessment and Access: Hispanics in Higher Education is divided into four parts. The first part of the book analyzes major elements and issues that affect Hispanic performance on tests and influence Hispanic access into higher education, with a focus on culture, language, reasoning skills, and the heuristic knowledge necessary to survive in and succeed in college. The paper by José P. Mestre and James M. Royer, "Cultural and Linguistic Influences on Latino Testing," attempts to shed light on why Latino students score significantly below the majority population in standardized tests of both academic aptitude and academic achievement. Mestre and Royer pay particular attention to what may be the most important mediators of academic achievement for Latino students: linguistic proficiency and the interplay of culture. The researchers describe specific ways in which language and culture can cause considerable levels of error in assessment techniques that do not take these factors into consideration for Hispanics. Several cogent examples of the problems encountered in tests are provided. Moreover, they report on a new approach for assessing linguistic proficiency, the Sentence Verification Technique (SVT), which they believe to be particularly well suited for the evaluation of students during the period in which they are gaining second language proficiency and are being acculturated into American culture, but have not acquired academic-level proficiency in English or sufficient familiarity with American culture to be accurately assessed by traditional tests. Mester and Royer's work is especially helpful for highlighting the factors involved in the attempt to assess Latino students under two conditions:

1) During the time that students are acquiring second language (English) proficiency and becoming acculturated to American culture.

2) For those Latino students who have already developed second language proficiency and who have achieved a degree of acculturation.

While Mestre and Royer focus on the important factors of "background differences," as Durán calls them, of language and cultural background, Durán's paper, "Diagnostic Testing of Reasoning Skills," discusses the potential of diagnostic tests of cognitive aptitudes that could provide information useful for all students, including Latino students, regardless of ethnicity, gender, or other background characteristics. In Durán's paper he describes a research program that is developing a computerized test of formal and informal reasoning ability that has the potential to lead us away from the concern for how different groupings of students compare in skill level, to attention on the ways in which to help individual students develop desirable aptitudes.

Raymond V. Padilla's paper takes us to the *hic et nunc* of students in their concrete college environments. Padilla's hypothesis is a highly intriguing one. He observes that assessment traditionally has been driven by the desire to predict which students are most likely to succeed in college and toward that objective tests have been designed to measure a student's aptitude in academic (usually book) knowledge. However, he argues that the association between scores on aptitude tests and subsequent college performance as indicated by college grade point average is quite modest, and as Durán (1983) has pointed out, disproportionately so for Hispanic students. It would be unwise for the institution and unfair to the student to predict the Hispanic student's chances of completing a college degree on such evidence alone. Moreover, the lack of predictive power of traditional assessment has not only negatively affected the credibility of traditional admissions criteria but has hurt the development of optimal support programs to help students succeed in college after they get there. In contrast, Padilla shifts the attention to retention and graduation, placing assessment within the broader perspective that encompasses not only academic knowledge but "heuristic knowledge," namely that which is required by students for success on a specific campus. Padilla develops a distinctive, original approach for learning what the necessary heuristic knowledge might be for campus academic success in its imparting.

The second section overviews several critical elements in test-construction as they affect Hispanics. For example, the element of time and time management has been documented as highly important to Hispanic test performance. The element of time management which is so critical on the standardized aptitude and achievement tests, as María Magdalena Llabre points out in her paper that reviews time as a factor in cognitive test performance of Latino college students, may reflect significantly different cultural differences between Hispanic and Anglo culture. Llabre reviews the notion of cultural differences in the concept of time as it has received attention from sociologists, cultural anthropologists, and social psychologists. Some studies have been conducted that document divergent standard errors in punctuality and time perception between Americans and Latin Americans. More specific to tests, Llabre reviews several factors that could negatively influence the performance of Hispanics on timed tests. These include the factor of longer amounts of time necessary for information processing among bilingual subjects even when they are competent in English; the factor of stress and fatigue negatively influencing performance in a second language to a greater extent than performance in the primary language; and the differential performance of Hispanics compared to Anglos which may reflect both cultural differences in the perception of time and test anxiety induced by the factor of speededness in test-taking.

I have referred earlier to the burgeoning field of "differential analysis," and its potential for addressing some of the most important issues that affect an accurate evaluation of the aptitudes and achievements of Hispanic students. The paper by Alicia Pérez Schmitt and Neil J. Dorans on factors related to differential item functioning (DIF) for Hispanic examinees on the SAT is genuinely a major effort, and probably the most important to date on the subject with respect to Hispanic test performance. It has been written by ETS researchers who are breaking ground in the field of differential analysis. The Schmitt and Dorans paper introduces the conceptual framework for DIF, summarizes recent research on DIF for Hispanic examinees, and presents the results of investigations for Hispanic examinees on the SAT. They document the existence of differential item functioning on the SAT Verbal for Hispanics and make a number of important suggestions for improvement, including combining statistical and judgmental screening procedures to detect DIF and working inductively, using that DIF that was detected to formulate hypotheses about Hispanic response style factors. Schmitt and Dorans also point out the DIF results can be indicative of educational areas that need to be stressed in the education of Hispanics or other minority groups. They judge that improved test-taking skills by Hispanics, informed by DIF research, might be achieved by special programs such as *TestSkills* that address both the assets and the problems that Hispanic students bring to the test-taking situation.

The paper by ETS senior research scientist William H. Angoff and his ETS associate, Linda L. Cook, conducts a highly sophisticated test equating between the English language SAT and its Spanish language analog, the PAA. The methodology made use of twice-translated versions of each test (first translating each set and then "back-translating" each set). The Angoff and Cook paper not only describes the method for and provides the results of this equating, it also describes the purpose and general approach to the matter of developing equivalent scores on two parallel forms of a test, with special attention devoted to the particular problems of equating tests for students of different languages and cultures. Finally, Angoff and Cook describe the uses and limitations of their equating study in its application to the problem of access to higher education for Latino students.

The third section, consisting of two papers by Richard R. Valencia and Sofía Aburto, represents a major, sustained analysis of the factors related to testing and Hispanic access into the teaching profession. The first paper, on competency testing and Latino student access into the teaching profession, provides a general overview of the problem—the "whitening" of American teachers that is occurring simultaneously with the "coloring" of the student population. In 1980, the combined ethnic minority K–12 enrollment nationally was 27% (Orfield, 1988) and by year 2000 this population is predicted to reach 33% (Smith, 1987), an increase of 22%. On the other hand the projections are that nationally the minority teaching force will *decrease* about 60% between the years 1980 and 2000. Valencia and Aburto present a rationale for the value of having Latino teachers and a demographic overview of Latinos in teaching. They also discuss the negative implications of teacher tests for prospective Latino teachers and the general obstacles to Latino teacher production.

Valencia and Aburto's second paper is a logical extension of their overview of Latino teacher and teacher training issues. Valencia and Aburto concentrate on the problems inherent in tests used for teacher licensure or certification. Among the problems that they review are the poor relationships between test (which may have high reliability but appear to document general knowledge) and ratings by supervisors, mentors of student teachers, and the like, which relate to the actual practice of teaching. Additional attention is devoted to the problem of predetermined cut scores for the purpose of licensing teachers. Another area of considerable interest currently in teacher testing is "performance assessment," a method quite different from traditional paper-and-pencil teacher tests or the teacher observation systems used in several states. Performance assessment is based on observations of teachers carrying out standard tasks designed to elicit their knowledge and skills. While performance assessment has certain potential advantages, the researchers also discuss the potential for linguistic and racial bias in this methodology. Finally, Valencia and Aburto review recent proactive efforts by teacher preparation institutions to begin a process of early identification, recruitment, diagnostic testing, and remediation of Latino and other minority students who plan to become teachers. The researchers describe the very positive results of some of these programs, particularly the significantly higher pass rates on teacher licensing tests on the part of minorities.

The fourth section focuses on the educational product jointly conceived and produced by the College Board, the ETS and the HHEC *TestSkills: A Kit for Teachers of Hispanic Students*. This product, which was published in the spring of 1989, is already being used in numerous places around the nation. It represents a first of its kind produced by the College Board and the ETS, namely a test-skills preparation kit that focuses directly on the ethnolinguistic factors that U.S. Hispanics bring into the test-taking situation, and most specifically, the PSAT/NMSQT, which approximately 1.4 million students take each year. Lorraine Gaire's paper on *TestSkills* reviews some of the historical background and research issues in the development of this program as well as its content. Gaire shows how elements that address the available research of test anxiety, test speededness, familiarity with different item formats, perceived probability of success, changing answers, confusion about appropriate guessing strategies, and other elements were addressed in *TestSkills* in order to eliminate as much as possible these extraneous factors in determining the aptitude of Hispanic and other students. *TestSkills*, based on current differential item functioning research of cognates, also incorporates strategies that permit Hispanic students or others with knowledge of Spanish, Latin, or another Romance languages to utilize those other-than-English language skills to advantage in the testing situation, particularly with respect to verbal aptitude or achievement tests.

The evaluation by Pennock-Román, Powers, and Pérez presents information about *TestSkills*, how it was used in a pilot evaluation in a number of school districts, and two key questions: whether the test-familiarization kit increased students' confidence and lessened their anxiety about test-taking and whether the kit increased the likelihood that students would take the PSAT/NMSQT. The evaluation showed that overall the response to *TestSkills* was very positive from students, teachers, and staff members.

Many of the papers in this book hopefully will introduce to a larger audience of educators and even interested community members topics which like differential item functioning, test speededness, or the issue of teacher preparation among Hispanics, has been cultivated primarily in highly research-focused journals or monographs. The case of *TestSkills* is even more likely to be of interest to a wide group of parents, students, teachers, and community members who are interested in preparing students to do the best that they are capable of on standardized admission tests to college.

Part I

Hispanic Access: The Factors of Culture, Language, Reasoning Skills, and Heuristic Knowledge

1

Cultural and Linguistic Influences on Latino Testing

~ ~ ~ ~

José P. Mestre and James M. Royer

The juxtaposition of two facts foreshadow a problem looming in American education. Fact one is that Latinos are the most rapidly growing minority group with demographic trends indicating that they will be the largest minority group in this country by the turn of the century. Fact two is that Latinos score significantly below the majority population in standard assessments of both academic aptitude and academic achievement. The challenge for our instructional and assessment systems is to address the problem described in the second fact by devising approaches to accurately assess and raise the educational attainment of Latino students. Indeed, this is an important challenge since maintaining the competitive edge that is crucial to the country's economic well-being requires a highly educated work force.

What is the cause of the academic underachievement of Latino students in the United States? If there were a simple answer to this question we could immediately set about making the appropriate changes in our educational system. Any reasonable attempt to formulate an answer to this question would need to draw on the interplay of socioeconomic, cultural, developmental, and linguistic factors. Research findings do point to linguistic proficiency as the single most important mediator of academic achievement for Latino students (Cummins, 1981, 1982; De Avila, 1988). However, we should heed De Avila's warning that "linguistic proficiency in English, although necessary, does not seem to be a sufficient condition [for academic achievement]" (116).

Because linguistic proficiency is such an important mediator of academic achievement, the ability to accurately assess linguistic proficiency among Latino students is of paramount importance. Although this will be a focal issue of this chapter, it is important to begin with an overview of ways in which culture and linguistic proficiency can affect cognitive performance, and to illustrate how assessment practices often overlook the influence of these two factors. We then describe a new approach for assessing linguistic proficiency, called the Sentence Verification Technique (SVT), that is particularly well suited for language minority populations, and discuss how this approach has been used successfully in a transitional bilingual education program. We conclude with some thoughts on the future of linguistic assessment among Latino students.

The Interplay of Culture in Cognitive Performance

The effect of culture on cognitive performance has been documented in various studies. At one extreme is the interesting example of the Oksapmin culture of Papua New Guinea. The Oksapmin were an isolated stone age culture until the latter part of this century when increased contact and trade with western civilization brought modifications to their culture. The influence of western culture was perhaps manifest most clearly in the Oksapmin number system (Saxe, 1985). The Oksapmin number system consists of twenty-seven body parts with no base structure. To count in this system, Oksapmin begin with the thumb of one hand and recite body part names moving around the upper periphery of the body. Although this system was perfectly suitable for their cultural needs (e.g., counting a set of valuables, or indicating the ordinal positions of two villages along a path), it was unsuitable for dealing with the base ten system required for monetary exchange during trading activities. Interestingly, observations of Oksapmin children attending "bush" missionary schools revealed that they were trying to adapt and use their body part counting system to solve base ten arithmetic problems. This example clearly illustrates how children use and adapt knowledge acquired in the home culture within an academic setting.

A similar cultural influence on mathematical problem solving can be found among the Ute Native American tribe of northeastern Utah (Leap, 1988). Leap found that Ute students often evaluated the "truth value" of a particular word problem and worked with that problem according to the findings of that evaluation. For example, when a Ute student was asked during a problem solving interview to determine how much money his brother would have to spend on gasoline if he wanted to drive his truck from the reservation to Salt Lake City, the student did not attempt to solve the problem based on the information presented in the request. Rather, he assessed the truth value of the request and answered, "My brother does not have a pick-up truck." According to Leap, such assessments are a common part of everyday life in the reservation and are related to the Ute language, which has very precise mechanisms for evaluating the "degrees of reality" of an event. Although it could be argued that the primary link to this behavior is language and not culture, this is clearly not the case: The Ute students in the study were not fluent in the Ute language, although Ute was used in the home. Thus, despite their lack of fluency in the Ute language, Ute children adopt tribal traditions and use them in their approach to mathematical problem solving.

Among Mexican-Americans, most studies of the role of culture on achievement have focused on familism (MacCorquodale, 1988). Familism refers to the relative importance of family members in determining an individual's values, goals, and orientation. Some argue that the family obstructs intellectual development because the needs of the family supposedly are placed above those of an individual family member (Grebler, Moore, and Guzman, 1970; Montez, 1960). There is evidence that Mexican-Americans who are more independent of their families exhibit greater educational achievements than those who maintain closer family ties (Schwartz, 1971). However, others argue that family orientation does not interfere with either aspirations or achievement (Lopez-Lee, 1972). Research findings support this view—Anglos and Mexican-Americans do not differ in educational values and aspirations (Aiken, 1979; Espinoza, Fernandez, and Dornbush, 1977; Juarez and Kuvlesky, 1969). Regardless of which view is correct, there does appear to be a clear difference between Anglo and Mexican-American family values in one area: Mexican-American parents are more traditional in their attitudes toward gender roles than Anglo parents are; Mexican-American girls are likely to be encouraged to pursue careers that will not interfere with their future family life (MacCorquodale, 1988).

In contrast to what one might expect given the performance differences between Anglos and Mexican-Americans in national assessments, research evidence suggests that Mexican-Americans are more likely than Anglos to do homework and that Mexican-American parents are very supportive of their children's education (MacCorquodale, 1984, 1988). These findings raise the interesting question, "To what can the differences in educational attainment between Anglos and Mexican-Americans be attributed?" MacCorquodale argues that Mexican-American parents are unable to translate their encouragement and support into concrete actions (e.g., helping their children with homework or advising their children on what courses to take in school), in part due to their limited educational background.

Although it could be argued that the examples discussed above would have an indirect effect on cognitive performance, there is evidence that culture can directly affect one of the more important instances of cognitive performance: reading comprehension. For example, one study investigated the reading comprehension of students from two distinctly different cultural groups (Americans and Asian Indians) on two stories, one based on their own culture and one based on the foreign culture (Steffensen, Joag-Dev, and Anderson, 1979). The two stories described a wedding in the United States and an Asian Indian wedding. After reading passages describing both weddings, subjects were able to recall considerably more material that was culturally similar to them, and also rated their understanding of the culturally familiar material higher.

Similar findings were obtained in a study of people's comprehension of baseball (Voss, Vesonder, and Spilich, 1980). When passages describing the events transpiring during a baseball game were read by individuals possessing high-knowledge and low-knowledge of the game of baseball, the high-knowledge individuals were better able to recall the salient features of the baseball passage. In this example, being well-versed in the "culture" of baseball served as a clear advantage in reading comprehension. Similar findings were obtained in a study of children's comprehension of a passage about spiders (Anderson and Shifrin, 1980). It therefore appears that the presence of material that is culturally foreign to students will adversely affect performance on tests, even though the students may have mastered the skills that the test is supposedly testing.

Culturally unfamiliar material has an adverse effect not only on performance but also on learning. A study of ninth grade Latinos learning algebra (Mestre, 1988) revealed that the students were not reading the textbook as a means of supplemental instruction. Because students did not read the textbook, the only instruction they received consisted of the in-class presentations by the teacher. Although readings from the textbook were assigned, students used the book only as a place to find problems assigned for homework. Upon closer scrutiny, it became evident that the context of the material in the textbook was largely unfamiliar to the students. When students were asked to explain the meaning of terms appearing in a typical section of the book, such as "shares of stock," "revolving charge account," "monthly payments," and "interest," it became clear that they had little idea what these terms meant. The context of the material in the textbook might be suitable for students from middle or high socioeconomic backgrounds, but it was totally unsuitable for the low socioeconomic backgrounds of the Latinos in that algebra class, a criticism that we are not the first to make (Taylor, 1978).

The Interplay of Language in Cognitive Performance

The lack of language proficiency can adversely affect cognitive performance through a variety of avenues, some more blatant than others. It is fairly easy to detect the more obvious ways in which language adversely affects cognitive performance, such as the case of a student asked to perform a task in a language with which she or he is not proficient. We will focus our discussion on the more subtle avenues through which language proficiency affects cognitive performance, since these are not as easy to detect.

Before proceeding further it is important to define language proficiency since studies often attribute the poor performance of language minority students to lack of language proficiency without ever assessing it (De Avila, 1988); clearly these studies equate language proficiency with ethnicity. We will define a language minority student to be *proficient* in the second language if that student's language proficiency level is equivalent to the "average" monolingual student of the same age. We take it as self-evident that a language minority student who is not *proficient* in the second language, as we have defined the term, will not perform as well on a task requiring language proficiency skills as will a mainstream monolingual student. The next obvious issue to consider is how likely it is for a language minority student to be *proficient*.

Most bilingual programs in this country are "transitional" programs, meaning that the school system has three years to bring the second language proficiency level of the students to a level where they can be mainstreamed. However, there is evidence that this is not nearly enough time to make students *proficient*. Indications are that it takes between five and seven years for language minority students to approach language proficiency levels equivalent to their monolingual peers (Cummins, 1982). Nevertheless, often language minority students are mainstreamed before they are *proficient*, and many subsequently exhibit below-average performance in mainstream classrooms and on assessments of academic achievement. The reason they frequently have difficulty can be found in the relationship between language proficiency and cognitive performance.

After approximately two years of exposure to English, many language minority students display sufficient skills in English to be able to communicate quite adequately with their monolingual peers in face-to-face situations. This type of "proficiency" is frequently presumed to be sufficient to allow students to enter the mainstream curriculum and compete favorably with monolingual students, a presumption that is inaccurate. According to Cummins (1980, 1981, 1982) it is important to distinguish between the language proficiency needed for face-to-face communications and the language proficiency needed for academic work. Face-to-face communication is "context-embedded" in the sense that there are many cues to aid communication (e.g., gestures and intonation). On the other hand, much academic work takes place within a "context-reduced" situation where the cues present in face-to-face communication do not exist. For example, in attempting to read and comprehend a complex text all a student has to go on are the words in the text. Ability to communicate in context-embedded situations will not necessarily help a language minority student perform in a context-reduced academic task.

This was the situation experienced by the first author, who was mainstreamed after spending two and one-half years in a bilingual program. He was able to communicate tolerably well with his monolingual peers, and even perform at "above average" level in school. In those cases where he did not understand the teacher's instruction or assigned work, he would turn to a neighboring student and ask for clarification. Thus, by forcing a context-reduced situation into a context-embedded situation, he was able to function quite well. However, it was in tests requiring substantial linguistic proficiency (both in-class and standardized) that problems arose. In these context-reduced assessments, the only cues available were the words on the paper. Particularly problematic were tasks where a passage was to be read followed by a series of "comprehension" questions; if several key words in either the passage or the questions were unfamiliar, there was nothing to do but guess and hope for the best.

In addition to the above unsolicited testimonial, there is research evidence of how limited English proficiency adversely affects performance on context-reduced academic tasks. One study with Latino college students revealed that some error patterns in solving math word problems were the result of language deficiencies; students were working out the problems incorrectly, but consistent with their interpretation (Mestre, 1986a). Similar evidence has led Dawe (1984) to hypothesize that, in order to perform well in cognitively demanding mathematical tasks, students must reach a threshold level of proficiency both in mathematical knowledge (i.e., mathematical concepts and how they are applied) and in the language used to express that knowledge. This language that is specific to mathematics has been termed the "mathematics register" and is comprised of the variety of language oriented to mathematics activities, including the various linguistic forms, along with their meanings and uses (Halliday, 1975; Spanos, Rhodes, Dale, and Crandall, 1988). Whereas it previously was thought that mathematics was a domain in which language proficiency played a relatively unimportant role, recent research suggests that this is not the case (Kintsch and Greeno, 1985). To be able to achieve in mathematics, students not only must be proficient in the English language, which is used throughout mathematics, but also must be proficient with the mathematics register, which defines the specific uses of the English language within mathematics.

Another example of how language interacts with cognitive performance emerged in a study of premise comprehension with both Anglo and Latino college students (Mestre, 1988). Findings from this study revealed that all students were using rules that govern the comprehension of natural discourse to interpret premises, rather than the rules of logic. For example, students were inclined to interpret the premise, "not all clerks are male" to mean "some clerks are male," rather than the appropriate interpretation, "some clerks are female" (the statement "not all clerks are male" is consistent with all clerks being female, thus it is incorrect to assume that some clerks are male). Although there were no significant differences between Anglos and Latinos in performance, an interesting difference emerged in evaluating an intervention strategy designed to improve performance.

The intervention strategy was a thirty-minute videotaped lesson that covered the rules for parsing and interpreting premises containing different number and types of negations. Immediately following the lesson, all Anglo students reached ceiling level performance on a post test assessing their ability to interpret premises. One week following the lesson, all Anglo subjects had retained a ceiling level performance. Six months later, 93% of the Anglo subjects had retained ceiling level performance. The pattern for the Latino subjects was different—only 65% reached ceiling level performance immediately following the lesson. Among those Latinos who had reached ceiling level performance after the lesson, only 38% were able to attain ceiling level performance six months after the lesson. This disparity in learning and retention from a context-reduced, linguistically laden lesson was attributed to the disparity in English proficiency between the Anglo and Latino groups; the average SAT verbal score of the Anglo group was a full 170 points higher than that of the Latino group. This study illustrates both the short- and long-term effects of linguistic deficiencies on learning and performance in academic situations.

Issues of Concern With Latino Assessment

The research reviewed in the previous two sections suggests that there are special considerations involved in the construction, use, and interpretation of assessment instruments among Latino students, particularly when those students are in the transition stage from first to second language proficiency. But it is equally evident that current assessment procedures are not responsive to these considerations. As Cummins states, "Most minority language students are still . . . assessed . . . with assessment tools and procedures that were designed only for children from the majority Anglo group" (1982, 1). These assessment instruments necessarily reflect the values and culture of both those who design the instruments and the mainstream population. For example, a passage in a reading comprehension test about a nature hike through the New England woods in winter may bear no overlap with the experiences of Latino students living in Puerto Rico or southern Texas. The Latino students may lack the mental schemata that facilitate interpreting and making sense out of that passage (Cabello, 1984; Steffensen, et al., 1979; Voss, et al., 1980).

Often, poor performance on these assessment instruments by bilingual students is used to reinforce myths, such as "bilingualism causes language handicaps," or "the best way for bilingual students to make progress in the second language is to eradicate the first language." There is research evidence that these myths are false (Cummins, 1981; Kessler, 1987; Leap, 1988).

Further, attempts to "patch up" assessment instruments designed for the majority population to make them suitable for Latino populations often are flawed. The most common patch-up consists of translating a test into Spanish. This practice places the student in double jeopardy—not only will the cultural values of the test remain intact, but there is now the risk that the translation will not be adequate for the target group (Cabello, 1984); for example, differences in the level of vocabulary across the two versions of the test, and the multiplicity of translations for particular words (e.g., "kite" could be translated as "papagayo," "cometa," or "papelote" depending on the country of origin of the translator), are just two of several possible limitations in translated tests (Wilen and Sweeting, 1986).

The analysis presented thus far suggests that current assessment procedures may be appropriate for Latino students when they have acquired academic-level proficiency in English and when they have acquired sufficient familiarity with American culture, but they are inadequate procedures for assessment during the period when the students are gaining second language proficiency and are being aculturated. Given the shortcomings with current assessment procedures, what would the ideal assessment procedure look like? The literature reviewed in the previous sections suggest two guidelines. First, the ideal assessment procedure would be sensitive to cultural experiences. This suggests that the ideal procedure would be tailormade to suit the cultural background of the target population. Mexican-American students in southern California might be assessed using one instrument, and children of Cuban background in Florida assessed with another. Second, the procedure should be sensitive to level of language proficiency. That is, the procedure should be able to trace the development of second language proficiency from the acquisition of "face-to-face" competence to the mastery of academic level proficiency.

In the section to follow we describe an assessment procedure that attempts to be responsive to these guidelines. The first part of the section will present a general overview of the technique. This will be followed by sections that describe how the technique is responsive to the guidelines set forth, and data will be presented that addresses the validity of the procedure as a measure of progress in a transitional bilingual education program.

Overview of the Sentence Verification Technique

The Sentence Verification Technique (SVT) is a recently developed technique for measuring reading and listening comprehension that was first introduced by Royer, Hastings, and Hook (1979). The technique entails developing one of four types of test sentences from each sentence appearing in a text passage. The first type of test sentence is called an *original* and it is a copy of a sentence as it appeared in the passage. The second type of test sentence, called a *paraphrase*, is constructed by changing as many words as possible in an original sentence without altering the meaning of the sentence. The third type of test sentence is called a *meaning change*, and it is constructed by changing one or two words in the sentence so that the meaning of the sentence is altered. The final kind of test sentence is called a *distractor* and it is a sentence that has a vocabulary level and syntactic structure that is similar to sentences in the passage and is consistent with the overall theme of the text passage, but the sentence is unrelated in meaning to any sentence that appeared in the passage.

An SVT test consists of a set of passages, each of which is followed by a set of test sentences. Each set of test sentences consists of equal numbers of each of the test sentence types. So, for example, most of the research using the SVT has used twelve sentence passages and either twelve test sentences (three each of the test sentence types) or sixteen test sentences (four each of the test sentence types). An examinee taking an SVT test reads or listens to the passage, and then in the absence of the text judges each of the test sentences to be "old" or "new" (the elementary school versions of SVT tests have recently started using "yes" and "no" as substitutes for old and new). Old (yes) sentences are defined as sentences that are the same as or mean the same as passage sentences (originals and paraphrases), and new (no) sentences have a different meaning than passage sentences (meaning changes and distractors). More details on the development and administration of SVT tests can be found in Royer, Greene, and Sinatra (1987), and in Royer (in press).

Theoretical Rationale for the SVT

The use of a verification technique as a measure of comprehension was shaped to a considerable degree by the theoretical assumption that comprehension is a "constructive" process that results in a memory representation that preserves the meaning but not the form of a linguistic message. The constructivist theoretical framework (e.g., Brown, Bransford, Ferrara, and Campione, 1983; diSibio, 1982; Jenkins, 1974, 1979; Kintsch and van Dijk, 1978; Royer, 1985; Royer and Cunningham, 1981) asserts that the process of comprehension entails an interaction between context, the linguistic message, and the knowledge base of the listener or reader. This interaction results in the construction of an interpretation of a linguistic message that preserves the meaning but not the surface structure of the message. This process of forming a memory representation is thought to occur more or less simultaneously with the reception of the message (e.g., Carroll, 1972; van Dijk and Kintsch, 1983), and it is largely unconscious except in instances where processing difficulties are encountered (e.g., Kintsch and van Dijk, 1978).

Constructive theory suggests that the "product" of comprehension is a memory representation that preserves the meaning of a linguistic message. This perspective, in turn, suggests that comprehension could be measured by determining if readers or listeners had successfully established a meaning preserving memory representation of something they had read or heard. The SVT was designed to accomplish this purpose.

If readers have comprehended a text and established meaning preserving memory representations of that text, then they should be able to correctly judge that original and paraphrase test sentences have the same meaning as their memory representations, and they should be able to correctly reject meaning change and distractor test sentences as having a meaning different from their memory representations. If, however, a reader has not successfully established a meaning-preserving memory representation, he or she should have great difficulty in correctly classifying the test sentences as having the same or a different meaning than a text sentence.

Scoring and Interpretation of SVT Tests

Two procedures have been used in scoring SVT tests. The first is a simple computation of proportion correct. Proportion correct can be computed for overall performance, for performance on separate passages, for performance on particular sentences within a passage, and for particular test sentence types (e.g., originals, paraphrases, etc.) within or across passages. Most of the research on the SVT has entailed calculating proportions correct, though for some purposes a more sophisticated test scoring procedure utilizing the theory of signal detection (TSD) (Swets, Tanner, and Birdsall, 1961) may yield more useful data. The scoring of SVT tests using TSD parameters may be a particularly attractive property if SVT scores were to be used as an index of the absolute comprehension of a passage. The scoring of SVT tests using TSD parameters is described in Royer (in press).

Research completed to date indicates that average readers get about 75% of the SVT items correct if the tests are based on material at grade level. With respect to listening performance, students typically can understand difficult material better when listening than when reading, but the difference between listening and reading comprehension diminishes as the students get older.

The Reliability and Validity of SVT Tests

The reliability of SVT tests has been assessed in a number of studies (Marchant, Royer, and Greene, 1988; Royer, Kulhavy, Lee, and Peterson, 1986; Royer and Hambleton, 1983; Royer, Tirre, Sinatra, and Greene, 1989) involving both children and adults. In the studies involving children, 1,150 students in the grades three through eight were tested. The average reliability for SVT reading tests in these studies was over 0.9 and the reliability for listening tests was over 0.7. The studies involving adults assessed U.S. Air Force enlistees and college students. The reliabilities of the reading tests, which were shorter than those used in the children studies, were in the range of 0.6 to 0.7.

The research assessing the validity of the SVT as a measure of comprehension has been conducted with Messick's (1980) observation in mind that test validity is ultimately a matter of construct validity and that " . . . construct validation is a continuous, never-ending process developing an ever-expanding mosaic of research evidence" (Messick, 1980, 1019). The construct validation research on the SVT is briefly outlined below.

• The SVT is sensitive to text readability (Royer, Hastings, and Hook, 1979, Experiments 1 and 2; Royer and Hambleton, 1983; Royer, Kulhavy, Lee, and Peterson, 1986).

• The SVT is sensitive to differences in reading skill (Royer, et al., 1979, Experiment 2; Royer, et al., 1986; Rasool and Royer, 1986; Royer and Hambleton, 1983).

• The SVT is sensitive to text characteristics (Royer, et al, 1984, Experiments 2 and 3).

• SVT performance varies as a function of working memory capacity (Lynch 1986, 1987).

• The SVT measures passage comprehension, not just sentence comprehension (Royer et al., 1984, Experiment 4).

• SVT tests have good divergent and convergent validity properties (Royer, 1986).

- The SVT can measure both listening and reading comprehension (Royer, et al., 1986; Royer, Sinatra, and Schumer, 1990; Royer, Carlo, Carlisle, and Furman, in press; Royer and Carlo in press).
- SVT tests measure educational gain (Royer, Lynch, Hambleton and Bulgarelli, 1984 Experiments 1 and 2; Royer et al., 1987).
- SVT tests predict future learning performance (Royer, Marchant, Sinatra, and Lovejoy, 1990; Royer, Abranovic, and Sinatra, 1987; Marchant, Royer, and Greene, 1988).
- SVT tests have diagnostic utility (Carlisle, 1989; Royer, Sinatra, and Schumer, 1990).

Virtues of the SVT as a Measure of Language Comprehension Performance with Latino Students

In an earlier section of this paper it was suggested that assessment procedures for use with Latino students involved in transitional bilingual education programs should be sensitive to differences in cultural background, and they should be able to assess the degree of second language competence attained by the Latino student. In this section we will consider the ways in which the SVT procedure meets these guidelines.

Developing Tests that are Sensitive to Cultural Background

From our perspective, local test development is the key to developing tests that are sensitive to cultural background. Local teachers and parents are the best judges of whether students have the cultural background that would allow them to understand a particular set of materials. Thus, teachers (possibly in conjunction with parents) could select materials that they believe to be consistent with the cultural experiences of their pupils and base tests on those materials.

The SVT lends itself quite well to this perspective. SVT tests can be based on virtually any text material. Moreover, it is easy to train local school personnel to develop SVT tests. This circumvents many of the problems associated with different uses of language among speakers of a language who have varying backgrounds.

As an instance of local SVT test development, the second author of this paper is involved in a research project on the island of Grenada that is assessing the impact of Computer Assisted Instruction in a developing country. This evaluation effort included developing reading comprehension tests for grades two through seven suitable for use in Grenada. The national language in Grenada is English, but there are striking differences between

English as spoken and used in the United States, and English as spoken and used in Grenada. The process of test development involved training Grenadian teachers to develop SVT tests and then having them develop tests based on materials selected from local sources. The tests developed by the teachers have been administered twice, and all of the evidence indicates the tests are valid indicators of progress in Grenadian schools (Greene, Royer, and Anzalone, 1990).

The Grenadian example described above, and the bilingual assessment study to be described later in this chapter, demonstrate how the SVT can be responsive to cultural background issues. The tests can be based on materials that local personnel judge to be consistent with the background experiences of the students, and the tests can be developed by people having linguistic and cultural experiences that are the same as the target population to be assessed. These procedures should result in culturally fair tests.

Developing Tests that Assess Degree of Second Language Competence

Earlier in this paper a distinction was made between face-to-face competence in a second language and academic competence in that language (Cummins, 1980, 1981, 1982). It was suggested that accurate decisions about which of these levels of competence had been attained was critical to the correct placement of Latino students. Those who have attained academic competence in English may benefit most from placement in mainstream classrooms. However, those who have only mastered English at the face-to-face competence level may undergo unnecessary educational hardship through placement in mainstream classrooms.

SVT tests provide a means of assessing the degree of language competence attained by students in the process of learning English. This is accomplished by administering both listening and reading comprehension tests. In our SVT studies with Latino students we have routinely administered listening and reading tests in both English and Spanish. The purpose of administering listening and reading tests in both languages is to attain a comprehensive portrait of a student's overall language ability. The listening and reading tests in Spanish provide indices of native language comprehension ability (performance on the listening tests) and reading comprehension ability. The performance on the English listening tests provide indices of face-to-face linguistic competence, and performance on the reading tests provide indices of academic competence in English. In our studies we have used audio tape recorders as a means of administering the listening tests. But if one wanted to increase the extent of "context-cues" present in the assessment session, the tests could be administered by having someone read the passages and tests.

This section has indicated how SVT tests can be responsive to some of the needs associated with assessing Latino students in the process of learning English. The next section will examine evidence that the tests are in fact fulfilling these needs.

Using SVT Tests to Track the Educational Progress of Students Enrolled in Bilingual Education Programs

This section will report the results of studies completed in the Holyoke, Massachusetts, public school system that evaluated the validity of SVT tests as measures of educational progress for students enrolled in a transitional bilingual education (TBE) program. The procedural details of the study will be described very briefly in this chapter. The reader interested in more detail on procedural matters and a more comprehensive description of the research results can find them in Royer and Carlo, in press; and Royer, Carlo, Carlisle, and Furman, in press.

The Holyoke, Massachusetts, public school system enrolls approximately 6,500 students, about 20% (1,400) of whom are enrolled in TBE programs. The large majority of the TBE students are native speakers of Spanish and virtually all of them are Puerto Rican. The school system has two types of TBE programs. The first is a traditional model involving six steps (Levels I, IIA, IIB, IIC, III, and mainstream) and the second is a "two-way" model in which TBE students spend considerable in-class time with native English-speaking students.

Students with little or no competence in English are placed in Level I of the TBE program where they receive all of their content instruction in their native language, combined with English as a Second Language (ESL) instruction. As they acquire competence in English, subject matter instruction in English is phased in beginning with mathematics, then science, social studies, and finally reading. The phasing in process in mathematics, science, and social studies occurs during level II (A, B, and C) of the program, and English reading instruction is encountered in Level III. Students are mainstreamed after the school system judges them to be competent in English.

When Spanish-speaking students enter the system they are tested with the Bilingual Syntax Measure (BSM) and interviewed. Evaluations of student progress are conducted twice a year. The criteria for exit from a TBE classroom to a mainstream class is a satisfactory score on the BSM and a grade equivalent score on the English form of the California Achievement Test (CAT) that is at least equivalent to the student's current grade placement. This latter requirement has been very difficult for many of the Spanish speaking students to achieve. Moreover, many of the native speakers of

English in the school system do not meet the requirement of grade level performance on the CAT.

Methodology

The test development phase of the studies began with having teachers from the school system select reading textbooks that could serve as the basis for SVT tests in English and Spanish. The books selected by the teachers were either in use in the system or they were judged to be very representative of the type of reading material both the TBE and mainstream students would be likely to encounter in their classrooms.

The research team then selected passages from the textbooks and edited those passages so that they were twelve sentences long and were "coherent" in that they had a beginning, middle, and end. The coherence editing was undertaken to avoid, as much as possible, the sense that the passages were excerpts taken from a larger text.

The next step involved developing SVT tests based on the passages. The tests were developed in accordance with the procedures described in Royer, Greene, and Sinatra (1987), and Royer (in press). The Spanish tests were developed by a graduate student who is fluent in both English and Spanish and who is a native of Puerto Rico. The English tests were developed by graduate students who are native speakers of English.

The listening and reading tests were developed using passages drawn from the same text source. When selecting passages for inclusion in the tests, two passages were selected that were judged to be parallel in difficulty. One of these passages then became part of the reading test and the second passage was included in the listening test. Tests for a particular grade level were constructed by "bracketing" a grade level. That is, the tests for a given grade consisted of passages that were thought to be easier than, equal to, and more difficult than the reading skill of the average reader.

After the tests were developed they were returned to the teachers for review and criticism. Following this review, final changes were made, both listening tests were recorded on audio tape by the bilingual graduate student, and the reading tests were prepared in booklet form.

The SVT tests have been administered to two student cohorts. The first cohort consisted originally of 115 5th grade TBE students who were administered SVT tests in February and May 1987, and in June 1988. The second cohort consisted originally of 120 students enrolled in the TBE program and to 260 students enrolled in mainstream classrooms. The second cohort, which consisted of students in grades three, four, five, and six, was administered SVT tests in December 1987, and the tests were readministered in June 1988. Mainstream students were given only the English listening and reading tests. The data reported here comes primarily from the second cohort, however, several issues will be examined using data from the first cohort.

Collection of Ancillary Information. The school system completed an information questionnaire for every student participating in the studies. This questionnaire asked for: (1) student age, (2) date of entry into school system, (3) Lau category, (4) TBE Level at the time the SVT tests were administered, (5) grade level of currently assigned reading book, (6) available standardized test scores, and (7) language spoken at home.

In addition to the information provided by the school system, the teacher of every student participating in the study rated each of his or her students on their listening and reading comprehension. Teachers of TBE students rated their students on listening and reading comprehension proficiency in both Spanish and English. Mainstream teachers rated their students only in English.

Indices of Test Validity

The purpose of the study was to assess whether SVT tests were valid indicators of educational progress for students enrolled in a bilingual education program. Such evidence would be present if the results followed the patterns described below.

(1) Performance of the TBE students on the English tests should vary in accordance with TBE Level. That is, Level I students should score lower than Level II students; Level II students should score lower than Level III students; and Level III students should score lower than native speakers of Spanish who are in mainstream classrooms.

(2) Performance of both TBE and mainstream students should vary on the reading tests as a function of level of assigned reading book. For instance, if one TBE student in the 4th grade is reading in a Spanish book at the 3.0 grade level, and a second student is reading in a 4.0 book, the second student should receive a higher score on the Spanish reading SVT test than the first student.

(3) Performance of both the TBE and the mainstream students should vary in accordance with teacher ratings of competence. For example, students rated as being highly competent in English reading should score higher on the English reading SVT tests than students rated at a moderate degree of competence, and students with moderate ratings should score higher that students with low ratings.

Two other issues, both of which provide part of the underlying rationale for the beneficial effect of bilingual education programs, can be examined in the context of the research effort. The first is the assumption that listening competence precedes reading competence. This assumption underlies the decision to provide ESL instruction prior to beginning systematic instruction in reading in English.

The second assumption is that academic skills acquired in one language will transfer to a second language when that language is acquired. Below are formal statements of these assumptions in terms of expectations about SVT performance.

(4) TBE students will have better scores on English listening tests than they will have on English reading tests during the time they are acquiring competence in English.

(5) Performance on the Spanish reading tests will be predictive of future skill on the English reading tests.

Results

SVT Performance on the English Tests as a Function of TBE Level. The Holyoke school system advances children through levels of the TBE program based on perceived increases in competence in English. Therefore, if the SVT tests in English were valid indicators of educational progress for the TBE students, SVT performance should vary in accordance with TBE Level. Figure 1 presents the results corresponding to this expectation. The data in the figure are average proportion correct on the SVT tests. The data is summed over the grade level of the students for ease of presentation, but graphs drawn separately for each of the grade levels depict essentially the same pattern as that presented in Figure 1.

The data in Figure 1 show the performance of the TBE students on the English SVT listening and reading tests administered in December 1987 (labeled "ENG LIS I" and "ENG RDG I" in the graph), and May 1988 ("LIS" and "RDG II" in the graph). In addition to showing data for TBE students at each level of the TBE program (the A, B, and C divisions in Level II of the TBE program have been collapsed), the graph also indicates the performance of Latino students in mainstream classrooms on the same tests, and it indicates the performance of native speakers of English on the tests. The Latino students in mainstream classrooms are students whom the teachers list as having Spanish as the language spoken at home. Many of these students undoubtedly were graduates of the TBE program, but it was not possible to sort out former TBE students from Spanish-speaking students who had never entered the TBE program.

As the graph shows, a clear relationship exists between placement in the educational program and performance on the SVT tests. Performance on both the listening and the reading English SVT tests increases as a function of advancement through the TBE program. Also, the mainstream

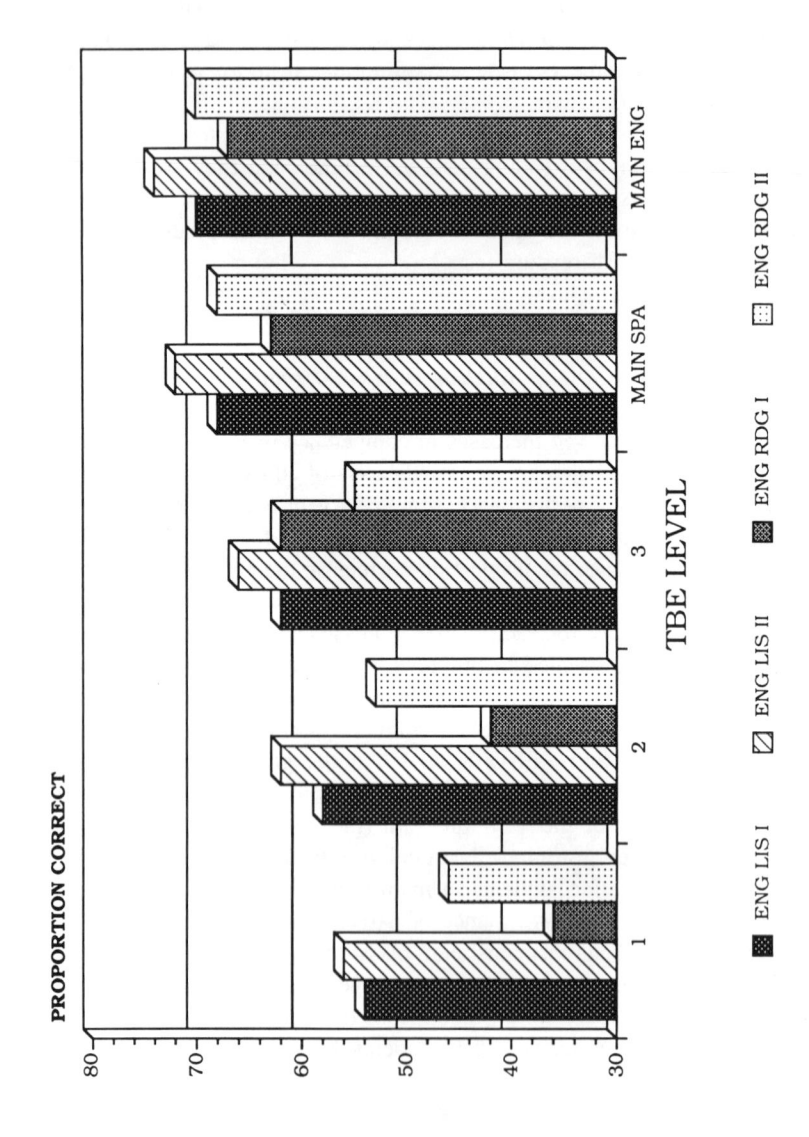

Figure 1. Average Performance on English SVT Tests as a Function of TBE Level

Spanish-speaking students are performing at approximately the same level as are the native English-speaking students.

Also interesting is the fact that listening performance consistently is superior to reading performance—congruent with the previously mentioned hypothesis that context cues associated with speech assist the understanding of linguistic material. Moreover, it is consistent with the educational goal of attempting to develop oral understanding of English through ESL classes prior to beginning formal reading instruction in English.

The only somewhat puzzling result is the decline in reading performance from the first to the second testing occasion for the students in Level III of the TBE program when every other group in the study showed a gain in performance. This might have happened because most of these students were in one fifth-grade classroom, and, according to the examiner, they were particularly unruly on the day the tests were administered.

The data presented in Figure 1 reports performance on the English tests. Similar analyses of performance on the Spanish tests have been conducted and they show no relationship between test performance and TBE level.

Performance on the SVT Tests as a Function of Teacher Assessments of Listening and Reading Competence. The teachers of the students who participated in the study were asked to rate every student with respect to his listening and reading comprehension skills. These ratings were made on a one to nine scale with the ratings of one and nine being anchored by the very best student in the class (rating of 9) and the very worst student in the class (rating of 1). After the teachers had made their ratings, the scales were collapsed to form three categories: low (ratings 1–3), medium (ratings 4–6), and high (ratings 7–9). Students in the TBE program were rated on both English and Spanish skills, whereas mainstream students were rated only on English skills.

If the SVT tests were valid indices of educational progress, performance on the listening and reading tests should vary in accordance with teacher judgments of competence. Figure 2 presents the data from the Spanish listening and reading tests. The data in the figure is average performance on the tests summed over grade. Similar graphs drawn separately for each grade show patterns much the same as the averaged data presented in Figure 2.

The graph shows that performance on both the listening and the reading tests increases as a function of teacher judgments of competence. Graphs similar to the one presented in Figure 2 have been plotted for mainstream students and for TBE students when rated on English skills and

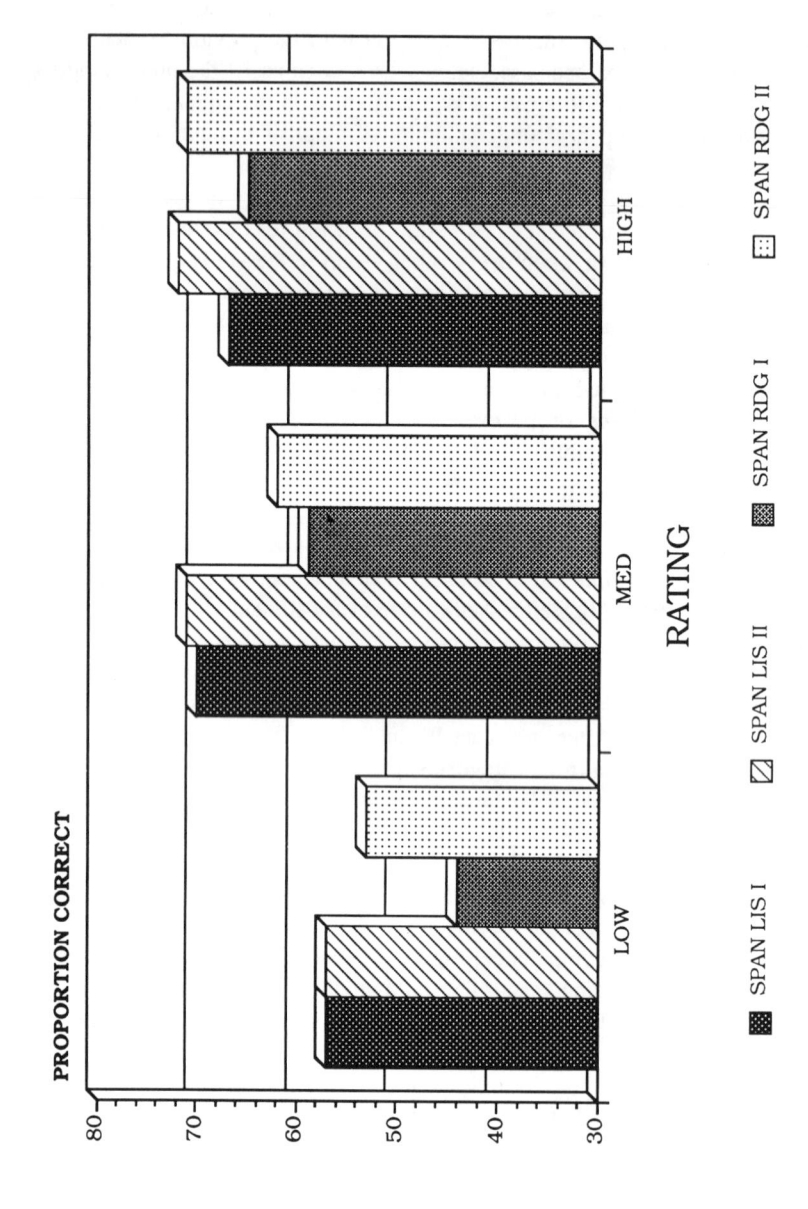

Figure 2. Spanish SVT Performance as a Function of Teacher Ratings

when tested with English tests. The data for mainstream students are even more striking than that for TBE students. There is a clear correspondence between performance on the tests and teacher judgments of competence.

The graph depicting the relationship between the TBE students' English SVT performance and teacher judgments were not nearly as orderly, probably because the TBE classrooms were segregated to some extent by TBE level: Some classrooms had a preponderance of students at upper levels of the TBE program while others contained mostly students at lower TBE levels, forcing teachers to make very fine competence discriminations. In some cases teachers were judging degrees of competence on a one to nine scale between students having virtually no English competence. In other cases teachers made discriminations on the same scale between students judged to be near mainstreaming. The net result was little relationship between the teacher judgments and SVT test performance.

Another interesting aspect of the data presented in Figure 2 is that there is a greater correspondence between teacher ratings of reading competence and SVT reading performance than there is ratings of listening competence and SVT listening performance. This data parallels other data that we have collected with mainstream students. Teachers seem to be better judges of who are better readers than who are better listeners, probably reflecting the generally greater emphasis placed on reading as an educational goal.

SVT Performance and Reading Book Level. One of the items of information collected in the study was the level of the reading book in which the students currently were working. If SVT reading tests were accurately measuring reading skill, test performance should vary in accordance with the level of the assigned reading book. The data on reading book level does not lend itself to summarization over grades because of variations in differing numbers of reading book levels represented at each grade. Given this, the data for only 6th grade will be presented. The graphs for the other grades show the same relationship between performance on the tests and reading book level. The data in Figure 3 shows the performance of 6th grade TBE students on the Spanish SVT tests. The reading book levels are in grade units (i.e., 4.0 is a beginning 4th grade level textbook) and are the levels of Spanish reading books in which the students are working. Very few of the TBE students were receiving reading instruction in English books.

The figure shows a clear relationship between performance on the SVT reading tests and the level of the reading book in which the students currently are working. It is also interesting to note a relationship between the level of the students' reading book and their performance on the Spanish listening tests. This result is again similar to that found in other studies

Figure 3. Average Performance on Spanish List and Rdg. SVT Tests as a Function of Reading Book Level (2nd Test Admin)

(e.g., Royer, Sinatra, and Schumer, 1990) where listening ability of good readers typically exceeds the listening ability of poor readers.

Graphs for mainstream students like the one presented in Figure 3 have been examined and there was a clear relationship between the level of the English reading book the mainstream students were working in and their performance on the English listening and reading tests.

Does Linguistic Competence Transfer? One of the most fundamental assumptions underlying transitional bilingual education programs is that educational skills acquired in a native language will transfer to a developing second language (e.g., Cummins 1983, 1984; Hakuta, 1986). Despite the importance of this issue, very little empirical research has been done in this area as noted by Hakuta in the following statement: "What is remarkable about the issue of transfer of skills is that despite its fundamental importance, almost no empirical studies have been conducted to understand the characteristics or even to demonstrate the existence of transfer of skills" (1986, p. 218).

The second author can verify Hakuta's observation. A very thorough search of the literature has not turned up a single convincing empirical demonstration of educational skills acquired in a native language transferring to skill in a second language.

The data acquired from the students tested in February and May 1987, and in June 1988 can be used to evaluate the transfer issue. One-hundred fifteen 5th grade TBE students were tested in February 1987. Unfortunately, only forty-nine of the original 115 students were available for testing in June 1988, and many of these students did not have a complete data record. Table 1 presents the results of pairwise correlational analyses which were computed using all available data. This means that the N contributing to each correlation will vary. The smallest N contributing to a correlation was twenty-nine.

The most interesting data in the table involves the relationships between the other test scores and performance on the English listening and reading tests administered in June 1988 ("Eng Lis 3" and "Eng Rdg 3" in the table). As the table shows, the only significant predictor of listening 3 SVT performance was listening 2 SVT performance, and the next best predictor was listening 1 SVT performance. This means that the best predictor of the TBE students' English listening competence in June 1988 was their English listening competence twelve months before, and the next best predictor was their English listening competence seventeen months before.

The predictions of listening performance can be contrasted to the predictions of reading performance. As the table shows, the best predictor of English reading performance was *Spanish* reading performance the year

Table 1
Correlations Between Spanish and English Listening and Reading Performance on Three Different Test Occasions

Variable	Correlations
	1 2 3 4 5 6 7 8 9 10 11 12
1 Span Lis 1	1.0
2 Span Rdg 1	.07 1.0
3 Span Lis 2	.14 .08 1.0
4 Span Rdg 2	.21 .16 .46* 1.0
5 Span Lis 3	.10 .28 .40* .15 1.0
6 Span Rdg 3	.32 .14 .00 .35* .32* 1.0
7 Eng Lis 1	−.10 .40* .02 .05 −.19 −.14 1.0
8 Eng Rdg 1	−.17 −.19 .08 −.16 −.18 .10 .14 1.0
9 Eng Lis 2	.07 −.22 .29 .26 .15 −.01 .09 −.01 1.0
10 Eng Rdg 2	.01 .24 −.07 −.11 .01 .08 .11 −.02 .23 1.0
11 Eng Lis 3	−.01 .16 .20 −.07 .05 −.17 .24 .16 .38* .19 1.0
12 Eng Rdg 3	.08 .12 .07 .29* −.08 .18 .19 .19 .25 .08 .17 1.0

* p equal to or < .05

before. Spanish reading performance was a better predictor than previous English reading performance.

These data must be interpreted cautiously given the small number of students involved and the magnitude of the relationships as illustrated by the relatively low correlational coefficients. The data certainly suggests, however, that the English listening competence that students acquire in and out of school translates into increasing ability to understand English, and they suggest that reading skill *acquired in Spanish* transfers to reading skills in English as the students improved their competence in English. The data collected in December 1987 and June 1988 from the much larger student cohort will be valuable in assessing the transfer issue in the future.

Summary of the Empirical Studies

In the early part of this section, three checks on the validity of SVT tests as indices of progress in bilingual education programs were suggested. The first check was that performance on the English versions of the tests should vary in accordance with placement of students in the TBE program. The second check was that performance on the tests should vary in accordance with teacher judgments of competence. And the third check was that performance on the reading tests should vary in accordance with the grade level of the assigned reading book.

Performance on the SVT tests were congruent with all three of these expectations. The TBE students improved in performance on the English listening and reading tests as they advanced through levels of the TBE program; performance on the tests varied in accordance with teacher expectations of listening and reading competence; and performance on reading tests was better for students assigned upper level reading books.

In addition to providing evidence regarding the validity of SVT tests in a bilingual context, the studies that have been conducted thus far provide some support for assumptions underlying TBE programs. Specifically, the results indicated that early competence in listening and understanding English was related to English listening competence a year later, and that reading competence in Spanish was predictive of subsequent reading competence in English. These results are consistent with the practices of providing ESL instruction as part of a TBE program, and with providing reading instruction in the native language during the period of acquiring competence in the second language.

Future Directions in SVT Assessment

Work that currently is underway will expand the scope of SVT assessment in three ways. First, we are examining whether SVT assessment is useful in content areas. In a pilot study using 7th grade TBE and mainstream students, SVT tests have been developed based on materials drawn from science and social studies text sources. If this study demonstrates that SVT tests can be used to assess the degree to which students can read and understand content area materials, we will expand the scope of this work to encompass more grade levels and content areas (e.g., mathematics). This research will build upon previous research which has shown that SVT test performance on content materials can be used to predict learning performance in that content area (Royer, Abranovic, and Sinatra, 1987; Royer, Marchant, Sinatra, and Lovejoy, 1990).

A second future concern is to develop better ways to train local school personnel to create their own SVT tests. We currently are working on two computer-based training programs. The first, the *SVT Test Maker* (Walczyk and Royer, 1989), is a program that automates many of the details associated with SVT test development. The test developer types in the text that is to serve as the basis for the SVT test, and the program parses the text and asks the developer several question about how the test should be arranged. After answering these questions, the program presents the developer with each sentence in the original passage and indicates that a test sentence of a particular type should be developed based on the presented sentence. The developer then types in the test sentence. After each test sentence has been developed, the program automatically formats the test, and prints it out, complete with instructions, in a form that is ready to be reproduced and administered. The *SVT Test Maker* currently exists only in an English version, but after further refinements our intent is to develop it in a Spanish version.

The second computer program, the *SVT Trainer*, will be a tutorial to train local school personnel to develop SVT tests. It will include an introduction to SVT testing, a brief description of prior research, and considerable practice with appropriate feedback on the development of SVT test items. The trainee also will receive instruction on constructing, administering, and scoring SVT tests, and interpreting test results.

The final SVT project envisioned for the future is a computer based reading diagnostic system that will include SVT listening and reading tests. This diagnostic system is designed to assist in diagnosing reading difficulties in students who do not seem to benefit from normal reading instruction. As with the other systems, the diagnostic system could be developed in Spanish as well as English.

Concluding Remarks

We view Latino testing as being divided into two separable concerns. The first concern is that tests used to assess Latino students be sensitive to cultural and linguistic influences *during the time the student is acquiring second language proficiency and being aculturated.* The second concern is that tests be developed that *are not systematically biased against Latino students who have developed second language proficiency and who have achieved a degree of acculturation.*

The first of the above concerns is critical to the effective education of Latino students and we believe that it can only be addressed at the local level. The introduction to this chapter reviewed evidence that culture and language can influence cognitive performance in general and test performance in particular. In our view there is no way that a single test can be truly fair to Latino students having differing cultural experiences and linguistic traditions. Our solution to this dilemma is to argue for tests that are tailor-made to fit the cultural and linguistic experiences of the target population.

Until recently, the argument for local based assessment would have been a hopeless expectation. Teacher-made tests are notorious for their poor reliability and validity, and local school systems do not have the resources to meet the enormous costs of developing reliable and valid tests using traditional psychometric procedures. We have presented evidence that SVT tests provide one means of meeting the need for local based assessment at a cost that local school systems can easily afford. We also are confident that once the idea that quality local assessment is possible, other procedures will be developed to meet this need.

We also believe that progress is being made on the development of standardized tests that are not systematically biased against minority students. For example, one area in which test makers are making considerable progress is in test bias detection. The Educational Testing Service recently has implemented a major effort for monitoring test bias through a technique called "differential item functioning." This technique compares the performance (at the test item level) of "target groups" (women, Blacks, Latinos, Native Americans, and Asian Americans) against that of the majority group. If either a target group or the majority group displays differentially lower performance on an item, that item undergoes close scrutiny; following the scrutiny, the item may be deemed inappropriate and not counted in the test.

In addition, recent positive steps have been taken by test makers to help Latino students in the areas of test familiarity and test-taking strategies. Standardized tests, such as the SAT, have very clear formats. Familiarity with the format of the various sections will reduce both the anxiety that a student will experience in taking the test and the time that student must spend figuring out what a particular test section is asking. For example, the SAT math has a section called "quantitative comparisons" where the test taker must compare two quantities and decide if: (a) the quantity in the first column is less than the quantity in the second column, (b) the quantity in the first column is greater than the quantity in the second column, (c) the two quantities are equal, or (d) there is not enough information to determine the relative sizes of the two quantities. A student walking into the SAT without being extremely familiar with the four answer categories for these items will be at a clear disadvantage because that student will have to spend considerable time looking back at the four options before responding to the items.

Further, there are sound test taking strategies that can help any student's performance in standardized multiple choice tests. For example, students who are familiar with the optimal "guessing strategies" in the types of tests that correct for possible guessing by subtracting a percentage of the incorrect answers from the correct answers will likely show a higher performance than students who are unaware of these strategies. One such strategy consists of instructing students in the advantage of guessing in those cases where the possible choices have been narrowed down to two or three from a field of five, while a complementary strategy consists of explaining to students why wild guessing will not help in the slightest. Finally, a wise strategy in timed multiple choice tests is not to spend too much time on any single item—a strategy which if ignored can increase the speededness of a test.

As in the case of monitoring possible item bias, the Educational Testing Service and the College Board are taking an initiative in helping Latino students in both of these areas. A recent Educational Testing Service-College Board publication entitled "Preparing for the PSAT/NMSQT for Latino High School Students" addresses these two specific issues for the Preliminary Scholastic Aptitude Test.

Despite these encouraging trends, there is a need for more research focusing on testing issues with minority populations, as well as more cooperation and communication between researchers and test makers. For example, more research should be conducted on test speededness and test validity. Because language minority students often read slower than majority students, they are likely to reach fewer items in a timed test and thereby exhibit a poor performance (Mestre, 1986b); it is therefore important to have a thorough understanding of the possible adverse effect of speededness on test performance for language minority students.

Test validity, which refers to whether or not a particular test is in fact an accurate measure of what it purports to measure, can be an unwieldy research area. It is conceivable that a test could be a valid instrument for a language minority group yet be insensitive in the cultural/linguistic dimension, or, conversely, that a test could be designed to be culturally and linguistically sensitive for a language minority group yet not be valid for that group. What is clear from existing research on validity is that tests that appear to be good predictors of future cognitive performance for majority students are not as good for predicting performance for minority students (Dalton, 1974; Hedges and Majer, 1976; Houston, 1980; Mestre, 1981). These studies suggest that caution must be exercised in how we interpret test scores among minority populations.

The impression with which we hope to leave the reader is that despite the enormous problems that remain in the area of testing language minority populations, progress is being made. We believe testing procedures now exist that will allow local school personnel to develop tests that are sensitive to the cultural and linguistic backgrounds of their students. We also believe that standardized tests developers are very concerned about issues of test bias and test validity as it relates to the assessment of minority populations, and that steps are being taken to reduce the possibility that standardized tests are biased and invalid measures of the abilities of minorities.

2

Diagnostic Testing of Reasoning Skills

~ ~ ~ ~

Richard P. Durán

Introduction

There is abundant evidence in the educational research literature that differences in the aptitude test scores of Latino students and non-minority students reflect true differences in skill development as well as possible differences related to language and cultural background of examinees (Durán, 1983). While concern about reducing the effect of background differences on test performance will remain important, it is also as important to find ways in which to make tests more sensitive to the legitimate learning needs of students regardless of their ethnicity, gender, or other background characteristics.

Existing tests of college aptitude, such as the SAT and ACT, stop short of providing diagnostic information on students' learning aptitudes that can be used to prescribe specific learning interventions for students. When we see that Latino and other minority students score below White examinees on the verbal scales of these test, we are not informed about specific ways in which educational interventions might be structured so as to improve the underlying skills of students. In contrast, diagnostic tests of cognitive aptitudes would provide information useful for these prescriptions, and indeed, it seems likely that emergence of such tests would be useful for all students and not just Latino students. Emergence of better diagnostic tests of skill development could help lead us away from an obsessive concern for explaining why groups differ on test scores, leading us instead to consider ways in which to help individual students develop target aptitudes.

Accumulating cognitive psychology research suggests that we can measure and assess complex reasoning and information processing skills that previously have not been well assessed by pencil and paper aptitude tests (Snow, 1988). As the field has evolved, increasing attention is being given to assessments of relatively specific kinds of skills that have established and generalized importance for academic learning tasks. Skills given attention include, for example, deductive and inductive reasoning ability and reading comprehension strategies. Additional cognitive research has emerged suggesting that these sorts of general skills are not acquired in the abstract, but that they are acquired through students' exposure to meaningful tasks that have face validity in immediate experience (Resnick, 1987). The implications for aptitude testing here are that diagnostic tests will more accurately reflect students' learning needs if they involve test items that emulate everyday learning and problem solving experiences in the classroom (Linn and Dunbar, 1990).

Assessment Goals

In this paper, I describe a collaborative research program with Russell Revlin and Michaele Smith developing and evaluating a computerized diagnostic test of formal and informal reasoning ability. The areas of *formal reasoning* covered by the test include ability to recognize instances of (a) valid and invalid conditional conclusions, (b) valid conclusions constituting paraphrases of text, (c) valid part-whole relationship conclusions, (d) invalid "false conversion" conclusions, and (e) invalid "false cause" conclusions. The areas of *informal reasoning* covered by the test include the ability to recognize instances of four kinds of fallacious conclusions stressed in textbooks on training of informal reasoning skills. These forms of fallacious informal reasoning included the fallacies of "many questions," "ambiguity," "composition and division," and "faulty generalization." Figures 1 and 2 define the forms of valid and invalid argumentation assessed in the project and give examples. Most of the forms of reasoning described have been subjected to intensive research, but diagnostic tests of students' ability to master these forms of reasoning are not readily available.

The computerized assessment procedure of the project presented college-aged student subjects with brief text passages. Each passage was followed by conclusions, presented one at a time, representing each of the types of valid or invalid conclusions identified in Figures 1 and 2. Students used a mouse control device to classify whether given conclusions either followed or didn't follow from text passages. The goal of the assessment was to determine a student's propensity to identify correctly whether conclusions of each type actually did or did not follow from passages.

Five expository text passages (approximately 250 words in length) were used. Each text passage was accompanied by ten conditional conclusions that were valid for a passage and four conditional conclusions that were not valid for the passage (see Figure 1). Also, each passage was accompanied by one valid paraphrase statement of information contained in the passage and one valid "set inclusion or part whole" statement based on the passage. In addition, each passage was accompanied by six instances of invalid conclusions that represented informal fallacies (see Figure 2).

Thus, across all five passages, a student subject was exposed to fifty instances of conclusions that followed with validity from passages and fifty instances of conclusions that were the results of invalid arguments. Accordingly, subjects were presented a total of 100 statements that they had to classify as "follows" or "doesn't follow." Each of the conclusions presented for a passage was displayed in a random order to each subject.

The remainder of this paper describes preliminary data regarding the performance of twenty-four native and twenty-four non-native English-speaking students on the reasoning skills assessment instrument. All students were undergraduates at the University of California, Santa Barbara. The native English group was composed of all lower division psychology undergraduates. The non-native English group consisted of students enrolled in ESL classes, seventeen of whom were from Asian backgrounds. I first present and discuss examples of the performance profiles of selected native and non-native English-speaking students. The profiles illustrate the utility of the assessment in diagnosing specific kinds of reasoning strengths and difficulties encountered by students.

Next, I describe performance differences between native and non-native English speakers on one reasoning task in the overall assessment—evaluating conditional conclusions that are the results of valid versus invalid arguments.

Performance Profiles

The responses of each student were scored as correct or incorrect by a computer program and were then assembled into a profile describing each student's propensity to correctly detect valid conclusions and invalid conclusions of each type. Table 1 shows a summary score profile for six native English-speaking college students (students are labeled NE-13 through NE-18). The table is divided into two parts. The top half of the table summarizes the ability of each student to correctly detect the occurrence of the fifty statements across passages that followed from valid arguments.

Figure 1
Formal Valid and Invalid Conclusions

CONDITIONALS
1. Formal arguments of the form 'If A, then B.'

Base statement	Invalid forms	Valid forms
If A, then B	If B, then A (affirming the consequent) If not B, then A If B, then not A If not A, then not B (denying the antecedent)	If not B, then not A

Valid Forms:

If A, then B — If a muscle is used, it burns up a bit of stored muscle sugar.

If not B, then not A — If stored muscle sugar is not burned up, then muscle is not used.

Invalid Forms:

If B, then A — If stored muscle sugar is burned up, then muscle is used.

If not B, then A — If stored muscle sugar is not burned up, then muscle is used.

If B, then not A — If stored muscle sugar is burned up, then muscle is not used.

If not A, then not B — If muscle is not used, then stored muscle sugar is not burned.

NONCONDITIONAL INVALID CONCLUSIONS

2. False Conversion.

Deduce from the fact that all cats are animals the additional information that all animals are cats. The converse of a statement, made by exchanging the subject and predicate, swapping a distributed term (covering the whole of its class) for an undistributed one.

All animals that exhibit allelomimetic behavior are birds.

3. False Cause.

The event is attributed to one cause whereas there could be multiple causes.

If someone tells you that she made a lot of money investing, then you know that it is only because she has an investment strategy.

Conversely, the bottom part of the table summarizes the ability of each student to correctly detect the occurrence of the fifty statements across the

Figure 2
Common Sense Fallacies
Definitions

1. **Many Questions**. For this fallacy, a statement embeds more than one yes/no question. The example is composed of more than one question: "Will rodents survive?" "Does the survival of rodents depend upon their ability to evolve allelomimetic behavior?" One of the key elements contributing to the fallacy of many questions is that the embedded questions do not necessarily follow from the text. Introduced in this form, the assumption is made that the embedded content is fact whereas it is usually contrary to the information given.

>The question of concern is whether or not rodents will be able to evolve allelomimetic behavior so as to be able to survive.

2. **Ambiguity**. This fallacy requires an ambiguous term or sentence which has the potential to shift meaning midstream in the discourse. In the passage on Investing Your Money, the author quotes a source as saying that "The first hurdle to get over [when investing] is the timidity hurdle." Processed with other information, this has the potential for being interpreted as follows.

>People who do not make investments are timid.

3. **Composition and division**. This is a pair of fallacies derived from collective versus distributive uses of a term. Often properties of a whole are applied to individual members. *Division* occurs when what is true collectively of a whole or a class is believed to be true of each part or member. *Composition* occurs when what is true of each part or member is believed to be true of the whole or class.

>If the executive committee finds that there is evidence to substantiate a case, then every member of the committee must have found the same.

4. **Generalization**. In this fallacy, a general rule that may not fit all cases, or one that is based on insufficient evidence is applied. Often some form of the term "always" is used.

>When people stop dieting, they always gain about ten pounds immediately.

---

passages that followed from invalid arguments. More careful inspection of the table shows the propensity of each subject to detect valid and invalid conclusions of each type identified in Figures 1 and 2.

Table 1
Sample Reasoning Skill Profiles of Native English Students

Valid Conclusions correct by subject (across 5 passages)

Conclusion Type	NE-13	NE-14	NE-15	NE-16	NE-17	NE-18
1a) A → B (If A then B)	5	5	5	4	3	5
2a: A → B	5	5	5	4	5	5
3a) A → B	5	5	5	5	4	5
4a) A → B	5	5	5	3	4	5
TOTAL (20 max correct)	20	20	20	16	16	20
1b) -B → -A (If not B then not A)	2	5	3	1	2	3
2b) -B → -A	5	3	3	3	3	4
3b) -B → -A	4	5	2	4	1	4
4b) -B → -A	3	3	2	4	1	3
TOTAL (20 max correct)	14	16	10	12	7	14
TOTAL FORMAL (40 max correct)	34	36	30	28	23	34
5) Valid Paraphrase	4	4	5	4	4	5
6) Valid Part-Whole Relation	3	3	4	2	4	3
TOTAL (10 max correct)	7	7	9	6	8	8
VALID TOTAL (50 max correct)	41	43	39	34	31	41

Fallacies correct by subject (across 5 passages)

Fallacy Type	NE-13	NE-14	NE-15	NE-16	NE-17	NE-18
False conversion	5	4	5	3	5	4
False cause	2	2	3	4	2	3
TOTAL (10 max correct)	7	6	8	7	7	7
1c) B → A (If B then A)	1	2	4	4	4	3
2d) -B → A (If not B then A)	5	3	5	4	5	5

Table 1 Continued

3e) B → -A (If B then not A)	5	4	5	5	5	4
4f) -A → -B (If not A then not B)	1	0	3	2	2	2
TOTAL (20 max correct)	11	9	17	15	16	14
Many Questions	2	3	4	2	4	3
Ambiguity	3	2	3	4	4	4
Composition/Division	5	3	3	2	5	4
Generalization	4	0	4	4	5	5
TOTAL (20 max correct)	14	8	14	12	18	16
FALLACY TOTAL (50 max correct)	32	23	39	34	41	37
CONCLUSIONS, TOTAL CORRECT (100 max)	73	66	78	68	72	78

Consider, for example, the performance profile shown for subject NE-13. This subject was exposed to twenty instances of a valid conditional conclusion of the form "If A, then B" over all five passages. These instances are coded 1a) through 4a) for passages because each occurrence was accompanied by occurrence of a separate valid conclusion of the form "If not B, then not A"—these are coded 1b) through 4b). Accordingly, subject NE-13 was exposed to twenty valid conclusions of the form "If not B, then not A."

Inspection of Table 1 shows that subject NE-13 correctly identified all twenty instances of valid conditional conclusions of the form "If A, then B," but only correctly identified fourteen instances of the corresponding valid conditional conclusions of the form "If not B, then not A."

Subject NE-13 was exposed to ten valid conclusions that were either paraphrases of passage information or set inclusion/part whole statements based on passage information. As Table 1 shows, subject NE-13 correctly identified seven out of ten of these occurrences across the five passages.

All told, subject NE-13 correctly identified forty-one out of fifty valid conclusions that he was asked to judge as following or not following from a passage.

As is shown by the information in the bottom half of Table 1, subject NE-13 was not as good at identifying fallacies (invalid conclusions) as he was at identifying valid conclusions. He identified seven out of ten occurrences of the fallacies of "false conversion" and "false cause." Further, subject NE-13 had difficulty in recognizing invalid conditional conclusions. His response patterns are interesting and reveal the potential diagnostic power of the assessment procedure. He was able to spot every invalid conclusion of the forms "If not B, then A," but he was poor at identifying invalid conclusions of the forms "If B, then A" and "If not A, then not B." In considering this pattern, recall that the top part of Table 1 shows that subject NE-13 had correctly identified all twenty occurrences of the corresponding valid conditional statements "If A, then B."

The pattern of performance of subject NE-13 in evaluating valid and invalid conditional conclusions has potential diagnostic value that needs further exploration. It suggests that the subject may be assuming a biconditional interpretation of the logical connective "then"—i.e., he may be interpreting "then" to mean "if and only if."

The remaining four entries in the bottom half of Table 1 show NE-13's ability to recognize the twenty occurrences of conclusion statements that are instances of the four informal fallacies of "many questions," "ambiguity," "composition/division," and "faulty generalization." NE-13 recognized fourteen of these occurrences. The performance pattern of NE-13 on these items indicates that he has most difficulty in identifying occurrence of the informal fallacy of "many questions." All told, then, subject NE-13 correctly identified thirty-two out of fifty fallacious conclusions presented him.

The overall performance profile for subject NE-13 indicates that he was better at identifying valid conclusions (forty-one out of fifty) than at identifying invalid conclusions (thirty-two out of fifty). But as the discussion above suggests, it is possible to identify some specific strengths and weaknesses in this subject's ability to reason that should influence the design of a training intervention to strengthen his reasoning skills. Diagnostic information of this sort is not readily available at present on widely used tests of college-level reasoning aptitude such as the analytic section of the GRE.

Comparison of the performance profiles of different subjects appears quite informative and useful in describing individual differences. For example, the performance patterns of subject NE-13 and NE-15 on valid and invalid conditional conclusions show striking similarities and differences that may have diagnostic value for training the reasoning skills of these two subjects. Both subjects are excellent at identifying valid conditional conclusions of the form "If A, then B," and both subjects show more difficulty in identifying valid conclusions of the form "If not B, then not A," though subject NE-13 (fourteen out of twenty) is better at this than subject NE-15 (ten out of twenty).

However, despite these similarities, subjects NE-13 and NE-15 show a different propensity to identify invalid conditional conclusions (see the bottom section of Table 1). Subject NE-15 is noticeably better at this. He correctly identified seventeen out of twenty invalid conditional conclusions, while subject NE-13 only identified eleven out of twenty of these invalid conclusions. Another example of similar, yet contrasting, performance patterns is evident if we compare the scores of subject NE-13 with subject NE-17. Subject NE-13 correctly identified seventy-three out of 100 valid and invalid conclusions. Subject NE-17 performed, overall, at a similar level, correctly identifying seventy-two out of 100 valid and invalid conclusions. Yet, careful inspection of the patterns of scores for the two subjects shows a striking difference in performance. Subject NE-17 identified ten fewer valid conditional conclusions than did subject NE-13. On the other hand, subject NE-17 was more successful in identifying invalid conditional conclusions than subject NE-13. NE-17 identified sixteen out of twenty of these invalid conclusions, while subject NE-13 identified only eleven out of twenty of these invalid conclusions.

Table 2 displays summary score profiles for six non-native English-speaking students (students are labeled NN-7 through NN-12). Student NN-7 shows the strongest performance, earning a total correct score of eighty out of a possible maximum of 100. This student performs almost equally well in detecting conclusions that follow from valid arguments (thirty-eight out of fifty) as when detecting conclusions that follow from invalid arguments (forty-two out of fifty). Two other students NN-9 and NN-10, however, show an interesting and contrasting pattern in comparison to NN-7. These two students are as good or better than NN-7 in identifying valid conclusions (NN-9, thirty-eight out of fifty; NN-10, forty-two out of fifty), but they are much poorer at identifying fallacious conclusions (NN-9, nineteen out of fifty; NN-10, twenty-four out of fifty) than NN-7 (NN-7, forty-two out of fifty). This unbalanced pattern of performance for students NN-9 and NN-10 resembles the pattern of performance of the native English student NE-14. This student identified forty-three out of fifty valid conclusion, but only twenty-three out of fifty invalid conclusions.

Statistical Comparisons of Performance

Differences in the performance profile of native English and non-native English students on a subsample of problem types were examined using analyses of variance. The problem types selected included valid conditional conclusions, labeled 1a) through 4a) and 1b) and 4b) in Tables 1 and 2, and invalid conditional conclusions labeled 1c), 2d), 3e), and 4f) in Tables 1 and 2.

Table 2
Sample Reasoning Skill Profiles of Non-English Students

Valid Conclusions correct by subject (across 5 passages)

Conclusion Type	NN-7	NN-8	NN-9	NN-10	NN-11	NN-12
1a) A → B (If A then B)	5	4	4	4	3	2
2a) A → B	4	5	4	5	4	4
3a) A → B	5	4	5	5	5	3
4a) A → B	5	5	4	5	4	3
TOTAL (20 max correct)	19	18	17	19	16	12
1b) -B → -A (If not B then not A)	4	2	4	4	2	1
2b) -B → -A	2	3	4	3	4	5
3b) -B → -A	1	2	3	3	2	4
4b) -B → -A	3	3	2	5	2	3
TOTAL (20 max correct)	10	10	13	19	10	13
TOTAL FORMAL (40 max correct)	29	28	30	38	26	25
5) Valid Paraphrase	5	5	4	2	4	3
6) Valid Part-Whole Relation	4	3	4	2	1	4
TOTAL (10 max correct)	9	8	8	4	5	7
VALID TOTAL (50 max correct)	38	36	38	42	31	32

Fallacies correct by subject (across 5 passages)

Fallacy Type	NN-7	NN-8	NN-9	NN-10	NN-11	NN-12
False conversion	5	3	1	4	4	2
False cause	3	4	2	3	2	3
TOTAL (10 max correct)	8	7	3	7	6	5
1c) B → A (If B then A)	5	2	2	2	2	3
2d) -B → A (If not B then A)	5	4	3	2	2	4

Table 2 Continued

3e) B → -A (If B then not A)	4	4	2	3	4	4
4f) -A → -B (If not A then not B)	4	3	3	1	3	1
TOTAL (20 max correct)	18	13	10	8	11	12
Many Questions	4	0	0	2	3	1
Ambiguity	5	3	2	3	5	3
Composition/Division	3	3	3	3	1	2
Generalization	4	2	1	1	3	0
TOTAL (20 max correct)	16	8	6	9	12	6
FALLACY TOTAL (50 max correct)	42	28	19	24	29	23
CONCLUSIONS, TOTAL CORRECT (100 max)	80	64	57	66	60	55

A first analysis examined whether native and non-native English students performed equally well in identifying valid and invalid conclusions. Table 3 shows the mean level of performance of native and non-native English students on two valid conditional conclusion forms ("If A, then B") and ("If not B, then not A") and on four types of invalid conditional forms collapsed into one category, simply labeled "Invalid."

An analysis of variance (Table 4) was conducted to test the hypothesis of no statistical differences among means. The results indicated that there was a statistically significant interaction between language background and ability to recognize valid and invalid conclusion types. Native English and non-native English students were equally and highly capable of identifying valid conditional conclusions of the form "If A, then B." In addition, both groups were noticeably poorer at identifying valid conclusions of the form "If not B, then not A" and invalid conditional conclusion forms in general. However, whereas native English students found it easier to correctly identify invalid conditionals than valid conditionals of the form "If not B, then A," the opposite proved true for non-English background students.

The results suggest the possibility that the non-native English students had a superior ability to analyze the logical function of double negation in

Table 3
Means for Conditional Conclusions

Forms	AB	NBNA	Invalid
Native English Students (N = 24)	17.13	10.83	14.71
Non-Native English Students (N = 24)	17.50	13.21	11.38

Valid Forms Included:
  AB: If A, then B
  NBNA: If not B, then not A

Invalid Forms Included:
  NANB: If not A, then not B
  BNA: If B, then not A
  NBA: If not B, then A
  BA: If B, then A

statements of the form "If not B, then not A" although more indepth study of this possibility is needed.

A second analysis of variance addressed the question of whether native English students uniformly outperformed non-native English students in correctly identifying each of four types of invalid conditional conclusions. Table 5 shows the mean number of correct judgements for native and non-native English students on each of the four invalid conditional conclusions forms. Table 6 presents the corresponding analysis of variance. The results

Table 4
Valid Formal Conclusions versus Invalid Formal Conclusions for Native and Non-native English Students
AB, NBNA, INVALID

Source	SS	df	MS	F	p
1 Between	223.083	47			
2 Native vs. Non-native	1.361	1	1.361	0.282	0.598
3 Error	221.722	46	4.820		
4 Within	1796.667	96			
5 Conclusion Type	756.542	2	378.271	41.490	<0.001
6 Interaction	201.347	2	100.674	11.042	<0.001
7 Error	838.778	92	9.117		
8 Total	2019.667	143			

Table 5
Means for Invalid Conditional Conclusions

	Invalid Conclusion Form			
	NANB	BNA	NBA	BA
Native English Students (N = 24)	2.292	4.542	4.583	3.292
Non-Native English Students (N = 24)	1.292	3.958	3.750	2.375

Invalid Forms:
NANB: If not A, then not B
BNA: If B, then not A
NBA: If not B, then A
BA: If B, then A

of this analysis indicated that native English students were significantly better at identifying invalid conclusions than non-native English students. This result, of course, was to be expected given the results of the earlier analysis of variance. However, and more interestingly, there was no statistically significant interaction between native and non-native English status and the relative difficulty of identifying different invalid conclusion forms. There was, however, a statistically significant main effect for invalid conclusion forms, because all students, regardless of language background, found invalid conclusions of the form "If not A, then not B" to be the hardest to identify correctly followed by invalid conclusions of the form "If B, then A." Invalid conclusions of the form "If B, then not A" and "If not B, then A" were the easiest for all subjects.

Table 6
Analysis of Variance Invalid Formal Conditional Conclusions
NANB, BNA, NBA, BA

Source	SS	df	MS	F	p
1 Between	130.979	47			
2 Native vs. Non-native	33.333	1	33.333	15.703	0.000
3 Error	97.646	46	2.123		
4 Within	314.000	144			
5 Conclusion Type	198.729	3	66.243	80.116	0.000
6 Interaction	1.167	3	0.389	0.470	0.703
7 Error	114.104	138	0.827		
8 Total	444.979	191			

Discussion

The pilot data described in this paper needs further investigation in order to connect the performance patterns of students to possible training interventions assisting students. The design of the reasoning assessment permits diagnosis of the propensity of students to detect several forms of conclusions that would follow from valid versus invalid arguments based on text passages similar to those encountered by students in everyday undergraduate college textbooks. The sample reasoning profiles which were discussed suggest that students show varied patterns of ability to detect valid and invalid conclusions of various types. The ability of the assessment to detect such patterns implies that the training of the reasoning skills of students could be tailored to emphasize acquisition of ability to detect conclusion forms that present the most difficulty.

Analysis of variance results indicated that non-native English background students were as good as native English students in identifying valid conditional conclusions that did not involve negation terms. Surprisingly, non-native English students were better than native English students at identifying valid conditional conclusions involving double negation. The reasons for this facilitation are unclear. One may speculate, that the predominance of Asians among the non-English student sample was allied with greater mathematics achievement and familiarity with the use of the contrapositive conditional form in mathematical arguments. This and other speculations would need more careful investigation in order to prove informative.

Another analysis of variance result was that non-native English students were significantly poorer at identifying valid conditional conclusions than native English background students. These results have yet to be investigated in detail, but they point out the possibility that the language used in stating conditional conclusions involving one negation term may be processed differently by native and non-native English background students. An alternative, and possibly related interpretation, is that non-native English students have greater difficulty than native English students in maintaining a functional memory for alternative interpretations of conditionals involving just one negation term. Such a result is consistent with research showing that bilinguals have greater difficulty in maintaining an accurate working memory for information presented in their less familiar language (Goldman and Durán, 1988). These and other alternative explanations of native and non-native students' performance on the assessment merit more rigorous evaluation as part of a program to create a truly diagnostic reasoning assessment.

3

Assessing Heuristic Knowledge to Enhance College Students' Success

~ ~ ~ ~

Raymond V. Padilla

Introduction

Historically, the assessment of college-bound students has been driven by the desire to predict which students are most likely to succeed in college. To that end, paper and pencil tests have been designed to measure a student's aptitude in selected areas of knowledge such as language, science, and mathematics. Aptitude generally is expressed as knowledge that the student acquires through books and the curriculum taught in the typical elementary and secondary school. It is assumed that this book knowledge is relevant to the knowledge that the student will acquire in college so that the more such knowledge a student possesses before entering college, the more likely it will be that subsequently he or she will succeed in college study.

The research evidence compiled over a number of years does indeed show that there is some positive association between scores on aptitude tests and subsequent college performance as indicated, for example, by college grade point average (Durán, 1983). The association, however, is quite modest, and it would be unwise to predict the average student's chances of completing a degree at a typical public college or university on such evidence alone. This relative lack of robustness in the predictive power of traditional assessment has left both practitioners and researchers with insufficient guidance not only for determining admissions criteria but also for developing support programs to help students succeed in college after they get there.

In this paper, the focus is not so much on assessment for the purpose of helping colleges and universities do a better job in selecting students, but on helping students to succeed after they enroll in a particular institution. Of course, this emphasis also has implications for institutions that are seeking ways to be more successful at retaining and graduating students. By shifting the focus to retention and graduation, assessment is viewed from a broader perspective that encompasses not only book knowledge but also what is commonly called "heuristic knowledge." Our attention is also drawn to the need for more "transparent assessment," i.e., assessment that is largely unseen by the subject because the subject actually is engaged in learning new knowledge while the assessment is going on. Transparent assessment is a by-product of learning rather than a separate, intrusive activity of little immediate value to the subject. The following sections first present the logic of the approach and then describe a general method for implementing it.

Knowledge: Compiled, Theoretical, and Heuristic

Following Harmon and King (1985), an individual's knowledge can be classified into three types: Compiled, theoretical, and heuristic. Compiled knowledge is a composite of the other two types and can be considered as " . . . information that is organized, indexed, and stored in such a way that it is easily accessed . . . [and] readily useful for problem solving" (Harmon and King, 1985, 30). In effect, compiled knowledge consists of chunks of information that can be permanently stored and easily retrieved for effecting goal-directed behavior. These chunks of information are accumulated from theoretical and heuristic knowledge.

Theoretical knowledge consists of information that typically is chunked as definitions, axioms, and laws and is expressed as principles and theories that apply to a particular discipline. Theoretical knowledge is learned through formal study, as in school or through books and other media. Having theoretical knowledge alone, however, does not guarantee that it can be applied successfully to practical problems because:

> General laws usually fail to indicate exactly how one should proceed when faced with a specific problem. Except in simple cases . . . formal axioms tend to generate problem spaces that are too large to search. (Harmon and King, 1985, 31)

Effective solutions seem to depend on both theoretical and heuristic knowledge. Heuristic knowledge is chunked and stored as rules of thumb that are domain specific and learned from experience or a mentor. The rules of thumb are effective because they " . . . prune search spaces to a manageable size." They also:

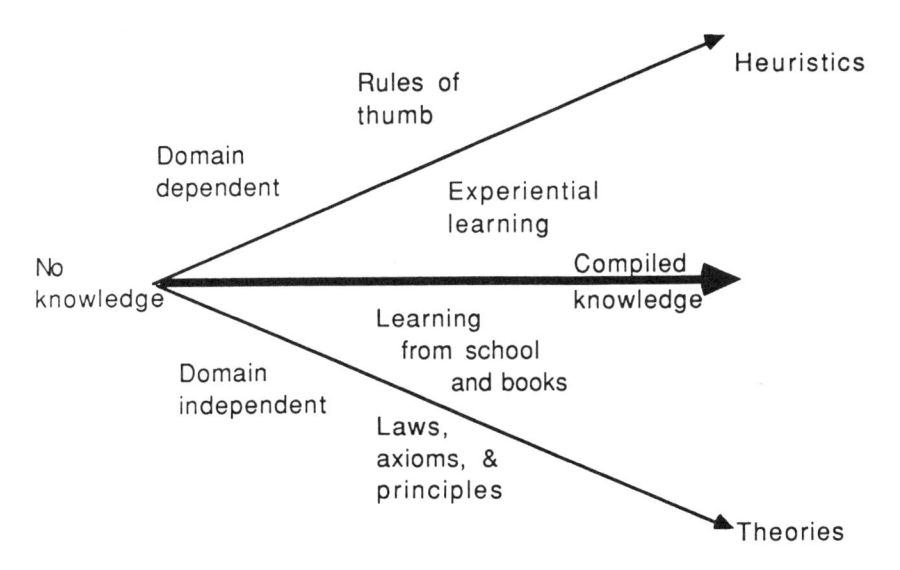

Figure 1. Compiled knowledge and its components (after Harmon and King, 1985, 30).

tend to focus attention on a few key patterns. . . . With domain experience, people become competent because they learn to focus quickly on the important facets of a problem, and because they learn the important relationships. (Harmon and King, 1985, 31)

Figure 1 shows graphically the relationship between the three types of knowledge. Note that heuristic knowledge is limited to a particular domain, typically thought of as "local" while theoretical knowledge is presumed to apply "universally." Interpreting Figure 1 from the point of view of college success, theoretical knowledge is largely book knowledge that will be learned on campus through course work and formal study, while heuristic knowledge is locally defined and acquired experientially.

Figure 1 shows that compiled knowledge, as well as heuristic and theoretical knowledge, can be seen as scaled from low to high levels. This raises the question of how much compiled knowledge a student must have in order to be admitted to a college as well as to graduate from it. Traditional precollege assessment focuses almost exclusively on determining the student's level of theoretical knowledge. Yet, heuristic knowledge may be just as important to a student's success.

High levels of heuristic and theoretical knowledge that result in effective problem solving can be designated as expertise. Expertise is thus performance based. For college students, such performance means simply that a student is successful in obtaining a college degree. To do so, a student must bring to campus, or acquire in the time allowed, the requisite theoret-

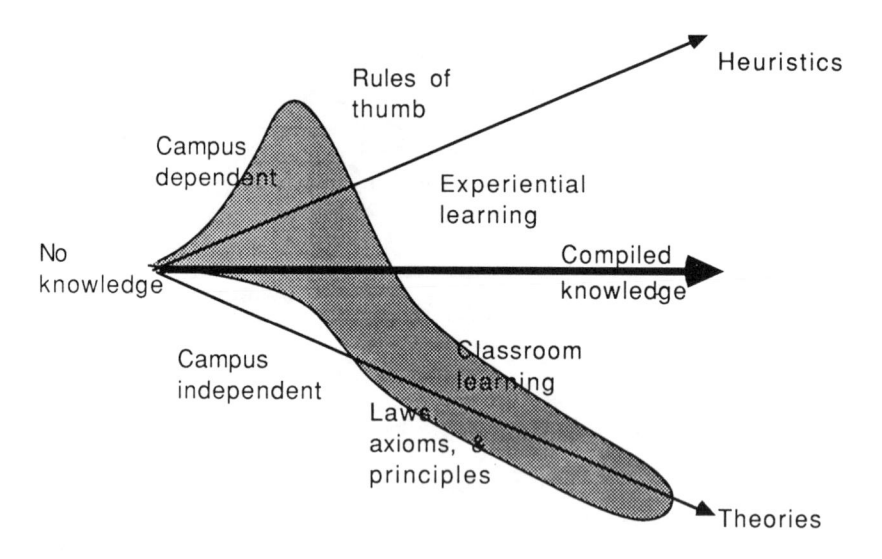

Figure 2. Suggested pattern of knowledge acquisition to become an "expert student" (adapted from Harmon and King, 1985, 33).

ical knowledge. At the same time, the student must acquire sufficient heuristic knowledge to overcome significant problems that are locally defined on campus or the campus/home environment. Following this line of reasoning, it may be that successful college students are simply individuals who have become experts in obtaining a degree; unsuccessful students lack such expertise. The knowledge characteristics of the "expert student" can be depicted as shown in Figure 2.

Observe that this conceptualization assumes that much of the heuristic knowledge is developed soon after the student's arrival on campus. It is important to acquire such knowledge early because the student must be socially and academically integrated into the campus environment fairly rapidly if he is to be successful (Tinto, 1987). Finding a satisfying social and academic "home" is necessary to further development of theoretical knowledge and degree attainment.

It is important to emphasize two salient characteristics of heuristic knowledge: its local domain and its experiential mode of acquisition. Localism confines heuristic knowledge to bounded spaces, situations, or phenomena. This means that heuristic knowledge has only limited transferability (applicability) from one location or situation to the next. For example, if a student is successful in obtaining a high school diploma, the heuristic knowledge acquired through this experience will have only limited applicability in obtaining a degree from a community college. Similarly, students who transfer from a community college to a four-year college will discover that the heuristic knowledge accumulated at the community college will have only limited applicability in the four year college campus.

Localism reflects the fact that all social situations include rules, norms, and sanctions to regulate individual and group behavior. The reality of a college student is that he or she must meet all of the "catalog requirements" (and the attendent academic and social requirements) of the institution in order to graduate. These requirements, and the social conditions under which they are expressed, are locally defined and sanctioned.

The localistic feature of heuristic knowledge leads to the experiential mode for learning it. One literally has to be there, *in situ*, to know the nuances, ambiguities, assumptions, and changing features of the situation. One learns by doing, by trial and error, by chance encounters, by good fortune, and misfortune. Knowledge takes the form of rules of thumb, ad hoc solutions, tricks of the trade, insider information, customs, norms, practices, and conventional wisdom. Having a good counselor, mentor, friend, buddy, soul sister, colleague, supporter, booster, etc., with experience on the scene is an effective means for rapidly acquiring such knowledge.

Heuristic knowledge is connected to the philosophic notion of *verstehen* or experienced reality. *Verstehen* implies that experienced reality is specific and concrete: The here and now. We survive by accumulating knowledge from each experience of the here and now. Thus, heuristic knowledge is concrete, specific, and bound to a particular domain. Any attempt to generalize it beyond the local situation (i.e., to render it unbounded) would result in abstract rules of limited applicability to a specific domain. To engage in such abstraction would be self defeating if the objective is simply to attain some goal in a concrete local situation that to a large extent is *sui generis*.

Assessing Heuristic Knowledge

If one considers heuristic knowledge as essentially similar to theoretical knowledge, then one might be tempted to approach the assessment of heuristic knowledge along the same lines as theoretical knowledge. One might proceed by developing some instrument to measure heuristic knowledge and then test each individual student to find out how much heuristic knowledge each one possesses. Unfortunately, this approach probably would prove ineffective simply because it largely ignores the two salient features of heuristic knowledge: its localism and the experiential mode of its acquisition. What is likely to be more effective is to develop a procedure that (1) assesses the heuristic knowledge that is relevant to a particular *campus* (as opposed to an individual), and that (2) provides an experience to students that helps them to acquire the relevant heuristic knowledge. This approach would focus on the campus as the entity to be assessed and in this way would define a bounded knowledge domain. Also, it would consider the student as an agent that must acquire heuristic knowledge experientially in order to be successful. Although the heuristic knowledge of the campus is acquired from the students and other relevant subjects, the assessment procedure essentially is transparent because the subjects will only be aware of a learning experience as they provide the assessment information.

Methodologically, this assessment strategy can be implemented by borrowing procedures from "dialogical research." Dialogical research (Freire, 1982; Reason and Rowan, 1981) attempts to involve researchers and subjects (participants) in a partnership to achieve greater understanding about a given situation. Through structured dialogue, participants are able to exchange views and information about a particular social setting. This permits the researcher to identify the heuristic knowledge valid in that social setting but, at the same time, the participants themselves gain important information about how to act successfully in the social setting that they inhabit.

The dialogical method can be made quite efficient if a matrix form of data collection is used and if the data are analyzed with the assistance of a computer (Padilla, 1987). Miles and Huberman (1984) have made a convincing case for displaying the results of qualitative data analysis in various well-defined formats, many of which take the form of a matrix. One can modify their approach to make it suitable for use with the dialogical method. The modification is simply to start with an *empty* matrix of the proper form in order to collect the desired data. In the context of assessment, to generate the proper form of the matrix requires the formulation of a well-formed assessment question by the researcher. This is the question that will be posed to the participating group of students as the initial subject for discussion. For example, the following might be a well-formed assessment question designed to tease out the heuristic knowledge relevant to a particular campus:

Think of a successful student on this campus. What barriers must this student overcome in order to be successful?

The collective responses of the participants are recorded in the empty matrix and backed up by audio tape recording. Figure 3 shows part of such a matrix; in this case only the lead data vector is shown. When filled, this vector will contain an unstructured listing of all the barriers that a successful student must overcome at the subject campus.

Barriers Overcome
by a Successful Student

Figure 3. The lead vector of a matrix designed
to capture heuristic knowledge about a
given campus.

By expanding the matrix, additional features can be studied for each of the identified barriers. For example, the participants may be asked to identify for each barrier the knowledge that a successful student possesses in order to overcome that particular barrier. Figure 4 shows the expanded matrix with two data vectors. The matrix does not necessarily have to be filled entirely by one group of participants. In fact, it may be desirable not to do so but to convene several small groups each of which contributes part of the information. This is similar to focus group research (Morgan, 1988). In this way, a broader representation of students can be included resulting in the construction of a more comprehensive heuristic knowledge base. In principle, the investigator can add as many data vectors as desired. As data vectors are added, the desired heuristic knowledge is "unfolded" from the starting point which is the well-formed assessment question, or in more conventional terms, the hypothesized cover term (Spradley, 1979).

This technique has been applied by the author to study successful Hispanic community college students. The lead question for the empty matrix

Barriers   Knowledge

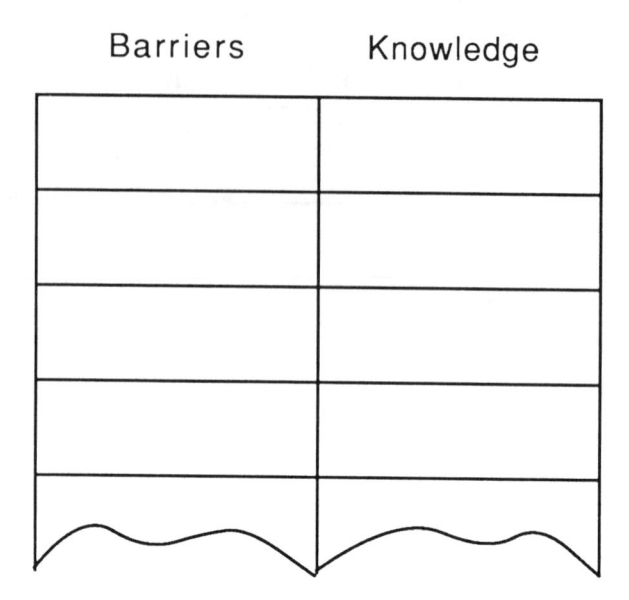

Figure 4. Empty matrix expanded with second data vector to capture the knowledge required to overcome each barrier.

was almost identical to the one suggested above. The matrix was expanded to include data about the incidence of each barrier overcome by successful students, the knowledge that successful students possess, and the specific actions that they take (see Figure 5). Note that by assigning each of two or more contrasting groups to complete separate matrices comparisons can be made between groups on a particular feature. Contrasts can be made on some salient group or site characteristic. For example, the author created contrast groups by comparing students, faculty, and staff between one another and across two campuses.

Analysis of the aggregated data revealed that the identified barriers could be classified into five types. They can be summarized as follows:

1. Barriers related to the institution or institutional processes (but not including the classroom). Some exemplars of this *institutional* class include:

> The admissions process
> Lack of mentors or role models
> Indoctrination to college life
> Students' lack of input into academic affairs
> Lack of parking

Barriers	Knowledge	Actions

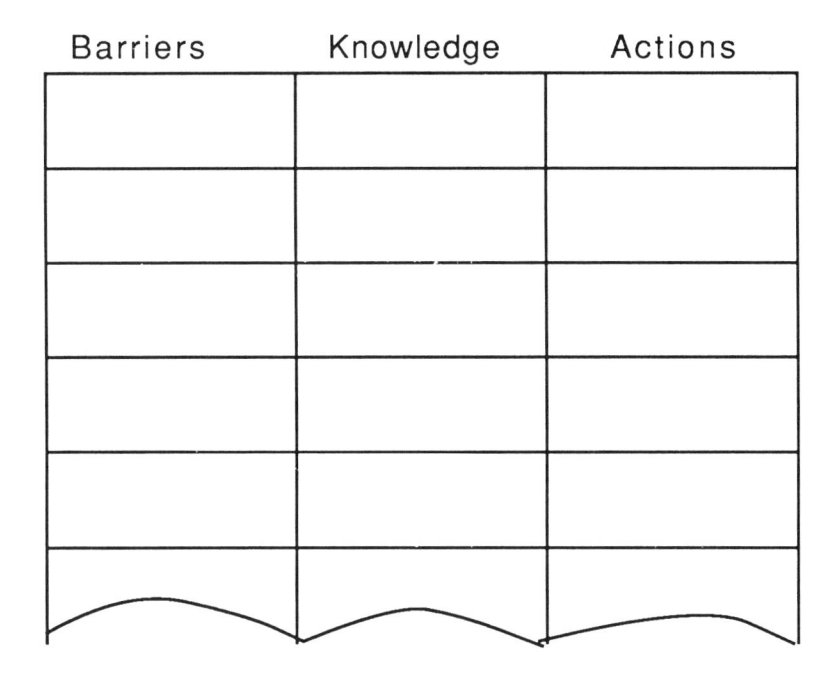

Figure 5. Part of an empty matrix used to study successful Hispanic students in a community college (source: Padilla and Pavel, 1988).

2. Barriers related directly to *classroom* functions and instruction. Some exemplars of this class include:

Lack of academic preparation
Lack of study skills
Instructor's delivery of instruction
Instructor's sensitivity to students

3. Barriers related to the student's *environment* outside the campus. Some exemplars of this class are:

Cultural differences
Lack of family support
Lack of social acceptance within the community

4. Barriers related to *financial* matters. Some exemplars of this class are:

Failure to qualify for financial aid
Need part-time job
Lack money-management skills

5. Barriers related to students individually in the sense of *personal* characteristics or traits. Some exemplars of this class include:

>Culture shock from lack of ethnics in classes
>Unclear educational goals
>Unable to manage time
>Lack of self-esteem
>"Unfair world" attitude

Notice that most of the barriers require heuristic knowledge to overcome them. Only some of the barriers listed under classroom can be aptly characterized as requiring theoretical knowledge to overcome them.

Analysis of the knowledge vector in the matrix revealed some specific characteristics of the heuristic knowledge that successful students apparently possess. Knowledge exemplars were classified into four types as follows:

1. *General* knowledge that restricts in meaningful ways the search space for a solution to a given barrier. This type of knowledge also can be likened to "awareness" of the general nature of a solution. Some exemplars of this class include:

>Know own personal values and goals
>Know about diverse student body at college
>Know available resources
>Know about Job Placement Center

2. *Specific* knowledge that points to a specific solution to a given barrier and, on a one-to-one basis, maps a barrier to at least one viable solution. Some exemplars of this class include:

>That students have to have an action plan
>That tutoring services are available and free
>Know how many hours you need to study
>That involvement leads to success
>Know that on-campus employment is best for retention

3. *Incremental* knowledge that implies the extension of a knowledge base, often simply the improvement of a particular skill. Some exemplars of this class include:

>More English
>Know math skills
>Library use

Textbook use
Note taking
Coping skills

4. *Procedural* knowledge that focuses on specific directions or the steps to be taken to overcome a barrier; this type of knowledge is more prescriptive in character. Some exemplars of this class include:

Know how to become a student
Know how to end-run problems
Cope with conflicts and stress
Learn to make decisions
Know how to organize notes

Note again that the knowledge required to overcome campus barriers is largely heuristic in character. Only knowledge of the incremental type can be easily linked to theoretical knowledge.

On the basis of this study, then, one can characterize heuristic knowledge as consisting of different types such as general, specific, and procedural with perhaps some of the incremental class. The latter, however, seems to be more closely related to theoretical knowledge. The "expert student" would probably possess a well-developed knowledge base built around these classes of heuristic knowledge. With heuristic knowledge the student sets general bounds to the search space for a solution to a particular barrier. This would constitute application of general knowledge that does not necessarily provide a specific solution to a barrier, but it does limit the possibilities for potentially effective solutions. The specific solution is contained in specific knowledge. Such knowledge works like a pointing index finger in that a specific solution to a given barrier is identified. Application of the solution presumably solves the problem, but not necessarily the general class of problems associated with it.

As already noted, procedural knowledge is more prescriptive. Solutions are not necessarily simple and straightforward. They may in fact involve complicated steps, delicate bureaucratic maneuvers, or complex strategies. Procedural knowledge perhaps reflects most clearly the experiential aspect of heuristic knowledge; it embodies the specific steps to be taken to implement an effective solution. This seems to be accomplished most successfully with experience.

Conclusion

These findings have been highlighted to show the richness of the data that can be acquired through the suggested procedure for assessing the heuristic knowledge required for student success on campus. The empty matrix approach not only produces evidence of the campus-specific barriers that successful students must overcome, and the specific knowledge that successful students possess to overcome these barriers, but it also provides the opportunity to describe in more general terms the content and structure of heuristic knowledge.

Moreover, since the procedure is dialogical in nature, participants who contribute the campus assessment data engage in a process that raises their own awareness and knowledge of how to be successful on campus. Obviously, one can use this technique not only as a research or assessment tool but also as a vehicle for imparting heuristic knowledge to students early in their college career.

The procedure meets our earlier criterion of assessing the heuristic knowledge required for success on a specific campus while helping students to acquire such knowledge. This seems to indicate that transparent assessment is a viable possibility in the assessment of heuristic knowledge.

Part II

Opening New Dimensions and Investigating
Advances in Test Construction on
Behalf of Hispanics

4

Time as a Factor in the Cognitive Test Performance of Latino College Students

~ ~ ~ ~

María Magdalena Llabre

In an article in *The Miami Herald* (November 12, 1988), the mayor of Coral Gables, Florida, commenting on the reason why a Cuban commissioner was not present at a meeting said: "We know that Hispanics don't like to get up early." Asked to explain his remarks, the mayor said: "In that culture, there are late awakenings, and they stay up later in the evenings." In communities with a large proportion of Hispanics, a distinction often is made between "American time" and "Hispanic time." The underlying idea behind these statements is the notion that Hispanics have a different concept of time than do Anglos, that they are less punctual than Anglos, and that they are less concerned with time limits than are Anglos.

The notion of cultural differences in the concept of time has received attention from sociologists, cultural anthropologists, and social psychologists. Frank (1939) first proposed the theoretical perspective that culturally determined attitudes and ideas about temporality are a major factor in the influence of culture on human behavior. This view still is upheld as Pronovost (1985) expressed: "The group to which individuals belong or relate to some extent determines their values and behaviour with regard to time . . ." (13). Empirical studies of cultural differences in time perspective have lent support to this theoretical view (Deregowski, 1979; Roberts and Greene, 1971; Sanders and Brizzolara, 1985). Levine, West, and Reis (1980) noted that differences in punctuality between Americans and Brazilians could be explained by divergent standard errors in their perception of time. They found that public clocks and watches were less accurate in Brazil than in the United States. Watchless Brazilians were less accurate than

Americans in estimating the time of day. Also, Brazilians were more often late for appointments or social gatherings than Americans.

If differences exist in the concept of time across cultures, and if time allocation is relevant to test performance (as is suggested by the testwiseness literature), it follows that time allocation differences on a test would be evident among different cultural groups. It also is conceivable that if these differences exist, they may be partly reflected in differential test performance.

Related Literature

That time allocation is relevant to test performance has received empirical support from the literature on testwiseness. In fact, the widely cited taxonomy of testwiseness proposed by Millman, Bishop, and Ebel (1965) includes *time-using* as one of the components that are independent of the test purpose. Intervention studies of testwiseness training that include Latino examinees in their sample generally demonstrate improved test performance for trained subjects (Oakland, 1972; Goldsmith, 1979; Dreisbach and Keogh, 1982; Maspons and Llabre, 1985; Benson, Urman, and Hocevar, 1986).

The effect of testing time on examinee performance has received limited attention in experimental studies. Large-scale research studies on the influence of time on test performance as a function of ethnic group membership have focused primarily on Black vs. White examinees. These studies have typically experimentally manipulated the amount of testing time available to create a speeded vs. an unspeeded condition and compared group performance on total test scores. Evans and Reilly (1972, 1973) used this approach on the reading comprehension section of the Law School Admission Test and on a special quantitative section of the Admission Test for Graduate Study in Business. They did not observe differential improvement in test scores for minority students in either study. These results were supported by the findings of Wild, Durso, and Rubin (1982) who found that increased time limits on special verbal and quantitative sections of the Graduate Record Examination did not differentially improve the scores of minority group examinees.

These studies of Black examinees seem to indicate that increased time limits are not related to differential performance. More recently, however, Schmitt, Bleistein, and Scheuneman (1987) and Schmitt and Dorans (1987) have noted a differential speededness effect between Black and White examinees on the verbal sections of the Scholastic Aptitude Test (SAT). In their studies of differential item functioning, the proportion of Blacks reaching the items at the end of a verbal section of the SAT tended to be lower than the proportion of White examinees of comparable ability as measured by the SAT total scores.

Studies of other cultural groups are few but suggest the importance of the time factor as it relates to examinee test performance. Immerman (1980), for example, found that the reading test scores of native American Indian examinees were improved by eliminating time constraints.

Specifically related to Latino students are a handful of studies that sample Mexican-Americans, Puerto Ricans, Cuban-Americans, or other Hispanics. If the notion that Latinos have a different concept of time than do Anglos holds true, and if Latinos are less concerned with time limits as was implied by the introductory remarks in this chapter, one could expect to observe differential test performance between Latinos and Anglos of equal ability on tests that impose time constraints. In an early study, Knapp (1960) investigated the effects of time limits on the Cattell Culture Free Intelligence Test given to 100 Mexican immigrants and 100 Anglos. The two groups were relatively similar in age (Mexican M = 27; Anglo M = 31) but quite dissimilar in the number of years of formal schooling (Mexican M = 4.9; Anglo M = 11.5). The results showed that while both groups scored higher under unspeeded conditions than under speeded conditions, the difference was significantly greater for the Mexicans (about 1.5 SD) than for the Anglos (about 1 SD).

Rincon (1979) compared 101 Mexican-American and eighty Anglo high school juniors under speeded (twenty-minute time limit) and power (forty-minute time limit) conditions with respect to their performance on the School and College Ability Tests. No significant differences between the speeded and unspeeded conditions were detected for either group with respect to the reliability and validity of the test. A significant but small difference between unspeeded and speeded performance was detected for the Mexican-American subjects having low to medium levels of test anxiety but not for Anglo subjects or Mexican Americans with high levels of test anxiety.

In a study of achievement, Wright (1984) examined the effects of increased time limits (an additional five and ten minutes) on the reading and writing sections of a practice test analogous to the College Level Academic Skills Test (CLAST) used in the state of Florida. His sample consisted of 181 college students classified as to sex, race (White, Black, and Hispanic), and native language (English and other). In general, test performance improved slightly (one to four points) with increased time limits. The improvement, however, was not greater for the Hispanic examinees, although the author did not test this interaction. Contrary to other studies with Latinos, the author concluded that increasing test time will not result in higher test scores.

Younkin (1986) studied the effects of increased testing time (ten minutes and twenty minutes) on the performance of 659 native and non-native speakers of English on the CLAST. The majority of the non-native speakers were Latino. Main effects due to time were observed on the reading, writing, and essay subtests of CLAST. A significant group by time interaction was observed on the computation subtest. The native speakers showed no improvement with increased time but the non-native speakers improved up to ⅓ SD with increased time. The author postulated that the level of semantic difficulty in the logic and word problems on the computation subtest was responsible for this interaction.

The recent work by Schmitt and Dorans (1987) on differential item functioning extended the results of differential speededness to Mexican-Americans and Puerto Ricans who reside in the United States and speak English as their primary language. These authors analyzed ten analogy items located at the end of a forty-five-item verbal section of the SAT administered in November 1983. In the study 278,166 Whites were compared to 2,963 Mexican-Americans and 3,230 Puerto Ricans. All ten analogy items were reached by a higher proportion of White examinees than of examinees in the Latino ethnic groups who were of equal ability, as measured by their total SAT scores.

Llabre and Froman (1987, 1988) have conducted two small-scale studies which compared Latino and Anglo college students with respect to time allocation to cognitive test items in order to determine whether this variable potentially can be used to explain differential test performance. In both studies, microcomputers were used as the vehicle for test administration.

Study One

Participants in the first study were twenty-eight Anglo and thirty-eight Latino students enrolled in a beginning algebra course at Miami-Dade Community College. All subjects responded to a sixteen-item multiple-choice test of reasoning ability that used items from the California Test of Mental Maturity (CTMM; Sullivan, Clark, and Tiegs, 1957). Subjects were given an unlimited amount of time to respond but were instructed to work as quickly as possible. Items were presented in a fixed order and examinees were unable to go back to previous items. The computer program designed for the study recorded the responses and the amount of time that elapsed from the moment the item appeared on the screen to the point when the examinee pressed a response key.

The time data were analyzed as a group-by-item split-plot design. The results revealed that the group-by-item interaction was statistically significant. Results of simple effects showed that the Latino examinees took longer to respond to all but five items. Ethnic differences on item difficulty indices were not significant. Analyses of total scores resulted in significant differences between groups for both total test score and total time. Latino examinees scored on the average one point less and spent approximately six minutes longer than Anglo examinees. Data were re-analyzed after imposing an arbitrary time limit of ten minutes. In this situation, Latino subjects would have scored six points less than Anglos. Pearson correlations between item time and difficulty were -.41 for Latinos and -.64 for Anglos. Although the difference between the two coefficients was not statistically significant, the trend indicated that Anglos might tend to budget their time according to the difficulty of the item to a greater extent than the Latinos. Taken together, the results suggested that imposed time constraints will work against the strategy employed by the Latino examinees, since they would have run out of time prior to responding to the last four items. And, relative to the Anglo examinees, the Latino subjects performed slightly better in these last four items.

Study Two, Phase One

The second study conducted by Llabre and Froman (1988) was done in two phases. Phase one was a systematic replication of the first study. In this study a fifty four-item computerized test (COMP) was used with items taken from the CTMM, Advanced Form S (Sullivan, Clark, and Tiegs, 1957) and the sequences and verbal reasoning subtests of the Test of Cognitive Skills, Levels 4 and 5 (CTB/McGraw-Hill, 1982). There were twenty-five nonverbal and twenty-nine verbal items and subjects were given an unlimited amount of time to respond. The Standard Progressive Matrices (SPM) test (Raven, 1978) was administered prior to the computerized test in an effort to control for cognitive reasoning ability between the ethnic groups. A questionnaire also was administered at the end of the testing session. The questionnaire contained items about country of origin of examinee and parents; length of time living in the United States; degree of English usage in the home, school and with friends; and specific attitudes about time and strategy used on six different test items. Subjects were either freshmen or sophomores of Hispanic or Anglo heritage attending Miami-Dade Community College. Seventy-seven subjects were used in the analyses of this study. Approximately half of the thirty-seven Latino subjects were born in the United States of Cuban parents. The remaining came from Cuba, Puerto Rico, Nicaragua, or other Central or South American countries. The number of years residing in the United States ranged from one to twenty-four with a mean of thirteen. Seventy percent spoke mostly Spanish with their families, but only 11% spoke mostly Spanish with friends.

The results demonstrated no significant ethnic group differences on the SPM or the total score on the computerized test. However, significant differences in total testing time were observed between the two ethnic groups, with Latino examinees taking longer than Anglos. The mean time for Anglos was 27.35 minutes and 33.68 for Latinos. Analyses at the item level revealed that Latinos took longer in all but seven of the items. The difference was significant for both the verbal and the nonverbal items.

Correlations between item difficulty and time showed the same trend as in study one. The values were -.58 for Anglos and -.41 for Latinos. The correlation between the number of years in the United States and the total time spent on the test was -.45 for the Latinos while similar correlations between years in the United States and SPM or COMP scores were nonsignificant.

Analyses of the questionnaire items did not reveal any important differences between the ethnic groups. Chi-squared statistics were used to test the relation between ethnicity and reported strategy used in each of seven items. All chi-squared values were nonsignificant, indicating similarity between groups in the particular strategies reported. Both groups also reported that time was "slightly important" when solving items and that they were "fairly conscious" of time. It is interesting that only one Latino subject reported having translated an item to Spanish before solving it.

Phase Two

In the second phase of this study, 142 subjects, 87 Anglos and 55 Latinos, participated. Within ethnic group, subjects were randomly assigned to either a structured or an unstructured time condition. The total time for both conditions (thirty-two minutes) was fixed based on the average time taken by all examinees in Phase One. In the structured condition, the time allowed per item was also fixed. A base time of fifteen seconds was allowed per item. The remaining total testing time was allocated to each item inversely proportional to the difficulty as determined from Phase One.

Characteristics of the Latino subjects in Phase Two paralleled those observed in Phase One. However, Phase Two subjects were not equal in ability to those in Phase One as evidenced by higher mean values on the SPM, particularly for the Anglo examinees. A time group-by-ethnicity Analysis of Variance on the SPM revealed a significant ethnicity main effect (F (1 and 138) = 5.8, p = .02), with Anglo examinees receiving higher scores (M = 52.64) than Latino examinees (M = 49.89).

Similar analyses were conducted on the COMP with and without SPM as a covariate. The results showed a significant ethnicity main effect: F (1 and 138) = 23.87, p = .001 without covariate; F (1 and 137) = 17.50, p = .001 with covariate. Means were 43.77 for the Anglo examinees and 37.11 for the Latinos. The effect of the time condition and the interaction were not significant.

Results from the questionnaire were almost identical to those observed in Phase One. For the most part, the Latinos did not translate the items before solving them and the strategies that they reported were similar to those reported by the Anglos. In contrast to Phase One results, both groups of Latinos reported being "slightly" more conscious of time and felt that time was "more important" than their Anglo counterparts.

The results from Phase One of Study Two replicate those observed by Llabre and Froman (1987). They indicate that Latinos take longer than Anglos of equal ability in responding to both verbal and nonverbal cognitive test items. Furthermore, if time is not restricted, the two groups do not differ significantly in test performance.

The results from Phase Two of the study indicate that structuring the time per item for the examinee may not be helpful. Although the difference in mean scores between the structured and unstructured conditions was not significant, COMP scores under the unstructured condition were generally higher than under the structured condition. This was contrary to expectations and may reflect a design weakness in the procedure used for estimating time per item. Imposing time constraints, whether structured or unstructured, resulted in ethnic group differences on the COMP test, with Latinos receiving lower scores. The difference persisted after adjusting for SPM scores.

Taken together, these results suggest that testing time is an important factor when measuring the cognitive test performance of Latino college students. Latinos take longer than Anglos to answer test questions and do not do as well under speeded conditions.

The longer time used by the Latinos is not spent translating the test items. The overwhelming majority of the Latino examinees said that they did not translate the items to Spanish before answering them. Also, the difference in allocated time was observed with both verbal and nonverbal items. The difference also is not due to any obvious difference in reported strategies used to solve the problems. The most plausible explanation at this point is a difference in familiarity or perception of testing time expectations. A negative correlation was observed between the number of years residing in the United States and time spent on the test (-.45) during Phase

One. It may be that as Latino examinees become more acculturated, they become more accustomed to testing procedures and are better able to conform to the time demands of the testing situation.

Methodological Issues

This area of investigation suffers from several methodological shortcomings. One of the problems is the need for control of the ability level of examinees from the different ethnic groups. Unless the ethnic groups are of comparable ability, it is not possible to determine the unique influence of the time factor upon test performance. This problem was recognized by Schmitt et al. (1987) who controlled for ability by using total SAT scores. Theirs is not a totally satisfactory solution, however, since the total score may be influenced by the speededness factor in the test. Using an untimed measure as was done by Llabre and Froman (1988) may be more appropriate but requires additional testing.

A second issue has to do with the specific time parameters used in experimental studies. In some instances (the Wright study is an example), the differences in time between conditions was very small (five minutes) relative to the total test length and total testing time (seventy minutes), thus producing weak treatment effects. In most studies, the rationale used to set time limits was not presented, in fact the limits appeared quite arbitrary. It then becomes very difficult to assess their appropriateness.

In studies where speededness is the dependent variable, its measurement is typically in terms of whether an item at the end of the test was omitted by an examinee. This definition assumes that the only reason for the omission is lack of time. The validity of this assumption needs to be addressed, particularly in testing situations where examinees also omit items throughout the test.

With some exceptions, the majority of the studies have done manipulations at the total test score level rather than the item level. This approach, although practical for the typical testing situation, precludes the understanding of item characteristics that may contribute to differential speededness. The studies by Schmitt et al. illustrate the potential value of working at the item level. The second study by Llabre and Froman further illustrates how additional information about the process used by examinees may be gained by monitoring item performance and querying examinees via computerized testing.

A problem introduced with an experimental computerized test, however, is the difficulty in obtaining large samples. The small sample size is a weakness in the Llabre and Froman studies. Working with operational forms of tests present the opportunity for analyzing large data sets but limit the experimental manipulations available to the researcher. Also related to the use of experimental situations is the external validity of results. Whether examinees will budget their time in a similar fashion under real as opposed to experimental conditions is questionable. For example, in the Llabre and Froman studies, the results of the test had no consequence for the examinees' future. Furthermore, their tests were easy for the level of the examinees. On the other hand, the SAT is a more difficult test that has important implications for students. Thus the level of motivation and anxiety will vary between the two testing situations. The external validity of these studies may be assessed by comparing the results obtained under both sets of conditions. The foregoing discussion seems to indicate that both types of studies are essential for understanding how time limits influence examinee performance.

In spite of the methodological shortcomings, a speededness effect has emerged for Latino examinees. Even with small samples, the Llabre and Froman studies revealed significant results. The results appear to be consistent even after controlling for cognitive ability. In spite of treatment level differences that are small and arbitrary, ethnic group differences have emerged from experimental studies. Finally, the differential speededness effect was confirmed by Schmitt and Dorans with an operational form of the SAT.

One additional point about generalizability needs to be considered. Latinos in the United States may be classified into four major subgroups: Mexican-Americans, mainland Puerto Ricans, Cuban-Americans, and other Latinos. Some of the research does not distinguish among these subgroups although there are cultural, linguistic, economic, and experiential differences among them. The Latinos in the United States not only differ in origin and the region in which they settled but also in their socioeconomic status and degree of bilingualism. Given these differences it may not be possible to make generalizations across subgroups. Yet cultural influences are powerful, and it may be that the perception of time generalizes across otherwise diverse subgroups of Latinos. The generality of this factor is an interesting and important topic in need of attention by test publishers.

Proposed Hypotheses

There are indeed cultural reasons why Latino students might be differentially affected by time limits on cognitive tests. Cultural differences in time perspective reported in the literature were noted earlier. There may also be linguistic reasons for the difference given that most Latinos are bilingual, with Spanish being the first language they learned. Information processing research conducted with bilingual subjects suggests that speed of processing is mush slower in a second language (Dordic, 1980). Furthermore, the research with bilingual subjects also indicates that factors such as stress and fatigue negatively influence performance in a second language to a greater extent than performance in the primary language. The fatigue factor has implications for studies of testing time when tests are long.

The linguistic hypothesis, however, appears to be weaker than the cultural hypothesis. The examinees in the Llabre and Froman study reported not having translated the items to Spanish. One could still argue that processing the information in English may have taken them longer. Yet with nonverbal items, the processing could have been done in their primary language and the time effect was still present. Although weaker, the linguistic hypothesis has not been ruled out by any of the studies examined here, since none of them evaluated it directly. There is also the possibility that both linguistic and cultural factors are operating simultaneously to produce an effect.

Whatever the reason, any individual responsible for the assessment of Latinos and the use of results to determine access to educational opportunities must give very serious considerations to the setting of time limits.

5

Factors Related to Differential Item Functioning for Hispanic Examinees on the Scholastic Aptitude Test

~ ~ ~ ~

Alicia P. Schmitt and Neil J. Dorans

Introduction

Identification of factors that differentially affect the performance of subgroups of examinees on items and consequently result in underestimation of their competence has been the focus of numerous investigations since the 1950s (Linn and Harnisch, 1981). However, not many of these differential item functioning (DIF) studies have identified general characteristics that explain differential performance by a specific subgroup (Linn and Harnisch, 1981; Scheuneman, 1982; Schmitt, 1988). The purpose of this chapter is to summarize recent research on DIF for Hispanic examinees. These research studies have been able to identify several item characteristics and relate them to the differential performance of Hispanic subgroups on the verbal portion of the Scholastic Aptitude Test (SAT). To provide a conceptual framework, DIF is defined and statistical procedures used to detect DIF are presented. Next, the results of investigations of DIF for Hispanic examinees on the SAT are presented. Lastly, implications of these findings for assessment practices and the education of Hispanics are explored.

The opinions expressed in this chapter are those of the authors and should not be misconstrued to represent official policy of either the Educational Testing Service or the College Board, the agencies that funded most of the research reported here.

Differential Item Functioning

Items that are harder for one group than for another group with the same level of ability or skill are defined as differentially more difficult or as functioning differentially between the two groups. Usually the majority group is referred to as the reference or base group and the minority group as the focal or study group. Since DIF indices take overall differences in ability into account by matching the groups before comparing their item performance, DIF indices identify items that might have construct-irrelevant characteristics. Judgmental evaluation of items with DIF may identify some possible causes of DIF.

Two statistical procedures currently used at the Educational Testing Service to assess DIF are the Mantel-Haenszel (MH) (Holland and Thayer, 1988) and the standardization (STD) methods (Dorans and Kulick, 1986). Both of these methods identify DIF after partitioning the reference and focal groups into subgroups with the same score on a relevant matching variable. The matching variable is usually the total score on a test closely related to the construct the item is intended to measure. While there are some differences between the MH and STD methods, such as the scale in which the item performance of the reference and focal groups are compared and the way that the individual differences between the subgroups are averaged, the DIF estimates computed by these methods are highly correlated (upper .90s) because they tend to yield the same rank order of items with respect to DIF (Wright, 1987; Holland and Thayer, 1988; Dorans, 1989).

The DIF findings summarized in this paper are based on results obtained using the standardization procedure. Because of the close theoretical relationship between the STD and the MH methods, similar DIF estimates would have been obtained with the MH method if that approach had been available at the time most of these studies were conducted. In addition to its similarity to the MH method, the standardization method provides a powerful descriptive statistical tool that can be used to pinpoint sources of DIF in an item via its standardized distractor analysis. For these reasons, it was the procedure used in these studies.

Standardization Methodology

In the traditional standardization analysis, an item is said to exhibit DIF when the probability of correctly answering the item is lower or higher for examinees from one group than for equally able examinees from another group. The focus of DIF analyses is on differences in performance between groups that are matched with respect to the ability, knowledge, or skill of interest. The basic elements of a standardization analysis of the keyed response are proportions correct at each level of a matching variable, such as total score, in a base or reference group and a focal or study group. Plots of these conditional proportions correct against score level in the focal and reference groups provide a visual indication of the extent of DIF that an item exhibits. A plot of differences in conditional proportions correct between the focal and reference group portrays the degree of DIF more directly. In addition to these plots, standardization provides numerical indices for quantifying DIF.

The prime numerical DIF index that standardization computes is the standardized p-difference, which is defined as

(1) $$DSTD = \Sigma\{W_s[P_{fs} - P_{rs}]\} / \Sigma\{W_s\},$$

where $[W_s / \Sigma\{W_s\}]$ is the weighing factor at score level s on the SAT used to weight differences in the proportions correct between the focal group (P_{fs}) and the reference group (P_{rs}), and Σ is the summation operator which sums these weighted differences across scores levels to arrive at DSTD, an index that can range from -1 to +1 or -100% to 100%. Negative values of DSTD indicate that the item disadvantages the focal group, while positive DSTD values indicate that the item favors the focal group. DSTD values between -.05 (-5%) and +.05 (+5%) are considered negligible. DSTD values outside the {-.10, +.10} or the {-10%, +10%} range are considered sizeable. For operational purposes, a $|DSTD| \geq .10$ is a recommended cutoff; for research purposes, a cutoff of $|DSTD| \geq .05$ should be used.

The weights, $[W_s / \Sigma\{W_s\}]$, which are applied to both P_{fs} and P_{rs}, are the essence of the standardization approach. Contrast this weighing constancy with what occurs in the computation of impact,

(2) $$IMPACT = P_f - P_b = \Sigma\{N_{fs}P_{fs}\} / \Sigma\{_{fs}\} - \Sigma\{N_{rs}P_{rs}\} / \Sigma\{N_{rs}\},$$

where N_{fs} and N_{rs} are the frequencies of score level s in the focal and reference groups. Thus, impact provides differences in performance between groups which have not been matched and *probably are not* comparable. In contrast, the standardization method focuses on comparing groups that *are* comparable. In addition, the particular set of weights employed for standardization depends upon the purposes of the investigation. Some plausible options are the following:

- $W_s = N_{ts}$, the number of examinees at s in the total group;
- $W_s = N_{rs}$, the number of examinees at s in the reference group;
- $W_s = N_{fs}$, the number of examinees at s in the focal group; or
- $W_s = $ the relative frequency at s in some reference group.

In practice, $W_s = N_{fs}$ has been used because it gives the greatest weight to differences in P_{fs} and P_{rs} at those score levels most often attained by the focal group under study. Use of N_{fs} means that DSTD equals the difference between P_f, the observed performance of the focal group on the item, and $P_{f'}$, the imputed performance of selected reference group members who are matched in ability to the focal group members.

In research on the SAT, two versions of DSTD have been computed. In the original version, all examinees, including those who do not reach the item, are included in the denominator of P_{fs} and P_{rs}, yielding $DSTD_1$. In the more recent version, an effort was made to adjust for speededness by excluding the not-reached examinees from the calculation of DSTD, yielding $DSTD_2$. Schmitt and Bleistein (1987) were the first to employ this correction, which has become the standard in operational DIF work on the SAT. Dorans, Schmitt, and Curley (1988) demonstrated that this correction partially adjusts for the speededness effect. Hence, $DSTD_2$ will be used in this report for all options except not-reached where only $DSTD_1$ makes sense.

The generalization of the standardization methodology to all response options, including omitting and not reaching the item, is straightforward. It is as simple as replacing the keyed response with the option of interest in all calculations. For example, a standardized response rate analysis on option A would entail computing the proportions choosing A (as opposed to the proportions correct) in both the focal and reference groups,

(3) $$P_{fs}(A) = A_{fs}/N_{fs}; \quad P_{rs}(A) = A_{rs}/N_{rs},$$

where A_{fs} and A_{rs} are the number of people in the focal and reference groups, respectively, at score level s who choose option A. The next step is to compute differences between these proportions,

(4) $$D_s(A) = P_{fs}(A) - P_{rs}(A).$$

Then these individual score level differences are summarized across score levels by applying some standardized weighing function to these differences to obtain DSTD(A),

(5) $$DSTD(A) = \Sigma\{W_s[P_{fs}(A) - P_{rs}(A)]\} / \Sigma\{W_s\},$$

the standardized difference in response rates to option A. In a similar fashion one can compute standardized differences in response rates for options B, C, D, and E, and for nonresponses as well.

For example, application of the standardization methodology to counts of examinees at each score who did not reach the item culminates in a standardized not-reached difference,

(6) $$DSTD(NR) = \Sigma\{W_s[P_{fs}(NR) - P_{rs}(NR)]\} / \Sigma\{W_s\}.$$

For items at the end of a separately-timed section of a test such as the SAT, these standardized differences provide measurement of the differential speededness of a test. Differential speededness refers to the existence of differential response rates between focal group members and matched reference group members to items appearing at the end of a section.

Results of Hispanic DIF Studies

Item Factors

True Cognates. Several studies have identified items with words with a common root in English and Spanish, i.e., true cognates, to be differentially easier for Hispanic examinees (Alderman and Holland, 1981; Breland, Stocking, Pinchak, and Abrams, 1974). More recently, Chen and Henning (1985) found the vocabulary subset of the English as a Second Language Placement Examination to be differentially easier for examinees who were native speakers of Spanish than for examinees who were native speakers of Chinese. In that study, all of the items that exhibited positive DIF for Hispanics contained "close" cognates. Schmitt (1985) also reported that true cognates favorably influenced item performance of Hispanic examinees. In two follow-up studies, this finding was supported (Schmitt, 1988; Schmitt, Curley, Bleistein, and Dorans, 1988). Findings from these studies will be summarized below and a modification to the general "true cognate hypothesis" will be offered.

In the first of these studies, Schmitt (1988) generated and tested the following hypothesis: "Cognates, or words with a common root in English and Spanish, will tend to favor Hispanic examinee item functioning. Example: music (música)" (4). Using the standardization method and results from two SAT-Verbal forms, the item performance of Mexican-Americans and Puerto Rican examinees who had identified themselves as having English as their best language were compared to the item performance of similarly-identified White examinees. A summary of the DIF statistics obtained in these studies are presented in Table 1, along with sample size information. Note that the number of extremely discrepant items (| DSTD | ≥ .10) across both of these SAT-Verbal forms is very small. One drawback of the original Schmitt (1988) investigation was that the study of item factors such as true cognates was restricted to the number naturally occurring in regular SAT-Verbal tests. The follow-up Schmitt et al. (1988) investigation attempted to remedy the limited naturally occurring item factors by developing items with these factors and administering them in non-operational SAT-Verbal sections.

Table 1
Summary of Standardized Differential Functioning between White and Hispanic Examinees on SAT-Verbal Forms I and II

	Mexican-American/White			Puerto Rican/White		
		$DSTD_1$			$DSTD_1$	
	# Items	Mean	SD	# Items	Mean	SD
		Total Test Form I[a]				
Total	85	.00	.03	85	−.00	.04
Positive	49 (3&1)	.02	.02	42 (5&1)	.03	.03
Negative	36 (5&0)	−.03	.03	43 (7&1)	−.03	.03
		Total Test Form II[b]				
Total	85	.00	.03	85	.00	.04
Positive	44 (4&0)	.03	.02	47 (7&1)	.03	.02
Negative	41 (10&0)	−.03	.02	38 (9&1)	−.03	.03

Note: The first value in parentheses identifies the number of positive or negative discrepant items using a criterion of |DSTD| ≥.05 and the second value uses a criterion of |DSTD| ≥.10. Data in this table has been excerpted from the Schmitt (1988) paper.

[a]The Form I analyses are based on 2,963 Mexican-American, 3,230 Puerto Rican, and 278,099 White examinees who speak English as their best language.

[b]The Form II analyses are based on 3,456 Mexican-American, 3,384 Puerto Rican, and 285,883 White examinees who speak English as their best language.

To assess the true cognate hypothesis, each verbal item across the two SAT-Verbal tests studied by Schmitt (1985, 1988) was classified by at least two bilingual judges. When the stem, key, or distractors of an item was comprised of more than one word, different coding procedures were followed depending on how many words comprised the part. For Antonyms and Analogies, where parts of the items included two words, half a point was given for each word defined as a true cognate. In Sentence Completion and Reading Comprehension, where the parts of the item were composed of a sentence or a clause, the complete stem, key, or distractor was classified as a true cognate only if the meaning of the part could be inferred from the true cognates. Possible true cognate values for any item type on the stem, key, or distractor ranged from zero (no true cognate) to one (all true cognates), with possible .5 values (if only one word was a true cognate). Both item content analyses and correlations between the true cognate classifications and the $DSTD_2$ value for all items in each of the two SAT-Verbal tests were done. Correlations of $DSTD_2$ with true cognates in both stem and item key and with an overall true cognate classification (sum of the factor across all the item parts (All-S,K,D)) are presented in Table 2.

Table 2
Correlations between Standardized Differences (DSTD$_2$) and True Cognate Factors in SAT-Verbal Form I and II

	SAT-Verbal Form I		SAT-Verbal Form II	
True Cognates	Mexican-American	Puerto Rican	Mexican-American	Puerto Rican
	Antonym (n = 25)			
Stem & Key	.42	.42	.41	.39
All-S, K, D	.38	.41	.44	.46
	Sentence Completion (n = 15)			
Stem & Key	.21	.40	.47	.63
All-S, K, D	.32	.35	.00	.21
	Reading Comprehension (n = 25)			
Stem & Key	.14	.25	−.03	.16
All-S, K, D	.02	−.04	.15	.06
	Analogy (n = 20)			
Stem & Key	.50	.45	M	M
All-S, K, D	.59	.57	.15	−.01

Note: Differences between these correlation values and the ones presented in the Schmitt (1988) paper are due to use of DSTD$_2$ values in the present table.

[M]Missing correlation values for Analogy items on Form II are due to insufficient number of items classified as having true cognates in both the stem and the key.

When true cognates were found in the item stem as well as in the key, the correlation between true cognate content and DSTD$_2$ was generally the highest value across all item type sections for both Mexican-American and Puerto Rican groups. The highest correlations between true cognate combinations in the stem and key and DSTD$_2$ are found across both groups for Sentence Completion items (ranging from .21 to .63) and Antonym items which were more consistent (ranging from .39 to .42). The Sentence Completion correlations are highest for the Puerto Rican group (.40 and .63 for Forms I and II respectively), while for the Mexican-American group the correlations are relatively lower (.21 and .47 for Form I and II respectively). The Analogy item type has correlations between true cognates in the stem and key combinations that are consistently in the high .40s for both Hispanic groups. Correlations of DSTD$_2$ with the overall true cognate classification are generally consistent with those found for the stem and key true cognate classification. The true cognate hypothesis was supported by these results. Note that true cognates affected the performance of Puerto Rican examinees more than the performance of Mexican-American examinees. A stronger reliance on Spanish as a second language by the Puerto Rican subgroup may be a possible explanation for that group's greater sensitivity to the true cognate effect (Arce, 1982; Ortiz and Gurak, 1982).

The purpose of the Schmitt et al. (1988) investigation was to provide a follow-up to Schmitt's (1985, 1988) studies by constructing and analyzing nonoperational SAT-Verbal sections in which the occurrence of several postulated factors, including true cognates, were rigorously controlled. In that study item pairs were constructed. Each item pair consisted of one item with the postulated factor and the other item without the factor. In every case the items within each pair were as parallel as possible. In most cases only one word was changed by replacing it with a synonym that had approximately the same language difficulty and frequency of usage in English. A total of two thirty-seven-item variants (ten Antonyms, five Sentence Construction, ten Analogies, and twelve Reading Comprehension) were constructed. Since, apart from true cognates, three other factors were under study, a total of only fifteen true cognate item pairs were constructed. These pairs were divided between the item types in the following fashion: four and three Antonyms, two and two Sentence Completion items, and two and two Analogies in each of the variants, respectively, had true cognates. In this study the matching variable was the score based on an external eighty-five-item SAT-Verbal test. Data consisted of item responses of self-identified White (44,341 and 40,511), Mexican-American (480 and 480), Puerto Rican (525 and 468), and Latin American or other Hispanic (614 and 574) examinees for Variants I and II, respectively. The samples were restricted to high school juniors and seniors who reported that either English or English and another language was/were their first language/s. Differences in $DSTD_2$ between the pair of items in Variants I and II were calculated for each of the White/Hispanic subgroup comparisons. Figure 1 presents differences in $DSTD_2$ for the true cognates for each of the three Hispanic subgroups and the total Hispanic group. Confidence bands are drawn on this figure, indicating that differences greater than 3% between the $DSTD_2$ values of the item pairs are statistically significant. Although there are only two Antonym item pairs that have differences that fall outside the confidence band for all the Hispanic subgroups, some of the other item pairs have differences in the postulated direction. Comparison of the true cognates with differences in the postulated direction versus those with no apparent DIF effect indicate that the true cognates that consistently made the items differentially easier were words with a higher frequency of usage in the Spanish language. Because of these results, the modification to the previously presented "true cognate hypothesis" consists of restricting the postulated effect to true cognates with higher usage in the Spanish language. In addition, the greater effect of true cognates on the performance of

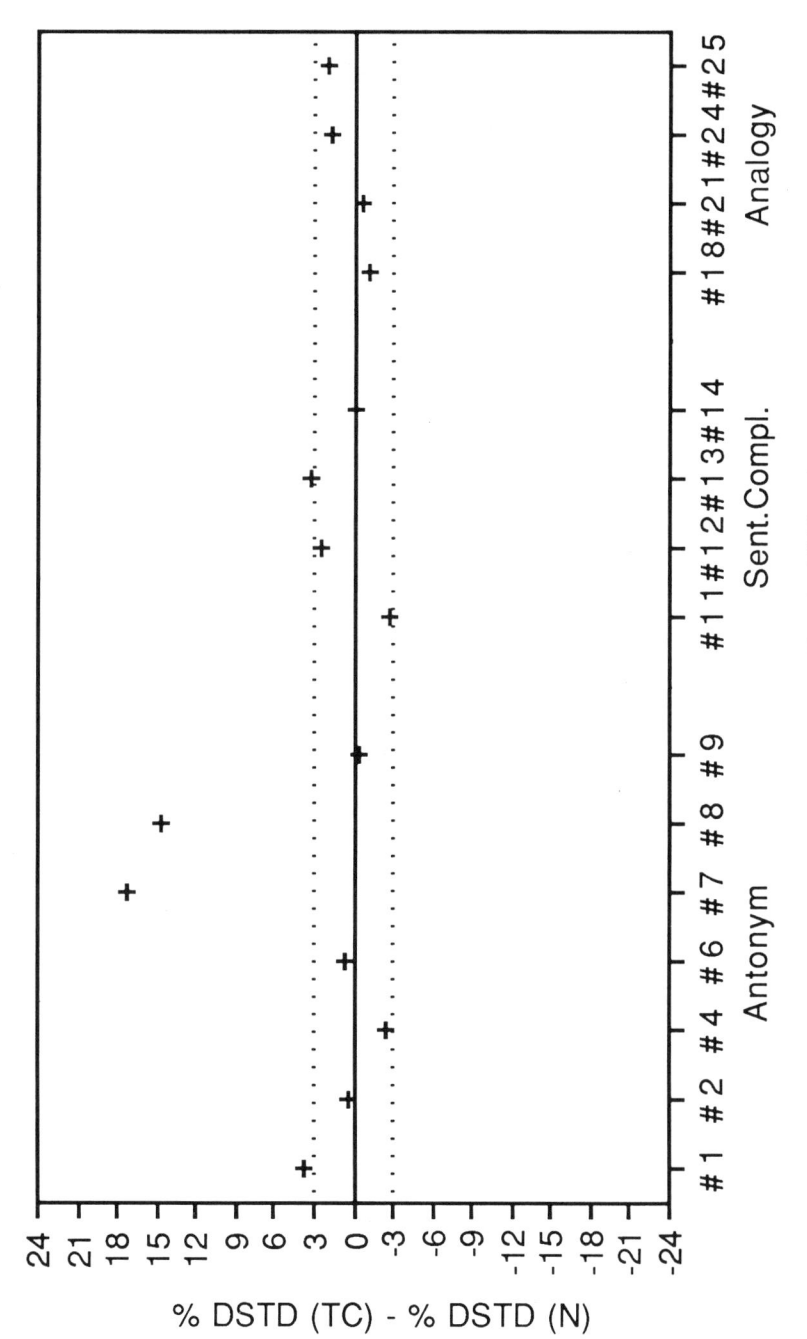

Figure 1. True Cognate Item Effects for All Hispanics

Puerto Rican examinees may be explained by the higher bilingual composition of this subgroup versus that of Mexican-Americans. Sixty percent of Puerto Ricans versus 40% of Mexican-Americans identified themselves as having *both* English and another (Spanish?) language as their first languages.

Several of the items with true cognates from the studies summarized are presented in Table 3 (Schmitt, 1988; Schmitt et al., 1988). Standardized distractor $DSTD_2$ values also are presented to help in the interpretation of DIF results. The first two items presented consist of true cognates on all of their parts. These items have high positive $DSTD_2$ values for Mexican-Americans and Puerto Rican examinees, indicating that they were differentially easier for these two Hispanic groups than they were for White examinees with comparable total SAT-Verbal scores. The last two items on this table have true cognates on both the stem and key. Both of these items also had positive $DSTD_2$ values. Further evaluation of the differential responses on these items indicate that, on most of these items, a differential omit effect is evident. This effect suggests that White examinees of comparable ability might opt to omit differentially more when the items are harder for them. This greater differential omission by White examinees on items differentially more difficult for them was first noted in a DIF study comparing responses of Black and White examinees (Schmitt and Bleistein, 1987). The differential omit effect will be discussed in more detail in the Examinee Response Style Factors section.

False Cognates. False cognates have been defined as words that appear to have the same root in English and Spanish but in reality have quite different meanings in each language. Because of these differences in meaning they have been postulated to be a source of confusion that negatively affects the item performance of Hispanic examinees and thus, to be related to negative DIF. Schmitt (1988) proposed the following hypothesis: "False cognates, or words whose meaning is not the same in both languages, will tend to impede the performance of Hispanic examinees. Example: enviable—meaning "sendable" in Spanish" (5). The same item classification procedures and data source used to study true cognates were used to evaluate the false cognate hypothesis. Because of the limited occurrence of false cognates in the forms studied, correlations of this item factor and $DSTD_2$ were deemed unstable and the evaluation of this factor was restricted to inspection of the level of DIF found in all of those items classified as having false cognates. Examination of the $DSTD_2$ values for these items indicated that the performance of Mexican-American and of Puerto Rican examinees was differentially lower than that of comparable White examinees but did not exceed the $|DSTD| \geq .10$ value.

Table 3
Examples of Items with True Cognate Factors

Item Type	Form	DSTD$_2$ MA	DSTD$_2$ PR	Item	Factor
Antonym	I			FACILITATE:	TC
		−.01	−.01	(A) intensify	TC
		−.03	−.04	(B) mobilize	TC
		−.03	−.06	(C) decline	TC
		.13	.19	*(D) complicate	TC
		−.00	−.01	(E) meditate	TC
		−.06	−.06	Omitted	
Antonym	II			AGGRANDIZEMENT:	TC
		−.01	−.01	(A) assessment	TC
		.01	.00	(B) leniency	TC
		.01	−.01	(C) restitution	TC
		.00	−.02	(D) annulment	TC
		.06	.11	*(E) diminution	TC
		−.07	−.08	Omitted	
Antonym	36			PALLID:	TC
		−.01	−.02	(A) moist	
		.02	−.01	(B) massive	FC
		.11	.17	*(C) vividly colored	TC
		−.02	−.03	(D) sweet smelling	
		−.02	−.02	(E) young and innocent	
		−.07	−.09	Omitted	
Antonym	31			ULTIMATE:	TC
		−.02	−.05	(A) implicit	TC
		.05	.13	*(B) initial	TC
		.01	−.02	(C) earthy	
		−.04	−.04	(D) flimsy	
		−.02	−.03	(E) irritating	TC
		.01	.02	Omitted	

Note: All items presented are either from disclosed SAT-Verbal forms or from specially developed variants that did not count towards operational scores.

To evaluate further the effect of false cognates, in the follow-up study, Schmitt et al. (1988) constructed nine item pairs with false cognates (one and three Antonyms, one and one Sentence Completion items, and two and one Analogy items in each of the variants, respectively). In the alternate version for each of these items, the false cognate was replaced with a synonym of comparable difficulty. Each of these sets of items are referred to as

Table 4
Examples of Items with False Cognate Factors

Item Type	Form	DSTD$_2$ MA	DSTD$_2$ PR	Item	Factor
Analogy	31			CONFERENCE:ADVISER: :	FC
		−.02	−.10	*(A) consultation:doctor	
		.01	.07	(B) sermon:priest	
		.01	.02	(C) reunion:school	
		.02	−.02	(D) suit:lawyer	
		−.01	.02	(E) truce:negotiator	
		−.01	.01	Omitted	
Antonym	36			CHARLATAN:	FC
		.01	.05	*(A) genuine expert	
		.05	.14	(B) uncommunicative person	
		.01	−.02	(C) fickle character	
		.02	.03	(D) benevolent being	
		−.01	−.03	(E) pathetic creature	
		−.07	−.16	Omitted	
Antonym	31			QUACK:	N
		.01	−.09	*(A) genuine expert	
		−.02	.03	(B) uncommunicative person	
		.00	−.02	(C) fickle character	
		.01	.02	(D) benevolent being	
		.00	.02	(E) pathetic creature	
		.00	.04	Omitted	

Note: Items presented are from specially developed variants that did not count towards operational scores.

a pair testing the false cognate hypothesis. Table 4 presents examples of the effect of false cognates in the Schmitt et al. (1988) study.

Standardized distractor DSTD$_2$ values are presented for each of the items. The second item in Table 4 is an Antonym item with the stem "CHARLATAN." This word has two possible meanings in Spanish. It's most usual meaning in Spanish is talkative person, while the meaning of quack is not as common. A special distractor was constructed to be especially attractive if the false cognate's meaning of talkative person could be a source of confusion. Distractor information shows that all Hispanic groups were drawn differentially to the "uncommunicative person" distractor while White examinees tended to omit this item more relative to Hispanics of comparable ability. The last item presented in Table 4 is the alternate pair to the "CHARLATAN" item. The stem of this item, "QUACK," is a noncognate (neither a true nor a false cognate). A negative DIF value was observed for the Puerto Rican examinees on the key and, as expected, the "uncommunicative person" distractor did not have a high $DSTD_2$ value for either Hispanic group. It appears that although the quack meaning of "charlatan" is not as common in the Spanish language, this meaning still is known and thus may have prevented Hispanic students from being differentially drawn toward the "uncommunicative person" distractor.

Although DIF on most of the false cognate pairs did not support the negative differential effect of false cognates, the Schmitt et al. (1988) study did increase our understanding of the differential effect of this factor on Hispanic item performance and of the factor itself. In practical testing settings, however, the occurrence of false cognates is very low. Moreover, it is very hard to come up with "good" examples of false cognates. Although the initial definition of false cognates states that these words have quite different meanings in both languages this might only be true for only one type of false cognates. Words in both languages that are composed by chance of the same letters but do not share a common origin can be referred to as "casual"[1] false cognates. A good example of a casual false cognate is the word "enviable" (sendable in Spanish). In other cases, the possible false cognate also could serve as a true cognate since the primary Spanish meaning was just a more archaic and lesser used English meaning. These words might share a common initial root between the two languages that evolved differently over time. Thus, specially constructed distractors used to test the confounding effect of these false cognates (archaic false cognates) could serve as another possible key, which violates a fundamental tenet of good test development practice. Although testing of this factor was very difficult, some of the differential responses found in the Schmitt et al. (1988) study do seem to support the confounding effect of both "casual" and "archaic" false cognates. Schmitt et al. (1988) summarize the difficulty of evaluating this factor by stating: "False cognates produce effects that are harder to evaluate and manipulate, in part because most false cognates tend to be homographs in Spanish, with one meaning being a false cognate and the other a true cognate" (19). It is expected that "casual" false cognates would be a greater source of confusion than "archaic" false cognates.

Homographs. A homograph is a word with the same spelling as another word but having different meanings and word roots. Items with words classified as homographs have been found to be related to negative DIF for Asian-American examinees (Bleistein and Wright, 1987; Schmitt and Dorans, 1990), Hispanic examinees (Schmitt, 1985, 1988; Schmitt and Dorans, 1990), and Black examinees (Schmitt and Bleistein, 1987). In all

Table 5
Correlations between Standardized Differences (DSTD$_2$) and Homographs and Vertical Relationships Factors for Analogies in SAT Form I and II

	SAT Form I Analogies		SAT Form II Analogies	
Factors	Mexican-American	Puerto Rican	Mexican-American	Puerto Rican
Homograph				
Stem	−.32	−.38	−.05	−.02
Key	−.26	−.34	—	—
Distractors	−.42	−.37	−.36	−.26
All-S, K, D	−.49	−.50	−.35	−.26
Vertical Rltn.				
Key	−.28	−.18	.14	.24
Distractors	−.30	−.46	−.08	.06

Note: Data presented on this table have been excerpted from the Schmitt and Dorans (1990) paper. Correlations in each column are based on twenty Analogy items.

these studies, items classified as having homographs were restricted to those items where the homograph word was testing a less frequently used meaning of the word. This is the type of homograph that will be assumed when the item-factor homograph is referred to in this chapter.

In the Schmitt (1988) study the following hypothesis was formulated and evaluated: "Homographs, or words that are spelled alike but which have different meanings, will tend to impede the performance of Hispanic examinees. Example: bark" (5). The data source in this study was the same as that used to evaluate the true and false cognate hypotheses. The Mexican-American and Puerto Rican sample compositions are footnoted in Table 1. At least two bilingual judges were used to classify homographs in the two SAT-Verbal forms used in the study. As with the true cognate hypothesis, both item content and correlational analyses were done. The stem or key variables took on zero or one as their values. The values for the distractor variable were obtained by summing up zero and one codes over distractors of the item. The value for the All-S,K,D variable was a sum of the stem, key, and distractor factor codes. Correlations between DSTD$_2$ values and homograph codes in the stem, or key or distractors were calculated for Analogy items (the only item type that had sufficient homographs). Correlational results for each Hispanic group are presented in Table 5. The consistent negative correlations presented in Table 5 indicate that Analogy items with homographs tend to be differentially harder for Hispanic examinees. Results for the Analogy items in Form I are more compelling than results for the Analogy items in Form II.

The Schmitt et al. (1988) follow-up investigation constructed items with homographs to evaluate their effect on Hispanic examinees (Mexican-Americans, Puerto Ricans, and Latin-Americans). The seven item pairs developed were divided into two and one Antonyms, one Sentence Completion, and two and one Analogy items in each of the variants, respectively. Although no consistent effect was found for these items across the Hispanic groups, a marginal effect of homographs was observed across several items. In addition, the differential attractiveness of distractors supported the hypothesized confusing effect of homographs on the item performance of Hispanics.

Several items with homographs from the Schmitt (1988) and Schmitt et al. (1988) studies are presented in Table 6. These items will be discussed in the section on vertical relationships presented below.

Vertical Relationships. When an item has a word or words in the stem that can be associated with a word in the key or any distractor and this association is independent of the analogical relationship between the two words in the stem, vertical relationships or word associations are present. These relationships are seen as strategies used by students when they are trying to guess the correct answer to an item. These associations were observed as strategies used by Black or White students when they encountered a word in the item stem that was especially difficult or esoteric or when there are other sources of confusion such as homographs (Schmitt and Bleistein, 1987). In the Schmitt and Dorans (1990) study, it was hypothesized that vertical relationships in distractors would be negatively related to $DSTD_2$, but that vertical relationships in the key would make the key more attractive and thus be positively related to $DSTD_2$. The correlation analyses calculated for Analogy items from the Schmitt and Dorans (in press) study are reproduced on the bottom of Table 5. Consistent negative correlations between $DSTD_2$ and vertical relationships in distractors are found across all groups for the Analogy items of Form I, while positive correlations between $DSTD_2$ and vertical relationships in the key are found for the Analogy items in Form II only. Because of the inconsistency of these results, the authors recommended that evaluation of possible interrelationships between other factors and vertical relationships needed to be explored. A study currently is in progress to further evaluate the effect of homographs and vertical relationships on the differential performance of several ethnic groups on Analogy items.

DIF information for two items with vertical relationships have been reproduced in Table 6. Interestingly, these two items have homographs as well as vertical relationship factors identified. On both of these items, negative DIF is observed for the key (more extreme for the Puerto Rican group)

Table 6
Examples of Items with Homograph and Vertical Factors

Item Type	Form	DSTD$_2$ MA	DSTD$_2$ PR	Item	Factor
Analogy	I			BARK:TREE: :	HM
		−.08	−.14	*(A) skin:fruit	
		.00	.01	(B) dew:grass	
		.04	.08	(C) seed:flower	VR
		.02	.02	(D) peak:hill	
		.02	.02	(E) wake:boat	
		.00	.01	Omitted	
	I			EXCERPT:BOOK: :	
		.02	.03	(A) type:page	
		.03	.01	(B) script:play	
		.00	.00	(C) solo:routine	
		−.07	−.08	*(D) clip:film	HM
		.00	.01	(E) drama:musical	
		.01	.03	Omitted	
	36			ANIMAL:HIDE	HM
		.03	.00	(A) egg:yolk	
		.00	.02	(B) deer:hunt	VR
		.02	−.03	(C) desk:top	
		.03	.11	(D) fugitive:shelter	VR
		−.08	−.13	*(E) fruit:rind	
		.00	.03	Omitted	

Note: All items presented are either from disclosed SAT-Verbal forms or from special variants that did not count towards operational scores.

while the distractors identified as vertical factors were selected differentially more, primarily, by Puerto Rican examinees. In most of the items on this table homographs are present either on the stem or on the key and a negative DSTD$_2$ value is observed.

Special Interest. According to Schmitt (1988), Hispanic students tend to find items with content that refers to Hispanic or to other minority groups or that is related to topics relevant to the Spanish culture to be differentially easier. In that study, items of two SAT-Verbal forms (Form I and Form II) were evaluated as to their special interest for Hispanics by two bilingual test development experts who considered whether the content referred to Hispanics, to other minority groups, or to topics relevant to the Spanish culture. All items were classified by using a code of zero for no special interest, one for possible interest (referring to other minority groups), or two for special interest particular to the Hispanic groups. All Reading Comprehension items from passages identified as being of special interest were classified in the same way. Using the same samples as with true and false cognates (see footnote for Table 1), $DSTD_2$ statistics were calculated and correlated with the interest codes. Correlational analyses were only relevant for Sentence Completion or Reading Comprehension item types due to the limited number of interest factors in the two vocabulary item types (Antonyms and Analogies).

Results from the correlation analyses showed that for both Mexican-American and Puerto Rican examinees there was a positive relationship between content of interest and DIF. The correlation values for the Sentence Completion items of Form II were .65 and .62 for the Mexican-American and the Puerto Rican groups, respectively. The correlations for the Reading Comprehension items were .56 and .34 (on Form I) and .22 and .24 (on Form II) for the Mexican-American and for the Puerto Rican examinees, respectively. Further evaluation of the Reading Comprehension items on Form I indicated that a five-item set corresponded to a passage that focused on changes in the life-style of migrant Mexican-American families. Four out of five items of this passage had positive $DSTD_2$ values for the Mexican-American group, indicating that all items were generally easier for this group when compared to a matched White group. The item set from Form II corresponded to a reading passage that referenced the work of a Black mathematician. Four of the five items on this passage had positive $DSTD_2$ values for both Hispanic groups. The only negative DIF item of this passage-item-set was only slightly negative with $DSTD_2$ values of -.00 and -.01 for Mexican-Americans and Puerto Ricans, respectively.

In an attempt to replicate these results, the Schmitt et al. (1988) study developed two Reading Comprehension passages with content of "special interest." The specific minority group referred to in one passage was varied in a parallel version. For example, in one version a passage by a Mexican-American reminiscing about ancestral heritage and cultural identity was slightly varied to express the point of view of Irish-Americans. Results of that study did not support the relationship of DIF and "special interest." Nevertheless, it is possible that the "special interest" effect was not apparent in these passages because of their diluted and general interest nature. For purposes of comparison, the parallel passages were maintained as identical as possible and had been originally selected or developed so that their focus of interest could easily be changed by only minor alterations. This study constraint might have prevented the specific focus on Hispanic interest required to cause an effect. In addition, it is possible that the topic of special interest needs to be not only more specific but perhaps also needs to exalt the specific ethnic culture, as did the passage about a Black mathematician in Form II. Further evaluation of these possibilities needs to be explored before conclusive decisions about this factor are reached.

Examinee Response Style Factors

Up to this point, the focus of this chapter has been on item factors or characteristics of items that might explain DIF for Hispanics on SAT-Verbal items. Now the evaluation of Hispanic DIF turns to examinee response style factors that may be related to DIF. These factors—differential omission and differential speededness—deal with how different groups' examinees approach the test-taking experience and how they deal with difficult items. After presenting evidence documenting the existence of these factors, correlational results relating these factors to DIF on the key and item difficulty are presented and discussed.

Differential Omission. When an examinee does not respond to an item but responds to subsequent items, that item is referred to as an omit. Data from Form I were used by Rivera and Schmitt (1988) to assess whether Puerto Ricans and Mexican-Americans were more or less likely to omit than matched Whites. As indicated earlier, all examinees in the DIF analysis spoke English as their best language. Standardization analyses were performed on omits using the $DSTD_1$ version of the standardized difference in which all data including examinees who did not reach the item were used in the analysis.

The results of this study were somewhat surprising because they contradicted conventional wisdom that held that Hispanics omit less than Whites—a conventional wisdom based on comparisons of groups that were not matched on total test. After matching on total test score, Rivera and Schmitt found that Mexican-Americans were less likely to omit than their matched White counterparts. For Mexican-Americans, more than twice as many items had negative differential omission rates than had positive differential omission rates, and five items had differential omission rates less than -.05. Interestingly, all five items contained true cognates. The results for Puerto Ricans were less conclusive because Puerto Ricans tended to omit slightly less than Whites on Antonyms and Reading Comprehension items, but slightly more on Sentence Completion and Analogies, producing a cancellation effect of no differential omission on the test overall.

The Rivera and Schmitt (1988) study was the first of its kind and involved only one test form. As part of a study investigating the relationship between item difficulty and DIF on the key, as measured by MH and STD, Kulick and Hu (1989) recently corroborated the Rivera and Schmitt (1988) findings for Hispanics (Mexican-Americans, Puerto Ricans, and Latin Americans groups combined). Based on an analysis that included nine SAT test forms, they found that Hispanics tend to omit less than matched Whites. Incidentally, they also found that DIF and difficulty are highly related for Hispanics, Blacks, and Asian Americans: Positive DIF tends to occur on hard items, while negative DIF tends to occur on easy items.

Differential Speededness. When an examinee does not respond to an item and does not respond to any subsequent items in a timed section, all those items are referred to as not reached. It is assumed that all examinees who do not respond to omitted items do so because the items are deemed too difficult. While some examinees may omit not reached items because they are difficult, it is assumed that most, if not all, examinees who do not respond to a not-reached item, do not, in fact, reach the item. Not-reached rates on items at the end of a timed section or test measure the section or test speededness for the group that took the test.

Differential speededness refers to the existence of differential response rates between focal group members and matched reference group members to items appearing at the end of a section. Schmitt and Bleistein (1987) found evidence of this phenomenon for Blacks, as compared to a matched group of Whites, on analogy items. Schmitt and Dorans (1990) reported that this effect also was found for Hispanics. Dorans, Schmitt, and Bleistein (1988) examined differential speededness results for Black, Hispanic, and Asian-American focal groups, compared to a White base or reference group. Data from that study, which used the $DSTD_1$ index of standardization to assess differential speededness on Forms I and II, are reported here.

Figure 2 depicts standardized differential not-reached rates on the last ten items of the two verbal sections of Form I that were observed for Mexican-Americans and Puerto Ricans. It is evident from Figure 2a that both Hispanic groups reach the last ten items of the 45-item Verbal 1 section at a lower rate than a matched group of White examinees. The standardized differential not-reached rate, $DSTD_1(NR)$, for Puerto Ricans hovers around .05 for all ten items. The $DSTD_1(NR)$ values for Mexican-Americans on these same ten items are slightly closer to zero.

Figure 2b depicts the standardized differential not-reached rates for the last ten items of the forty-item Verbal 2 section. In contrast to Figure 2a, the differential speededness phenomenon builds up from no effect for either group at item thirty-one to a clear separation of the groups by item forty. Once again, the effect is most pronounced for Puerto Ricans and minimal for the Mexican-Americans.

Figure 3 depicts standardized differential not-reached rates on the last ten items of the two verbal sections of Form II that were observed for

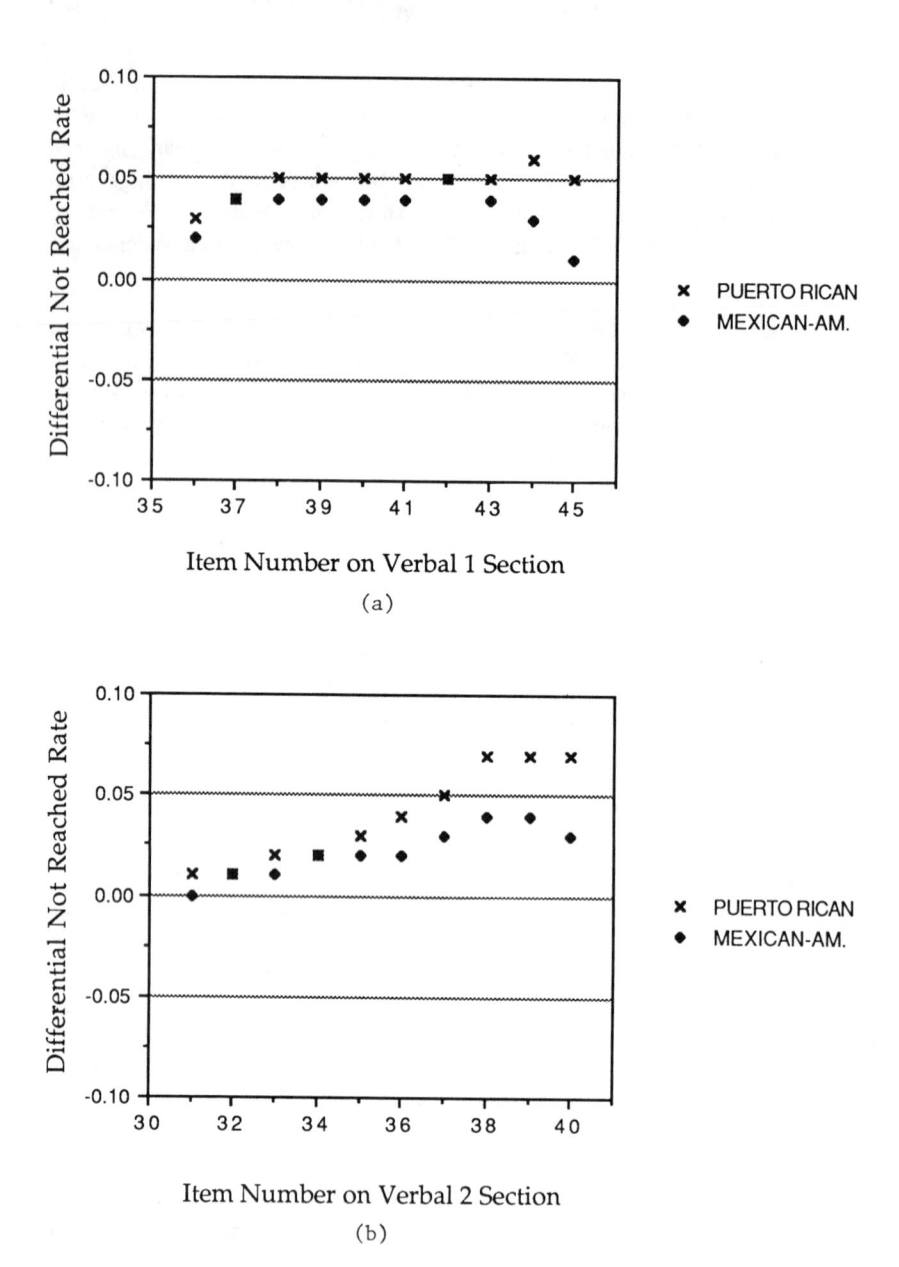

Figure 2. Differential Speededness for Hispanics on SAT Form I.

(a)

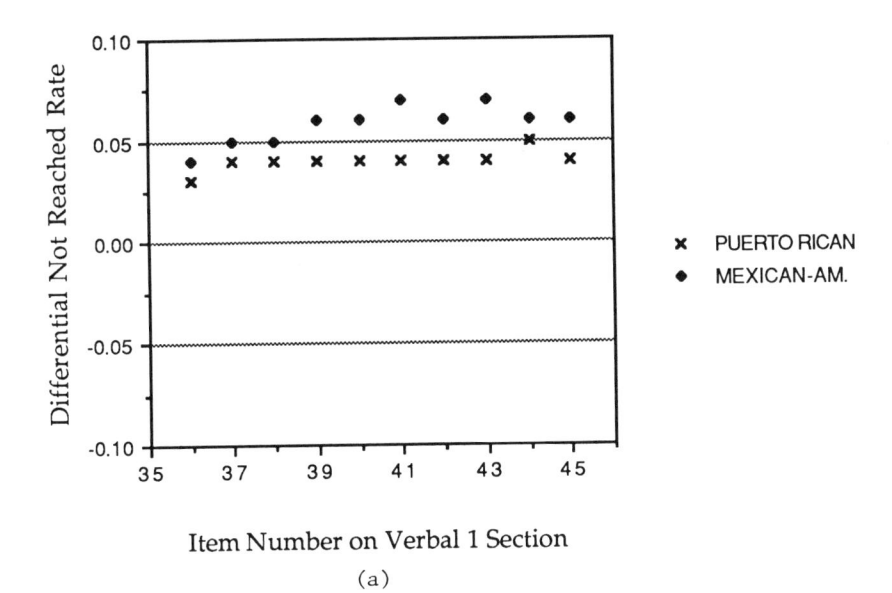

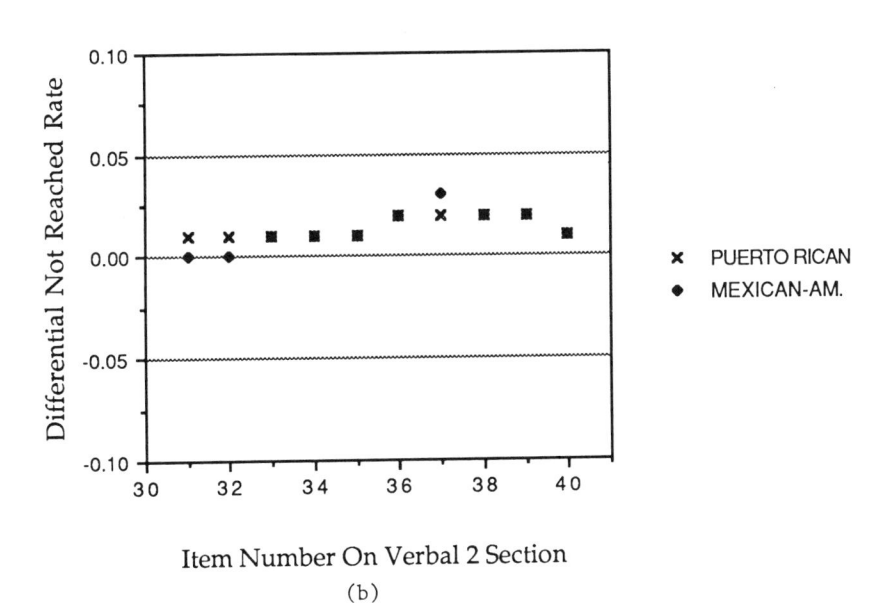

(b)

Figure 3. Differential Speededness for Hispanics on SAT Form II.

Mexican-Americans and Puerto Ricans. Figure 3a depicts the rates for the last ten items on the forty-five-item Verbal 1 section, while Figure 3b displays the rates for the last ten items on the forty-item Verbal 2 section. Both Hispanic groups have standardized differential not-reached rates near or above the .05 level on the Verbal 1 section with the Mexican-American group having the higher rates and the Puerto Rican group having the lower rates. This pattern reverses that seen for Form I in that the two Hispanic groups have exchanged locations on the plot. On the Verbal 2 section in Figure 3b, differential speededness is barely noticeable for either group.

DIF, Easiness, Differential Omission, and Differential Speededness. Table 7 contains intercorrelations among standardized indices of DIF, $DSTD_2(K)$; easiness (focal group percent correct); standardized differential omission, $DSTD_2(0)$; and standardized differential speededness, $DSTD_1(NR)$, by item type across both Hispanic groups and across both forms. Eight intercorrelation matrices are presented for each combination of form by item type. Within each matrix, the correlations for Mexican-Americans appear above the diagonal, while the correlations for Puerto Ricans appear below the diagonal.

For Antonyms, the most consistent finding is the significant negative correlation between DIF on the key and differential omission for both Hispanic groups. The consistent positive relationships between differential omission and item easiness for Mexican-Americans is also noteworthy.

The positive item easiness/differential omission relationship for Mexican-Americans is also consistent on Sentence Completion items, where a significant negative item easiness/differential speededness also occurs on Form II.

While no significant intercorrelations occurred for Reading Comprehension items on Form I, results for this item type on Form II reveal a strong negative relationship between differential omission and differential speededness for both Hispanic groups. In addition, consistent with findings on Sentence Completion items, Mexican-Americans, again, have a strong positive relationship between item easiness and differential omission, while Puerto Ricans have a strong negative relationship between item easiness and differential speededness.

Many significant results occur with Analogy items. The most consistent finding is—as it was for the other vocabulary item type, Antonyms—a strong negative relationship between DIF on the key and differential omission. A consistent and strong negative relationship between item easiness and DIF on the key occurs across both Hispanic groups on Form I, while only Puerto Ricans have this negative relationship on Form II. In addition, both groups exhibit a strong positive relationship between item easiness and differential omission on Form II, but only Mexican-Americans have this positive relationship on Form I.

Table 7
Intercorrelations between Omit and Not Reached DSTDs, Key DSTD$_2$, and Item Difficulty in SAT-Verbal Form I and II

	SAT-Verbal Form I			Focal	SAT-Verbal Form II			Focal
	K-D2	Omit	NR	P	K-D2	Omit	NR	P
Antonyms (n = 25)								
DSTDs:								
Key (D2)	1	−.48*	−.23	.06	1	−.80*	.02	−.21
Omit (D2)	−.68*	1	.33	.51*	−.75*	1	−.07	.48*
NR (D1)	.22	−.30	1	.32	−.06	−.08	1	.21
Focal P	.11	−.02	.12	1	−.15	.35*	.10	1
Sentence Completion (n = 15)								
DSTDs:								
Key (D2)	1	−.21	−.21	−.47*	1	−.36	.23	−.03
Omit (D2)	−.22	1	−.45*	.71*	−.21	1	−.37	.55*
NR (D1)	−.29	−.15	1	−.09	.25	.17	1	−.54*
Focal P	−.36	−.01	−.11	1	−.25	.02	−.54*	1
Reading Comprehension (n = 25)								
DSTDs:								
Key (D2)	1	−.35*	.05	.31	1	−.07	.15	.17
Omit (D2)	−.31	1	−.20	.14	−.22	1	−.43*	.58*
NR (D1)	.17	−.19	1	−.23	.03	−.40*	1	−.27
Focal P	−.03	.16	−.25	1	.30	.18	−.45*	1
Analogy (n = 20)								
DSTDs:								
Key (D2)	1	−.65*	.04	−.60*	1	−.75*	.00	−.37
Omit (D2)	−.62*	1	−.09	.47*	−.82*	1	.01	.64*
NR (D1)	.22	−.26	1	−.15	−.01	.11	1	−.16
Focal P	−.62*	.14	−.25	1	−.76*	.71*	−.10	1

Note: Within each intercorrelation matrix the values above the diagonal are for the Mexican-American group while the values below the diagonal are for the Puerto Rican group.
*p ≤ .05.

The most striking finding in Table 7 is the strong negative relationship between DIF on the key and differential omission that occurred across both forms for both groups on the two vocabulary item types, Antonyms and Analogies. Hispanics are less likely to omit than Whites on items that have positive DIF, items that are relatively easier for them than for a group of matched Whites. Kulick and Hu (1989) replicated this finding using data from nine other SAT forms. Before concluding that Hispanics should omit less in order to have more positive DIF, it is important to realize that this strong relationship may be somewhat artifactual for the following two reasons. First, a mathematical dependency exists between selecting the key and omitting an item that may contribute to this negative correlation. Secondly, and perhaps more importantly, both the MH and the common version of the standardization index treat omits as wrong answers in their calculations, which may give spuriously high (in magnitude) DIF values on items in which differential omission occurs. In sum, this strong relationship between differential omission and DIF on the key may be due, in part, to a mathematical dependency and statistical artifact caused by erroneous treatment of omitted responses by the DIF indices in current use.

Another striking finding in Table 7 is the consistent strong relationship between item easiness and differential omission observed for Mexican-American examinees. The more difficult the item is, the more likely it is that Mexican-American examinees will omit less than matched Whites. A comparable finding does not occur for Puerto Rican examinees. Could there be a cultural explanation for why Mexican-American examinees are less willing to let a difficult item defeat them than are Whites or Puerto Ricans examinees?

A few more observations are worth noting. Significant correlations are more frequent among Mexican-Americans than Puerto Ricans, which could be due to the greater salience of differential omission in the former group. Differential omission is by far the variable with the most significant correlations. Analogies is the item type with the greatest proportion of significant relationships.

Summary of Main Findings

Results of several studies were summarized. Item and examinee response style factors were evaluated for their relationship with DIF. The main finding from the item factors studied was the consistent positive effect of true cognates on the DIF of Hispanic examinees. Furthermore, it was observed that true cognates with a higher frequency of usage in Spanish had the most consistent and positive effect on Hispanic DIF. Because of these results, a modified "true cognate hypothesis" was presented that postulates that the effect of true cognates would be stronger if those words had a higher usage in the Spanish language. In addition, the greater effect of true cognates on the performance of Puerto Rican examinees was found to be consistent with the bilingual composition of this subgroup versus that of Mexican-Americans and Latin Americans. Sixty percent of Puerto Ricans versus forty percent of either Mexican-Americans or Latin Americans identified themselves as having both English and another (Spanish?) language as their first language.

Only marginal support was obtained for the other item factors studied. Although DIF results on most of the false cognate items studied did not support the negative differential effect of false cognates, the Schmitt et al. (1988) study did provide further information for understanding the differential effect of this factor on Hispanic item performance and of the confounding effect of the factor itself.

Negative correlations between $DSTD_2$ and homographs indicated that analogy items with homographs tend to be differentially harder for Hispanic examinees. Although no consistent effect was found for these items across the Hispanic groups and forms, a marginal effect of homographs was observed across several items (Schmitt, 1988). In addition, the differential attractiveness of distractors supported the hypothesized confusing effect of homographs on the item performance of Hispanics (Schmitt, 1988; Schmitt et al., 1988).

The effect of vertical relationships was not consistent. Further evaluation of this factor and its interrelationship with other factors was recommended. In addition, the Schmitt et al. (1988) study did not support the relationship of DIF and "special interest." A more restricted focus of the stimulus of special interest was recommended. It is possible that the topic of special interest needs to be not only more specific but perhaps also needs to exalt the specific minority culture. Further evaluation of these possibilities must be done before conclusive decisions about these factors are reached.

Results about examinee response styles indicated that Hispanics, primarily Mexican-Americans, tend to omit differentially less and to reach differentially fewer items or to have a differential speededness effect.

Implications

Assessment Practices

Statistical and judgmental item screening procedures are two methods that should be used in conjunction to screen items for DIF and to examine possible causes of differential item functioning. Currently at the Educational Testing Service (ETS) both of these methods are used in the SAT.

Statistical Screening. Many large testing programs already use statistical procedures to screen items for DIF at the pretest stage or at the score reporting stage just before scores are released. Items with large DIF values (both positive and negative) are routinely excluded from tests at the pretest stage. In addition, items are sometimes dropped from screening at the score-reporting stage. At the ETS, the MH statistic is used to flag items for exclusion or deletion. The standardization approach, particularly standardized distractor analyses, is employed as a statistical tool for assessing whether hypotheses about DIF are consistent with the data, which is particularly useful at the score-reporting stage where deletion of an item has consequences on the scores that examinees receive.

The research conducted on Hispanics to date has implications for the statistical screening processes. A statistical process that is blind to explanations in the data is likely to discard, on the basis of Hispanic DIF, some items that fit the true cognate hypothesis and some items that are homographs or are susceptible to vertical relationships. Is this desirable? We don't necessarily think so, as we mention in the next section. Blind statistical processing is most likely to occur at the pretest stage where there is less time to spend evaluating a flagged item and where the immediate cost of not evaluating these flagged items is small. The long-term costs, however, may be rather high for several reasons. Some items might be flagged due to sampling error, i.e., in larger datasets they would be statistically adequate. Some items might be flagged because of statistical deficiencies with the flagging methodology. For example, the MH method has a tendency to flag too many easy items, and may misclassify items on which there are large omission rates. Other items will be flagged because they have DIF, which on further examination would be viewed as acceptable because the item is construct relevant. For example, most items with true cognates are often construct relevant as are many items with homographs. Blind screening at the pretest stage is likely to have many undesirable consequences in the long run.

Statistical screening also can have a detrimental effect on the process of generating explanations for DIF if only items with large DIF are studied. It is critical to dip into the non-DIF pool to see if DIF hypotheses generated on DIF items really hold water.

In sum, statistical screening is a positive way of reducing DIF, but it has its pitfalls. The screening process should not be blind to existing research and should be applied carefully. Methodological improvements and enhancements also are needed.

Judgmental Procedures. The test-development process of most standardized testing programs involves a routine judgmental item evaluation process. At the ETS every test is reviewed to eliminate references or language that might be stereotypical or objectionable to any subgroup of the population (Hunter and Slaughter, 1980). This judgmental method generally is referred to as the Sensitivity Review Process. It is possible that once factors related to DIF are understood more clearly, then, this item-screening process also could be used to eliminate or control these factors.

Elimination of all items with factors found to be related to DIF might not be the best option available. Only when these factors are *not related* to the construct the test is measuring would their elimination be appropriate. On the other hand, in those cases where the factors are *directly related* to the construct measured by the test, their elimination might reduce the validity of the measurement. Also, in the long run, the indiscriminate elimination of these factors might reduce educational standards. Because of these considerations, responsible DIF screening decisions need to be made carefully. For example, results presented in this review of factors related to the DIF of Hispanic examinees indicates that true cognates favorably influence the item performance of these examinees. Reliance on Spanish as a second language might have given these examinees an added advantage in understanding true cognate words. Would it be appropriate to eliminate these Latin words from a test in which one of its intents is to evaluate knowledge of vocabulary? Shepard (1987) raises the question as to "what constitutes a 'fair' proportion of Latinate words on the test" (3). She proceeds to suggest that these true cognate words be balanced proportionally with the number of these words found in standardized written English. Shepard (1987) states: " . . . a conscious effort should be made to have the proportion of Latin roots mirror what is found, say, in typical freshman reading assignments" (3). Balancing rather than eliminating is only one of several possibilities on how to deal with factors related to DIF.

Education of Hispanic Students

Another alternative is to consider these factors as indicators of educational areas that need to be stressed in the education of Hispanics or other minority groups. For example, greater emphasis on learning vocabulary could reduce the possible confounding effect of false cognates and homographs, so that the performance of Hispanics on items with these factors could be similar to comparable White examinees. In addition, programs specifically geared to improve test-taking skills might help reduce the differential omit and speededness effects by Hispanics. Improved test-taking skills by Hispanics might be achieved by special programs developed to improve their exposure to standardized testing as well as to provide specific advice on how to approach the test. One such program has been developed specifically for Hispanics. The kit, "Test skills: A kit for teachers of Hispanics," was developed to provide guidance on preparing to take the Preliminary Scholastic Aptitude Test/National Merit Scholarship Qualifying

Test (PSAT/NMSQT). In this kit, a set of lesson plans was developed specifically to improve such test-taking skills as using time effectively, eliminating wrong answers and choosing among the remaining alternatives, and the appropriate use of cognate knowledge (College Entrance and Examination Board and Educational Testing Service, 1989).

Conclusions

The following statements summarize the main points that have been made in this paper: (1) We can detect DIF reasonably well but could do it better; (2) DIF exists for Hispanics on the SAT-Verbal test; (3) item and response style factors have been found to be related to Hispanic DIF; (4) knowledge of DIF results needs to be integrated into assessment practices; and (5) educational curriculums may need to consider these DIF results.

The best approach to effective action based on these conclusions would be to combine statistical and judgmental screening procedures to detect DIF; to use the detected DIF to formulate hypotheses about factors related to DIF that could then be tested in studies such as the ones reported in this paper; and to use corroborated findings to develop appropriate guidelines for assessment and education.

6

Equating the Scores of the College Board *Prueba de Aptitud Académica* and the College Board *Scholastic Aptitude Test*

~ ~ ~ ~

William H. Angoff and Linda L. Cook*

This chapter describes a study designed to yield equivalent scores on the College Board Scholastic Aptitude Test (SAT), administered to English-speaking students applying for admission to U.S. colleges, and the College Board Prueba de Aptitud Académica (PAA), a test parallel to the SAT, but constructed in Spanish and administered to Spanish-speaking students applying for admission to colleges and universities mainly in Puerto Rico. The study was undertaken in a manner similar to that conducted by Angoff and Modu (1973) and was intended as a check on the earlier results. It differed

---

*The authors would like to express their deep appreciation for the fine work of the many professionals who have contributed to the success of this study: The professors of English and mathematics in Puerto Rico who accomplished the difficult and sensitive task of translating the test items from English to Spanish and from Spanish to English; the several members of the test development staff at Educational Testing Service (ETS) who coordinated the assembly of the equating tests and worked with the translations; the members of the statistical staff of ETS who coordinated and produced the statistical analyses for the study; and finally, the staff of the College Board Puerto Rico office for their dedicated involvement and able support throughout the course of the study. Tables and figures reprinted with permission from College Board Report No. 88-2, *Equating the Scores of the* Prueba de Aptitud Academica *and the* Scholastic Aptitude Test by William H. Angoff and Linda L. Cook. Copyright (c) 1988 by College Entrance Examination Board, New York.

from the earlier study, however, in that it utilized more modern methods of examining items for equivalence and of equating test scores.

The paper is organized into four sections. The first describes the purpose and general approach to the matter of developing equivalent scores on two parallel forms of a test—i.e. equating the two forms; the second considers the particular problems of equating tests for students of different languages and cultures; and the third gives a description of the particular method adopted for the present study and a presentation of the resulting tables of equivalent scores. The last section describes the uses and limitations of the study in its application to the problem of access to higher education for Latino students.

Introduction

It is sometimes the task of an admissions officer at a university in the United States to evaluate the credentials of an applicant who has attended elementary and secondary schools in a foreign country. Difficult as this task may be, it is made significantly more difficult when the language and culture of the other country are different from those of the United States. Occasionally, the need to make such an evaluation develops when a Spanish-speaking student from Puerto Rico applies for admission to a college or university in the United States. Ordinarily, such a student would have taken the College Board Spanish-language PAA, a test administered, typically, to Puerto Rican students who are applying for admission to universities in Puerto Rico. The U.S. admissions officer, however, is not ordinarily familiar with the PAA; the scores he or she deals with are usually those earned on the College Board English-language SAT, a test usually taken by many applicants to colleges and universities in the United States. In order, then, to permit the admissions officer to evaluate the student's academic record in terms of the SAT norms he or she knows and understands, it seemed reasonable to seek a conversion of scores between the PAA and the SAT. The present study was designed as an attempt to develop such a conversion. In this sense it purports to provide a psychometric solution to one of the problems of access for Latino students to education in the United States. In the process of finding this solution, it was necessary to confront the difficult problem of bridging the cultural and linguistic differences between the United States and Puerto Rico.

Although the study of cultural differences has been of central interest to educators and social psychologists for many years, attempts to develop a deeper understanding of such differences have been frustrated by the absence of a common metric by which many such comparisons could be made. The reasons for this are clear. If two cultural groups differ from each other in certain ways that cast doubt on the validity of direct comparisons between them in other respects—if, for example, they differ sharply in language, customs, and values—then those very differences also will defy the construction of an unbiased metric by which we could hope to make such comparisons.

We find, however, that there are times when comparisons nevertheless are made, even though the basic differences in language, customs, and values, for example, that sometimes invalidate these comparisons are known to exist. The study described in this chapter has been designed in an attempt to develop a method to help make such comparisons in the face of these difficulties by providing a metric common to the two cultures. Specifically, it purports to provide a conversion of the verbal and mathematical scores on the PAA to the verbal and mathematical scores, respectively, on the SAT. Both tests, it is noted, are administered to secondary school students for admission to college. It was expected that if conversion tables between the score scales for these two tests were made available, direct comparisons could be made between students or subgroups of the two language-cultures who had taken only that test appropriate for them. For the immediate purpose, however, it was expected that these conversion tables would help in the evaluation of the probable success of Puerto Rican students who were interested in eventually attending college in the United States and were submitting PAA scores for admission. The study was conducted in an effort to repeat the earlier study by Angoff and Modu (1973), but with some modifications and improvements in method, and to confirm that the earlier results still are valid.

Interest in developing conversions such as these has been expressed in various other contexts, usually in the assessment of the outcomes of education for different cultural groups living in close proximity: for example, for English- and French-speaking students in Canada, for English- and Afrikaans-speaking students in South Africa, and for speakers of one or another of the many languages in India or in Africa. No satisfactory methods to satisfy this interest have been available until recently, however, and the problems attendant on making comparisons among culturally different groups are far more obvious and numerous than are the solutions. For example, to provide a measuring instrument to make these comparisons, it is clearly insufficient simply to translate the test constructed for one language group into the language of the other, even with adjustments in the items to conform to the more obvious cultural requirements of the second group. Nuances of expression and subtleties of custom are unwittingly embodied in words and phrases and often have particular meanings for one group but not for the other. It can therefore hardly be expected, without careful and detailed checks, that the translated items will have the same meaning and relative difficulty for the second group as they had for the original group before translation.

A method considerably superior to that of simple translation has been described by Boldt (1969). It requires the selection of a group of individuals judged to be equally bilingual and bicultural and the administration of two tests to each individual, one test in each of the two languages. Scores on the two tests are then equated as though they were parallel forms of the same test, and a conversion table is developed relating scores on each test to scores on the other.

One of the principal drawbacks with the foregoing procedure is that the judgment "equally bilingual and bicultural" is extremely difficult, perhaps impossible, to make, except in those relatively rare instances where an individual is perfectly proficient in both languages. More than likely, the individual members of the group, and even the group as a whole, will on average be more proficient in one of the two languages than in the other.

The present study represents an attempt to overcome such difficulties. In brief, it calls for administering the PAA to Puerto Rican students and the SAT to U.S. students, using a set of "common," or anchor, items to calibrate and adjust for any differences between the groups that should be considered in the process of equating the two tests. It is noted that these items are common only in terms of the operations used to develop and select them. By the very nature of things they had to be administered in Spanish to the Puerto Rican students and in English to the U.S. students. Therefore, to the extent that there is any validity in the notion that a set of test items can represent the same psychological task to individuals of two different languages and cultures, to the extent that the sense of the operations used to develop and select the items is acceptable, and to the extent that the operations themselves were adequate, the study will have achieved its purpose. Another concern is that the Puerto Rican and the U.S. groups chosen for the study may appear to differ so greatly that with the limited equating techniques available, it unlikely that any set of common items, however appropriate, can make adequate adjustments for the differences.

The final concern is about the generalizability of a conversion between tests that are appropriate for different cultural groups. In the usual equating problem, a conversion function is sought that will simply transform scores on one form of the test to the score scale of a parallel form of the test—an operation analogous to that of transforming Celsius units of temperature to Fahrenheit units of temperature, also parallel measures, but in the sense that they are both measures of heat. When the two tests in question are measuring different types of abilities or when the tests may be unequally appropriate for different subgroups of the population, the conversion cannot be unitary, as is the temperature-scale conversion, but would be different for different subgroups (Angoff, 1966). In the present equating attempt, it is entirely possible that the use of different types of subgroups for the equating experiment—Mexicans and Australians, for example, instead of Puerto Rican and U.S. students—would yield conversion functions quite different from those developed in the present study. For this reason the conversions developed here should be considered to have limited applicability and should not be used without verification with groups of individuals different from those studied here.

The General Problem of Equating

In any testing program in which a number of different forms or editions of the same test are used it is inevitable that there will be variations in difficulty from form to form. Therefore, if the scores of individuals who take the different forms are to be compared with one another for the evaluation of their relative abilities, it is necessary in the interests of equity at least to calibrate, or "equate," the scores on the different forms.

The process of equating is a statistical one that in most testing programs ultimately yields an equation for converting raw scores to scaled scores. Thus, if there is no random error in the equation, one can assume that a student who has earned a scaled score of, say, 560 on a particular test form would have earned that same scaled score whether he or she had taken a more difficult or less difficult form of the test than the one actually taken. Viewed slightly differently, the purpose of equating is to maintain a constant scale over time in the face of changing test forms and different kinds of students. Only if this purpose is achieved will it be possible to compare students tested today with students tested five years ago, to aggregate data from different test forms, to plot trends, and to draw conclusions regarding, for example, the effects of practice, growth, changing curriculums, or changes in the composition of the student group over the course of time.

It was mentioned earlier that the end product of an equating process is often a transformation by which raw scores on a test form are converted to scaled scores. The methods followed in the equating process are designed to produce an equation that is characteristic of the test form itself, unaffected by the nature of the group of individuals from whom the data were collected. For example, the result of the calibration of two thermometers has generality and is therefore useful only to the extent that it is independent of the particular data used in the calibration. The conversion of Celsius (C) to Fahrenheit (F), if properly carried out, should be $F = 9/5 C + 32$, however the calibration was done and whatever the data were that were used for the calibration. If this condition holds, then the equation will also characterize the "pure" relationship between the two scales of temperature and will therefore be applicable to all objects—air, water, oil, molten steel, etc.—for which a measure of temperature is desired.

Similar requirements are imposed on score equating. Ideally, the data used for equating are drawn as two random samples from the same population. One sample (Group A) is given Form X of the test, the other (Group B), Form Y. Raw scores on Form X are then equated to raw scores on form Y (X→Y) by assuming, quite reasonably, that the two groups are equivalent. This is often done by means of a linear procedure (if the forms are very nearly parallel in difficulty) or by a curvilinear (i.e., equipercentile) procedure if not. If, in the operational testing program, X is the new form and Y is an old form for which there already exists a conversion equation, making it possible to go from raw scores on Form Y to scaled scores (Y→SS), we can, by using Y as the link, combine the two conversions, X→Y and Y→SS, in such a way as to allow the conversion to go directly from X to the scale (X→Y→SS, or, briefly, X→SS).

In the usual testing program, however, we are not at liberty to divide a total population into two random subsamples and administer a different form to each. Ordinarily, all the students at a given administration (Group A) take the same operational form (say X), and the task is to equate X to a parallel form, Y, that had been given operationally to a different group of students (Group B) at a prior administration in the testing program.

The equating of raw scores on the two forms requires an assessment of the relative difficulty of those forms, an assessment that is easily accomplished if the two forms are administered to very nearly equivalent groups—groups that, for example, are drawn at random from the same population. However, two groups that choose to take the tests at different administrations are very likely to be different, with respect to both average ability and dispersion (spread) of ability. Therefore, any evaluation of the relative difficulties of the forms on the basis of a direct examination of the data for these two groups could well be misleading and biased. Such an evaluation could easily result in a conversion equation for Form X that is contaminated by the characteristics of the groups rather than one that is based solely on the characteristics of the test forms. For example, if the group taking Form X is more able than the group taking Form Y, we might erroneously decide that Form X is easier than Form Y. Some means is therefore needed to adjust for differences between the two groups in level of ability.

The device used for making these adjustments is a short "equating," or "anchor," test administered to both groups at the time that they take the regular operational test. Sometimes the equating test is a separately timed test administered during the course of the administration, while other times it is a collection of items interspersed throughout the operational tests and common to both the old and the new test forms. This collection of common items is nevertheless treated statistically as though it were a separate test. At the time that the equating of the operational forms (Forms X and Y) is carried out, scores are obtained for the two groups on *both* the equating test *and* the operational forms that were administered to them. Appropriate formulas are then applied to the statistics observed for the two groups to yield estimates of the characteristics of the two forms as though they had been administered to the same group.

In applying these formulas, differences in the performance of the two groups are observed and used in making the adjustments necessary in the estimations of the required statistics for the two forms. Once these adjustments have been made it would be expected that the estimations are relatively free of contamination and bias attributable to differences in the abilities of the two groups, and the conversion relating raw scores on Form X and Form Y can be assumed to be, within the limits of random error, independent of the particulars of the equating experiment. This being the case, the conversion can also be assumed to be appropriate to all situations in which Forms X and Y are applicable—in the same sense that the equation for converting Celsius to Fahrenheit is appropriate to all situations calling for a measurement of temperature.

Because of its crucial role in the equating process, considerable care must be exercised in the choice or construction of the equating test. For reliable equating, the items that it comprises should themselves provide a reliable score. A recommended rule of thumb is that no fewer than twenty items or no fewer than 20 % of the items in the operational test—whichever choice yields the larger number of items—should be used for the equating test. There are other, more subtle requirements as well. The items that form the equating test should as a totality represent, insofar as possible, a parallel miniature of the operational forms, which themselves must be parallel forms. The items also should, in terms of the total equating test as well as the individual items that constitute it, represent the same psychological task to the groups taking each of the two operational forms—i.e., the directions for administering the test and for guessing, the time limits, the relative order of the alternatives within the items, etc., must be the same for the two groups.

Thus the quality of equating depends crucially on the parallelism of the two operational forms, the quality of the equating test, and the similarity of the two groups of students taking the two operational forms.

In the present study the conditions for ideal equating do not prevail. In it we attempt to equate two *different* tests, designed for students of different language, culture, and customs, and who are also characteristically different in average levels of academic ability, as measured by the PAA and the SAT. Clearly, it is unreasonable to assume, contrary to our general observations, that they may be taken as random samples drawn from the same population. The only alternative is to construct an equating test to use in making statistical adjustments in the averages and dispersions of scores for these two groups of students on the operational tests administered to them. The question is how to construct an equating test that although not literally the *same* for both groups, does present the "same psychological task" to both groups.

Method

The method followed in this study for deriving conversions of scores from the verbal and mathematical scales of the PAA to the verbal and mathematical scales of the SAT was similar in broad outline to that followed in the Angoff-Modu (1973) study referred to above. The 1973 study was conducted in two phases. The first phase called for the selection of appropriate anchor items for equating—preparing sets of items both in Spanish and in English, translating each set into the other language by Puerto Rican educators proficient in both languages, and administering both sets in the appropriate language mode to Spanish- and English-speaking students. On the basis of an item analysis of the data resulting from this administration, groups of verbal and mathematical items were chosen to fulfill the principal requirement that they be equally appropriate, insofar as this could be determined, for both student groups. Beyond this requirement, the usual criteria for the choice of equating items as to difficulty, discrimination, and content coverage were adhered to. Also, care was taken to produce sets of anchor items reasonably balanced as to Spanish or English origin. Once the anchor items were chosen, the second phase of the study was undertaken, which called for a second test administration and an analysis for equating based on the data resulting from that administration.

Phase 1: Selection of Items for Equating

In accordance with the foregoing plan, 105 Spanish verbal items, 110 English verbal items, 62 Spanish mathematical items, and 62 English mathematical items were drawn from the file and submitted to bilingual experts in Puerto Rico for translation. Two experts were assigned to translate the Spanish verbal items into English, and two experts were assigned to translate the English verbal items into Spanish. After this initial translation was completed, the two sets of experts independently back-translated each other's work into the original language. All translations were then sent to Educational Testing Service (ETS), where Spanish-language experts compared the back-translated items with the original items. Adjustments were made in the initial translations by the ETS staff and by the staff of the College Board Puerto Rico Office when the comparisons revealed inadequacies. In some instances it was judged that revisions could not be made adequately, and as a result a number of items were dropped from further use. The same process, including the back-translation procedure, was carried out for the mathematical items. Because of the smaller number of mathematical items, only two translators were used—one for translating items from Spanish to English and the other for translating items from English to Spanish. Eventually two complete sets of items were compiled, 160 verbal and 100 mathematical; each set appeared in both languages and, to the extent that this could be observed at an editorial level, was equally meaningful in both languages.

The 160 verbal items were of four types, paralleling the item types usually appearing in the operational forms of the PAA and the SAT: antonyms, analogies, sentence completion, and reading comprehension. The 100 mathematical items fell into four content categories; arithmetic, algebra, geometry, and miscellaneous. Detailed quantitative information on the pretested items is given later in this report.

The 160 verbal items and the 100 mathematical items were subdivided into four forty-item verbal sets and four twenty-five-item mathematical sets and administered to randomly equivalent samples of regular College Board examinees. The test items in Spanish were taken by candidates for the Spanish-language PAA at the October 1984 administration; the same test items, in English, were taken by candidates for the English-language SAT at the January 1985 administration. All of the foregoing sets of items were administered in thirty-minute periods. All PAA and SAT examinee samples consisted of about 2,000 cases.

Item response theory (IRT) methods were used to compare performance on the verbal and mathematical items taken by the SAT and PAA groups. Items that functioned most similarly for the two groups were selected to constitute the forty-item verbal and twenty-five-item mathematical equating tests.

Of all the methods currently available for selecting items that function similarly for two groups of examinees, the three-parameter IRT method (Lord, 1977; Petersen, 1977; Shepard, Camilli, and Williams, 1984) used in this study was deemed to be most preferable. This is so because it minimizes effects related to differences in group performance that seriously confound the results of simple procedures such as the delta-plot method (Angoff and Ford 1973) used in the previous study.

As just indicated above, IRT methods may be used to compare two groups of examinees with respect to their responses to a particular item for the full ability (theta) continuum. Item response curves, such as those shown in Figure 1, describe the relationship between the probability of a correct response to an item (shown on the vertical axis) and the degree of ability measured by the item (shown on the horizontal axis). The curves, typically falling along on S-shaped pattern, are described by the values of three items parameters: a, b, and c. These parameters have specific interpretations: b is defined as a function of the proportion of examinees who answer the item correctly, and is taken as a measure of item difficulty. If there is no guessing on an item, b corresponds to the ability level at which 50% of the examinees are expected to answer the item correctly. The b-parameter, which represents the placement, horizontally, of the item response curve on the scale of theta, usually takes on values between -3 (representing very easy items) and +3 (representing very hard items). The a-parameter which describes the steepness of the item response curve, represents the degree to which the item provides useful discriminations among individuals. Items with high a-values are highly discriminating; items with low a-values (close to zero) are not very discriminating. The c-parameter represents the probability that an examinee with very low ability will obtain a correct answer to the item. For this reason it is sometimes referred to as the guessing parameter.

Studies of differential item difficulty—to determine whether the items in the equating, or anchor, tests are equally difficult to students of the same ability in the two groups—were undertaken by estimating the item response curves of the pretested items separately for the PAA and SAT groups. Theoretically, if the item represents the same task—i.e., has the same meaning—for the two groups, the probability of a correct response should be the same for examinees of equal ability (i.e., for any value of *theta* along the continuum). Panel A of Figure 1 contains a comparison of item response curves obtained for a verbal item given to the PAA and SAT groups. Examination of the item response curves in Panel A shows that for all levels of ability *theta* the PAA group has a higher probability of obtaining a correct answer to that item—i.e., the item is seen to favor the PAA group. Panel B of Figure 1 provides a comparison of the item response curves obtained for a mathematical item given to the PAA and SAT groups. In contrast to the curves shown in Panel A, the item response curves for the mathematical item given to the two groups of examinees are almost identical—i.e., individuals at all levels of ability in both groups have the same probability of obtaining a correct answer to the item. In that sense, the item favors neither of the two groups, and therefore would be an ideal item to include in the equating test for this study; the item illustrated in Panel A would not.

Equating the Scores

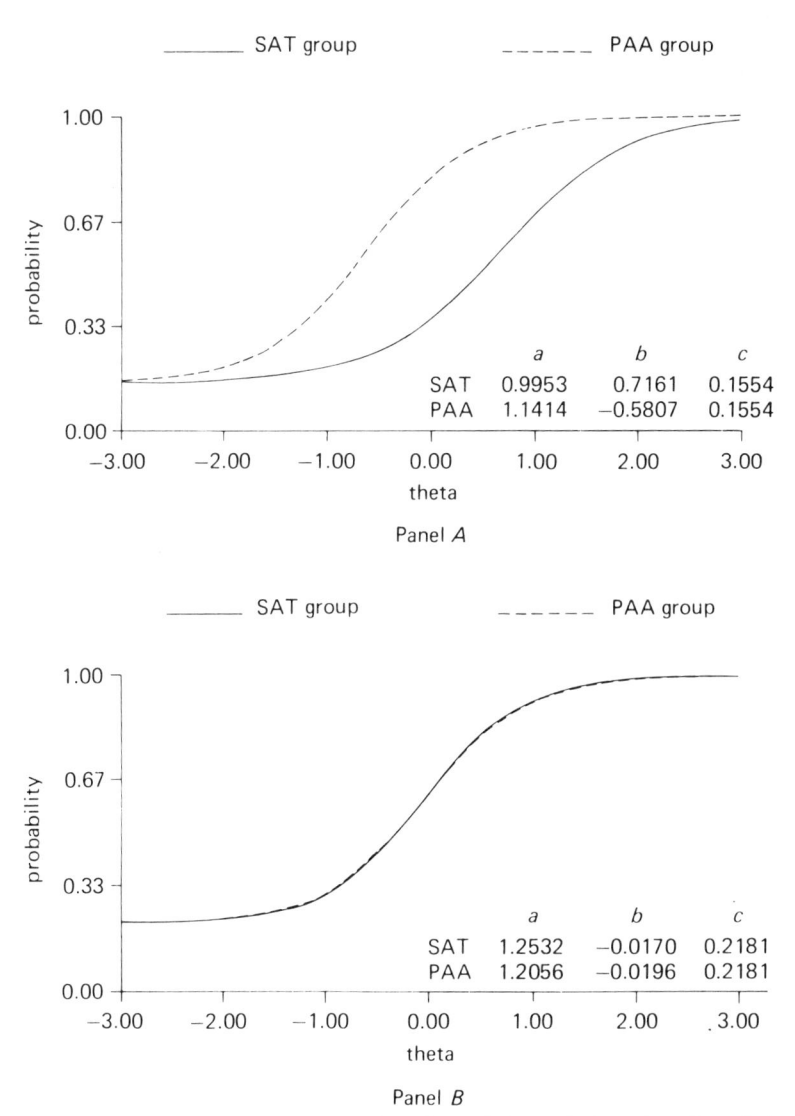

Panel A

	a	b	c
SAT	0.9953	0.7161	0.1554
PAA	1.1414	−0.5807	0.1554

Panel B

	a	b	c
SAT	1.2532	−0.0170	0.2181
PAA	1.2056	−0.0196	0.2181

Figure 1. Plots of item response functions for verbal (Panel A) and mathematical (Panel B) items given to PAA and SAT groups, illustrating poor and good agreement between groups.

For this study, item parameters and examinee abilities were estimated by use of the computer program LOGIST (Wingersky, 1983; Wingersky, Barton, and Lord, 1982). LOGIST produces estimates of a, b, and c for each item, and an ability estimate, *theta*, for each examinee. Estimates of item parameters obtained from separate calibrations (LOGIST runs) were placed on the same scale using the item response curve transformation method developed by Stocking and Lord (1983).

Several items were eliminated from the entire pretest pool as result of the LOGIST calibration. Because of the nature of the item responses, it was not possible to obtain estimates of the items parameters for fifteen verbal items and seven mathematical items. In addition, three verbal and two mathematical items were found to be so easy for both groups that stable r-biserial correlation coefficients could not be assured, and consequently, these items also were removed from the study. As a result, the pretested item pools were reduced to 142 verbal and ninety-one mathematical items.

The next set of steps was undertaken to identify the items in the verbal and mathematical pools that represented most nearly the same psychological task, or meaning to the two cultural-linguistic groups. For this purpose a procedure described by Lord (1980, chapter 14) was followed. Briefly, the procedure consists of the following steps:

1. Estimate the item difficulties (b-parameters), item discriminations (a-parameters), and the guessing parameters (c-parameters), for the total group of examinees, i.e., for the PAA and SAT group, combined.

2. Fixing the estimates of the c-parameters at the values obtained in Step 1, estimate the a- and b-parameters separately for the PAA and SAT groups.

3. Using the estimates of the a-, b-, and c-parameters, generate the entire item response curve for each item. Compare the estimates of the a- and b-parameters (obtained in Step 2), as well as the entire item response curves, for the PAA and SAT groups.

The comparison called for in Step 3 was accomplished by computing a chi-square statistic (Lord, 1980, chapter 14), testing the hypothesis that there are no differences between the corresponding parameters in the two groups. In addition, and as indicated in Step 3, the response curves for each item were also compared. This comparison was made by computing an index of the similarity between them, defined operationally as the mean of the absolute difference between the two curves (in their entirety) for each item. (See Cook, Eignor, and Petersen, 1985, for a detailed description of this index.) For each test (verbal and mathematical), items were ranked according to their chi-square values. From the set of items with the smallest chi-squares, those with the smallest values of the discrepancy index defined above—i.e., the mean absolute difference between the two curves—were chosen to constitute the equating tests. The verbal equating test, so constituted, consisted of thirty-nine items; the mathematical equating test consisted of twenty-five items. (It should be mentioned here that the original plan was to select forty verbal items and twenty-five mathematical items. However, after the selections were completed, but before the tests were administered, it was deemed necessary to drop one of the verbal items because it needed extraordinary revision to make it useful. As a consequence, the number of verbal equating items was reduced from forty to thirty-nine.)

Summary statistics for all pretested items as well as for those items eventually chosen to constitute the verbal and mathematical equating tests are illustrated in Figures 2 and 3 and presented in detail in Tables 1, 2, and 3. Figure 2 shows the 142 b-values (IRT estimates of item difficulty) for the English verbal items plotted against the corresponding b-values for the same verbal items as they appeared in Spanish. Figure 3 gives a similar plot for the ninety-one mathematical items. As may be seen from these figures, the verbal plot shows much more scatter in the off-diagonal direction than the mathematical plot, and represents a substantially lower correlation for the verbal items. ($r = .66$) than for the mathematical items ($r = .90$). In general, the correlation between the b's is a measure of the degree to which the items represent the same rank order of difficulty in the two languages. If the two groups had been drawn at random from the same population, one would expect to see correlations between item difficulty indices in the neighborhood of .98 or even higher, depending on the size of the sample on which the indices were calculated. The low correlation obtained in this study for the verbal items indicates that these items do not have quite the same psychological meaning for the PAA and SAT groups. Mathematics, on the other hand, with its higher correlation in these data, appears to be a more nearly universal language.

In a sense, these two correlations represent one of the more significant findings in this study because they reflect the very nature of the difficulties that are likely to be encountered in cross-cultural studies, especially when verbal tests are used. With respect to this study in particular, some doubt is cast on the quality of any equating that could be carried out with tests in these two languages and with groups as different as these. Since the equating items are used to assess and adjust for differences in the abilities of the PAA and SAT groups, a basic requirement for equating is that the items have the same rank order of difficulty in the two groups; and it is clear that for the verbal items, this requirement is not met. The verbal items were considerably improved by discarding the most aberrant items and retaining those that showed the smallest differences between the PAA and SAT groups in their item response curves. If one refers to Figures 2 and 3, one can see the effects of dropping the most discrepant items from the plots. (Items that were retained and actually used for the equating are represented by the boxes drawn in the plots.) It should be noted that even after dropping

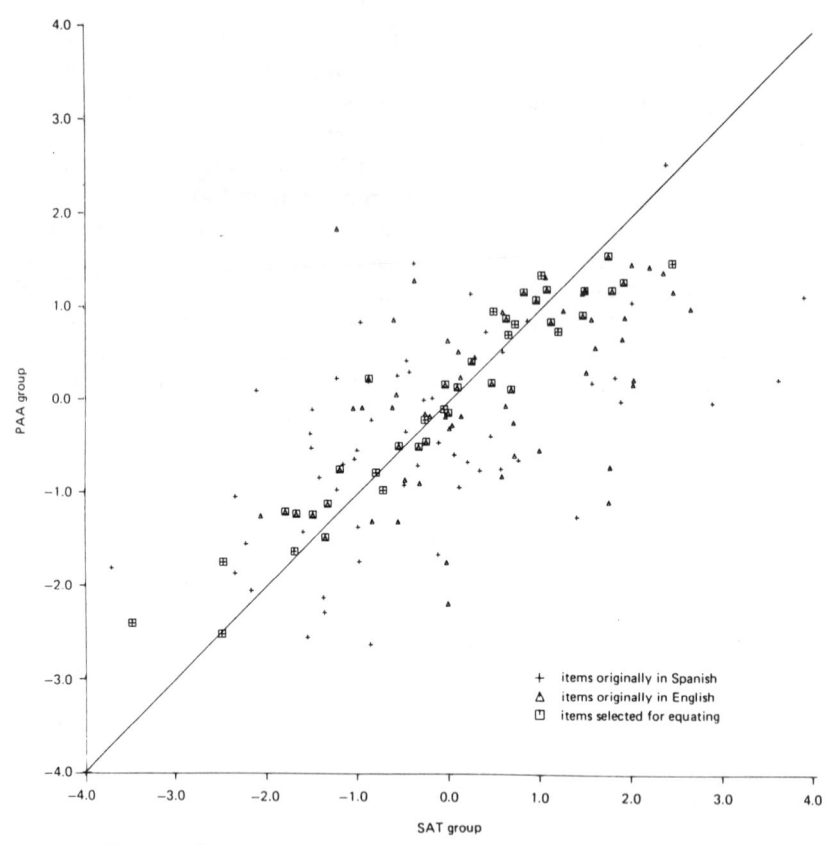

Figure 2. Plot of b's for pretested verbal items (number of items = 142).

the discrepant items, the items that were retained for the verbal equating still show considerable scatter. Hence, the concern remains that the verbal equating may be much less trustworthy than would be expected of an equating of two parallel tests intended for members of the same language-culture.

As mentioned previously, these results were not entirely unexpected; the observation has often been made that verbal material, however well it may be translated into another language, loses many of its subtleties in the process of translation. Even for mathematical items some shift in the order of item difficulty is to be expected, possibly because of differences between Puerto Rico and the United States with respect to the organization and emphasis of the mathematics curriculum in the early grades.

A summary of item difficulty indices (p-values) and item discrimination indices (r-biserials) is presented in Table 1 for both the verbal and mathematical items. The item difficulty index summarized in Table 1 is a

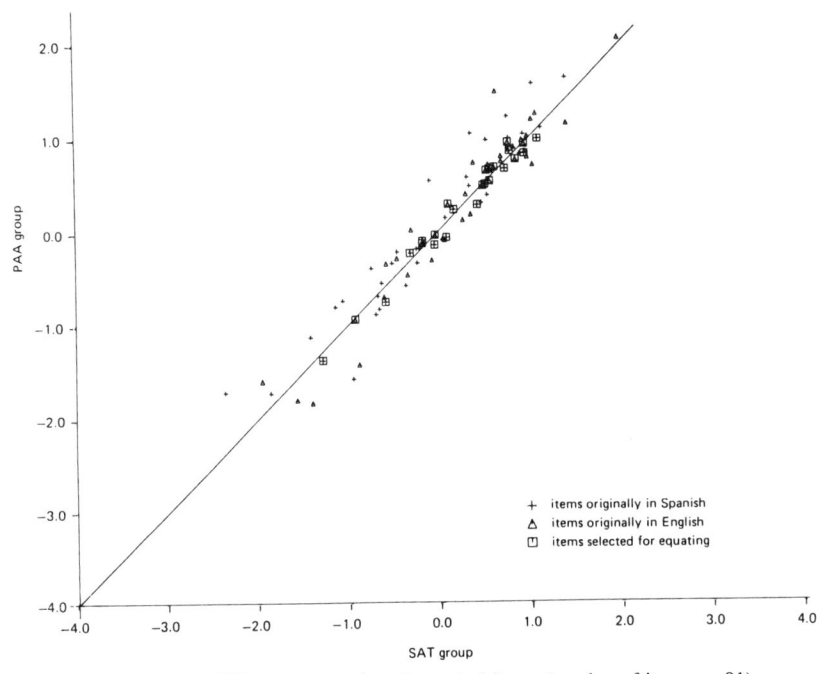

Figure 3. Plot of b's for pretested mathematical items (number of items = 91).

traditionally used estimate of the item difficulty and is simply the proportion of examinees choosing a correct answer to an item. The item discrimination index presented in Table 1 is the familiar item-test biserial correlation. Difficulty and discrimination indices are presented separately for the verbal and mathematical items and, within those categories, separately by each item's language of origin. There is also a summary of those indices for the thirty-nine verbal and twenty-five mathematical items selected for the equating tests. Also found in Table 1 are the means and standard deviations of the index of discrepancy (the mean absolute difference) between the two item response curves. This index, it is recalled, was one of the indices mentioned previously, used as the basis for selecting the equating items. Finally, Table 1 gives the correlations between the estimates of the b-parameters for the PAA and SAT groups, again by category of items.

As can be seen from the mean p-values given in Table 1, the items are, on the average, considerably more difficult (lower mean p-values) for the PAA candidates than for the SAT candidates. It also is seen that the difference between the mean p-values for the verbal items given to the PAA and SAT groups is smaller than the difference observed for the mathematical items given to samples of the same candidate groups. Finally it is interesting

Table 1
Summary Statistics for Pretested Items, by Language of Origin, before and after Selection of Equating Items

All Pretest Items	No of Items*	Difficulty Values (p) Mean PAA SAT	Difficulty Values (p) SD PAA SAT	Item-Test Correlations (r_{bis}) Mean PAA SAT	Item-Test Correlations (r_{bis}) SD PAA SAT	Discrepancy Indices Mean	Discrepancy Indices SD	Correlations between b's
Verbal								
Originally English	74	.43 .53	.20 .24	.37 .47	.14 .10	.13	.11	.61
Originally Spanish	68	.50 .63	.21 .21	.41 .42	.13 .14	.13	.11	.66
All verbal items	142	.46 .58	.21 .23	.39 .45	.14 .12	.13	.11	.66
Mathematical								
Originally English	44	.28 .54	.17 .18	.36 .57	.14 .09	.04	.03	.96
Originally Spanish	47	.33 .62	.20 .20	.43 .60	.16 .11	.05	.04	.89
All mathematical items	91	.31 .58	.19 .19	.40 .59	.15 .10	.04	.03	.90
Items selected for equating								
Verbal	39	.43 .60	.22 .23	.37 .47	.15 .09	.06	.03	.96
Mathematical	25	.28 .56	.15 .17	.40 .60	.11 .07	.03	.01	.99

*Three of the 145 verbal items and two of the ninety-three mathematical items were so easy for both groups that stable *r*-biserial correlation coefficients for these items could not be assured. Consequently these indices were not calculated for the items in question.

to note that for both the verbal and mathematical items and for both the PAA and SAT groups, the items originating in Spanish are easier (have higher mean p-values) than the items originating in English.

As mentioned previously, a summary of the item-test correlations (r-biserials) for the items in their Spanish and English forms also is found in Table 1. In general, both the verbal and the mathematical items—particularly the mathematics items—appear to be more discriminating for the SAT candidates than for the PAA candidates. These differences also are present in the group of selected items. It is observed that the mathematical items, at least for the SAT group, have higher mean r-biserial correlations, on average, than do the verbal items.

As the column summarizing the discrepancies between the item response curves for the two groups shows, the mean discrepancies between the curves for the verbal items are larger than those for the mathematical items, a finding that is consistent with the lower correlation between the b-values for the verbal items when compared to the correlation between the b-values for the mathematical items. Also, it may be observed that the items selected for equating show smaller mean discrepancies than is observed in the entire group of pretested items. This observation reflects the fact that the items were chosen largely on the basis of the agreement between the two item response curves.

The last column in Table 1, which gives the correlations between the b's, expresses numerically what has already been observed in Figures 2 and 3. Here we see again that the correlation between estimates of the b-parameters is much lower for the verbal items than for the mathematical items. And again, we see that the correlations between the b-values for the selected items—especially the verbal items—are higher than for the unselected items.

Table 2 is a summary of the same data as shown in Table 1 but classified by item type rather than by language of origin. The greater difficulty of the items for the PAA group, particularly the difficulty of the mathematical items, is readily observable in this table. It also is clear that the items in all four verbal and mathematical categories are more discriminating for the U.S. students than for the Puerto Rican students. It is interesting that the four verbal types arrange themselves into two distinct classes insofar as the correlations between their b-values are concerned: the higher correlations are characteristic of the sentence completion and reading comprehension items while the lower correlations are characteristic of the antonyms and analogies. This result is intuitively reasonable since verbal items with more context probably tend to retain their meaning, even in the face of translation into another language.

Although the item groups are too small to permit easy generalization, it appears that there is considerable variation from one verbal item type to

Table 2
Summary Statistics for Pretested Items, by Item Type

		Difficulty Values (p)				Item-Test Correlations (r_{bis})				Discrepancy Indices		Correlations between b's
		Mean		SD		Mean		SD		Mean	SD	
All Pretest Items	No. of Items[*]	PAA	SAT	PAA	SAT	PAA	SAT	PAA	SAT			
Verbal												
Antonyms	43	.44	.47	.22	.23	.37	.43	.13	.13	.18	.13	.59
Analogies	34	.41	.59	.19	.24	.42	.45	.15	.12	.13	.10	.62
Sentence completion	29	.49	.63	.25	.23	.36	.45	.14	.12	.15	.11	.73
Reading comprehension	36	.51	.66	.16	.17	.41	.45	.12	.13	.08	.06	.75
Mathematical												
Arithmetic	21	.29	.58	.16	.20	.42	.60	.19	.10	.05	.03	.93
Algebra	37	.34	.62	.20	.19	.40	.58	.13	.11	.04	.04	.96
Geometry	26	.28	.54	.19	.19	.38	.60	.14	.09	.05	.03	.92
Miscellaneous	7	.29	.54	.16	.23	.35	.53	.18	.07	.03	.01	.99

[*]Three of the 145 verbal items and two of the ninety-three mathematical items were so easy for both groups that stable r-biserial correlation coefficients for these items could not be assured. Consequently these indices were not calculated for the items in question.

Table 3
Distribution of Pretested Items, by Item Type and Language of Origin

	Originally English	Originally Spanish	Total
Verbal			
Antonyms	21	22	43
Analogies	19	15	34
Sentence completion	16	13	29
Reading comprehension	18	18	36
Total	74	68	142
Mathematical			
Arithmetic	11	10	21
Algebra	15	22	37
Geometry	13	13	26
Miscellaneous	5	2	7
Total	44	47	91

another with respect to the similarity of the task presented to the PAA and SAT groups. The analogy items especially, and to some extent the sentence completion and reading comprehension items, were more difficult than the antonym items for the Puerto Rican students than for the U.S. students. This effect appears to be a subtle one, very likely characteristic of the item type itself. It does not appear to be a function of the origin of these items or their increased relative difficulty upon translation into the other language. As shown in Table 3, very nearly the same proportion of the items for each of the categories was drawn from each language.

Phase 2: Equating

Once the thirty-nine verbal and twenty-five mathematical items that were to be used as "common"—more properly, "quasi-common"—items were chosen, the equating of the PAA to the SAT was carried out in the following manner. Two samples of candidates were chosen from the December 1985 administration of the SAT—one to take the verbal items in English (N = 6,017) in a thirty-minute period, the other to take the mathematical items in English (N = 6,172), also in a thirty-minute period, in addition to the regular operational form of the SAT given at that time. Similarly, two samples of candidates were chosen from the October 1986 administration of the PAA—one to take the verbal items in Spanish (N = 2,886) in a thirty-minute period, the other to take the mathematical items in Spanish (N = 2,821), also in a thirty-minute period, in addition to the regular operational form of the PAA given at that time. The scaled score means for the SAT samples were 405 verbal and 455 mathematical, compared with their parent group means of 404 verbal and 453 mathematical. The scaled score means for the PAA samples were 466 verbal and 476 mathematical, compared with their parent group means of 465 verbal and 485 mathematical.

Clearly, the SAT sample means for the verbal and mathematical tests agreed quite closely with their parent group means. Similarly, the PAA sample mean for the verbal test agreed closely with its parent group mean. The PAA sample mean on the mathematical test, however, showed some disagreement when compared to the parent group mean, but the degree of disagreement was not considered serious enough to cause concern.

Prior to equating the PAA verbal and mathematical scores to the SAT verbal and mathematical scores, the items of the equating section (the common items) were again evaluated to determine if they were functioning in the same manner for the PAA and SAT samples. The evaluation was carried out by examining plots of item difficulty indices (delta values[1]). Common items in this study were defined as "equally appropriate" to the Spanish- and English- speaking groups on the basis, it is recalled, of the similarity of their rank-order position among other items for the two groups. Five verbal and 2 mathematical items that were considered "outliers," after examining plots of verbal and mathematical item deltas, were deleted from the common-item sections, thus reducing further the number of verbal equating items to 34 and the number of mathematical equating items to 23.

Tables 4 and 5 contain information that may be used to evaluate the extent to which the common items and the operational tests were appropriate for both groups of examinees. Table 4 contains frequency distributions and summary statistics for the operational and common-item sections of the SAT- and the PAA-verbal. It can be seen from the verbal common-item (equating section) data in Table 4 that the U.S. sample is the higher scoring of the two groups. Also, we see that the difficulty of the sixty-six-item PAA appears to be just about right, on average, for the Puerto Rican sample; the average percentage-pass on the test was .49. The eighty-five-item SAT, on the other hand, is clearly difficult, on the average, for the U.S. sample; the mean percentage-pass on that test was .40.

The correlations observed in Table 4 between the scores on the common items in English and the scores on the SAT and between the scores on the common items in Spanish and the scores on the PAA (.84 and .81, respectively) suggest that each of the verbal common-item sets is reasonably parallel in function to the operational test with which it is paired.

The data presented in Table 5 describe frequency distributions and summary statistics for the operational and common-item (equating section) mathematical sections of the SAT and the PAA. The operational and

Table 4
Frequency Distributions and Summary Statistics for Verbal Operational and Equating Sections of the SAT and PAA

| | Mainland U.S. Sample || Puerto Rican Sample ||
Raw (Formula Score)	Operational SAT	Equating Section	Operational PAA	Equating Section
81–83	3			
78–80	16			
75–77	23			
72–74	28			
69–71	39			
66–68	67			
63–65	87			
60–62	122		15	
57–59	137		33	
54–56	185		90	
51–53	217		83	
48–50	277		141	
45–47	333		193	
42–44	333		201	
39–41	363		241	
36–38	416		209	
33–35	459	44	239	
30–32	441	216	260	5
27–29	405	495	219	31
24–26	404	625	233	47
21–23	362	804	164	126
18–20	327	939	152	244
15–17	263	874	166	337
12–14	245	863	94	502
9–11	190	500	80	424
6–8	128	345	45	459
3–5	78	212	20	400
0–2	29	71	7	209
−3−−1	27	26	1	100
−6−−4	9	2		2
−9−−7	4	1		
Number of cases	6,017	6,017	2,886	2,886
Mean	33.80	17.72	32.41	10.58
SD	15.91	7.17	12.64	6.56
Correlation: Operational vs. Equating		.841		.806
Number of items	85	34	66	34

Table 5
Frequency Distributions and Summary Statistics for Mathematical Operational and Equating Sections of the SAT and PAA

	Mainland U.S. Sample		Puerto Rican Sample	
Raw (Formula Score)	Operational SAT	Equating Section	Operational PAA	Equating Section
59–60	19			
57–58	14			
55–56	20			
53–54	33			
51–52	56			
49–50	74		5	
47–48	79		9	
45–46	106		24	
43–44	101		28	
41–42	160		49	
39–40	160		44	
37–38	211		51	
35–36	248		92	
33–34	258		80	
31–32	300		116	
29–30	323		92	
27–28	366		153	
25–26	336		121	
23–24	416	206	159	2
21–22	369	486	190	10
19–20	341	320	183	10
17–18	370	505	201	25
15–16	321	439	178	27
13–14	320	511	229	40
11–12	248	613	205	75
9–10	257	556	183	119
7–8	200	677	165	172
5–6	187	554	90	295
3–4	136	571	90	444
1–2	64	460	47	733
−1–0	47	188	29	550
−3–−2	15	82	4	272
−5–−4	7	4	2	45
−7–−6	1		2	2
Number of cases	6,172	6,172	2,821	2,821
Mean	24.17	10.82	19.56	2.92
SD	12.48	6.72	10.71	4.43
Correlation: Operational vs. Equating		.879		.740
Number of items	60	23	50	23

common-item mathematical data in Table 5 indicate even more than do the verbal equating data in Table 4 that the U.S. sample is the higher-scoring of the two. Also, note that unlike the verbal test, the operational PAA-mathematical test was as difficult for the PAA sample (the percentage-pass was .39) as was the SAT-mathematical test for the SAT sample (the percentage-pass on the mathematical test, similar to the percentage-pass on the verbal test, was .40).

Unlike the results shown for the verbal tests in Table 4, the correlations shown in Table 5 between the SAT and the common items in English (.88) and between the PAA and the common items in Spanish (.74) suggest that the common-item set may be considered parallel in function to the SAT but not quite so parallel to the PAA.

Two kinds of equating were undertaken, linear and curvilinear. Of the several linear methods, two were chosen for use, one attributed to Tucker (see Angoff, 1984, p. 110), the other, to Levine (1955). In addition, two curvilinear methods were used: equipercentile equating (see Angoff, 1984, p. 97) and IRT equating (Lord, 1980, chapter 13). Although the results of all the methods were evaluated, only the IRT results were used. Consequently this is the only method and these the only results described in this report.

It should be noted that IRT assumes that there is a mathematical function that relates the probability of a correct response on an item to an examinee's ability. (See Lord, 1980 for a detailed discussion.) Several different mathematical models of this functional relationship are possible. As mentioned in the preceding section, the model chosen for this study was the three-parameter logistic model.

The following is one of the underlying properties of IRT that make it useful for equating applications: If the data (in this study, the responses to PAA and SAT items) fit the three-parameter logistic model, referred to previously, it is possible to obtain an estimate of an examinee's ability (theta) that is independent of the difficulty level of the particular subset of items to which the examinee responded. Therefore, it does not matter if an examinee has taken a difficult or easy test; his or her theta estimate should be the same, apart from measurement error, once the estimates of the item parameters have been placed on the same scale. For this study, parameter estimates used for the PAA and SAT equating were placed on the same scale using a procedure referred to as "concurrent calibration." For IRT concurrent calibration, all estimates of the item parameters for the two test forms to be equated (the PAA and the SAT) are obtained in a single LOGIST run. (See Petersen, Cook, and Stocking, 1983; and Cook and Eignor, 1983, for a description of this and other IRT equating procedures.)

Because any ability score (theta) can be mathematically related to an estimated true score, it is possible to use estimates of theta (the outcome of the concurrent calibration described above) to establish the relationship between (i.e., to equate) estimated true scores for the SAT and the PAA. Of course, in practice, an examinee's true score is unknown. For this reason, the relationship established using the estimated true scores on the PAA and SAT forms was applied to the actual observed raw-scores obtained on these two test forms.

Results

The final outcome of the IRT equating of the PAA verbal and mathematical tests to the SAT verbal and mathematical tests was the production of two conversion tables: One table relates raw scores on the PAA verbal to raw scores on the SAT verbal, and the second table relates raw scores on the PAA mathematical to raw scores on the SAT mathematical. Conversion tables showing the relationship between scaled scores on the respective PAA and SAT tests were derived from the raw-to-raw conversion tables, as shown in the following schematic: Score Scale$_{PAA}$→Raw Scores$_{PAA}$→Raw Scores$_{SAT}$→Score Scale$_{SAT}$, or, in brief, Score Scale$_{PAA}$→Score Scale$_{SAT}$. Scaled score conversions for the verbal and mathematical tests are presented in Table 6. It is clear from the Table 6 list of verbal equivalences that the difference between the two scales is as much as 180 to 185 points at a PAA score of 500. The differences are smaller at the extremes of the score scale.

The equivalences for the mathematical tests also show striking differences between the PAA and the SAT scales. In the vicinity of a PAA mathematical score of 500 there is also a difference of 180 to 185 points. As is the case for the verbal equivalences, the differences between the mathematical scales are smaller at the extremes of the score scale.

Graphs of the verbal and mathematical IRT equating results appear in Figures 4 and 5. It is evident, even from a cursory glance at these figures that the conversions between the PAA and SAT are markedly curvilinear, typical of the results of equating two tests that differ sharply in difficulty. Such conversions, which are likely to be very nearly the same irrespective of the particular method of equating employed, are seen to be concave upward when the easier test is plotted on the horizontal axis and the more difficult test on the vertical axis. In this instance the PAA clearly is the easier test, and—inasmuch as the concavity is deeper for the mathematical test—it appears also that the mathematical tests are more different in difficulty than the verbal tests.

Some attention should be given to the meaning of the differences in the PAA and SAT scales. That a 500 score on the PAA corresponds to a

Table 6
Final Conversions between the PAA and SAT

Verbal		Mathematical	
PAA Scaled Scores	Equivalent SAT Scaled Scores	PAA Scaled Scores	Equivalent SAT Scaled Scores
800	785	800	785
787	757	790	743
774	709	779	676
761	660	768	629
749	617	758	593
736	584	747	564
723	557	736	539
710	535	726	518
697	516	715	499
684	500	704	482
672	485	694	467
659	472	683	453
646	460	672	440
633	449	662	429
625	438	651	418
617	428	640	408
609	419	630	399
601	410	619	390
592	401	608	382
584	393	598	374
576	384	587	366
568	376	576	359
560	369	566	353
552	361	555	346
544	354	544	340
535	347	534	334
527	340	523	329
519	333	512	323
511	326	502	318
503	319	491	313
495	313	480	308
487	307	470	303
478	301	459	299
470	295	448	295
462	289	438	290
454	283	427	286
446	278	416	282

Table 6 Continued

Verbal		Mathematical	
PAA Scaled Scores	Equivalent SAT Scaled Scores	PAA Scaled Scores	Equivalent SAT Scaled Scores
438	272	406	278
430	267	395	274
421	262	384	269
413	257	374	265
405	252	363	261
397	248	352	257
389	243	342	253
381	238	331	249
373	234	320	245
364	229	310	241
356	225	299	237
348	221	288	232
340	216	278	228
332	212	267	224
324	208	256	220
316	204	246	216
307	200	235	212
299	196	224	209
291	192	214	205
283	188	203	197
275	184	200	188
267	180		
259	176		
250	172		
242	168		
234	163		
226	158		
218	155		
210	152		
202	150		
200	148		

lower-than-500 score on the SAT says simply this: If one can assume that the SAT and PAA scale values have been maintained precisely since their inception, it can be concluded that the original scaling group for the SAT was generally more able in the abilities measured by these aptitude tests than was the original scaling group for the PAA. It does not by itself imply

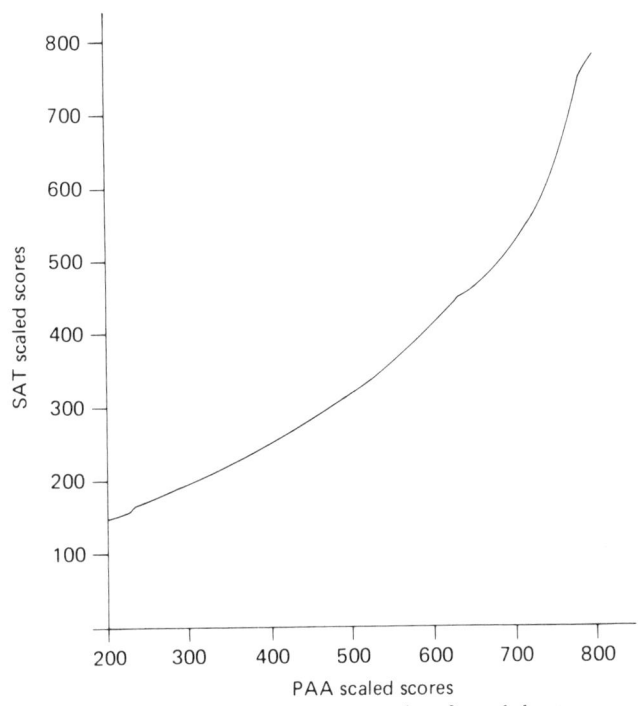

[Figure: plot with SAT scaled scores on y-axis (100-800) vs PAA scaled scores on x-axis (200-800), showing a monotonically increasing curve]

Figure 4. Item response theory conversions for verbal tests.

that the SAT candidate group today is necessarily more able than the PAA group, although this appears to be the case; average scores on the common items (the equating tests), for example, are higher for the SAT examinees than for the PAA examinees (see Tables 4 and 5). Nor does it necessarily suggest any generalization regarding the large populations from which these two examinee groups were selected—e.g., that the 12th grade students in the United States score higher than do the twelfth graders in Puerto Rico. We know that the number of high school seniors taking the SAT in current years is about two-fifths the size of the 12th grade population in the U.S. and is therefore a more self-selective group than is its PAA counterpart, which represents almost all (over 95 percent) of the 12 grade population in Puerto Rico. On the other hand, this is not to say that there are no differences between the two 12th grade populations. There is some evidence, however crude, that marked differences do exist, but this evidence is outside the scope of this study.

In view of these and other possible sources of misinterpretation of the data of this report, it will be useful to restate the limited purpose for which

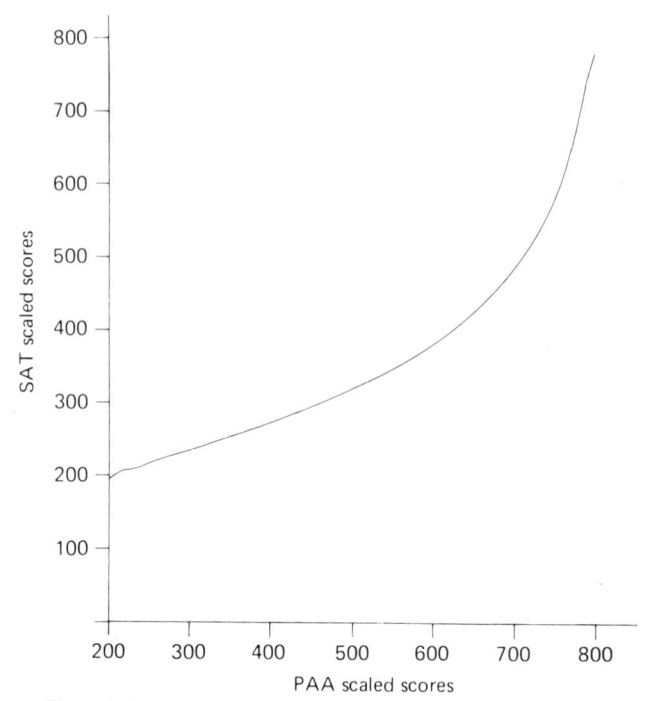

Figure 5. Item response theory conversions for mathematical tests.

the present investigation was undertaken: to derive a set of conversions between two similar-appearing scales of measurement—one for tests of one language and culture, the other for tests of a different language and culture. Clearly, the accuracy of these conversions is limited by the appropriateness of the methodological theory used to derive them and the data assembled during the course of the study. It is hoped that these conversions will be useful in a variety of contexts, but (as suggested by the examples cited here) to be useful, they each will need to be supported by additional data specific to the context.

At this point it is natural to question how well the equivalences developed in this study compare with those developed in the 1973 Angoff-Modu study. In the earlier study, two linear equating methods were used in addition to a curvilinear method. The final conversions reported there were taken to be an average of the three, essentially weighting the curvilinear results equally with the average of the two linear results. With the benefit of improved IRT techniques for equating and somewhat greater understanding of equating theory, the entire operation in the present study was based on the curvilinear equating as determined by the IRT procedure. The results of this study yielded substantially lower conversions to the SAT verbal scale than was the case in the earlier study, especially in the large middle range between about 450 and about 750, while conversions to the SAT mathematical scale showed better agreement with the earlier results. One can only speculate regarding the reasons for these results. One reason is the change in equating method. Another reason is the possibility of drift in the equating of either the PAA verbal scale or the SAT verbal scale, or both, over the intervening fifteen years. Yet another reason is that verbal equating across two languages and cultures is more problematic than is mathematical equating. In any case, we suggest that for a variety of reasons, the present results are probably more trustworthy than those given in the earlier Angoff-Modu report.

Summary and Discussion

The purpose of this study was to establish score equivalences between the College Board SAT and its Spanish-language equivalent, the College Board PAA. The method employed involved two phases: (1) the selection of test items equally appropriate and useful for Spanish- and English-speaking students for use in equating the two tests and (2) the equating analysis itself. The method of the first phase was to choose two sets of items, one originally appearing in Spanish and the other originally appearing in English; to translate each set into the other language; to "back-translate" each set, independently of the first translation, into the original language; and to compare the original version of each item with its twice-translated version and make adjustments in the translation where necessary and possible. Finally, after the items were thought to be satisfactorily translated (some items that appeared to defy adequate translation were dropped), both sets of "equivalent" items—one in English and the other in Spanish—were administered, each in its appropriate language mode, for pretest purposes. These administrations were conducted in October 1984 for the PAA group and in January 1985 for the SAT group, and samples of candidates were drawn from those who took the PAA or the SAT at regularly scheduled administrations. These samples provided conventional psychometric indices of the difficulty and discriminating power of each item for each group. In addition, they provided two item response curves for each item—one as it appeared in Spanish and was administered to the Spanish-speaking candidates and one as it appeared in English and was administered to the English-speaking candidates. Both curves were arranged to appear on the same scale so that discrepancies between them could easily be observed. Finally, indices of agreement between the curves and measures of goodness-of-fit of the data to the item response curve also were made available.

On the basis of the anlayses of these data, two sets of items—one verbal and the other mathematical—were chosen and assembled as "common," or "anchor," items to be used for equating. In the second, or equating, phase of the study these common items, appearing both in Spanish and in English, were administered in the appropriate language along with the operational form of the SAT in December 1985 and the operational form of the PAA in October 1986. The data resulting from the administrations of these common items were used to calibrate for differences in the abilities of the two candidate groups and permitted equating the two tests by means of the IRT method. The final conversion tables relating the PAA verbal scores to the SAT verbal scores and the PAA mathematical scores to the SAT mathematical scores are given in Table 6. Because of the scarcity of data at the upper end of the distribution of PAA scores, score equivalences in that region are not considered highly reliable.

The general approach followed in conducting this study requires special discussion, perhaps all the more so because the method is simple, at least in its conception. On the other hand, from a psychological point of view the task of making cross-cultural comparisons of the kind made here is highly complex. In the extreme the task is inescapably impossible; and although the present study may represent a reasonably successful attempt, it should be remembered that the cultural differences (between Puerto Rico and the United States) confronted by the study were relatively easily bridged. If, for example, the two cultures under consideration in the study were very different, then there would be little or no common basis for comparison.

Given that the cultures studied are similar to some extent, and that there is a basis for comparison, the approach and method offered appear to have some likelihood of success. Indeed, the method itself is useful in providing a type of metric for utilizing the common basis for comparison. For example, it allows a comparison of the two cultures only on a common ground, or only on those items whose item response curves were relatively similar, thus removing from consideration those characteristics of the two cultures that make them uniquely different. Thus, while we are afforded an opportunity to compare the two cultures on a common basis—i.e., on the item that are "equally appropriate"—we are also afforded an opportunity to examine the differences in the two cultures in the terms provided by the divergent, or "unequally appropriate," items. It is noteworthy that what emerges from this study is that the method described here also yields a general measure of cultural similarity, expressed in the index of discrepancy between the two item response curves for any particular item. The index—rather, the reciprocal of the index—summarizes the degree to which members of the two cultures perceive the item stimulus similarly. Additional studies of the similarity of any two cultures would have to be based on other stimuli examined in a wide variety of different social contexts.

The method clearly has its limitations, as do, therefore, the results of this study. For example, the present study has relied on the usefulness of translations from each of the two languages to the other, with the assumption that any biases in translation tend to balance out. Quite possibly, however, translation may be easier and more free of bias when it is made from Language A to Language B than in the reverse direction. If this is the case and items do become somewhat more difficult in an absolute sense as a result of translation, this effect would be felt more keenly by speakers of Language A than by speakers of Language B. Also implicit in the method of this study is the assumption that language mirrors all of the significant cultural effects. It is possible that the translatability of words and concepts across two languages does not accurately or entirely reflect the degree of similarity or difference in the cultures represented by those two languages. If, for example, there are smaller (or greater) differences in the languages than in the cultures, then again the method may be subject to some bias.

Aside from matters of methodology and possible sources of bias, a point made earlier in this report deserves repeating: In this study the comparison was made between Puerto Rican and U.S. students; the resulting conversions between the PAA and the SAT apply only between these two groups of students. Whether the same conversions also would have been found had the study been conducted on other Spanish and other English speakers is an open question. It is also an open question whether the conversion obtained here also applies to variously defined subgroups of the Puerto Rican and U.S. populations—liberal arts women, engineering men, urban Black adults, and so on.

We also hope that the conversions between the two types of tests will not be used without a clear recognition of the realities: A Puerto Rican student with a PAA verbal score of 503 has been found here to have an SAT verbal score "equivalent" of 319. This is not to say that that student would actually earn an SAT-verbal score of 319 were he or she to take the SAT. The student might do better or worse, depending, obviously, on the student's facility in English. The conversions do offer a way, however, to evaluate a general aptitude for verbal and mathematical materials in terms familiar to users of SAT scores; depending on how well the student can be expected to learn the English language, the likelihood of success in competition with native English speakers in the United States will vary considerably. Continuing study of the comparative validity of the PAA and the SAT for predicting the performance of Puerto Rican students in U.S. colleges and universities is indispensable to the judicious use of these conversions.

Finally, it will be helpful to describe the ways in which the conversions may be used appropriately. Intelligent use of the table requires the additional knowledge of the student's facility in English. For this purpose scores on a test like the Test of English as a Foreign Language (TOEFL), measuring the student's understanding of written and spoken English, would be useful. (Another possibility is a test that can accurately predict how rapidly a student is likely to learn a foreign language.) If the Spanish-speaking student's TOEFL scores are very low indicating little or no facility in English, these conversions may probably be taken at face value with appropriate cautions for their generalizability, as described earlier. If, however, the student's English-language ability is high, the conversions given here will be underestimates. Further, it would be expected that inasmuch as the SAT verbal test depends more heavily on English language ability than does the SAT mathematical test, the verbal conversion for the PAA to the SAT will be more sensitive to the student's facility (or lack of facility) with English than will be true of the mathematical conversion. These guidelines are, at best, based on educated intuition; as already indicated, the continuing conduct of validity studies will yield the best guidance for the proper use of these scores.

Part III

Testing and Hispanic Access to the Teaching Profession

7

Competency Testing and Latino Student Access to the Teaching Profession: An Overview of Issues

~ ~ ~ ~

Richard R. Valencia and Sofía Aburto

A major contemporary schooling problem facing the Latino community in the United States is characterized by a sharp paradox.[1] As the Latino school-age population dramatically expands (as well as the general ethnic minority population), the teaching force is becoming increasingly White (Zapata, 1988). As Andrews (1983) has noted, in 1980 minority teachers composed about 12.5% of the K–12 (kindergarten to grade 12) national teaching force (Blacks, 8.6%; Hispanics, 1.8%; American Indians and Asian Americans, less than 1%). Observers warn that if (a) the current very high failure rate of minorities on teacher tests continues unabated, and (b) the present rates of attrition via retirements stabilize, and (c) the present substantial percentage of 33% of newly certified teachers continue to select careers other than teaching, then by the year 2000 the national combined minority teaching force might be sharply cut to 5% or less—a reduction of about 60% in only two decades (Andrews, 1983; Smith, 1978).

The paradoxical aspect of this impending crisis is that as we see the whitening of the teaching force, we will likewise see a coloring of the elementary and secondary school population. In 1980, the combined ethnic minority K–12 enrollment nationally was 27% (Orfield, 1988), and by the year 2000 the minority K–12 population is predicted to reach 33% (Smith, 1987)—an increase of 22%. In short, during the time frame between 1980 and 2000, the projections are that nationally the combined ethnic minority teaching force will *decrease* about 60% while the combined ethnic minority K–12 public school population will *increase* by over 20%. The growing minority student/minority teacher disparity has been a subject of great concern in the educational literature. The predominant view is that the growing minority teacher shortage—coupled with the explosive increase in the minority student K-12 population—is creating serious issues for educational equity, particularly in the sense that a multicultural exposure for *all* students is being greatly hampered by the absence of significant numbers of ethnic minority teachers (e.g., Mercer and Mercer, 1986). One scholar has even gone so far as to describe the negative impact of teacher testing on prospective minority teachers as a new form of institutional racism. Commenting on the teacher shortage vis-á-vis the Black community, Mercer (1983) claims: "To operate a public school system without black teachers is to teach white supremacy without saying a word. If racism excludes black teachers from schools, no American can have a quality education, since only a racist system would tolerate the inequality that stifles the talents of any group of Americans" (p. 71).

With respect to a Latino student/Latino teacher comparison, there are striking disparities between the percentages of the Latino school-age population and the Latino teaching force. For example, in the huge Los Angeles City Unified School District, Latinos comprise one of every two K-12 students, yet only one in ten teachers are Latinos (Crawford, 1987). Although there are other hurdles (e.g., low and declining college-going rate), a major obstacle blocking Latino access to the teaching profession is the teacher competency test (e.g., California Basic Educational Skills Test [CBEST] and Pre-Professional Skills Test [PPST]). Latino performance on teacher tests is exceedingly clear:[2] Latinos score considerably and consistently lower than their White peers (more on the access problems created by teacher testing will be provided in the section "Obstacles to Latino Teacher Production"). The available data are alarming. For example, in California in 1986–87, 66% of Blacks, 41% of Chicanos, and 49% of other Latinos failed the test (CBEST) that is required to obtain a teaching credential. In contrast, only 19% of Whites failed the examination (Smith, 1987). In Texas, from March 1984 through June 1987, 68% of the Black students and 53% of the Latino students who wished to enroll in teacher education programs failed the admissions examination (PPST). The failure rate for White students was considerably lower at 19% (Smith, 1987). Based on some recent data, the high failure rate of Latinos on teacher tests continues. In Texas, for example, about 3,000 teacher education candidates took the Texas Academic Skills Program test (TASP, a new replacement for the PPST) in September, 1989. The fail rates for Latinos and Whites were 39% and 14%, respectively (Garcia, 1989). In sum, the disproportionate failure rate of Latinos on teacher tests combined with the tremendous increase in Latino school-age enrollment, present critical questions about potential negative impact in providing equal education opportunities for Latino students (e.g., delivery of bilingual education due to bilingual teacher shortage; see Olsen, 1988). Particularly, schools are very likely to find themselves in precarious predicaments in the delivery of multicultural education (especially bilingual education). Unfortunately, conditions down the line do not look bright. As Zapata (1988) admonishes about bridging the Latino student/teacher gap, "Projections for the future are generally bleak" (p. 20). Of course, such pessimism is couched in the presumption that the status quo in teacher testing will remain undisturbed in the years ahead—a supposition, we argue, that needs to be challenged.

The purpose of this chapter is to describe and analyze the problems associated with Latino access to the teaching profession, a significant contemporary issue dealing with career-specific pathways for Latino college students. A major area of concern that is covered is teacher competency testing. This overview of issues is a companion paper to chapter 8 of this volume, which provides a discussion of proactive measures that are likely to improve Latino access to teaching.

This chapter provides the following sections, listed in the order in which they appear: a rationale for the importance of having Latino teachers, a more full discussion of the negative implications of teacher tests vis-à-vis Latinos, a demographic overview of Latinos in teaching, and a discussion of obstacles to Latino teacher production, with a focus on teacher tests.

The Value of Having Latino Teachers: A Rationale

We think, and hope, that most people in the nation believe it is desirable to have an ethnically diverse teaching force, especially at a time when our school-age population is becoming increasingly ethnically diverse. An impatient advocate of the need for more Latino teachers might argue that the only rationale required for increasing the proportion of Latinos in teaching is one of a moral imperative—that is, it is simply the right thing to do. We have some disagreement with a moral argument, as such. Because the problem of the low and falling proportion of Latino teachers is so grave, the argument needs to be couched in theory, research, and practice so educational policymakers can be as informed as possible. We are fearful that moral rhetoric alone will not move policymakers in the right direction in producing equitable ways to enhance Latino access to the teaching profession.

Where does one begin in developing an informed rationale that lays out arguments for the value of having Latino teachers? We tackle this in several ways: by examining some theoretical discourse on the notion of "shared identity" between teacher and learner, by probing the notion of teacher role models, and by exploring the pedagogical raison d'etre for a culturally pluralistic curricula.

Shared Identity

In his recent book, *The Practice of Teaching*, Philip Jackson (1986) presents six stimulating essays whose paths parallel and often cross. The first chapter (essay), "On Knowing How to Teach," asks in a broad fashion, "What must teachers know about teaching?" One facet of this inquiry has to do with the similarity between teacher and student, or as Jackson calls it, "the presumption of shared identity."

According to Jackson, the presumption of shared identity carries this implicit idea: "the existence of a match between teachers and students along several dimensions at once: cultural, psychological, and physiological" (p. 22). Regarding the dimension of psychological functioning, teachers often presume that their students are similar to themselves—(e.g., the way they think and feel; what motivates them to laugh, to cry). With respect to physiology, teachers assume a similarity with their students in ways that the latter become fatigued, tolerate stress, become excited, and so forth. The third aspect of the presumption of shared identity—the one that has most relevance for our discussion on the match between Latino student/ Latino teacher—is what Jackson refers to as "our common cultural heritage." Jackson elaborates on this provocative expression this way:

> What that heritage contains is rather difficult to say with precision, but certain of its elements are clear enough. It includes a common language and a large part of the kind of common sense knowledge about which much already has been said. It includes a knowledge of cultural heroes, popular tastes, and everyday customs and conventions, all of which enable people to feel at home and to behave understandably within a specific cultural context. (p 22.)

The implication of the presumption of shared identity—if it is met—according to Jackson, is that teaching for the teacher becomes easier and more efficient (and we assume enhances the student's learning). In other words, Jackson argues that when teachers teach students who are very similar to themselves, a great deal of learning how to teach is provided by common sense or by knowledge of the subject matter to be taught. Jackson does not downplay the importance of having pedagogical techniques, per se. He simply is contending that if the presumption of shared identity is met, most but not all of what teachers need to know about learning to teach comes from other sources (e.g., subject matter knowledge). But Jackson asks, what might occur when the presumption of shared identity is invalid—(i.e., not met)? His response:

> there may be quite a lot to learn about how to proceed. The knowledge called for under these circumstances is genuinely knowledge about teaching *per se*. It is not a part of what most people would call common sense, nor is it deductible from knowledge of the material to be taught. Instead, it has to do with such things as the developmental characteristics of students and how to adapt instructional procedures in the light of those characteristics, how to handle social situations involving the potential for conflict, how to proceed in the face of disagreement of the purposes and goals of instruction, and so forth. (p. 26)

Jackson continues by asking: In that no two people are exactly alike, might a teacher operating on the presumption of shared identity run the risk of making an error in some cases? Jackson agrees that this is an important question, but the answer—it seems to him—is that we must have a starting point. It is a given that teacher and student do not fully share the same outlook, background, psychological makeup, etc. The answer is that some expression of the presumption of shared identity needs to remain unquestioned in order for teacher-student social interactions to occur. In other words, Jackson contends, the issue is not whether the presumption of shared identity is valid or invalid. Rather, he posits: "To what *extent* is it valid? What are its limits? What this turns out to mean is simply that some teachers are more like their students than others. The question is: which are which?" (p. 27).

Jackson answers this final question, in part, by referring to certain dimensions of dissimilarity that have been widely accepted as hindrances in the communications process between teachers and students, such as social class, race, ethnicity, among others.[3] Conversely, "teachers who share with their students a similar social class background have a *great advantage* [italics added] insofar as presumed identity is concerned" (p. 28). Furthermore, we would add, given that ethnicity or race are often a proxy for social class, there should be little quarrel that these former variables might also be advantageous insofar as presumed identity is concerned.

Although we do not necessarily underestimate the importance of pedagogical knowledge as does Jackson, his theoretical discourse on the presumption of shared identity, particularly the "common cultural heritage" dimension, provides a window to look into and around in order to understand why it is important to have Latino teachers. Making generalizations from Jackson's global treatise on the presumption of shared similarity to the specificity of the Latino situation, it is not difficult to posit from a general theoretical perspective that Latino teachers, compared to their White peers, would tend to have an advantage in working with Latino students. In no way do we mean to imply that *only* Latino teachers can and should teach Latino students, nor are we implying that *only* White teachers can and should teach White students. The generalization, and hence the implication, that we truly wish to draw is simply this: Insofar as the presumption of shared identity is concerned, it appears that other factors being equal, Latino teachers are likely to have some advantage teaching and enhancing the learning of Latino students, with whom they share similar backgrounds.[4] If this is a reasonably plausible thesis—and we believe it is—then a fairly sound argumentative foundation can be laid as to why Latino teachers are valued, especially at a time when school failure among Chicano and Puerto Rican students is so pronounced.

Role Models

For our ensuing discussion, a logical pedagogical extension of the presumption of shared identity deals with the phenomena of modeling, " . . . the imitation of others' behavior—and vicarious experience, learning from others' successes or failures" (Slavin, 1986, 130). Bandura (1969, 1977), the developer of social learning theory, contends that much of what humans learn is indirectly or directly learned from models. One aspect of modeling is "model-client similarity." Research in this area has shown that similarity in model-learner attributes tends to improve learning outcomes (Rosenthal and Bandura, 1978). More precisely, Bandura (1977) contends that when an individual is exposed to a role model that has similar characteristics—and when the model performs a task successfully—the learner expectations about his/her ability to perform the task are enhanced.

Going from the generality of modeling to the specific context of modeling in the school setting, research has shown that teachers can and do serve as role models (e.g., Barton and Osborne, 1878; Brophy and Putnam, 1979). Going further to the schooling of minority students, a justifiable assertion is that minority students would profit in a more direct manner from a teacher role model if there is an ethnic match between student and teacher (Graham, 1987). Furthermore, it can be argued that White students will benefit from being taught by minority teachers. These opportunities and experiences can provide White students familiarity with minorities in teaching situations, particularly in learning the same lesson that minority students do: Minority adults can occupy positions of respect and authority (Graham, 1987; Middleton, Mason, Stilwell and Parker, 1988).

In sum, the intersection of the presumption of shared identity and role models helps shape a strong argument why it is important to have Latino teachers. We now move to an exploration of a pedagogical raison d'être for a culturally pluralistic curriculum for Latino students and the vital role Latino teachers should have in the conceptualization and delivery of such curricula.

Multicultural Education

In a recent comprehensive analysis of multicultural education in the United States, Sleeter and Grant (1987) found numerous problems in the available literature—e.g., virtual absence of research studies on what occurs when teachers implement multicultural education in the classroom. Notwithstanding these problems, Sleeter and Grant found a few positive indicators. One particularly good sign is that as a whole, the field of multicultural education "is becoming an accepted and articulated concept among teacher educators and teachers, in part because of the increased attendance of students of color in our schools" (p. 439).[5]

One example of the proponent view of multicultural education is Gay (1988), who conceptualizes its essence as "the diversification of the content, contexts, and techniques used to facilitate learning to better reflect the ethnic, cultural, and social diversity of the United States" (p. 332). Gay and a growing number of scholars (e.g., Banks, 1984; Gonzalez, 1974; King and Ladson-Billings, 1988; Suzuki, 1984) contend that the rationale for multicultural education rests on two firm foundations—valuative and ideological. The valuative foundation refers to the need to develop knowledge and to foster appreciation of ethnic and cultural diversity. The ideological aspect refers to the need to equalize educational opportunities—that is, the importance of linking multicultural education goals of excellence and equity for diverse learners.

In the case of Latino students and multicultural education, Gonzalez (1974) presents an informed, well-reasoned developmental and sociological rationale for culture-based curricula.[6] In brief, Gonzalez' thesis is that from a developmental perspective, children require a cultural or ethnic set of reference points from which to base and build learning. The premise here is that the child's cultural heritage and/or current ethnic experience need to be taken into consideration. Furthermore, instruction must begin from where he/she currently is and proceed onward. From a a sociological perspective, Gonzalez argues that a culture-based curricula is needed because they can assist the White child in reducing, perhaps reversing racial prejudice, and assist the Latino child in fending off racist behavior and actions. In sum, Gonzalez' rationale for a culture-based curricula is based on individual, group, and societal needs.

With this as background, we can now ask: What is the linkage between multicultural education and Latino teachers? Multicultural education, as other forms of curricula, has standard components, namely: rationale, goals and objectives, content, learning activities, and means of evaluation (Gay, 1988). The prime mover of this delivery system is the teacher. Given what we discussed earlier on the presumption of shared identity and role models, we would say that, as a whole, Latino teachers would have some advantage over White teachers in the delivery of multicultural education. Latinos, by their backgrounds and experiences, are: more likely to have had interactions with other Latinos in general, more able to empathize with Latino students, and more likely to share a common cultural heritage. In contrast, White teachers—as a whole—are more likely to have certain disadvantages in teaching multicultural education. On this topic, King and Ladson-Billings (1988) share their experiences as teacher educators in an elite university setting:

> Most of our teacher education students . . . lack experiences with people from backgrounds different from their own. They are not only limited by their white middle-class "ethnic encapsulation" but the elite, monocultural education they have experienced has created certain ideological blind spots which limits their ability to critique prevailing educational practices that contribute to the persistent educational problems of "minorities." Their social and educational background also limits the ability of our students to empathize with poor and culturally different students. (pp. 2–3).

There are two additional reasons, in the context of multicultural education, why it is important to have Latino teachers. These justifications are related to the limited preprofessional training in multicultural education teachers receive, and the disinterest many current preservice teachers have in receiving training in multicultural education. Regarding the limited training issue, Olsen (1988) reports that most teachers are inadequately prepared to implement international or multicultural curricula perspectives. A case in point: According to Olsen, only 5% of prospective teachers in California take any course in international or multicultural education. Mahan and Boyle (1981) provide further evidence. In a twenty-five-state study, it was concluded that more than 80% of beginning teachers were deemed, by students teaching directors, as unqualified to teach in urban settings. Perhaps the limited preservice training in multicultural education received by prospective teachers explains, in part, teacher prejudice against minority students. For example, Olsen (1988) notes that more than a third of her total sample ($N = 360$) of California immigrant students (ages 11–18) reported racial incidents of what they believed were teacher prejudice (e.g., punished or embarrassed for using their native language; cultural clashes; derogatory or stereotypic comments in front of the class).[7]

With respect to the issue of disinterest, the study by Mahan and Boyle (1981) is informative. The authors surveyed student teaching directors ($N = 66$) in twenty-five states. It was found that two of three directors believed somewhere between 60 to 100% of students in teacher education programs did not desire preparatory experiences in multicultural education. As King and Ladson-Billings (1988) argue, such resistance to multicultural education training does not justify its exclusion from teacher education programs.

In summary, the rationale we have developed plus the extant empirical data offer convincing evidence for the importance of having Latino teachers. The needs and problems in multicultural education underscore the critical role Latino teachers can serve in meeting the challenge of cultural diversity, particularly with respect to Latino students.

Negative Implications of Teacher Testing for Latinos

Smith (1985) notes that 1978 was a significant marker in the history of the nascent teacher competency movement. The U.S. Supreme Court in 1978 upheld the use of the National Teacher Examinations for certification of teachers (U.S. v. State of California, 434 U.S. 1026). This major judicial decision gave life to teacher testing, a movement that would spread quickly throughout the country. According to Eissenberg and Rudner (1988), presently twenty-four states require some type of teacher test as a condition for admission to a teacher education program, thirty-six states require teacher testing only upon graduation as part of state certification, and eighteen states require both entrance (admissions) and exit testing (certification). Shepard and Kreitzer (1987) note that three states mandate teacher competency testing for teachers currently practicing (recertification).

Since 1983, the literature on teacher education has increasingly concerned itself with the negative impact of teacher testing on minority would-be teachers. Sometimes implicit, sometimes explicit in this literature is the contention that the absence of minority teachers contributes negatively to the quality of education of all students in a pluralistic society (e.g., Bass de Martinez, 1988; Mercer, 1983; Mercer and Mercer, 1986; Middleton et al., 1988; Nava, 1985; Pressman and Gartner, 1986; Smith, 1985). The argument goes something like this: Minority teachers serve as positive role models, particularly to students of their own ethnicity; they are important in passing on cultural heritage and instilling minority pride; they can assist in the promotion of racial understanding among all students and help to discourage cultural misconceptions and prejudices (cf. Mercer and Mercer, 1986).

With respect to the negative implications teacher testing has on prospective Latino teachers, we will discuss two issues: the reduced or nondelivery of multicultural (particularly bilingual) education, and the impact on access to Latino leadership roles in the schools.

Issue of Multicultural Education and Equal Educational Opportunity

The old educational adage, "Those who can, do; those who can't teach," recently has been challenged to read, "Those who can, do; those who understand, teach" (Shulman, 1986). With respect to the dwindling Latino teaching force as affected by teacher tests and the concomitant negative impact on the delivery of multicultural education, perhaps the maxim should read, "Those who aren't there, can't teach." Next, we offer some insights to the consequences resulting from teacher testing (i.e., Latino teacher shortage) and the schooling of language minority students (i.e., Limited-English Proficient [LEP] Latino students).

Nava (1985) argues that because Latino college students, compared to their White peers, disproportionately pursue bilingual/multicultural teaching careers, and because Latinos' failure rates on teacher tests are so high, bilingual education programs are beginning to experience severe and worsening shortages of teachers.[8] Nava discusses the case of Texas, a state that is experiencing the effects of the teacher shortage of fully credentialed bilingual teachers. Up until 1984, Texas had slightly more than 9,000 bilingual teachers. Nava reports, however, that there are more than 630,000 LEP students in bilingual education in Texas between five and seventeen years of age (99% of these students are of Latino origin, predominantly Chicano). According to Nava, the bilingual teacher shortage is so acute that, "An additional 20,000 bilingually certified/endorsed teachers are needed to provide adequate equal education opportunities for these linguistically and culturally different groups" (p. 34).

Texas is not alone with its bilingual teacher shortage problem. In 1987 in California, for example, there were 613,324 LEP students (approximately 73% of these were Latino students), and fewer than 10,000 credentialed bilingual teachers were available to serve these students' needs (Olsen, 1988). Because of the severe teacher shortage, less than 25% of the LEP students were in classes staffed by bilingual teachers; the remaining 75% received little, if any, instructional support in their primary language. According to Olsen, the critical effects of the shortage of bilingual teachers will be felt far into California's future. For example, in the year 2000, it is predicted that there will be approximately 18,000 bilingual teachers. Yet, the actual demand to meet the needs of the thousands and thousands of LEP students will be about 30,000 bilingual teachers—a projected shortfall of

12,000 teachers. It is likely that in Texas, California, and elsewhere, the high failure rate of Latinos on teacher tests will continue to be a major contributing factor in blocking access to teaching careers in bilingual education—unless this obstacle to access is dealt with vigorously. In any event, the negative effects of teacher testing on the Latino community are here now. Nava (1985) incisively captures the issue this way when speaking of the crisis in Texas:

> Ultimately, if minority certificated and non-certificated persons fail these tests in disproportionate number, second language minority students at the elementary and secondary levels will be greatly affected. Teachers without special linguistic skills and cross-cultural competencies have not been effectively responsive to the needs of these students. Culturally and linguistically different students need teachers and administrators who are familiar with their language and culture. (p. 34)

Issue of Access to Latino Educational Leadership Roles

An overlooked but significant implication of teacher testing is that the reduced number of minority teachers is very likely to result in a reduction of minority principals and superintendents (Smith, 1985).[9] It is typical for states to require two to three years of classroom teaching experience as a prerequisite for certification as an administrator. Thus, it is probable that the high failure rate of Latinos on teacher tests exacerbates the already difficult time Latinos have in gaining access to top positions in educational administration. In 1980 ("pre" era of teacher competency testing), Latinos nationally comprised only 2% of the total public elementary and secondary school principals (Orum, 1986).[10] Current national data on the percentage of Latino principals (and superintendents) is not available, but one could surmise the national percentage is down. Our intent here is not to argue that Latinos' access to principalships and superintendentships is totally blocked. One could contend, however, that because of the Latino teacher shortage, the available pool of those Latino teachers who may aspire to become principals and/or superintendents has shrunk and will continue to shrink.

The predicted reduction in the numbers of Latino principals and superintendents has far-reaching implications for the schooling of Latino students. Let us take the case of the principalship. Studies have shown that in general (e.g., Edmonds, 1979, 1986) and for language minority students, such as Latinos (Carter and Chatfield, 1986; Garcia, 1988; Garcia, Flores, Moll and Prieto, 1988), one major correlate of effective schools is the role of the principal.[11] As Edmonds (1986) notes, "The main difference is that principals of effective schools are the instructional leaders in their buildings, whereas those in ineffective schools are not" (p. 97). Garcia et al.

(1988; as cited in Garcia, 1988) report a school effectiveness study involving Chicano elementary school children in Phoenix, Arizona. Among several key findings was that the principals tended to be well versed in their schools' curriculum and instructional strategies, were very supportive of their teachers, recognized that teacher autonomy was important, and held high standards of accountability. Given the persistent, pervasive, disproportionately low achievement of Latino school-age students (cf. Orum, 1986), it makes sense to have Latinos in proactive leadership roles, such as principals. Unfortunately, at a time when Latino educational leadership is sorely needed, the mobility pipeline appears to be increasingly clogged as an indirect result of the disproportionately high failure rate of Latinos on teacher tests.

Latinos in Teaching: A Demographic Overview

To underscore the severity of the current escalating shortage of Latino teachers, it is necessary first to couch the statistics in a broader demographic picture of the Hispanic population in the United States.[12] Using information collected in March 1986 and 1987, the Bureau of the Census (1987) notes that the Hispanic civilian noninstitutional population increased by 4.3 million (or 30%) from 1980 to 1987, compared with 6% for the non-Hispanic population. It is clear that nationally Latinos are the fastest growing major ethnic minority group—increasing at a rate in the 1980s about five times the rate of the non-Hispanic population. Currently, this heterogeneous population numbers nearly 19 million people. By the year 2080, it is projected that the Latino population will surpass Blacks, becoming the nation's largest ethnic minority group (Cannon, 1986).[13] In light of these dramatic increases in Latino population, it is a given that in the very near future the school-age Latino population will begin to occupy a sizeable proportion of the total school-age enrollment. The need to provide Latino teachers as role models will become an even more pressing social and educational concern.

Composition of the Teaching Force

National data on the racial and ethnic composition of the elementary and secondary teaching force vary widely depending on the source and surveying methodology. Drawing on early survey data from the Equal Employment Opportunity Commission (EEOC), Orum (1986) reports that in 1980, Hispanics comprised only 3.5% of "full-time" (i.e., professional and paraprofessional staff) employees in the nation's public elementary and secondary schools. With respect to the teaching force, Hispanics were 2.6% of all elementary school teachers and 1.7% of secondary school teachers. Only 2% of the principals and 2.5% of central office administrators were Hispanic. Hispanics were employed in larger proportions, however, in noncertified and noninstructional job classifications, comprising 7.9% of the nation's teacher's aides and 4.4% of school clerks and secretaries.

The American Council on Education (1987), using slightly more recent EEOC data, indicated that in 1982, 2.6% of the teaching force was Hispanic. Unfortunately, it is not clear whether this percentage refers solely to elementary school teachers, as in the Orum (1986) report, or if it is a combination of both grade levels. Thus, it is difficult to determine if these data indicate stability or a decline in the number of Hispanics in the teaching force. These data also showed that in 1982, 0.6% of the teaching force was Asian American, 0.2% was American Indian, and 11.1% was Black. Whites comprised 85.4% of the full-time classroom teachers.

Using 1985 data, Mingle (1987) reports slightly higher percentages than Orum, with Hispanics representing 2.7% of all elementary teachers and 3.2% of secondary teachers. Also using data from 1984–85, the Department of Education reports 85% of the classroom teachers were White, 9.9% were Black, and 4.4% were "other" (American Council on Education, 1987). Unfortunately, the reported "other" data were not disaggregated for Hispanics, Asian Americans, and American Indian.

A more accurate and consistent accounting is needed on the racial and ethnic composition of the nation's teaching force. As will be shown below, however, even when the highest estimates of minority teachers are compared with the racial and ethnic composition of the nation's students, it becomes clear that the number of minority teachers is low and falling while the percentage of minority school-age children as a proportion of the total school population continues to grow dramatically.

Racial/ethnic composition of public schools

As reported by the Center for Education Statistics (1987), the racial and ethnic composition of the nation's public schools underwent considerable change between 1976 and 1984. Continuing the trend from previous decades, the proportion of White students declined, while the proportion of minority students increased. In particular, the percentage of Asian American students increased by more than 85%, and the percentage of Hispanic students increased by 28.2%, going from an enrollment of 6.4% in all public school districts in 1976 to 9.1% in 1984. In contrast, the proportion of Black students declined by nearly 6%.

Orfield (1988), examining a combination of earlier and more recent federal data on the race and ethnicity of students, further substantiates this

Table 1
**Percent of National Enrollment by Race and Ethnicity,
Fall 1968 – Fall 1986**

Race/Ethnicity	1968	1980	1986	Change
Hispanic	4.6	8.0	9.9	+5.3
Black	14.5	16.1	16.1	+1.6
White	80.0	73.2	70.4	−9.6
Asian and American Indian	.9	2.7	3.7	+2.8

Note: From "The Growth and Concentration of Hispanic Enrollment and the Future of American Education" by G. Orfield, July 1988, paper presented at the National Council of La Raza Conference, Albuquerque, New Mexico.

trend by noting that while Hispanics made up 4.6% of the national school enrollment total in the 1968–69 school year, they accounted for 9.9% in the 1986–87 school year (see Table 1). In other words, the Hispanic share of the total U.S. public school enrollment doubled in an eighteen-year period. Thus, while eighteen years ago there were more than three times as many Blacks as Hispanics in the school population, now the Hispanic enrollment is approaching two-thirds of the Black numbers. Even more striking is the fact that while eighteen years ago there was one Hispanic student for every seventeen White students, in 1986–87 there was one Hispanic for every seven White students.

In terms of raw numbers, Orfield (1988) notes that between 1968 and 1986 the number of Hispanic students in public schools grew from 2,003,000 to 4,064,000, an increase of about 2.1 million students, while White enrollment dropped 5.6 million and Black enrollment increased only 0.3 million. In other words, during this period Hispanics increased by 103%, Whites dropped by 16%, and Black enrollment was up 5%. As Orfield (1988) summarizes, "Should these trends continue very long they will fundamentally change the social structure of American education. Hispanics will become the nation's largest minority group and the proportion of Whites will fall substantially. All signs show that these changes are continuing" (p. 6).

While the Hispanic general population and Hispanic school enrollment are growing nationally, in reality only a small number of states will be heavily affected by this growth. Orfield (1988) notes that eight states (containing about 40% of the nation's total population) enroll a total of 3.57 million Hispanic students, representing 88% of the national Hispanic total (see Table 2). Among the states with large Hispanic populations, enroll-

Table 2
States with Largest Hispanic Enrollments, 1970 and 1986

State	Year/Enrollment 1986	Year/Enrollment 1970	Change No.	Change %
California	1,318,100	706,900	674,200	95
Texas	1,086,200	565,700	520,500	92
New York	384,700	316,600	68,100	21
Illinois	157,000	78,100	78,900	101
Arizona	154,700	85,500	69,200	81
Florida	149,500	65,700	83,800	127
New Jersey	132,000	59,100	72,900	123
New Mexico	128,900	109,300	19,600	18

Note: From "The Growth and Concentration of Hispanic Enrollment and the Future of American Education" by G. Orfield, July 1988, paper presented at the National Council of La Raza Conference, Albuquerque, New Mexico.

ment from 1970 to 1986 almost doubled in California and Texas, with both states enrolling three of every five Hispanic students in 1986–87; the increase was least rapid in New Mexico and New York. With the exception of New Mexico, which already has the largest proportion of Hispanic students within any state (45% in 1986), all the states have had substantial increases during the first six years of the 1980s (Orfield, 1988).

The concentration of Hispanics, and minority students in general, can further be traced to a few large school districts. The Center for Education Statistics (1987) reports that when examining all school districts nationally in 1984, the proportions of White and minority students were about 71% and 29% respectively. By comparison, when examining only the twenty largest school districts, the proportions essentially were reversed, with enrollments of 30% White and 70% minority students.

Minority Student/Minority Teacher Comparisons

Table 3 shows the percentage of the nation's various racial/ethnic school-age enrollments, accompanied by their respective percentages of racial/ethnic teaching forces. It is clear that for the two time frames (i.e., 1980/1980; 1984/1986), White teachers are overrepresented compared to the percentages of White students. In contrast, for minority teachers of *all* racial/ethnic backgrounds, there are severe underrepresentations. It is also clear from Table 3 that Latino teachers are the most severely underrepresented ethnic group. For example, in 1986 the national Latino school enrollment nationally was about 10%, while Latinos comprised only 2.5% of the national teaching force—a disparity of 75% (underrepresentation).

Table 3
Minority Public Elementary and Secondary School Enrollment and Minority Elementary and Secondary Teaching Force

Race/Ethnicity	1980 %School pop.[1]	1980 %Teaching pop.[2]	% Disparity	1986 %School pop.[1]	1984 %Teaching pop.[3]	% Disparity
White	73.2	87.5	20.0	70.4	85.0	21.0
Black	16.1	8.6	−47.0	16.1	8.9	−45.0
Latino	8.0	1.8	−78.0	9.9	2.5	−75.0
Asian and American Indian	2.7	2.1	−22.0	3.7	2.9	−22.0
All Minorities	26.8	12.5	−53.0	29.7	14.3	−52.0

Note 1: The student data in columns 1 and 4 are from "The Growth and Concentration of Hispanic Enrollment and the Future of American Education" by G. Orfield, July 1988 paper presented at the National Council of La Raza Conference, Albuquerque, New Mexico.

Note 2: The teacher data in column 2 for 1980 are from "The Condition of Education: A Statistical Report, 1987" by the U.S. Department of Education, Office of Educational Research and Improvement.

Note 3: The teacher data in column 5 for 1984 are from the "Sixth Annual Report on Minorities in Higher Education, 1987" by the American Council on Education, Office of Minority Concerns.

Implicit in these data from Table 3 is the conclusion that in no state with a large Latino population does the percentage of Latino teachers come even close to the percentage of Latino students. Although data are not readily available on a state-by-state analysis, some information exists for California. Based on 1987–88 data, Latino students in K–12 comprised 30.1% of the total public school enrollment in the state. For the same year, Latino teachers in K–12 were 6.9% of the total California teaching force (Watson, 1988). In terms of a student/teacher disparity analysis, Latino teachers were underrepresented by a huge 77%—a figure very close to the national disparity for Latinos (see Table 3). In contrast White teachers in California during 1987–88 were overrepresented by 64%—a figure well above the national disparity for Whites (see Table 3).

Despite the sketchy data, these trends clearly indicate that all students will see fewer minority teachers throughout their educational experience. As Smith (1985) notes, an average child during his/her K–12 schooling experience has about forty teachers. If the underrepresentation of minority teachers continues, by the mid 1990s—a time when minority students will be about one of every three students nationally—the average child over the

K–12 years "can expect only 2 of these 40 (teachers) to be from *any* minority group" (Smith, p. 128).

Analysts agree that the nation can only anticipate additional declines in the number of minority teachers. At the same time, the percentage of schoolchildren who are members of minority groups continues to grow as a proportion of the total school population. This grim statistic on the ethnic and racial mismatch between students and teaching force comes at a time when a general shortage of teachers seems imminent (American Council on Education, 1987). The demand for new hiring of teachers is expected to rise principally because of student enrollment increases, pupil/teacher ratio improvements, and educational reforms. Between 1986 and 1990, the estimated demand for elementary and secondary school teachers is expected to outweigh the supply, with educators expecting a shortage of 172,000 new teacher graduates. The greatest demand for new teachers is expected to rise by 42% between 1985 and 1990. Although the demand for secondary teachers is expected to decrease by 16%, there already are shortages in certain fields, such as mathematics, physics, and chemistry. The trend is expected to reverse itself between 1990 and 1993, when the demand for elementary teachers is expected to decline by 9% and the demand for secondary teachers is expected to increase 30% (American Council on Education, 1987). In conclusion, minority children rapidly are making up more than half of the public school's enrollment in numerous states, thus increasing the nation's diversity and, in particular, making it more heavily Hispanic. Yet the data clearly indicate that this trend is coupled with a national shrinking of teachers from all minority groups. The impact of this phenomenon can only lead to fewer children learning from a teacher who shares their culture, language, or appearance. Unless steps are taken now to reverse this situation, the growing disparity between the number of Latino students and Latino teachers will continue. The following section provides further insight to those barriers creating access problems for prospective Latino teachers.

Obstacles to Latino Teacher Production

Orum (1986) has identified three major factors contributing to the low and falling proportion of Latinos in the K–12 teaching force: the low and declining college-going rate for Latino students, the declining preference rate of Latino college students who pursue careers in K–12 teaching, and the major subject of this chapter, the very high rate of failure of Latinos on state-mandated, standardized teacher competency tests (i.e., admissions and certification tests). We now present discussion on each of these obstacles to Latino teacher production.

Low and Declining College-Going Rate

The size of the applicant pool of any professional occupational force is strongly related to the number of people who enter and pursue preprofessional training in the respective field. With regards to the number of prospective Latino teachers who flow through the postsecondary pipeline, their eventual applicant pool size is likewise influenced by the rate at which they enter the pipeline (i.e., initial college enrollment).

A contributing factor to the low and declining proportion of Latinos being hired as teachers is the low and declining college attendance rate of Latino high school graduates. In 1972, 26% of Latino high school graduates participated in college (Mingle, 1987).[14] The Latino college participation rate peaked to 36% in 1976, dropped considerably and sharply to 30% in 1980, and plummeted further to 26% in 1985 (Mingle, 1987). In other words, using 1972 as a base-line date and 1985 as another reference point, a "no change" rate can be seen in Latino college participation rate over a thirteen-year period. Using the decade from 1976 to 1985 as reference points, the college participation rate of Latino high school graduates dramatically declined 28%. The irony of the current decline is that it is occurring at the same time the Latino and other minority college-age cohorts are rapidly increasing. In 1970, the combined minority college-age population (18–24 year olds) was 13%. By 1980, it had increased slightly to about 15%. Current projections are that by the year 2000, the minority college-age cohort will be about 30%, and almost 40% in 2025 (Mingle, 1987).

It is beyond the scope of this chapter to discuss in any great detail the access and retention issues pertinent to Latino college students. The interested reader can refer, for example, to the exemplary works by Duran (1983), Mingle (1987), Orum (1986), Payan, Peterson, and Castille (1984), and Olivas (1986a). It would be informative, however, to take a few moments to glean from the literature the salient points that have been identified as contributing access and retention problems for Latino college students, in general:

1. High school preparation. The Latino eligibility pool for college entrance is severely reduced in that 75% of Latino high school seniors have not completed high school curricula of a college preparatory nature. Furthermore, about 33% of Latino high school graduates have "D" or "F" grade-point averages in one or more key academic subjects (Orum, 1986).

2. Dropout rates. The low college-bound rate of Latinos is exacerbated by the extremely high dropout rate in high school. In 1985, Latinos nationally had a high school completion rate of 62%, below that of Blacks (75%) and well below that of Whites (83%) (Mingle, 1987).

3. Type of college matriculation. As of 1984, Latinos—compared to *all other* ethnic groups—had the highest percentage of students enrolled in two-year collegiate institutions. In fact, in 1984 the *majority* of Latino college students (54.4%) were enrolled in two-year colleges. For each of the other ethnic groups (except American Indian, 54.2%), the percentages of students enrolled in two-year institutions were under 50% (Mingle, 1987). So, two-year colleges serve as a major entry point to the collegiate pipeline for the majority of Latino students. It has been documented, however, that community colleges have inherent problems in facilitating access to four-year institutions (e.g., Mingle, 1987; Olivas, 1986b). This uneven distribution of Latinos within higher education institutions presents one other obstacle in providing access to professional careers, such as teaching.

4. Testing and admission standards. Research has shown that Latino students: are less likely to take standardized college entrance tests, and when they do take such tests, Latino students score substantially lower than White students (Orum, 1986). Furthermore, complicating the linkage between predictors and college performance is Duran's (1983) finding that high school graduation and admissions test scores are not as good predictors of college grades for Latinos as they are for Whites.

5. Persistence patterns. "Normal" persistence refers to being on the "fast track." That is, a student enrolls in college following high school graduation and completes the college degree without interruption (i.e., does not drop or stop out; does not shift from full to part-time enrollment). Contrary to belief, normal persistence is not typical. Based on 1980 data, the fast track rates for the various ethnic groups were: Asians (one of three), Whites (one of five), Blacks (one of seven), Latinos (one of ten), and American Indians (one of twelve) (Mingle, 1987).

In short, once in the collegiate pipeline, there appears to be tremendous variability among the various ethnic groups as to persistence patterns. Research has shown there are particular social, psychological, and institutional factors connected with persistence variability. For Latino college students, some of these are likely related to financial aspects (Orum, 1986; Payan et al., 1984), stress (Muñoz, 1986) and a host of other personal and institutional variables (cf. Duran, 1983). Taken together, a number of factors may negatively impinge on a Latino college student's mobility pattern as he/she negotiates through the collegiate pipeline. The worse case scenario is that some Latinos will never complete the collegiate degree. Orum (1986) reports that in 1982, the majority of Latino males (57%) and Latino females (54%) did not graduate from college. Orum also reports that in 1984, Latinos in ten states where most Latinos reside, had substantially lower college graduation rates than Whites.

In conclusion, if we move from the global to the specific, there is evidence that the applicant pool of prospective Latino teachers is being reduced in part by the low and declining proportion of Latinos entering college. This most basic point of entry for prospective Latino teachers needs to be opened widely, and proactive measures must be implemented during the collegiate experience to ensure Latino college student success (see chapter 8 of this book).

Declining Preference Rate for Teaching Careers

For the total higher education student population, as well as for minorities, the most popular degree fields have shifted in recent years. In particular, education as an intended field of study has become less attractive to many college-bound students. While a slight upward trend reversal was reported in 1986, the freshmen of recent years were less likely to major in education that their counterparts were a decade ago; in 1985, 7% of entering freshmen planned to major in education compared to reports of 10–13% in 1974 (American Council on Education, 1987; Ottinger, 1987). For minorities, though education and the social sciences still represent the two most frequently chosen fields, there has been a significant shift to other fields, such as business/management at the undergraduate level, and professional schools at the graduate level (American Council on Education, 1987).

Data for degrees conferred from 1975–76 to 1984–85 at the baccalaureate and master's levels indicate a continuing trend away from education and social sciences and towards business and management for degree recipients as a whole. Bachelor's degrees awarded in education have been declining steadily; during the decade between 1974–75 and 1984–85, the number of degrees awarded in this field declined by 47%. Over this ten-year span, bachelor's degrees conferred in education dropped from a high of 167,015 in 1974–75 to a low of 88,161 by the year 1984–85 (Center for Education Statistics, 1987).

When examining minority baccalaureate recipients, the data indicate that in 1975–76, education was the most frequently chosen field, but by 1984–85 it had slipped to third. Business/management was by far the most popular area of concentration in 1984–85 for all minority degree recipients. Latinos followed this same general pattern, increasing their concentration of degrees in business/management by 127.6%.

Table 4 compares the number of baccalaureate degrees in education awarded to Whites, Blacks, and Latinos for the years 1975–76 and 1984–85 (American Council on Education, 1987). The data show that Black students demonstrated the largest decline (61.6%) in education degrees awarded, while Whites were second in decline (42.7%). Although Hispan-

Table 4
Bachelor's Degrees Awarded in Education by Race/Ethnicity, 1975–76 and 1984–85

	1975–76 Total Education Degrees		1984–85 Total Education Degrees		Decline
	No.	%	No.	%	%
White	135,464	16.7	77,531	9.4	42.7
Black	14,209	24.0	5,456	9.5	61.6
Hispanic	2,831	15.7	2,533	9.8	10.5

ics showed the smallest decline (10.5%), it is nevertheless, a decline. Readers are advised that while in past years the overwhelming majority of newly graduated teachers were education majors (Center for Education Statistics, 1987), the use of an education degree as proxy for a teaching career likely overestimates the latter.

Degrees awarded at the master's level to minorities followed the same general trend set at the baccalaureate level. Between 1975–76 and 1984–85 nearly all racial/ethnic groups doubled or tripled the number of master's degrees received in business and management and made moderate to large gains in engineering. Although the number of master's degrees was down dramatically in education for Blacks (53.3%), and significantly for Asians (11.5%), Hispanics gained 20% (American Council on Education, 1987).

Very High Failure Rate on Teacher Tests

Before assessing the impact of testing on the national minority teaching force, it is important to examine the primary factors leading to the development of state teacher competency programs. Andrews, Lyle, and Langland (1984) suggest four overlapping possibilities, briefly discussed here: one historical, one related to how the role of the teacher is conceptualized, one related to the leadership of the state education agency, and one related to the public's demand for accountability. The historical factor arises because many people believe that the knowledge and skills a teacher needs can be specified and demonstrated through a written or performance test. While many educators are uneasy about competency tests, little argument exists over the assumption that one cannot teach what one does not know; therefore, written tests should at a minimum be able to measure the knowledge component in each of the specific teaching fields (e.g., mathematics and English).

The second factor according to Andrews et al. (1984) follows a belief that teaching is an occupation that can be divided into discrete tasks. The idea is not new and dates back to the 1920s when the teacher-training institution was viewed as a vocational school, because it trained teachers to perform vocational functions, or objectives. In short, while the recent focus is on competency tests, it should be noted that in the past many states had permitted institutions of higher education to establish their own competency-based teacher education and certification programs. The third factor, leadership from state education agencies, has also evolved over time. State certification officials have moved beyond their role of reviewing candidates' transcripts and are now involved in approving entire teacher training programs. Concern that these policies blur the distinction between the responsibilities of the preparatory institution and those of the certifying agency led many states, beginning with Georgia in 1972, to develop a series of competency tests that would more appropriately represent the state's role.

Finally, because of the continuing criticisms of America's teachers and schools, (e.g., *A Nation at Risk*, 1983, National Commission on Excellence in Education), the public is demanding assurances from its state agencies that teachers who are licensed and certified actually are competent. The change most often suggested for improving certification systems, and thus the quality of teachers in elementary and secondary schools, has been competency tests. So great has been the states' response to this suggestion that the number of states now requiring either admissions or certification tests (or both) has grown from only ten before 1980 to forty-six in 1988. Specifically, in the past two years thirteen states have implemented either admission or certification testing programs (Eissenberg and Rudner, 1988). The remainder of this section explores the variety of competency testing approaches being taken nationwide and highlights the disproportionate number of minority candidates failing admission and teacher certification tests.

The most important juncture at which tests limit minority access to teaching is initial state licensure or certification; the second is the earlier obstacle of gaining admission to a teacher education program (Haertel, 1988). The examinations used for licensure and certification may be organized into four major categories, with the largest typically testing the "basic skills" of reading, writing, and arithmetic. The most commonly used examinations in this category are the communications test from the core battery of the National Teacher Examinations (NTE), covering reading, writing, and listening; and the general knowledge test from the NTE core battery, covering literature and fine arts, basic mathematics, science, and social studies. Other tests used include, for example, the CBEST and the PPST. A second category of examinations for licensure is professional knowledge tests, most often the professional knowledge test from the NTE core battery. The test primarily covers planning instruction, implementing instruction, and evaluating learning outcomes; general familiarity with laws governing classroom practice; and knowledge about the teaching profession. A third category of tests covers teachers' expertise in their content areas of specialization. The most common content knowledge tests are the NTE specialty area tests and customized tests. The final category includes classroom observations of the teacher's proficiency in each of a series of teaching competencies. Typically they are based on observer ratings during a series of brief, announced or unannounced classroom visits (Haertel, 1988). As reported earlier in this chapter, Table 5 (adapted from Eissenberg and Rudner, 1988) indicates that thirty-six states now have initial licensing or certification tests, with Massachusetts intending to use them in 1989, and Ohio and Michigan by 1991; twenty-seven states report testing basic skills; at least twenty-three states test professional skills; and twenty-four states test specialized content knowledge.

In order to enter a teacher training program, candidates in a number of states are required to take and pass an examination at or above some cutting score. Such tests may be required over and above the general admission requirements of the college or university through which the program is offered. According to Sandefur (1986; cited in Haertel, 1988), twenty-five states require or plan to require testing for admission to their teacher education programs. In four of those states, admission requirements have not gone into effect. Of the remaining twenty-one states, three require the Scholastic Aptitude Test or American College Testing, six require the PPST, one requires the communication skills and general knowledge tests of the NTE core battery, and eleven require some other test of general educational achievement, including CBEST, Comprehensive Tests of Basic Skills, and California Achievement Tests, among others (Haertel, 1988).

Given the established presence of competency testing, a crucial question to ask is, "What has been the impact of teacher competency tests on minorities?" The answer to that question can be found by critically examining the percentage of minority candidates failing admission and certification tests, especially in comparison to White candidates, and paying close attention to the *numbers* these percentages represent. For those states providing data, Eissenberg and Rudner (1988) report that the average (unweighted mean) pass rate for all candidates combined on admission tests, is approximately 76%, ranging from a low of 55% in Connecticut, to a high of 95% in Nevada. The average pass rate for all candidates on initial teacher certification tests is approximately 83%, ranging from a low of 69% in Delaware to a high of 94% in Kansas (see Table 5).[15]

While the reciprocal of these pass rates—fail rates—may not seem very low, they can translate into literally thousands of candidates not entering teacher education programs or the teaching profession. Furthermore,

Table 5
Teacher Education Testing Requirements

State	Date Revised	Admissions Tests Test	Admissions Tests Pass Rate	Certification Tests Test	Certification Tests Pass Rate	Coverage Basic	Coverage Prof	Coverage Subj
Alabama	1987	Custom	80%	Custom	85%		Yes	Yes
Alaska	1987	—		—				
Arizona	1987	PPST	79a	Custom	78b	Yes	Yes	
Arkansas	1987	—		NTE			Yes	Yes
California	1987	CBEST	77a	CBEST	74a	Yes		
Colorado	1988	CAT	58a	—				
Connecticut	1987	Custom	55a	NTE				Yes
Delaware	1987			PPST	69c	Yes		
Florida	1988	SAT,ACT		Custom	82d	Yes	Yes	Yes
Georgia	1987	—		—	78e			Yes
Hawaii	1987	—		NTE	73a	Yes	Yes	Yes
Idaho	1988	—		NTE		Yes	Yes	
Illinois	1987	—		Custom		Yes		Yes
Indiana	1988	—		NTE	88	Yes	Yes	Yes
Iowa	1987	—		—				
Kansas	1988	—		PPST,NTE	94a	Yes	Yes	
Kentucky	1987	CTBS	63b	NTE	93b	Yes	Yes	Yes
Louisiana	1988	NTE		NTE	90a	Yes	Yes	Yes
Maine	1987	—		NTE		Yes	Yes	
Maryland	1988	—		NTE		Yes	Yes	Yes
Massachusetts	1988	—		i				
Michigan	1988	—		f				
Minnesota	1988	—		PPST		Yes		Yes
Mississippi	1988	COMP		NTE		Yes	Yes	Yes
Missouri	1987	SAT,ACT		—				
Montana	1988	—		NTE	92a	Yes	Yes	
Nebraska	1988	PPST		PPST				
Nevada	1987	PPST	95b	PPST		Yes		Yes
New Hampshire	1988	—		PPST	74a	Yes		
New Jersey	1988	—		NTE	83a	Yes		Yes
New Mexico	1987	Misc.		NTE	88b	Yes	Yes	Yes
New York	1988	—		NTE	79a	Yes	Yes	
North Carolina	1988	NTE		NTE	80b	Yes	Yes	Yes
North Dakota	1988	Misc.		—				
Ohio	1987	Misc.f		f				
Oklahoma	1987	Misc.		Custom	81g			Yes
Oregon	1987	CBEST	77a	CBEST	80a	Yes		
Pennsylvania	1988	—		NTE,Custom		Yes	Yes	Yes

Table 5 Continued

State	Date Revised	Admissions Tests Test	Pass Rate	Certification Tests Test	Pass Rate	Coverage Basic	Prof	Subj
Rhode Island	1988	—		NTE		Yes	Yes	
South Carolina	1988	Custom	81h	NTE,Custom			Yes	Yes
South Dakota	1988	—		—				
Tennessee	1988	PPST		NTE		Yes	Yes	Yes
Texas	1987	PPST	71h	Custom	85h		Yes	Yes
Utah	1987	Misc.		—				
Vermont	1988	—		—				
Virginia	1988	—		NTE		Yes	Yes	Yes
Washington	1987	Custom SAT, ACT		—				
West Virginia	1988	PPST, COMP	81h 95h	Custom	88h			Yes
Wisconsin	1987	PPST		—				
Wyoming	1988	CAT		—				
Totals		26	76j	38	83j	27	23	24

a = 1986; b = 1985; c = 1983–86; d = 1980–87; e = 1981–86; f = Planned for 1991; g = 1982–85; h = 1987; i = Planned for 1989; j = Mean totals.

ACT = the American College Testing Program. CAT = the California Achievement Test. COMP = the College Outcomes Measure Project. CTBS = the California Test of Basic Skills. SAT = the Scholastic Aptitude Test. PPST = the Pre-Professional Skills Test. CBEST = the California Basic Educational Skills Test.

Passing rates may be cumulative, per administration, or for the most difficult subtest. Because of the different definitions, the mean value is only approximate.

Note: Adapted from "State Testing of Teachers: A Summary" by T. E. Eissenberg and L. M. Rudner, 1988, *Journal of Teacher Education*, 39.

when the data are analyzed by ethnic or racial group, it becomes evident that minorities, particularly Blacks and Latinos, make up the disproportionate number of students failing. Smith (1987) estimates that typical first-time pass rates on admission and certification tests ranged nationally from 15 to 50% for Blacks, 39 to 65% for Latino candidates, 37 to 77% for Asian American candidates, and 20 to 70% for American Indian candidates, compared to 71 to 96% for White candidates. In terms of actual *numbers*, Smith's study of nineteen states documented the alarming teacher test failure of nearly 38,000 members of minority groups within approximately the last five years, including 21,515 Blacks, 10,142 Latinos, 1,626

Asian Americans, 716 American Indians, and 3,718 members of other minority groups. Because many states do not disaggregate results by racial/ethnic group, and because some are able to provide data for only one or two administrations of their tests, Smith estimates that if data were available for all test administrations in all states, the numbers of minorities failing would be much greater. This exclusionary impact is observed regardless of the state and of the type of examination being used. In short, it is a national phenomenon.

Table 6 shows the passing certification rates by race/ethnicity for six states with large Latino populations. The data reflect a mixture of different years and examinations, such as basic skills (e.g., CBEST, PPST) state customized tests of professional knowledge (e.g., Arizona's Test of Professional Knowledge) and classroom observation scales (e.g., the Florida Performance Measurement System). The data appear to indicate that, in general, failure rates are higher for tests of basic skills and general knowledge but tend to decrease with examinations more closely assessing teaching (e.g., professional knowledge examinations and classroom observations). There appears to be variability in pass/fail rates between types of examinations (e.g., basic skills v. professional knowledge) within and across states, but similar rates across states within type of examination. The data indicate that pass rates for Latinos and minorities are far below that of Whites on basic skill tests heavily used to determine entry into teacher training programs and licensure (see Table 5). For example, in California and Texas, recent results show that not quite four in ten Latinos pass basic skills tests. In contrast, in these two states nearly eight in ten Whites pass them. The conclusion is obvious: State-mandated testing is one of the major reasons contributing to the minority teacher shortage.

Conclusions

Smith (1988) states that given the current state of affairs, the prospects for sustaining any semblance of a minority teaching force are indeed dim. As we described very early in this chapter, the projection is that minority representation in the national teaching force will be reduced to 5% by the year 2000—largely because of the impact of state teacher testing. This reduction will come at a time when the combined ethnic minority school enrollment in the nation will be about 33%.

We agree with Smith (1988) that the issue is not that a 95% White teaching force will be unable to teach Latino and other ethnic minority students. Rather, the issue is ". . . that the traditional informal interactions between the teacher and the community will be severed. Historically, mi-

Table 6
Teacher Competency Test Pass Rates by Ethnicity for Six High-Density Latino States

	Year	Whites (Non-Hispanic)	Asians (Non-Hispanic)	Blacks	Hispanics	American Indians	All	
Arizona	1/6/83	73	50	24	42	22	66	ATPE Basic Skills
	7/9/83	70	25	21	36	19	59	ATPE Basic Skills
	1985	80	70	44	56			ATPE Basic Skills
	1983	98	100	84	97	85		ATPE Prof. Know.
	1985	99	68	91	96			ATPE Prof. Know.
California	1982/1983	76	50	26	39	67	68	CBEST (ETS)
	1985	76		30	38			CBEST (ETS)
Florida	1982	92	67	37	57	90	85	FTCE
	1983	90	63	35	51	100		FTCE
	1985	90		40				FTCE
	1985	95		90				FPMS
New Mexico	1985	71			51		63	Not Identified
New York	1985–86							
Commun. Skills		86	40	49	75/42/49(2)	69	81	NTE (ETS)
General Knowledge		80	59	42	33/36/42(2)	77	75	
Profess. Knowledge		89	64	60	83/51/50/(2)	83	87	
Texas	1985	73	49(3)	23	34	49(3)	65	P-PST (ETS)
	1986	99		81	94		97	TECAT (Recertification)

Note: Adapted from "Minorities in Higher Education: Sixth Annual Status Report" by American Council on Education, 1987, Office of Minority Concerns, Washington, DC.

Note: (2) in the New York data indicates the first pass rate for each subtest is for Mexican Americans, the second pass rate is for Puerto Ricans, and the third is for Hispanic and other Latin American candidates; (3) indicates that Asian and Native American candidates are reported in a combined "Others" category in the Texas reporting system.

ATPE = the Arizona Teacher Proficiency Exam.
CBEST = the California Basic Educational Skills Test.

Table 6 Continued
Teacher Competency Test Pass Rates by Ethnicity for
Six High-Density Latino States

FTCE = the Florida Teacher Certification Exam.
FPMS = the Florida Performance Measurement System.
NTE = National Teacher Examinations.
P-PST = Pre-Professional Skills Test.
TECAT = Texas Examination of Current Administrators and Teachers.

nority teachers who have lived where they worked have had a powerful presence and encouraged, even exhorted, children and parents alike to attend to the business of school achievement'' (Smith, 1988, 166).

Notwithstanding some variability in academic achievement within the Latino school age population, the norm for this group is characterized by considerable underachievement—extremely high dropout rates from secondary schooling, very low academic performance, and very low and falling college-bound rates (Valencia, 1991). As we argued earlier, there are many good reasons for having Latino teachers. It is clear to us that a shortage of Latino teachers only exacerbates the many schooling problems Latino students already face.

In this chapter, we have underscored the plight of prospective Latino teachers and the implications of the worsening Latino teacher shortage. Describing and analyzing the problems, however, is only half the story. The next step is a discussion of proactive suggestions to improve access for Latinos to the teaching profession, a task we attempt in the following chapter, ''Research Directions and Practical Strategies in Teacher Testing and Assessment: Implications for Improving Latino Access to Teaching.''

8

Research Directions and Practical Strategies in Teacher Testing and Assessment: Implications for Improving Latino Access to Teaching

~ ~ ~ ~

Richard R. Valencia and Sofía Aburto

In the previous chapter, Valencia and Aburto provided a comprehensive overview of teacher testing, focusing on the negative implications of such testing for Latinos. It was underscored that the high failure rate of Latino college students and teacher education program graduates is a major contributing factor to the severe and worsening shortage of Latino kindergarten to 12th grade teachers. This chapter is a logical extension of that overview. Here, our focus will be on reform—the identification and discussion of research directions and practical strategies in teacher testing and assessment that are likely to increase access for Latino college students aspiring to become teachers. Our discussion will focus on four areas.

We begin with the subject of reliability and validity research on existing paper-and-pencil teacher tests. We briefly will discuss the current state of the art, as well as the feasibility and worthwhileness of conducting test bias research across ethnic groups so as to improve the psychometric properties of teacher tests. We conclude that the existing psychometric research is, in general, weak and irrelevant, and that although there have been attempts to debias existing tests, differential criterion validity research across ethnic groups is sorely needed.

Second, we will offer a discussion on one of the most controversial decision-making aspects of teacher testing—standard setting, the development and use of a predetermined cut score in order to decide who passes and fails a particular test. Along technical, political, and equality lines, the cut score has become the linchpin of the decision-making process, and as we will see, a double-edged link at that. One side in omnipotent is deciding who passes and who fails, while the other side is brittle, open to attacks that the cut score is indefensible in how the standard is technically determined. Criticisms also have been directed at standard setting, alleging that the cut score is arbitrarily set and the decision-making process results in racially discriminatory practices. In this subsection, we will attempt to bring clarity to these debates. Our main intent, however, is to discuss various ways in which cut scores can be modified to increase Latino access to teaching.

Third, we will explore the new, developing form of teacher testing subsumed under the rubric of "performance assessment," a method based on observations of teachers carrying out standard tasks designed to elicit their knowledge and skills (Haertel, 1988a). This type of assessment rests on a conception of teacher testing that differs substantially from traditional paper-and-pencil teacher tests and the teacher observation systems used in several states. We will examine the potential advantages and disadvantages of performance assessment with respect to increasing the number of permanently licensed minority teachers. Because such assessment methods may involve, at times, direct observations of minority teachers by examiners, bias may enter the evaluative process; we will discuss, in particular, the potential for linguistic and racial bias.

Finally, another strategy that is likely to increase access for aspiring Latino teachers (as well as other ethnic minority teacher aspirants) involves an affirmative action type of student outreach, intake, and preparation prior to teacher testing. In this subsection we will examine ongoing efforts of teacher education programs that deal in whole or in part with the process of early identification, recruitment, diagnostic testing, and remediation of Latino and other minority students who plan to become teachers. Such proactive efforts by teacher preparation institutions are gaining attention, and in some instances are resulting in quite positive consequences—the pass rates of minorities have risen.

Reliability and Validity of Paper-and-Pencil Teacher Tests

Any review of the literature examining the psychometric properties of measurement instruments must acknowledge the gradual evolution of the theoretical conceptions of reliability and validity and their subsequent impact on testing practice. As pieces by Anastasi (1986), Cronbach (1984), and Messick (1989) clearly illustrate, both test developers and users are currently in the midst of reexamining their roles in the entire assessment enterprise. Thus, while the evidence reviewed here oftentimes paints a bleak picture of both the testing industry and the consumers of teacher tests, likely improvements appear forthcoming.

As noted in the previous chapter, existing admissions and competency tests are preventing a large number of prospective teachers—both from majority and minority groups—from entering the profession. It is essential to understand what accounts for the significant variations in performances of different groups in the population. A logical place to begin is the test itself.

Tests make an easy target for criticism in attempting to explain differences among ethnic/racial groups, challenging the testing industry and program administrators to assure the public that such differences are not the result of bias in the test instruments themselves. While it is easy to attack allegedly biased tests, a competing hypothesis holds that the tests measure real differences in the quality of education available to different groups in our society. Hence, some people in the measurement community believe that test results reflect real differences in knowledge of groups of individuals (Allan, Nassif, and Elliot, 1988). This section will examine the available evidence for judging the psychometric adequacy of current certification tests for selecting teachers—majority and minority. For reasons of space limitation, we will focus on certification tests. As will be seen, while there is a large volume of content and criterion validity studies treating teacher candidates as a homogeneous population, literature examining the properties of certification tests in relation to minority subgroups is virtually nonexistent.

As Haertel (1988b) notes, in all testing the two primary concerns are reliability and validity for intended use (e.g., the selection of teachers). Objective paper-and-pencil tests of basic skills, professional knowledge, and pedagogy have all proved to be quite reliable psychometric instruments (Haertel, 1988b). Two commonly used tests of basic skills, the Pre-Professional Skills Test (PPST) and the California Basic Educational Skills Test (CBEST), share virtually identical test specifications and similar moderate reliabilities. Peterson (1984) reports internal consistency reliabilities for the PPST and CBEST Writing tests of .89 and .69, respectively. CBEST Reading and Math reliabilities are reported as .88 and .89, respectively. The Educational Testing Service (ETS) (1987) reports PPST reliability estimates of: Reading, .88; Mathematics, .89; Writing-multiple choice, .84; and Writing- essay, .28-.76. In reference to professional knowledge tests, Haertel (1988b, p.13) cites Nelson (1985) as reporting that " . . . the internal consistency and reliability of the [NTE] tests is uniformly high, greater than .90 for every Core Battery and Specialty Area test."

While all of the licensure tests in use appear to have acceptably high reliability coefficients, Haertel (1988b) points out that for purposes of licensing decisions, high reliability does not necessarily imply consistent classifications when evaluating tests for use in licensing teachers. The coefficient of reliability is less relevant than the consistency with which the test classifies examinees as proficient versus nonproficient. Haertel notes that tests designed with an eye toward high internal consistency (or test-retest) reliability coefficients may not be optimum for making consistent classifications with respect to a given cut score.

Criterion-Based Validation

Of the teacher licensing tests currently in use, the National Teachers Examinations (NTE) are more widely used than any other set of related examinations and have been researched more thoroughly than state developed examinations. Since its introduction nearly fifty years ago, there have been numerous studies of its criterion-related validity—investigations that have related scores on the test to criteria indicative of actual teaching (Haertel, 1988b).

A comprehensive review by Quirk, Witten, and Weinberg (1973) and additional studies since then arrive at the same summary conclusion: A teacher's total score on the NTE Common Examinations has no predictive relation to how competent or effective a teacher is in the classroom. In other words: "NTE scores correlate moderately well with undergraduate grade point averages (median correlation about .55), but virtually zero with grades assigned during practice teaching, with university supervisors' ratings, or with principals' or supervising teachers' ratings of on-the-job performance" (Haertel, 1988b, 34). The discouraging aspect of the latter statement is underscored by Johnson (1988) who reminds us that to determine how useful teacher certification tests are in selecting good teachers, one would expect these tests to be validated by criterion-based procedures that use successful teaching performance as a criterion. Haertel (1988b) similarly argues for the importance and necessity of criterion-related validity in justifying where to set the line between adequate and inadequate teaching. Criterion-related validity is viewed as a requirement in establishing the empirical accuracy of a cut score, that controversial and varying point which, in theory, distinguishes between candidates who will perform adequately and those who will perform inadequately in the classroom. In short, although it seems that academic ability should be related to teaching performance, the use of examination scores for teacher selection has been questioned by a number of researchers (e.g., Haertel, 1988b; Johnson, 1988; Quirk et al., 1973).

A thorough and recent review of available criterion related validity research can be found in Haertel (1988b). Two examples reflective of typical findings are offered for purposes of illustration. In the first, Andrews,

Blackmon, and Mackey (1980; cited in Haertel, 1988b) report a few significant correlations between NTE scores (prior to the 1982 revision) and ratings of student teacher performance ($N = 269$). In analyzing correlations between scores on each of seven Area Examinations and on each of twenty-two ratings of teaching performance, the authors report that of 176 correlations, ten were significantly greater than zero and three were significantly less than zero (using a .05 level of significance). Haertel estimates that the number of significant findings Andrews et al. report are barely more than would be expected by chance. If in fact the actual values of all the correlations between NTE scores and performance ratings were zero, then about nine would be expected to be statistically significant at the .05 level of significance purely by chance. We join Haertel in agreeing with the authors' conclusion that the combination of few significant positive relationships between the NTE scores and teaching performance ratings, coupled with a few negative relations, tends to undermine confidence in the expected relations.

The second example is from Browne and Rankin (1986) who used multiple regression techniques to analyze the relative contributions of scores on the NTE Area Examination for elementary school teachers (Education in the Elementary School Specialty Area Test) and of teacher supervisory ratings in predicting elementary school teaching employment within the first year after graduation. Correlations between the independent variables and success or failure in obtaining a job were computed for 111 students from five state or private universities. The authors report moderate correlations between area examination scores and supervisor ratings of student performance, with supervisor ratings being a more valid predictor of employment than the NTE examination score. The authors interpreted the correlation between the total rating scale score and success in finding a job as likely due to the independent use of similar criteria by both supervisors and those who hire teachers. Perhaps there is a global factor that similarly makes the supervisor evaluate a student as competent and the employer perceive the student as worthy of hire (Browne and Rankin, 1986). The authors concluded that more information is needed on whether employers actually make use of the prevalent test and rating information available, because according to this study's data, personality factors may have been more important than tested knowledge in determining whether or not the novice teachers received a position.

Content-Based Validation

Because problems associated with validating tests of general educational background, of professional knowledge, and of specialized information are similar, the type of validation studies and validity evidence gathered is very similar across the three types of examinations, without substantial variations in the validations carried out by different states. Content validation procedures most commonly are employed in constructing and validating teacher examinations, with major evidence coming from: a review of test content relative to the curriculum of the state's teacher education program, a review of test content relative to the job of teaching in the state, a sensitivity review, and a judgmental standard setting process, sometimes referred to as "Knowledge Estimation" (Haertel, 1988b). This section examines the rationale for the first three types of test evidence; a later section (pp. 207–212) will examine the adequacy of judgmental standard setting.

Content validation of tests based on the congruence between the test content and the curricula of teacher training programs relies on a model that uses expert panels of teacher educators and teachers for evaluating the test specifications and test questions in relation to teacher training institution curricula. Panels then estimate the percentages of minimally knowledgeable candidates in their institutions who would be expected to know the answer to each individual item. Both content appropriateness and item estimates are used in arriving at a statistical estimate of the score that would be expected of a minimally knowledgeable examinee (Rosner and Howey, 1982).

While these content-based procedures are acknowledged as a useful piece of a total validation plan, they have been criticized as insufficient for primary validation of state licensing examinations by a number of authors (e.g., Haertel, 1988b; Johnson, 1988). As Johnson (1988) points out, content validation procedures are used with achievement tests—i.e., tests designed to determine whether specific content has been learned. Yet, teacher certification tests are being used as measurements of achievement to predict classroom performance which research has shown to be unrelated to candidate scoring on the test. Haertel (1988b) acknowledges that the curricula of teacher education programs could represent a consensus of what educators believe teachers need to know in order to function effectively in the states' classrooms, but points out that in fact content review panels are *not* asked to judge whether each item's content was needed in teaching, but only whether the opportunity for learning had been present.

Panels of teachers and/or administrators also have attempted to judge the correspondence of the knowledge and skills covered on a test to the job of beginning teachers in a number of states (e.g., "crucial," "important," "questionable," or "not relevant"). While the attempt is laudable, Haertel (1988b) again raises a number of concerns and criticisms over the rationale for the approach, only one of which is noted here. He acknowledges that if the knowledge and skills elicited in a licensure test are a representative sample of the tasks actually required in the job of teaching, then job performance may be predicted from test performance based on statistical inference. He warns, however, that in fact the content validity evidence provided by reviews of test items is not as direct as it appears. Because what teachers do is quite different from answering multiple-choice questions, the reviews are in fact relying not only on the judges' knowledge of teaching, but also on their inferences about the psychological processes of answering test questions. As Messick (1989) points out, inferences regarding behaviors require evidence of response or performance consistency and not just judgments of content, whereas inferences regarding processes require construct-related evidence. As a general rule, content-related inferences and construct-related inferences are inseparable, yet the evidence offered for licensure examinations is rarely contextualized as part of a broader set of construct-related evidence supportive of score inferences.

In addition to the types of state validation studies described above, empirical studies examining the relation between basic skills and achievement test also could serve to identify how adequately a particular admissions or certification test samples or represents some domain of knowledge or skills, or perhaps some domain of test items. For example, findings indicate that the PPST, which purports to measure reading, writing, and mathematics, has high correlations with achievement tests such as the American College Test (ACT), whose subtests include English, Social Science, Science, and Mathematics. In investigating relations between scores on the PPST subtests and ACT scores, Stoker and Tarrab (1985) found the ACT composite scores correlated highly with all three PPST scores and highest with the total PPST score. Pearson product-moment correlations ranging from .68 to .77 were found between the PPST and ACT. Aksamit, Mitchell, and Pozehl (1987), using canonical correlation analysis and double cross validation procedures, also provided evidence of significant shared variance between the PPST and ACT. The highest correlate of PPST Reading was the ACT composite score (.74); for PPST Writing it was the ACT English score (.72), and for PPST Mathematics it was the ACT Mathematics score (.76). Using published KR-20 reliabilities for the ACT and PPST, the authors calculated disattenuated correlations of .83, .85, and .84, respectively—leaving very little variance unaccounted for. Aksamit et al. recommend using the ACT in place of the PPST to avoid the expenditure of additional time and money, citing the tests' high comparability and the ACT's added comprehensiveness over the PPST.

In a study primarily intended to examine the characteristics of teachers who passed and failed the CBEST, Bruno and Marcoulides (1985) also contribute evidence for understanding the type of knowledge CBEST requires of teacher candidates and teachers. Bruno and Marcoulides worked from the premise that for a true certification test, one should expect each of three major subject matter areas (in the case of CBEST, writing, reading, and math) to be equally represented or weighted for passing the test. To determine the type of knowledge that best classifies applicants who pass CBEST from those applicants who fail CBEST, the authors performed a discriminant analysis of the data. The sample of 160 (the majority percentage were ethnic minority) was divided into four groups: fail-CBEST-employed, fail-CBEST-not employed, pass-CBEST-employed, and pass-CBEST-not employed; scale scores on the CBEST for Mathematics, Writing, and Reading were used as classifying variables. Results showed that high scores on the mathematics test best described the two passing groups; reading added somewhat to describing the groups, while writing scores did not seem to discriminate between any of the four groups. Bruno and Marcoulides conclude "that the CBEST is little more than a mathematics test" (p. 161), with candidates scoring low in mathematics failing the test, while those scoring high pass the test. The reading and writing scales added very little to the pass-fail classification. Though not described as such by Bruno and Marcoulides, the authors conclude by offering content validity advice for CBEST's revision: The examination must be made more discriminating on the writing and reading knowledge portions and less discriminating on the mathematics knowledge portion. As this study suggests, CBEST is not a basic skills test in reading, writing, and mathematics; it is essentially a test measuring the latter.

Bias and Sensitivity Studies

In the process of developing teacher certification tests, most developers will include potential bias as one of the several criteria for the review of test materials. The purpose is to avoid bias against members of groups, defined for example by sex, race and ethnicity, or linguistic background. That is, at a general level, "If two examinees possess the same level of the knowledge or skills to be assessed, they should have the same chance of passing the test even if they belong to different groups" (Haertel, 1988b, 25).

As defined in the literature, methodologies aimed at detecting item bias and test bias appear superficially different but do not necessarily imply different conceptualizations of bias. For purposes of this section, the authors concur with Shepard's (1982) more inclusive approach to test bias that notes items are not fundamentally different from tests; therefore, the entire process of establishing that sets of items are unbiased is the same as the process of construct validation for the test. That is, Shepard draws the parallel between unbiased tests and unbiased items by conceptualizing lack of bias in test items as equal construct validity across groups.

In general, development efforts aimed at identifying and preventing item and test bias usually take one of two forms. One procedure involves a logical/judgmental method; the other relies on an empirical/statistical approach. The judgmental approach uses a separate review committee that reviews draft or existing materials for language, content, or stereotypes likely to offend members of minority groups. These "sensitivity reviews" address only the appearance of bias or discrimination, without reference to the actual performance of examinees from different groups in responding to an item. They are an established part of development for each new form of the NTE and as part of some states' validations for a number of tests (Carlton and Marco, 1982; Haertel, 1988b). It is important to note that while sensitivity reviews may appear laudable and important in test development, there is little evidence in the measurement literature that this form of expert panel review has any differential effect upon the distributions for different groups, or even that designated groups perform especially poorly on the items identified by the panels (Haertel, 1988b; Reynolds, 1982). In a broader psychometric sense, the identification of bias through judgmental bias procedures typically cannot be confirmed by the more rigorous and valid statistical bias procedures (Berk, 1982).

Bias in tests also may be detected by subjecting test results from field tests and actual administrations to a number of statistical treatments meant to identify items that have differential characteristics. Shepard (1982) describes statistical techniques for finding biased items as internal methods designed to ensure that the meaning *individual* items contribute to the total test *score* is the same for all groups. That is, statistical techniques are used to find aberrant items in what are believed to be homogeneous sets of items, thus detecting flaws in the original logic and inference. A consistent strategy used by these methods involves adjusting for differences in overall group means and then considering additional differences as a sign of bias. Item bias methods function by detecting items that are anomalous; whatever it is that the rest of the items measure, the biased item functions differently (Shepard, 1982). Numerous empirical methods have been proposed for operationalizing item bias (e.g., differential differences in item difficulty; group differences in item discriminations; and comparisons of item characteristic curves) (Carlton and Marco, 1982; Shepard, 1982), yet the caveat remains that these item bias methods cannot detect pervasive bias because they lack an external criterion (Shepard, 1982).

Bias in tests also may be detected by subjecting test results from field tests and actual administrations to a number of statistical treatments meant to identify items that have differential characteristics. Item bias is defined by Haertel (1988b) as differential item functioning for members of different groups. The ETS and other major publishers routinely analyze for this type of differential item functioning, occasionally leading to removal or nonscoring of an item even after its inclusion in an operational form of a test (Berk, 1982; Haertel, 1988b; Shepard, 1982). Examinations of item bias are not to be confused with sensitivity reviews, since sensitivity reviews address only the appearance of bias of discrimination, without reference to the actual performance of examinees from different groups in responding to an item (Haertel, 1988b).

A third possible type of bias study examines a test's differential validity, which is demonstrated when the validity coefficients of major and minor groups differ significantly from one another (Jensen, 1980). In relation to teacher certification examinations, Haertel (1988b) notes differential validity studies examining criterion-related validity could be used to help detect test bias. Test bias is determined to be present if the relation between test performance and some external criterion varies across groups defined by some identifiable characteristic (e.g., race or ethnicity). Should one group consistently obtain higher test scores than another without corresponding differences in job performance, it follows that a common decision rule across all groups is biased in favor of some groups and against others (Rebell, 1988). In the case of teacher examinations, studies of test bias would determine the relation of test scores to classroom performance, separately for examinees from different racial or ethnic groups. Admittedly, the fact that current examinations do not claim to predict classroom performance and also fail to show predictive validity with *any* group may seem to make conducting this type of study with these examinations irrelevant and possibly foolish. Yet in conjunction with improvements in assessment, this final type of study seems crucial in understanding what aspects of performance are contributing to the observed differences in past rates.

In conclusion, while psychometric evidence exists on current certification examinations, none of it is strong. In the case of reliability, while internal consistency estimates are high, cut score reliability has not been thoroughly examined. Criterion-related validity is extremely weak and, as has been pointed out primarily by Haertel (1988b), much of the content validity evidence is irrelevant to the uses made of licensure tests. Although current item bias studies and sensitivity review panels contribute to removing bias from existing examinations, no test bias research (defined as differential criterion validity for different groups) exists.

Some readers may view the negative evaluation of achievement tests such as the NTE as simply knocking over a straw man. The NTE does not claim criterion validity. As a standardized test of academic preparation for teaching, it should and does correlate with courses and grades in college.

That teacher preparation courses and grades do not correlate with "successful teaching" is lamentable, and clearly an indication of very real limitations not only in existing teacher tests, but also teacher education programs and the educational community's conception of what constitutes a measurable criterion of successful teaching. Yet the fact that such examinations are nevertheless used as screens for keeping candidates from teaching necessitates an analysis of their worth. Based on the available evidence, the sole use of these tests to determine licensure is a practice difficult to justify.

Modification of the Cut Score of Paper-and-Pencil Teacher Tests

Before we turn to the heart of the matter—perspectives on cut score modification vis-á-vis Latino access to teaching—it is first necessary: to place the debate in social and political contexts, to describe briefly how standard setting is done, and to comment on the growing controversy in the measurement community about the defensibility of the development and use of cut scores.

As noted earlier, in teacher testing the " . . . cut score becomes the linchpin in the decision process" (*Standards*, 1985, 50).[1] Drawing from the analyses of Airasian (1987) and Marcoulides and Bruno (1986), it can be argued that the uses of teacher testing and test results have generated great controversy. For example, Airasian contends "there is a constant tension between the goals of quality and equality . . . "(p. 407). That is, attempts to assess teacher competence through teacher tests via the cut score inevitably clash with those goals of equalizing educational opportunity, such as striving for ethnic diversity in the teaching force. In short, the nature of teacher testing is such that it has become highly politicized. The desire for quality in teachers and the desire for social justice (i.e., diversity in the teaching force) are inconsistent with respect to the criteria driving each goal. The former goal (teacher screening) presently is based on absolute standard setting (i.e., rigidity, uniformity, and constancy), while the latter goal (teacher diversity) needs to be based on flexible standard setting (i.e., pluralism, conditional aspects, and differential attributes). Thus, given that teacher testing has taken on a powerful role in the distribution and redistribution of educational benefits (Airasian, 1987), it appears that the cut score (i.e., the linchpin) holding the decision-making process together needs to be scrutinized for modification as a mechanism of greater inclusion for Latinos who wish to become teachers. Now that we have placed the present discussion of cut score modification in the social and political contexts, we move next to a brief overview of how standard setting is done.

From a measurement perspective, a cut score (also referred to as pass score) on a teacher test can be chosen from one to three general methods:

methods based on judgments about test questions, methods based on judgments about individual test-takers, and methods based on judgments about a group of test-takers (Livingston and Zieky, 1982). Because it is beyond the scope of this chapter to discuss the theories guiding these methods and their technical features, we will confine our brief presentation to the essential features of the most commonly used methods—those based on judgments about test questions.[2]

Methods based on judgments about test questions rely on the notion of the "borderline" test-taker (or sometimes referred to as the "minimally competent" examinee). "This test-taker is the one whose knowledge and skills are on the borderline between the upper group and the lower group" (Livingston and Zieky, 1982, 15). The basic idea here is quite simple: Test-takers in the upper group have a strong tendency to score higher than people who belong in the lower group. Therefore, the cut score is that point in the distribution that would be marginal or borderline—that is, the score that separates the upper from lower groups. The three most commonly discussed methods in the literature that use judgments about test questions are the "Nedelsky method," the "Angoff method," and the "Ebel method." Each method consists of five fundamental steps: the selection of judges (also known as panelists), the definition of "borderline" skills and knowledge, the training of judges in the chosen method, the collection of judgments, and the combination of the judgments to choose a cut score (Livingston and Zieky, 1982). The first two steps are invariant for all three methods; the remaining three steps differ across methods.

Although the Nedelsky, Angoff, and Ebel methods are well known in the measurement community and often discussed in the scholarly literature, when it comes to practice just about all teacher testing standard settings have utilized some variant of the Angoff method (Haertel, 1988b). This method is succinctly described by Haertel as follows:

> Under this procedure, each panelist working independently imagines a group of minimally competent examinees, that is, candidates who should be right at the intended cutting score, and then judges, for each item, the proportion of such candidates who would be expected to answer them correctly. These item-level probabilities are then summed to obtain the average score for the entire test implied by that panelist's judgments. Next, these scores are averaged across panelists to obtain a final cutting score. (p. 55)

Sifting through what we described thus far, the reader is likely to see from this discussion of standard-setting methods that human judgment is a salient feature. As Haertel (1988b) notes, these are usually judgmental situations in which members of panels are provided no information whatsoever on which to base their judgments in regards to the actual performance of test-takers (referred to as "judgmental" methods). In only some standard-setting situations of teacher test validation are judges given performance data (e.g., provided information on the proportions of test-takers who were found to respond correctly to different items; referred to as "judgmental-empirical" methods). It is exactly this element of the linchpin—the human judgmental process used to derive the cut score—that is at the center of the growing controversy about the adequacy of cut scores in teacher tests. We discuss this contentious issue next.

In the earlier subsection, we noted that teacher tests need to be reliable and valid. Given the critical use of the cut score in teacher tests, it also is essential that it results in rates that are acceptably low in false positive and false negative classification errors (Haertel, 1988b).[3] Or stated a bit differently, the cut score needs to be set at such a level that it produces "acceptably low probabilities of misclassifications" (Haertel, p.11). Does this occur? According to Haertel, the proposition that the cut score must yield acceptably low probabilities of classification errors is not supported at all by the available evidence. A number of other specialists in the measurement community (e.g., Berk, 1986; Glass, 1978; Shepard, 1980, 1984) have indicated that the process of standard setting is open to repeated criticism, particularly along lines of the difficulty in executing the process and defending it psychometrically.

The major problems in standard setting, as voiced by its critics, appear to center around the vagueness of the notion of "competence," the subjectivity of human judgment, and the resultant variability in accuracy. When judges are asked to speculate on the competence of unknown (sometimes make-believe) test-takers and provide probability statements of item accuracy, "there is simply no evidence that people can perform this kind of task with accuracy" (Haertel, 1988b 60). In sum, there are serious problems in the procedures used to develop the linchpin of teacher testing. From a measurement perspective, the following critique by Haertel (1988b) captures matters well:

> I see absolutely no basis for asserting that the judgments of individual panelists about individual items are unbiased estimates of performance for the imagined target population of minimally competent teachers. I consider attempts to derive a meaningful cutting score by aggregating panelists' judgments to be at best a meaningless misapplication of statistical theory (p. 61).[4]

It is very likely that notwithstanding all the technical criticisms leveled against standard setting practices in teacher testing, the cut score will reign as the linchpin in the decision-making process. This is predictable because, as Airasian (1987) points out, in the testing certification arena the important debate is about "issues" (accountability, and competency) and "ends" (testing with absolute standards), *not* "problems" (equal educational opportunity, and diversity in teaching force) and "means" (pluralistic assessment standards). Until the time comes when there is a social consensus between the goals of educational quality and equality (Airasian, 1987), and a balance between the political demands to certify teachers with personnel demands for school staffing (Marcoulides and Bruno, 1986), "technical" solutions will win over "value-based" solutions. In light of, and in spite of, this pessimistic portrayal, one must push ahead in the development of *defensible* teacher testing standard setting procedures and uses. Such improvements should prove beneficial to the field of teacher testing, as a whole, and particularly vis-á-vis prospective Latino teachers. We turn our attention now to some ideas about short-term and long-term cut score modification solutions that are likely to improve Latino access to the teaching profession.

Clearly, one of the simplest solutions to the access problem—and one with immediate, positive results—is to lower the cut score on tests like CBEST and PPST. Before laying out the arguments for this debatable, and likely unpopular recommendation, it is important to ask several questions. First, are cut scores of teacher tests derived in a technically defensible manner? To iterate our earlier, lengthy discussion, the answer strongly appears to be "no." Second—and a question that follows from the first—are cut scores set arbitrarily? Scholars such as Bruno and Marcoulides (1985), and Haney (1978; cited in Bruno and Marcoulides) would argue "yes." For example, Haney contends that the final determination of the cut score on basic skills type tests comes about often as a compromise between seemingly acceptable expectations of pass rates and failure rates that seem to be politically tolerable.[5] Third, is there empirical evidence that the methods used to establish cut scores result in acceptable rates of misclassification errors? Again, based on our previous discussion, the answer is strongly, "no."

Therefore, given these standard-setting limitations of technical indefensibility, arbitrariness of cut score determination, and nonexistent evidence for establishing the decision rule vis-á-vis classification errors, then cut score level modification appears reasonable as a short-term solution. In that existing cut scores on teacher tests appear to be needlessly high and cause adverse impact on the prospective Latino teaching force, the lowering of the cut score would be a logical manner in balancing the mechanics of cut score determination with the need to have more Latino teachers.

We can illustrate this perspective by referring to Bruno and Marcoulides (1985) who offer a more analytic and humane approach to establish the cut score (in this case, on the CBEST). Essentially, their approach takes into consideration three aspects: the subtest cut score, "marginal passes," and total test cut score. Their data indicate that although examinees pass each subtest at substantial proportions (e.g., a 73% pass rate on the writing subtest), these results are not reflected in the overall, low ethnic minority pass rate in the CBEST.[6] Their study also presents convincing data and arguments that through total cut score modification (lowering), the pass rate can be raised without revising the cut scores on the various subtests. In their suggested procedure, the lowering of the overall cut score need only be a few points. Furthermore, the authors' recommendation also contains this feature: "Subsequently, over time, cut-scores can be 'fine-tuned' and raised progressively as the problem of teacher shortage decreases and as the number and 'quality' of students graduating from teacher education programs increases" (p. 163). On a final point, there is evidence that lowering cut scores on teacher tests will increase dramatically the pass rate for minorities (cf. Spellman, 1988). Although the discrepancy of pass rates among racial/ethnic groups remains, we believe in this case that the ends justify the means.

A second related cut score modification procedure deals with those examinees who score in the "marginal range," that area of the score distribution that prevents a person with a one-point or so difference from passing a teacher test. Haertel (1988b) argues that because of small biases in test scores of "marginal" test-takers, additional evidence of skill should be used in conjunction with results of performance on the teacher test. Haertel also suggests "provisional licensure" to improve the accuracy of classifications that deal indirectly with our notion of cut score modification. This procedure, which is pertinent only to licensure, not admissions, cases, "would treat those scoring below it [the cut score] only as *having failed to demonstrate* an adequate level of knowledge or skill, rather than regarding them as *having demonstrated* inadequate skill" (pp. 12–13). As such, the candidate would be offered a provisional licensure, and once they enter teaching, additional documentation would be collected to determine teaching competence. Provisional licensure is an attractive strategy, but credentialing agencies need to be extremely cautious about creating an underclass of teachers who receive a lower wage for doing the same job as fully certified teachers.

In sum, we urge the recommendation of the three previously cut score modification procedures—lowering of the overall cut score, marginal range considerations, and provisional licensure. These approaches can provide short-term relief for the adverse impact teacher testing is having on Latino and other minority examinees. To our critics who assuredly will counter that these recommendations are going to result in a "lowering of the standards," we respond in several ways. First, the current standards are not standards in the traditional sense—that is, they are not defensible and they are not objective. Second, the positive social consequences—i.e., greater diversity in the teaching force—far outweigh any possible social costs. Third, "lowering of the standards" connotes verticality—levels of competence. We prefer to see the issue as connoting a horizontal state—one of creating broadness and diversification.

Performance Assessment

If criterion-related evidence is weak and the majority of content-validity studies are irrelevant to the uses made of licensure examinations, it is necessary to consider the availability of alternative assessment methods and alternative forms of evidence of teacher competence. In fact, in addition to general education background tests, professional knowledge tests, and tests of specialized content knowledge, a number of states are turning to a fourth category of assessment for licensure that depends on observing teachers' classroom performance. These structured classroom observations usually are administered to beginning teachers during their first year of teaching. The assessments are classroom observations of a teacher's proficiency in each of a series of teaching competencies. Typically, they are based on observer ratings during a series of brief announced or unannounced classroom visits. Candidates are observed by trained personnel, usually a mentor teacher, the principal, and/or an education professor. The purpose of these assessments usually is to assist the beginning teacher as well as to determine whether the beginning teacher will be eligible for regular, nonprovisional certification (Center for Policy Research, 1987). As noted by Sandefur (1986), fourteen states now require some demonstration of competence on the job as part of their mandated teacher competency assessments.

Pioneering developmental efforts in Georgia exemplify the use of performance-based teacher certification of this type. Acting within its role as a licensing agency, the Georgia State Board of Education announced in 1972 a need to certify personnel on the basis of demonstrated competency, going beyond the formal training implied by an earned degree. In addition to grade-level subject matter examinations, all teachers planning to enter the profession also must pass an on-the-job assessment focusing on the teacher's capabilities to organize, plan, and implement instruction, and to manage the classroom and establish positive interpersonal relationships with students (Leach and Solomon, 1986). Among the tests developed to meet this mandate were the Teacher Performance Assessment Instruments (TPAI), which are composed of the Teaching Plans and Materials Instruments, the Classroom Procedures Instrument, the Interpersonal Skills Instrument, the Professional Standards Instrument, and the Student Perceptions Instrument. In total, sixteen competencies are addressed by the TPAI, with fourteen identified to be required for certification. Competencies range from planning instruction to achieve selected objectives to helping learners develop positive self-concepts. The selected fourteen are from among an initial set of twenty identified as generic and essential for all subgroups (i.e., across grade levels, teaching fields, and job settings) (Leach and Solomon, 1986).

In examining reliability and validity studies on the TPAI and other performance assessments of this type, the evidence appears supportive. Andrews, Lyle, and Langland (1984) indicate that three sets of indicators have been used in studies related to the TPAI: student perceptions of the classroom, student engagement in learning, and student achievement (defined as achievement gain on teacher-made tests, performance on norm-referenced tests, and performance on criterion-referenced tests). The authors report that high correlations between two of the TPAI instruments, Classroom Procedures and Interpersonal Skills, and student perceptions of the classroom have been found consistently. Performance on the TPAI also was significantly correlated with student engagement rates (in three of four studies) and with student achievement gains. Reliabilities of the instruments' scores as well as of the decisions made based on the TPAI are also reported as quite adequate. The one reported technical weakness of the TPAI and similar instruments lies in the validity of the decision actually made—a problem identified by Haertel (1988b) in all the currently used major licensure examinations. Andrews et al. (1984) report there is no available evidence concerning whether the present minimal performance levels and cut scores are the most valid in terms of their relation with a criterion variable such as student achievement. The authors also report that with respect to Georgia's subject matter certification examinations, almost no relation has been found between scores on "content" and ratings on the ability to "put it over" in the classroom.

The standing of Latino and other minority candidates on these types of performance assessment measures may offer some hope for a more equitable evaluation of their knowledge and skills. An example can be found in the state of Virginia, where Blacks scored at or above the level obtained by Whites on fourteen generic competencies on the Beginning Teacher Assistance Program (BTAP), a classroom observation approach as previously described (Jones, 1986). In the fall of 1985, 57% of the Black teachers and 55% of the White teachers successfully passed all competencies. Johnson (1988) reports similar differences in favor of Black candidates were found in 1986. Educators have cited a number of possible explanations for the findings, including Johnson's idea that the validity of performance assessment measures for Black candidates may be greater for them than the validity of standard paper-and-pencil tests. Virginia educators offer a second interpretation. They observe that the findings do not contradict each other but instead merely confirm what Black educators have contended throughout about Black performance on other written certification examinations: "Blacks can teach as well as Whites, though their educational background may make it harder for them to pass standardized tests" (Jones, 1986).

While observing teachers' classroom performance in this manner seems a valuable addition to certification examinations, a number of individuals and groups support a much broader vision of "performance assessment" (e.g., Carnegie Forum on Education and the Economy, 1986; ETS, 1988; Holmes Group, 1986). One example is the work of the Teacher Assessment Project (TAP; Lee Shulman, principal investigator) at Stanford University, sponsored by the Carnegie Forum on Education and the Economy. The work rests on the assumption that approaches to assessment must mirror as accurately as possible the complexity and richness of teaching. It also rests on a conception of teaching that differs substantially from those currently employed for such assessments as the NTE or the teacher observation systems in place in a number of states. The primary critique against the direct observation of practice as currently in place is its almost invariable use of a global scale that ignores differences in context attributable to the subject matter being taught or the age or level of the learners (see Shulman, 1987; Shulman, Haertel, and Bird, 1988 for a more complete description of the TAP).

These futuristic views of teacher assessment envision an ongoing set of procedures possibly including written assessments, assessment center exercises, documentation of performance during supervised field experiences, and direct observation of practice by trained observers (Shulman, 1987). Of special interest here are the potential advantages associated with using performance center exercises and the documentation of field-based work, not only for improving the evaluation of all candidates, but particularly that of minority candidates. In brief, performance assessment centers are used in such professions as business, school administration, emergency medicine, the foreign service, and architecture (Aburto and Haertel, 1986). Performance assessment of this type uses methods of simulation to represent aspects of the functions to be performed in a given occupation. As Shulman (1987) explains in describing the TAP's pioneering work on assessment centers for teachers, candidates come to a center and participate in simulation exercises. Yet, unlike traditional exercises in which a candidate responds by selecting an alternative to a multiple-choice item or writes an essay that describes what one would do under certain circumstances, assessment center activities—primarily set up as interview simulations—instead require candidates to respond as they would on the job. For example, in a planning exercise, candidates must plan; in a group problem-solving exercise, candidates deliberate together; in a teaching exercise, they teach.

An additional form of documenting the performance of candidates in classrooms is being sought through observing and recording a teacher's accomplishments during a supervised residency period (Shulman, 1987). For example, a teaching candidate may have to demonstrate that certain goals have been attained through the testimony of supervisors, be they cooperating teachers, university supervisors during student teaching, or on-site mentors during an initial period of residency. Documentation evidence, in the form of portfolios, is likely to include such features as lesson plans, examples of student work, or videotapes of teaching, with attestation comments by mentors or supervisors.

The new approaches to teacher assessment, such as the ones briefly mentioned here, usually are justified on a number of grounds. For example, among other beliefs, the TAP group perceives a need for a more comprehensive view of teaching and a new form of assessment that will instill teacher educators with a desire to aim higher in creating their curricula and designing their programs. While the motives are not contested, the reality is that these new assessments are yet more screens that would have a positive or negative effect on the participation of minority groups in teaching. One easily can see that these new studies offer perhaps the most promising opportunity for minimizing unwarranted biases in assessment and for revealing relevant strengths of minority candidates that might not have appeared in other types of tests for teachers. By the same token, performance assessments offer a dangerous opportunity to perpetuate a disregard for bias studies while simultaneously failing to validate minority performance as displayed in the new forms of assessment. That these new assessments offer alternate forms of evidence there is no doubt; what is of concern is what evaluators will choose to see and how they will then form their evaluations.

In summary, the emerging forms of performance assessment have the potential to offer more equitable and pluralistic ways to assess beginning Latino and other minority teachers. In particular, they offer the opportunity to exhibit competence through more than one avenue, and allow for the possibility of assessing knowledge, skills, beliefs, and orientations to teaching that are likely correlated with cultural background. Notwithstanding these positive assessment features and certification outcomes, there are potential problems with performance assessment. As noted earlier, a major aspect of performance assessment involves a great deal of observing and interviewing of candidates by trained examiners. Given these close observational formats, we are concerned that some bias against minority candidates may creep into the assessment process, working against the final licensing or certification outcome. These potential issues are discussed next.

Potential Linguistic and Racial Bias in Performance Assessment

The potential problems we raise here about performance assessment stem from issues we have identified in the literatures of sociolinguistics and race relations. One of the most pervasive findings in these bodies of study is that dominant group members—through their evaluative reactions in intergroup settings—typically will stereotype and downgrade the linguistic and other behavior of minority group members.[7] These negative attitudes and behavior on the part of dominant group members often can and do result in diminished opportunities for success and social advancement for minority people.

The major concern to be discussed centers around potential linguistic bias against Latinos, with particular focus on Chicano-accented English.[8] We need to preface the following discussion with a caveat: To date, we know of no research studies that have investigated whether linguistic bias against Latinos operates during any form of performance assessment.[9] There is, however, a rich body of literature from experimental studies in educational and other settings that has identified such linguistic bias. Our intent here is not to generalize these findings to performance assessment settings. Doing so would violate principles of external validity. Although we cannot demonstrate that linguistic bias exists in performance assessment, we can speculate that based on the broader theoretical and empirical bases, such bias *may* occur. In short, we are introducing some research issues that can be refined as research agendas for empirical investigation. Given that performance assessment appears to be a developing alternative in teacher testing, we offer the ideas in this chapter as points of discussion to those developers and researchers involved in this field. Our discussion begins with a brief overview of the pervasiveness of how evaluative reactions of certain listeners are differentially biased against certain speakers of certain language varieties. This is followed by a synopsis of pertinent research findings in which Chicano-accented English is downgraded and stereotyped. We conclude with some points on what this may mean for Latinos who are evaluated within a performance assessment framework.

"The way we speak and how listeners interpret our manner of speaking have important consequences for our interactions with other people" (Ryan, Carranza, and Moffie, 1977, 267). This proposition has been examined fairly extensively by sociolinguists and other scholars. As Carranza (1982) notes, the subject of language attitude research has received much attention since the 1970s and has immensely helped shape the growth of sociolinguistics.[10] Carranza also states that the field of language attitude research is still in a nascent stage, particularly along lines of measurement techniques and theoretical development. Notwithstanding the developmental status of research on this topic, it is quite apparent that language attitudes do indeed shape language behavior (Carranza, 1982). "It is evident that different language varieties occupy distinctive positions of perceived social status. Language varieties that are seen as less prestigious and are associated with the lower classes are usually downgraded in preference to other varieties." (Carranza, 1982, 63). Differential linguistic evaluations are so pervasive that dominant group language bias toward regional, foreign, or lower-class accents and dialects has been identified in research studies in many parts of the world, including Canada, Italy, Egypt, England, and the United States (for references of primary studies, see Brennan, Ryan, and Dawson, 1975; Ryan, 1979).[11]

Why and how does such differential linguistic evaluation operate? It is well beyond the intent and scope of this chapter to present detailed perspectives on this important explanatory aspect of language attitude research, but we will offer in brief some theorizing by Williams (1970), who posits a conceptual framework that makes good sense to us.[12] In its simplest terms, Williams' thesis is: "we associate types of speech with types of people"(p. 381). The links in this theoretical framework are speech, attitudes, and social structure. In short, as viewed by Williams, our speech offers an abundance of social and ethnic correlates—each of which contains attitudinal correlates for the listener's and our own behaviors. With this configuration, speech becomes a reminder to others and ourselves of ethnic and social boundaries, and therefore constitutes one part of the process of social maintenance (or change). Extending this logic, a "stereotype hypothesis" is central to Williams' framework. That is, a person's evaluative reactions to another's speech are stereotyped versions of his/her attitudes toward the collective users of the particular speech. Placed in a sequential schema, Williams links speech, attitudes, and social structure as follows: "in a situation, (1) speech types serve as social identifiers. (2) These elicit stereotypes held by ourselves and others (including ones of ourselves). (3) We tend to behave in accord with these stereotypes, and thus (4) translate our attitudes into a social reality" (p. 383).

With the preceding as background, we now can examine briefly the literature on language attitudes vis-á-vis Latino language varieties. Our focus will be on attitudes and evaluative reactions toward speakers of Latino accented English, the most extensively studied area in Latino language varieties.[13] The generalizations we draw are about Chicanos, as Puerto Ricans were not a target group in the available research. Based on a small but rich body of empirical investigations, there are at least five pertinent findings we are able to glean from the literature on the topic of language attitudes towards Chicano-accented English:

1. One need not be a linguist or trained listener to be able to detect varying degrees of accentedness. Research by Brennan et al. (1975) and Ryan et al. (1977) found that nonlinguistically trained (naive) White college students are capable of making rather fine discriminations in discerning varying degrees of accentedness in English. The target linguistic groups were eight bilingual Mexican-American college students who read a formal-style excerpt in English. The stimuli readings constituted a wide range of accentedness, and each speech sample was known to have certain features of Spanish phonological interference (Brennan et al.). The major finding was that " . . . nonlinguistically trained listeners give reliable judgments of the accentedness of speech samples, and they are in agreement as to what constitutes various levels of accentedness" (Brennan et al., p. 33). The implications of this result—as well as the other findings below—with respect to performance assessment of Latinos will be discussed later.

2. Chicano-accented English speech—compared to a more standard variety of English speech—elicits negative evaluative reactions by Whites.[14] That is, research has consistently found that Whites negatively stereotype and downgrade accented English spoken by Chicanos (e.g., Arthur, Farrar, and Bradford, 1974; Brennan, 1977; Galván, Pierce, and Underwood, 1975; Politzer and Ramirez, 1973a, 1973b; Ryan and Carranza, 1975; Ryan et al. 1977).[15] For example, in Arthur et al. (1974), forty-eight White university students enrolled in undergraduate linguistics classes rated four pairs of matched guise voices (standard English guise and Chicano-accented English guise) on fifteen bipolar adjective scales (e.g., friendly-hostile; intelligent-stupid; dependable-unreliable.)[16] The evaluators were informed ahead of time that the speakers (on tape) were Mexican-Americans from the Los Angeles area. A major finding was that the voices elicited two dramatically different character profiles, with the speakers of the Chicano guise—compared to the standard guise—eliciting less favorable evaluative reactions. For example, the Chicano-accented English guise was negatively stereotyped as such: "working class," "uneducated," "low self image," "stupid," "untalented," "narrow minded," "unreliable," "lazy," and so on. A good point made by the authors was that the stereotyped reactions were not to ethnicity, per se, in that the evaluators were informed prior to the rating sessions that the speakers were Mexican-Americans. That is, "The negative reaction of the raters was not towards Mexican-Americans but towards Mexican-Americans who speak a dialect heavily laden with non-standard phonetic features" (p. 262). In sum, the downgrading of Chicano-accented English speech appears to be a wide-

spread phenomenon. Mendoza-Hall (1980) succinctly captures this critical social issue in this manner:

> there seems to be a negative attitude in this country toward Chicano-accented speech, evidenced by the consistent devaluation of Chicano-accented speech as compared to "un-accented" speech. This negative evaluation of speech accentedness appears to generalize into negative evaluations of behavioral characteristics of the speaker. (p. 97)

3. There appears to be a strong positive correlation between degree of accentedness and the strength of the negative stereotype. For example, Ryan et al. (1977) had 100 college students (presumably all White) rate ten matched guise Spanish-English bilingual speakers (presumably all Mexican-American) representing a wide range of accentedness. The authors found that small increments in accentedness were statistically associated with increasingly less favorable evaluations of solidarity (friendship), status (eventual occupation), and speech characteristics (accentedness, pleasantness, and fluency). The research finding of Ryan et al. is consistent with other investigations (e.g., Brennan and Brennan, 1981a, 1981b) that found as the degree of accentedness increases, so does the degree of negative stereotypes and downgrading.

4. Stereotyping and downgrading of Chicano-accented English speech appears to be age independent. As Brennan (1977) notes in her review of pertinent literature, "The downgrading pattern has been shown to appear consistently at different developmental levels" (p. 6). Politzer and Ramirez (1973a, 1973b) found downgrading of accented English (compared to standard English) among 3rd-and 6th-grade children. Brekke (1973) reported downgrading evidence among pre-adolescents (elementary students) and adolescents (high school students). Furthermore, Brekke found a developmental trend (i.e., toward greater negative evaluations of the Chicano-accented English by the older students). As we discussed previously, downgrading of accented English has been found among young adults (e.g., Arthur et al., 1974; Ryan et al., 1977). Finally, Flores and Hopper's (1975) investigation provided evidence that downgrading persists into later adulthood. In this study, the subjects (i.e., evaluators) included sixty-two Mexican-American adults, ages sixteen to seventy-four years. The mean evaluative ratings for nonstandard dialects (accented English and "Tex-Mex"—Texas Spanish) were lower compared to the standard dialects (standard English and Spanish).

5. Although Mexican-Americans have been found to downgrade Chicano-accented English, such negative evaluative reactions appear not to be as great as those by Whites. Downgrading of accented speech—in

comparison to standard speech—by Chicanos has been observed in several studies (e.g., Brekke, 1973; Flores and Hopper, 1975; Politzer and Ramirez, 1973a, 1973b; Ryan and Carranza, 1975). Notwithstanding such downgrading by Chicanos, there is evidence that Chicanos compared to Whites were somewhat more favorable in their ratings of Chicano accented English (see Brekke, 1973; Politzer and Ramirez, 1973a; Ryan and Carranza, 1975). For example, in the study by Brekke (1973), Chicano adolescents, compared to their White peers, rated Chicano-accented English speakers significantly more favorable on six of ten speaker characteristics scales. For the preadolescent group, Chicanos, compared to their White peers, rated accented English more correct, more acceptable, and more valuable on all three speech characteristics scales.

Within-Chicano group differences have also been observed. In the investigation by Flores and Hopper (1975), an all Mexican-American sample was utilized. Significant differences in evaluations were observed according to the subjects' most preferred self referent (i.e., "Latin," "American," "Mexicano," "Mexican-American," or "Chicano"). The results showed that least tolerant of the nonstandards (accented English and Tex-Mex) were the "Latin" and "American" self-referent groups. The "Mexicano" and "Mexican-American" groups were favorable to accented English, but not to Tex-Mex. Finally, the "Chicano" self-referent group was favorable to both accented English and Tex-Mex, especially the latter.

With the preceding overview of language attitude research in mind, what might be some implications with respect to potential performance assessment problems vis-á-vis Latinos? The most glaring concern one can raise deals with potential discriminatory assessment of Latino examinees who speak English with an accent. Given what is known from the existing literature on evaluative reactions to Chicano-accented speech, it appears quite appropriate to ask whether the downgrading of such speech also may occur in performance assessment settings. Because the finding of accentedness speech downgrading in the available scientific experiments is so robust, we hypothesize that similar downgrading and negative stereotyping are likely to occur during performance assessment. As we described earlier, broadly conceptualized, performance assessment contains a considerable amount of examiner-examinee direct contact and interaction. Because performance assessment relies heavily on interview and simulation activities such as the actual teaching of students, a considerable amount of examinee speech is spoken. In short, given the very close contact between examiner and examinee, coupled with the pervasiveness of examinee speech samples, it appears warranted to predict that performance assessment settings may become fertile grounds for negative evaluative reactions of Latino-accented English.

If downgrading and stereotyping of Latino-accented English is likely to occur during performance assessment, how might the process work? In the absence of empirical data and developed theory, we can only speculate at this time. First, a key player is the observer—the examiner who evaluates the candidate. Based on the previously discussed language attitude research, those examiners who have the least familiarity with Latino culture, particularly nonstandard dialects and accented speech, will likely demonstrate the highest degree of downgrading. Second, there is the Latino examinee. For those Latinos who speak English with an accent, it will be those who speak with the greatest amount of accentedness who are likely to experience the most downgrading. Third, there is the actual setting. It is important to keep in mind that in the scholarly literature the typical design called for a matched guise technique in which the subjects (the raters) reacted to various speech samples on audio tape. That is, the actual persons of the voices were not in visual view of the subjects. The voices served as the stimuli, and in some cases the raters were provided actual information (e.g., ethnicity) or contrived information (e.g., social status) of the person behind the voice. On the other hand, in performance assessment the examiner has full view of the person—voice and all.

Taking these three features together—background of examiner, degree of accentedness of examinee, and nature of the interactive setting—we can speculate further about the probable process of negative evaluations. First, because the performance assessment setting is far removed from the experimental and contrived setting seen in the scientific literature on evaluative reaction studies, the psychological processes of downgrading by the examiner are likely to be more subtle. Assuming the tenability of Williams' (1970) previously discussed stereotype hypothesis, it is probable that stereotyping as an evaluative reaction will gain salience as a psychological process in the performance assessment setting. Following the theorizing by Williams, speech (in our case, accented speech) provides an index of stereotypes for the examiner. This triggers an opening to a catalog of what the examiner has generalized about the status of similar others. Furthermore, at the same time the presence of additional cues—the most salient being racial/ethnic membership—provides the basis for quick hypothesizing about the status of the newly encountered examinee. (Later, we will present further thoughts on how racial/ethnic membership of examinees may influence the examiner's evaluation).

Second, in addition to the theoretical value of the stereotype hypothesis in understanding linguistic downgrading and stereotyping of Latino-accented English, another potentially fruitful area may be related to the concept of "negative affect in speech." This notion was introduced by Sebastian, Ryan, Keogh, and Schmidt (1980; cited in Carranza, 1982). In this study, the subjects were engaged in color-recognition accuracy tasks while listening to either standard speakers or accented speakers. Voices were heard through a noisy background. The results showed that accuracy on the color-recognition tasks was significantly influenced (i.e., hampered) by both noise and accent singularly, and in combination. Carranza (182) summarizes the study's results and implication:

> Speakers heard through a noisy background were downgraded suggesting that negative affect associated with a speaker leads to negative evaluation. Accented speakers received more negative responses than standard speakers on most measures, including several social evaluation scales. These findings suggest that serious attention be given to the negative affect mechanism involved in the social evaluation of nonstandard speech styles. (p. 80),

This finding by Sebastian et al. (1980) is most interesting for the present discussion on performance assessment. Taking some theoretical liberties here, we could surmise that the interaction between examiner and examinee during performance assessment is largely a process of communication. The examiner listens to and observes the examinee while getting on with the task of assessing the latter's teaching skills. In some cases, examinee-accented speech may operate as a perceived interference to the examiner's task of evaluating the examinee. That is, drawing from the Sebastian et al. finding, we too propose that concerted attention be paid to the idea that accented speech may operate as a negative affect mechanism during performance assessment. The really important issue, which we will cover later, is how to sensitize examiners to not allow accentedness to take on negative affect in their evaluations.

The third and final area in which we wish to offer some conceptual woodcutting with respect to an understanding of how Latino-accented English may be downgraded and stereotyped during performance assessment, deals with racial/ethnic prejudice and discrimination. The two major concerns we raise here are straightforward in their propositional elements: Linguistic bias against Latino-accented English speakers is likely to be influenced by the examiner's reactions to racial/ethnic cues—skin color and other physical characteristics. In short, racial/ethnic bias against Latinos is likely to have an exacerbating effect on linguistic bias. Also, even for Latinos who do *not* speak English with an accent, there is some probability that racial/ethnic bias will occur during performance assessment when observed by examiners who are prejudiced against Latinos. Space does not permit us to explore these two speculations about racial/ethnic bias in any detail. We merely offer a few glimpses of this research.

As Montalvo (1987) notes, racial/ethnic prejudice and discrimination against Chicanos and Puerto Ricans have been documented by numerous scholars (e.g., Acuña, 1981; Barrera, 1979; DeLeon, 1983; Longres, 1974). Of course, whether such negative bias generalizes to the performance assessment setting is an entirely different issue. About the closest one can come in order to draw any possible theoretical linkages is to examine the personnel psychology literature, particularly those studies that have investigated what transpires during the employment interview process (for pertinent reviews see: Arvey, 1979; Rothwell, 1987; Schmitt, 1976). Although the bulk of the available research has utilized laboratory settings in which college students (serving as "interviewers") interacted with or read about hypothetical job applicants, several key findings are noteworthy. Summarizing the review by Schmitt (1976), Parsons and Liden (1984) cite the following as important factors in the interview:

1. Interviewers give too much weight to negative factors.
2. Decisions in the interview occur as early as the first four minutes of the interview.
3. Judgments made by interviewers are too often based on superficial characteristics that are unrelated to subsequent job success.
4. Interviewers form stereotypes concerning the requisite characteristics necessary for job performance and attempt to match the character of job candidates to those perceived characteristics. (p. 557)

The obvious conclusion from these findings that Parsons and Liden point out is interviewers can be greatly influenced by the "physical characteristics, behavior, and other nonverbal cues that are not necessarily directly job-related" (p. 557).

With respect to the effect of applicant race, Arvey (1979) found only a few investigations in which race (Black and White) was a variable of study. To date, no studies of Latino/White companions have been identified in the literature. The major conclusion drawn by Arvey was that Blacks were not unfairly rated lower than Whites during the interview. This conclusion, however, needs to be tempered with caution. As Parsons and Liden (1984) and Rothwell (1987) admonish, past research investigating race effects may have been fraught with methodological problems, thus obscuring the existence of true substantive findings. Such methodological limitations include: the interviewer may have figured race to be a key variable under study, thus social desirability (i.e., being fair to Blacks) may have resulted; the lack of realism in laboratory studies; the use of between-subject designs in which the interviewers viewed only one stimulus condition.

In addition to these methodological issues, there have been recent studies since the Arvey (1979) review that did find negative bias against Blacks in the interview process (McConahay, 1983; Parsons and Liden, 1984). The study by McConahay is informative in that White college students' ("interviewers") scores on a valid measure of racial prejudice, the Modern Racism Scale (McConahay, Hardee, and Batts, 1981), were negatively correlated with the hiring evaluations of Blacks.[17] Regarding the Parsons and Liden study (which also found negative bias against Blacks), it is interesting to note that of the eight nonverbal cues examined—e.g., poise, clothing, eye contact, articulation, and pauses—the speech characteristics variable—articulation and proper pauses—were the best predictors of hiring evaluations for the aggregated sample. In conclusion, given the methodological problems described earlier and the conflicting substantive findings, it appears that the subject of race effects in the interview literature remains an open issue.

Granted, it is a leap from the sociolinguistics and personnel psychology literature on interviewing to the developing field of performance assessment of beginning teachers to argue that linguistic and racial/ethnic bias will be operative. We iterate, however, that we are not making claims, but rather raising some potential warning flags. From the scholarly literature (both theory and practice), much is known about linguistics bias, the history of racial prejudice and discrimination in the United States, stereotype formation, interpersonal attractiveness, the interview process, and so on. Given this knowledge, it seems quite reasonable to contend that those individuals and agencies who will direct performance assessment should be well aware of the potentialities of linguistic and racial/ethnic bias against Latinos and other ethnic minority examinees. Assuming that our concerns have merit, it would be important and timely for those involved in performance assessment to begin to ask a number of research questions, such as: What proportion of Latino examinees are expected to speak in accented English? What is the expected racial/ethnic backgrounds of the examiners? What percentage are expected to be bilingual (Spanish-English)? If linguistic and racial/ethnic bias does occur during performance assessment, are there particular locations or segments that may serve as "hot spots"? How might the subtleties of bias work? Can (and should) examiners be screened for potential bias? If research is done to address some of these concerns can (and should) it be done unobtrusively?

Suffice it to say that we heartily encourage these and many other research questions about potential bias in performance assessment. Research, however, is just one aspect—and a time-consuming and expensive one at that. Until such research is underway (and we say this with cautious optimism), we think it is important for leaders in performance assessment to begin quite early implementing proactive preventive measures. Some possibly fruitful areas are:

1. Sensitivity training. All examiners (regardless of racial/ethnic background, but with focus on Whites) should undergo some form of sensitivity training and awareness workshops designed to understand the cultural diversity examinees may bring to the assessment setting (e.g., interaction, and teaching styles). Furthermore, examiners' negative preconceived notions about minority groups (e.g., linguistic aspects) and related stereotypes need to be discussed and resolved in informed manners. Specialists in intergroup relations should organize and facilitate such training.

With respect to the issue of linguistic bias, very special attention should be given to the perceptions of White examiners. A case in point is the previously discussed study by Arthur et al. (1974) in which White college students significantly downgraded and negatively stereotyped Chicano-accented English. Arthur et al. ask:

> What would be the cost of dialect change in terms of student effort and what would be the probability of success? Perhaps a more important implication of this study concerns the education of Anglo-Americans. The ratings given by UCLA students do suggest that even those students who have studied linguistics cannot escape a false doctrine of verbal correctness and a certain verbal snobbery which has been associated with standard English. (p. 270)

2. Minority Examiners. In a vigorous manner, Latino and other minorities should be sought out to serve as examiners, particularly those who have had direct exposure to and knowledge of nonstandard dialects and accented speech. Providing a force of culturally and linguistically diverse examiners is a must.

3. Calibration. In order to minimize the examiners' use of nonessential characteristics (e.g., accented speech and physical characteristics) in the formation of their evaluations, it is critical that all examiners undergo extensive calibration sessions to ensure that all are evaluating examinees in the same manner and on the same essential criteria.

4. Interexaminer reliability. Although systematic, rigorous calibration techniques are likely to prevent problems of disparate evaluations, a system should be in place so an independent examiner can verify the accuracy of an examiner at any point in time. Such checks can be done randomly. Particular attention should be placed in establishing interexaminer reliability of minority examinee evaluation.

In sum, the nascent field of performance assessment brings with it an exciting and potentially promising alternative to the conventional paper-

and-pencil teacher tests—tests that have become to be a bottleneck for Latino and other minority people who are pursuing teaching careers. At the same time, however, because performance assessment brings human beings closely together in an evaluative setting, there appear to be probabilities of bias against Latinos and other ethnic minorities. We encourage the technical development of performance assessment, but we also encourage—along each step of the way—that close attention be paid to ways of reducing, even eliminating if possible, linguistic bias and racial/ethnic bias against minority group members.

Early Identification, Recruitment, Diagnostic Testing, and Remediation.

In this final subsection, we will discuss practical strategies associated with the identification, recruitment, diagnosis, and remediation of Latino and other minority teacher candidates. Our discussion will begin with a brief overview of the growing attention such efforts, among others, are being given. Following this will be a description of common features of these practical strategies, as well as comments on several model programs. The discussion ends with an overall assessment of these strategies, placed in the context of wider school reform.

Fortunately, the development of programs designed to attract minorities into the teaching profession is gaining national attention. As Spellman (1988) notes, both the Holmes Group (1986) and the Carnegie Forum on Education and the Economy (1986)—writers of recent national teacher reform proposals—have set goals and presented recommendations in attempts to increase the number of minority teachers. For example, the Holmes Group and the Carnegie Forum recommend that greater monetary incentives be offered to prospective teachers, particularly minorities (Spellman, 1988). In addition to national reform proposals, there is a growing concern in the scholarly literature about the need to implement programmatic efforts to recruit and retain minority teacher education students. A case in point is the article by Stewart (1988) that lists and annotates nearly two dozen published articles and Educational Resources Information Center (ERIC) documents (1983 to 1987) describing and discussing features (and in some instances, actual programs) of strategies designed to provide access to teacher education and teaching opportunities for minorities. Next, we will glean from the literature the central features of these strategies. Particular focus will be given to those programs that have been implemented.

In our review of the pertinent literature, we have identified at least sixteen elements of collegiate outreach and intake efforts that speak to the subject of increasing the numbers of minority teachers. In no particular order of sequence, the features are as follows:

- early identification and recruitment of minority high school students (e.g., Anrig, 1986; Morehead, 1986; Zapata, 1988)
- career/academic advising of college students (e.g., Morehead, 1986)
- personal advising and support services (e.g., Case, Shive, Ingelbretson, and Spiegel, 1988)
- diagnostic and predictive tests for basic skills assessment and remediation (e.g., Nava, 1985; Salinger and Heger, 1986).
- learning/developmental centers for remedial study (e.g., Anrig, 1986)
- scholarships and/or "forgiveness" loan programs (i.e., minority students who pursue a teaching credential and teach for a specified period after graduation need not repay their student loans (e.g., Baratz, 1986)
- test-taking skills development (e.g., Hackley, 1985; Morehead, 1986; Pressman and Gartner, 1986)
- role models (e.g., minority teachers present guest lectures in teacher education courses) (Morehead, 1986)
- leadership by college president or chancellor (e.g., Anrig, 1986; Hackley, 1985)
- institution-wide responsibility (e.g., Anrig, 1986)
- complete curricula review and modification of entire teacher education program (e.g., Hackley, 1985)
- more rigorous standards of admissions to teacher education program (e.g., Spencer, 1986)
- in-service training for faculty in areas of test development and monitoring of student progress (e.g., Spencer, 1986)
- educational "warranty" (i.e., the teacher training institution "guarantees their product" to the employing school district) (e.g., Hackley, 1985)
- recruitment and status upgrade (i.e., credentialing) of minority teacher aides (Haberman, 1988)
- partnership cultivation between two-year and four-year institutions (e.g., Haberman, 1988)

As one can see, the preceding list of proactive strategies are quite varied in focus and scope. For the sake of analysis and convenience, the logic of Spellman (1988) is helpful in compressing the above features into two general categories of recommendations: those that "(a) Optimize conditions on campus that will encourage successful completion of the teacher education program by minority candidates, and (b) develop programs to recruit more qualified minorities into teacher education" (p. 62). What follows is a description of several highly successful programs that have increased minority access to teaching in some form or another.

To date, the most comprehensive and successful programs designed to improve access for aspiring minority teachers are located in several southern Black colleges. Two exemplary programs are at Grambling State University (GSU) in Louisiana and the University of Arkansas at Pine bluff (UAPB). We will only touch on the highlights of these efforts, as the programs have been described in detail elsewhere (e.g., Hackley, 1985; Spencer, 1986). In 1979, GSU adopted the NTE as its licensing examination. At that time, only about 5% of the teacher education program's graduates passed the NTE. By 1983, however, the pass rate had risen to 85% (Spencer, 1986). These outstanding results came about by a university-wide commitment to excellence. The transformation of the GSU teacher education program involved, in part, a number of the sixteen features we previously described—e.g., more rigorous admissions standards, diagnostic testing, remediation, test-taking skills development, faculty in-service, scholarships, student recruitment, educational warranty, and administrative leadership (Pressman and Gartner, 1986; Spellman, 1988; Spencer, 1986). GSU's efforts have been so successful that the teacher education program is the fastest growing unit in the university. Enrollment hit a low of 200 students in 1981. As of 1986, 850 students were in the teacher education program (Spencer, 1986).

The teacher education unit at UAPB, a historically Black university, represents another model program designed to increase access for prospective minority teachers. When NTE cut scores were first set by the board of education in Louisiana, test validators had predicted a pass rate of 20% for UAPB (Hackley, 1985). In 1983, two years after UAPB began its institutional overhaul, the NTE pass rate was 42%. In 1984, it rose to 73%. The programmatic reform at UAPB contains a number of the same features seen in GSU's efforts (e.g., test-taking skills development, educational warranty, and curricula reform). Also, as seen at GSU, the reform at UAPB had strong backing by the chancellor. In fact, the chancellor (Hackley) provided a strong leadership role in conceptualization of the reform efforts, as well as their implementation (Hackley, 1985).

With respect to outreach-intake efforts designed for prospective Latino teachers, there appears to be no comprehensive programs such as those at GSU and UAPB. There are, however, some programmatic components in various stages of development. Such efforts appear to be largely confined to Texas. The University of Texas at San Antonio (UTSA) has an early identification and recruitment program underway for Latino teacher candidates, while the University of Texas at El Paso (UTEP) has in place a screening, advising, and remediation program for Latino students who are aspiring to become teachers.

The UTSA program—*Project: I Teach*—is a collaborative undertaking by UTSA, the ETS, and the San Antonio and Edgewood Independent School Districts (Zapata, 1988). At this stage of development, *Project: I Teach* is largely an early identification and recruitment program. Its overall goal is to increase the number of Latino students pursuing careers in teaching. The project intends to accomplish this major task by these goals:

1. To provide academic support to Hispanics wanting to pursue teaching as a career but who lack the academic skills to do so.

2. To provide test-taking and study skill development . . .

3. To provide emotional and psychological support . . .

4. To provide knowledge about, if not actual, financial support . . .

5. To facilitate the transition from high school to college . . .

6. To provide Hispanic role models . . . (Zapata, 1988, pp. 20–21)

During the first year of operation of *Project: I Teach*, student identification and recruitment were main goals. By programmatic design, a modest number of students ($N = 21$) were participants. Targeted students were high school juniors; they were nominated by either themselves, teachers, or counselors. The first year was largely devoted to program orientation, self-assessment with respect to qualities needed for teaching, a field trip to UTSA, and frequent meetings on local school campuses. A "Summer Camp" followed the first year activities (Zapata, 1988). The Summer Camp was held at UTSA; students stayed in university housing. Camp activities included: writing/reading, problem-solving strategies, test-taking/ study skills, guest speakers, and special cultural events.

The second year of *Project: I Teach* focused on reinforcement of previous experiences, particularly those of the Summer Camp. Special attention was given to test-taking skills and preparing students for the transition to college (i.e., UTSA). Each student was assigned a "mentor" (student from UTSA). Plans for the students' admission to UTSA were also made (Zapata, 1988). Mentoring will continue, as well as support groups; the ETS will continue to provide assistance in study skills and test-taking development. Students' performance on the SAT and PPST will provide a set of evaluative data. Of the original twenty-one students, nineteen are still with the program; sixteen are still committed to pursuing a career in teaching.

The screening/advising/remediation program at UTEP was developed as a response to the high failure rate of minority students on the PPST in Texas. UTEP is an ideal location for such efforts because the total university enrollment is about 50% Latino (predominantly Mexican American), with a higher proportion in the College of Education (Salinger and Heger, 1986). The UTEP program offers a one-semester hour course, "Orientation to Education." In the course, students are tested in basic skills—mathematics and reading. The tests used are the Salinger-Burns Tests: "developed from the same public domain specifications as the P-PST, the Salinger-Burns Tests assess students' chances of passing each P-PST subtest and diagnoses specific weak skill areas" (Salinger and Heger, p. 121). These tests are used widely in Texas at more than seventy institutions, and elsewhere. Commercial forms are available (Burns, 1983, 1985; Salinger, 1983, 1985). The Salinger-Burns Tests appear to be excellent predictors of teacher candidate success on the PPST. For example, on the Salinger Reading Test (Form A), 95% of students who scored thirty correct of a possible forty points passed the PPST reading subtest at first attempt. Observed correlations between the Salinger-Burns Tests and the PPST range from moderate to strong magnitudes (.50 to .80; Salinger and Heger, 1986).

The remediation component at UTEP appears to be well thought out and comprehensively implemented. This unit—the Study Skills and Tutorial Services—works closely with the College of Education (M. Dubree, personal communication, April 27, 1987). After students are tested on the Salinger-Burns Tests in the "Orientation to Education" course, those who score below the cut score are referred to the Study Skills and Tutorial Services for remediation. The program consists of a six-week/eighteen-hour preparation workshop that is team taught. Each session is devoted to writing and reading development, and one-on-one sessions can be made available. Major emphases also are placed on opportunities for practice on test-taking skills and test-taking sophistication. The Study Skills and Tutorial Services also offer a free, eight-week reading course for students whose skills are not at college level. In all, the screening/advising/remediation program at UTEP appears to be a laudatory one in design and scope. Although Salinger and Heger (1986) claim that the UTEP student pass rate has been higher than expected, no data are provided.

To conclude this subsection on early identification, recruitment, diagnosis, and remediation, we offer these observations and recommendations:

1. Although there is a growing attention paid in the scholarly literature to the subject of outreach-intake measures designed to improve access to teaching careers for minorities, there is only a paucity of actual programs being implemented. The exemplary efforts at GSU, UAPB, UTSA, and UTEP are the exceptions, not the rule. Certainly, such endeavors need to be

implemented in much broader and more extensive fashion across the nation. We applaud and encourage any activities of this nature. Suffice it to say that the establishment and implementation of such programs are not easy. The accomplishments of GSU and UAPB, for example, inform us that extensive resources and extraordinary commitment are required to place proactive programs in motion. A case in point is GSU. In the realization of GSU's goals, it was necessary to secure grants from the U.S. Department of Education in order to buy computers and software for remediation and instruction in the development of test-taking skills (Spencer, 1986).

There are some other bright spots, however, appearing on the horizon. In addition to the programs at UTSA and UTEP, other activity is underway in Texas. Pan American University at Edinburg—a high density Latino university—recently has proposed that $50,000 be earmarked to develop a basic skills preparatory program in order to reduce the high failure rate of its students on the PPST (Nava, 1985). Also, Nava reports that Prairie View A & M in Texas—a predominantly Black institution—has adopted some features of the UTEP model, and students there have shown significant gains in PPST pass rates. Finally, in the summer of 1987, the Texas Education Agency made available grant money totaling $320,000 for projects designed to identify and recruit minority students who are interested in pursuing teaching careers (Zapata, 1988).

2. The outstanding accomplishments at GSU and UAPB are quite telling with respect to the need for university-wide commitment and administrative leadership. In both cases, the chief executive officer (chancellor/president) of the institution—in collaboration with the teacher education program and the entire education department—was very active in seeing the program developed and carried out. The apparent lesson here is that in such institutional reform, the candle needs to burn at both ends. A top-down strategy, working in concert with a bottom-up strategy, appears to offer comprehensive, sweeping reform and results in significant positive impact. We recommend that institutions planning to develop related programs strive to garner the support of the entire university, as well as strong leadership by the chief executive officer.

3. Of the previously described sixteen outreach-intake features we identified from the literature, they all have merit because they appear reasonably suited as measures to increase access to teaching careers for minorities. Some of them, however, appear to us to be particularly critical. Early identification and recruitment of students is essential. We agree with Witty (1986) that recruitment efforts should begin as early as the 7th grade. In general, early outreach efforts appear to be quite successful in getting young students in college preparatory tracks. Maeroff (1983; cited in Spellman, 1988), in a discussion of the University of California's Partnership

Program, reported that students participating in the program were more likely to earn higher grades and take college preparatory courses than their peers who did not participate.[18]

Identification and recruitment efforts can and should vary, according to the institutional needs and resources, as well as the student clientele. Ideas that have been discussed, and in some cases attempted, include: personal contacts and follow-ups (Witty, 1986), career days (Kortokrax-Clark, 1986–87; Warren, 1985), minority alumni recruiters (Nakanishi, 1986; Warren, 1985), university-public school system linkages (Nieto, 1986; Rodriguez, 1984), two-year/four-year college linkages (Haberman, 1988), and the formation of Future Teacher Clubs at middle and secondary schools and community colleges (Mercer and Mercer, 1986). In sum, early identification and recruitment of Latino and other minority students who are interested in pursuing careers in teaching should become a national educational priority. Programs such as *Project: I Teach* (Zapata, 1988) appear promising, and we encourage that similar efforts are started as soon as possible.

Another essential strategy we wish to underscore as a proactive measure are those activities dealing with the diagnostic testing, advising, and remediation of minority students. Such experiences at GSU, UAPB, and UTEP inform us that these kinds of efforts are very fruitful in increasing the pass rates of Black and Latino students on teacher tests. The model at UTEP appears to be a particularly fine program, in which a unique relationship exists between the College of Education and the Study Skills and Tutorial Services. These practices at UTEP and elsewhere hold great promise for increasing the number of Latino and other minority teachers. Again, we commend those institutions that have implemented or are implementing diagnostic testing, advising and remediation measures. More importantly though, we strongly encourage other institutions to follow suit. We are in agreement with Rebell (1986) who advocates that states should provide minority students with assistance in test preparation and remediation, if necessary. "In all competency testing situations, extensive preparatory materials such as study guides, sample questions and counseling should be provided at *state expense* [italics added] for minority students who have not had an opportunity to develop sophisticated test-taking skills" (p. 399). On the issue of remediation, we also concur with Rebell, who suggests: "More importantly, an extensive program of remedial assistance aimed at improving basic skills in areas of identifiable weaknesses should be offered to all who fail in initial administration of the test" (p. 399).

In the final analysis, the numerous practical strategies discussed in this subsection—particularly early identification, recruitment, diagnostic testing, and remediation—represent significant vehicles for increasing access for Latinos and other minorities pursuing teaching careers. The model programs at GSU, UAPB, UTSA, and UTEP have provided and continue to provide positive results, but these programs are too few in number. It is urgent that other institutions develop and implement similar methods. The comprehensive programs at GSU and UAPB with their university-wide support and administrative leadership, the fine early identification and recruitment model at UTSA, and the excellent screening, advising, and remedial components at UTEP can serve as beacons of reform for other universities.

On this topic, we leave the reader with a final observation. It is important to place these outreach-intake efforts in the context of the broader subject of school reform. We agree with Haberman (1988) that recruitment and retention programs are important, but they should be viewed only as short-term solutions to the low and falling percentage of minority teachers. What is truly called for is great attention to deep school reform—the need to deal proactively with the massive schooling problems (e.g., segregation, curriculum differentiation, and school financial disparities) faced by Chicano, Puerto Rican, Black, and American Indian students. Given that the vast majority of minority students attend segregated, urban schools, it is *there* that future teachers (as well as all students pursuing various careers) should be provided basic educational opportunities, identified, and inspired. Haberman's point is well taken: The shortage of minority teachers is just one manifestation of the poor schooling minority students receive in inadequate elementary and secondary school systems. In sum, short-term recruitment efforts need be coupled with long-term reform agendas. Haberman (1988) puts it succinctly:

> While we concern ourselves with the valid and important problems of recruiting and preparing more minority teachers, we must necessarily address the pervasive and exacerbating problem of dismal urban schooling, which effectively precludes potential college graduates and future teachers before they get to middle school. Until the schools that serve the urban poor start providing adequate elementary and secondary education, even our most creative ideas will serve as palliatives rather than cures. (p. 39)

Conclusions

As Smith (1988) notes, "For the nation to plunge headlong into the 21st century with a public school system devoid of minority teachers is unacceptable" (p. 168). This severe underrepresentation of minority teachers is certainly where we are heading unless concerted efforts are made by the measurement community, teacher training institutions, and policymakers to increase access for prospective Latino and other minority teachers. Furthermore, it is clear that the shortage of minority teachers clearly is linked to the wider problems of inferior schooling in urban areas. In short, understanding the problems as well as finding solutions to the minority teacher shortage present major challenges as we approach the next century.

In this chapter, we have extended our discussion about the plight of prospective Latino teachers by presenting proactive suggestions to improve access for them. The negative impact of teacher testing on Latinos and other minorities and the need for informed action has best been captured by Smith (1988):

> The use of pencil-paper competency tests to certify teachers has forced both educators and the public to challenge the most cherished premise underlying the philosophy of public education in a democratic society: That persons regardless of socioeconomic status, race, or creed, are guaranteed both excellence and equity in their pursuit of education . . . excellence in teaching has been operationally defined in the narrowest sense, a high score on a pencil-paper test. . . . Collaborative leadership . . . must challenge new ways to perpetuate old inequities and must seek solutions to the dilemma of achieving excellence and equity simultaneously. Signs of the time foretell a brewing controversy and point to the need for reexamination of the competency testing movement and its long-term impact on the American promise of equity. (p. 169)

Part IV

TestSkills: The First Course of Instruction Directed Specifically to the Improvement of the Test-Taking of Hispanics

9

The Development of *TestSkills*: A Test Familiarization Kit on the PSAT/NMSQT for Hispanic Students

~ ~ ~ ~

Lorraine Gaire

The Beginnings

TestSkills grew out of a series of meetings held between representatives of the Hispanic Higher Education Coalition (HHEC), the College Board, and Educational Testing Service (ETS). These meetings were convened to discuss issues concerning access to higher education for Hispanic students, and they resulted in consensus regarding projects to address access in different ways and at different age levels.

The members of the Coalition believed strongly that the first project should be the development of materials designed to prepare and encourage Hispanic students to take college admission tests. Since the Preliminary Scholastic Aptitude Test/National Merit Scholarship Qualifying Test is itself a preparatory activity for the Scholastic Aptitude Test (SAT), and since PSAT/NMSQT results are important in the selection of students for scholarships, especially the National Hispanic Scholar Awards Program, it was decided that the test preparation materials would be based on the PSAT/NMSQT. This would provide early encouragement to Hispanic high school students to enter the college-going pipeline. Also, since the PSAT/NMSQT results are used by many colleges in their recruiting efforts, the students would begin to receive frequent and continuing reminders of the possibility of attending college in the form of college promotional materials.

The original plan for this project was to assemble materials already available at ETS and the College Board into a kit that would be made available to Hispanic students. The final product is considerably more structured and complex. TestSkills is a series of twenty-three lesson plans accompanied by an instructor's guide and related student materials, exercises, practice tests, and five additional supplemental math lesson plans. The difference between the project as originally envisioned and as completed grew out of reviews of existing research, a related research project (described later), and discussions with Hispanic educators about effective ways of presenting test preparation information to students.

Early in the planning process it was decided that it would not be useful to present the materials as stand-alone test preparation for the target audience. Several such products are widely available in bookstores throughout the country: large volumes with suggestions, strategies, and numerous practice tests and items for drill and practice. They present a rather daunting prospect and are of very limited value to the average student. Instead, we chose to present a mediated and structured opportunity for the students by formulating the materials into lesson plans for delivery by teachers, guidance counselors, or staff at community organizations that tutor Hispanic students to improve their academic skills. Developing lesson plans meant taking statements and suggestions that had been made to students in various publications by the College Board and working them into instructional materials and procedures. It also required consideration of the probable educational level and experiences of the students who would be on the receiving end of the lesson plans.

Building on the Research Base at ETS, Beatriz Clewell (1988) was doing research on the characteristics of the Hispanic students selected by the National Hispanic Scholar Awards Program. These were high-achieving students who had been very well prepared for college admission tests, so they were not in need of additional attention in this area. In contrast, those students falling in the lowest percentiles of classroom performance would have significant educational deficits, to the point that it was unlikely that helping them develop strategies for pacing and guessing, or for reasoning with analogies, would be a good use of their time. Therefore, the lesson plans were aimed at the students of mid-range ability, roughly the two middle quartiles.

A review of the existing research by Charlene Rivera, the first project director, turned up little that was useful in identifying specific test-taking problems for Hispanic students, and even less that provided direction for the development of specific instructional strategies and materials. However, she did find general direction in a paper presented at the Sixth Annual RACHE Conference by Edward Rincon that stated that "factors that represent inadvertent sources of test difficulty for Hispanics and other ethnic minority groups can also lead to decreased performance on standardized tests. These factors include test speededness, familiarity with different item formats and directions, test anxiety, perceived probability of success, and confusion about appropriate guessing strategies. In addition to decreased test scores, this relative lack of test sophistication among Hispanics further decreases accuracy in the measurement of scholastic ability."

Rincon's research indicated that, for the most part, the sources of Hispanic difficulty were congruent with the content of the typical test preparation program, largely based on part of Jason Millman's (1965) test-wiseness taxonomy, i.e., attention to the generic test-taking skills of timing and pacing, guessing strategy, dealing with an answer sheet and familiarization with the specific item formats that the student will meet on the test. It also suggested however, that the proposed test preparation materials should deal specifically with test anxiety, and should attend to affective as well as cognitive structure and content.

Test Anxiety

The research on test anxiety by Mandler (1952), Wine (1971), Richardson (1977), and Sarason (1972) presents a convincing and practical explanation for the differences in our personal responses to the testing situation. It is called the "attentional interpretation of test anxiety," and basically states that the attentional focus on high and low anxious subjects differs under threat. The threat in the case of a test is the extent of the evaluatory dimension of the testing situation, i.e., the perceived effect of the test results on self-esteem or on future educational plans. This relates two of the factors cited by Rincon: test anxiety and the perceived probability of success. Low test-anxious persons focus attention on the task in front of them, high test-anxious persons focus attention internally on self-evaluative, self-deprecatory thinking and on perception of their autonomic responses, such as sweaty palms, perspiration, trembling, upset stomach, etc. High and low test-anxious people are so defined by their responses to self-report instruments such as the Text Anxiety Questionnaire developed by Mandler and Sarason (1952) and Sarason's (1972) Test Anxiety Scale. Examples of items from these instruments are:

"I seem to defeat myself while working on important tests."

"While taking an important exam I find myself thinking of how much brighter the other students are than I am."

"During tests I find myself thinking of the consequences of failing."

"After important tests I am frequently so tense that my stomach gets upset."

Liebert and Morris (1967, 1969, 1970) present a consistent view of test anxiety and its effects on performance. They suggest that test anxiety is composed of two major aspects: worry, which is described as cognitive concern over performance; and emotionality, which is the autonomic arousal aspect of anxiety (sweaty palms, etc.).

What is interesting here is that it is worry, the cognitive component, that interferes with performance by directing the test-anxious person's attention to their internal state. The emotional or autonomic response is a reaction to this attentional focus. It follows that reducing test anxiety is essentially a cognitive activity of interfering with and replacing the worry state with positive self-statements and redirecting the attentional focus to the task at hand, i.e., the test. The other strong implication for dealing with test anxiety in the test preparation situation is that students should become so familiar with the test—its item formats, the item directions, the answer sheet, the way the items look on the page, the length of the testing period, etc.—that the actual test holds no surprises that would call up the worry state. Therefore, TestSkills has a strong focus on duplicating the test experience in many ways in the classroom, including use of the answer sheet with all exercises and practice tests that simulate actual timing and testing conditions. It also contains a supplemental section of test anxiety materials designed to make students conscious of their feelings and aware of the effects of negative self-statements on their performance, and to help them develop strategies to replace those self-statements with positive ones.

In designing instructional materials that would have a positive affective approach, we expected that thorough familiarity with the test and its environment would itself produce affective rewards, in terms of comfort and confidence with the test. We also explored the success that Arthur Whimbey (1986) has had in improving the thinking and reasoning skills of special admission college students. His approach, which seems to work on all age levels and with both verbal and mathematical skills, is to pair or group students and have them help each other to increase the precision with which they can state or describe their reasoning processes. One student attempts to verbalize the thinking process as he or she attempts to solve a problem or answer a question, and the other student(s) ask questions that require the thinker to be increasingly clear, precise, and logical in stating and dealing with the problem. TestSkills borrowed a page from Whimbey in suggesting that many of the classroom exercises be performed in small groups or in pairs, and that the students be encouraged to provide and verbalize the logic required to respond to items such as analogies.

Guessing

Another area of concern raised in reviewing the research literature was that of guessing, and whether there was a systematic difference in the way that Hispanic students approached guessing on multiple-choice tests. While the question had been addressed by researchers, there was nothing conclusive to guide the teaching of a guessing strategy. Charlene Rivera (1988) was interested in this question and with Alicia Perez Schmitt conducted a study which was published in August 1988 as "A Comparison of Hispanic and White Non-Hispanic Students' Omit Patterns on the Scholastic Aptitude Test." Questions that are omitted are differentiated from questions that are not reached and are, therefore, an indirect measure of guessing behavior, since a decision to omit an item indicates that the student chose not to guess on that item. This study concluded that the Hispanic students tended to omit less on the SAT verbal test than white students of comparable ability. Items that had unexpectedly extreme lower omit rates for Hispanic students were flagged and examined for commonalities that might explain the difference. There were six of these items, and five of them contained true cognates or words in the item that have a common root in Spanish and English. Cognates were located in at least the stem, key, and/or distractors. Those five items also had been subjected to a differential item functioning (DIF) analysis and were found to be differentially easier for Hispanic students.

The conclusions that we drew from the Rivera/Schmitt study were that Hispanic students did not seem to need any additional encouragement to guess, but introducing a reasonable guessing strategy would probably be useful. Although the study was exploratory in nature and limited in terms of numbers of items, it suggested that the presence of cognates in test items represented a source of advantage to Hispanic students. They should therefore be made aware of the existence of cognates, and encouraged to apply any knowledge of Spanish in interpreting words that were cognates. As a result, TestSkills contains a lesson plan that describes the formation of cognates, and it encourages students to view their Spanish language skills as an advantage in the testing situation.

Changing Answers

Another area of interest for development was the research concerning the efficacy of changing answers in the test situation. In discussions with teachers, we found that they tend to hold the unsubstantiated and probably inaccurate view that one's first response to a test question has some special validity or accuracy, and therefore students should be told not to change their answers when they review their work on a test. Benjamin (1984) summarized the findings of thirty-three separate investigations on changing answers as follows: "In fact, the evidence uniformly indicates that (a) the majority of answer changes are from incorrect to correct and (b) most students who change their answers improve their test scores. None of the 33 studies contradicts either of those conclusions."

Since research contradicts this popular fallacy, we wanted to provide a better strategy to the students. This was problematic since both guessing and changing answer behavior are highly idiosyncratic (the research results are averages; while the majority of students improve scores as a result of guessing or changing answers, other students lose points). Therefore, we set up the practice tests so that students would be encouraged to practice guessing strategy and to change answers when they thought they had a better one, marking these questions with a symbol for guessing or changing answers. During the review of the practice test the students use the guessing correction factor to calculate the effect of these strategies on their score, and determine for themselves whether these strategies have a positive or negative effect.

Also, the research generally supported the concept that specific feedback on test results can lead to improved performance, motivation, and understanding, and this is addressed in TestSkills by immediate feedback of answers and rationales for class exercises, as well as by the use of the practice test results for feedback and additional educational planning.

Other considerations that informed the development of TestSkills involved the variety of environments in which the materials might be used, the probable level of skill of the instructor, and the desirability of providing sufficient flexibility to allow the user to add or subtract material depending on the needs and educational experiences of the students and the instructor.

Organization of TestSkills

The resulting first draft of TestSkills contained an instructor's guide and twenty-two lesson plans. Each plan had a statement of purpose and objectives, a list of students materials keyed to the plan, suggestions for preparing to teach the plan, a discussion of the content that the plan addresses, and a series of procedural steps to be used in instruction. While we hoped that teachers would consider this information thoughtfully in terms of their students needs and previous experiences, the basic intention was to organize the material so as to simplify review and preparation by the instructor. The plans are structured around the PSAT/NMSQT item formats, and integrate generic test-taking skills—such as pacing, guessing, and changing answers—into exercises on antonyms, analogies, sentence completion questions, and reading comprehension questions. Each item format is introduced with sample questions that model the thinking process required to reach the answer.

The students are then given a page of practice questions to be worked through in groups or for homework. The instructor is encouraged to continue the process used in the sample questions of verbally modeling the reasoning process used to reach the answer. The sample and practice questions are drawn from disclosed PSAT/NMSQT tests, but in some instances, such as the lesson plan that was developed to help students develop skills at drawing inferences, simpler reading material is used so that the difficulty of the reading passage would not be an obstacle to demonstrating the meaning of inference.

In many lesson plans, the material provided goes beyond the review of educational skills to suggestions on addressing deficits. For example, in the lesson plans on reading comprehension, students are shown how test questions that require them to identify the main idea in a reading passage differ from questions that require them to locate specific detail. For students who need work on more elemental reading skills, there are suggestions on exercises to help develop skimming and outlining techniques. The student materials are included with the lesson plans, and a second reproducible set is included in the kit, with permission to reproduce sufficient copies for the class.

The instructor's guide contains the objectives for the kit, suggestions for use of the materials, a summary of test-taking skills, a discussion of test anxiety with suggestions for classroom activities, and an explanation of the lesson plan format and suggested scheduling.

While the lesson plans were developed with the traditional forty-five minute classroom period in mind, the timing is dependent on student needs for more or less instruction on any area of skill.

The math section of TestSkills was structured around the statement of math concepts that is provided in the student bulletins for the PSAT/NMSQT and the SAT. The instructor reviews these concepts with the students, then provides a Quick Test to determine if the student's math preparation is sufficient for the test. If the students are able to complete the Quick Test, the instructor provides material on strategies to use on different kinds of math questions. Originally, we expected that the instructors would be able to supplement TestSkills with mathematical material that they had found effective in working with students who were deficient in math skills. However, as a result of some early pilot tests with the materials and the suggestions from the evaluation of those pilots (Pennock-Roman, Powers, and Perez, 1989), we decided to add additional material in mathematics.

Five additional lesson plans were keyed to the Quick Tests, and designed to be added by the instructor when the students exhibit a need for a more exhaustive review of the basic mathematic concepts tested by the PSAT/NMSQT.

A twenty-third lesson plan was added after the evaluation of the kit. Since these materials mostly likely would be used with high school sophomores who would be taking the PSAT/NMSQT in their junior year, this last lesson plan is designed as a review activity for the following September, immediately prior to the test administration. It provides a summary of test-taking strategies, and a final practice test to help the students review their skills and be ready to do their best on the test.

Review and Evaluation

TestSkills was reviewed extensively by the staff and members of the three collaborating institutions. At ETS, test developers, statistical analysts, program directors, and editors reviewed the draft. At the College Board, reviewers included program directors, field office staff, and members of the Advisory Committee on Minority Affairs and the SAT Committee. The HHEC staff reviewed the materials, conducted a conference during which Hispanic educators reviewed and reacted to the materials, and arranged to send the draft to many other Hispanic educators as reviewers.

The kit was piloted over a two-year period, first at sites in California and Texas, and, in the second year, at Hartford, Connecticut, and at several sites in California that were conducting pilot projects in response to the Tanner legislation.

Additional information was supplied by the evaluation, and all of this information was used in preparing the final version, which was received from the printer in April 1989 and is being marketed by the College Board.

10

A Preliminary Evaluation of *TestSkills*: A Kit to Prepare Hispanic Students for the PSAT/NMSQT*

~ ~ ~ ~

María Pennock-Román, Donald E. Powers, Monte Pérez

Introduction

A collaborative effort to improve access to college for Hispanic youth on the part of the College Board, The Educational Testing Service (ETS), and the Hispanic Higher Education Coalition resulted in a test-familiarization pilot kit titled *Preparing for the PSAT/NMSQT for Hispanic High School Students*. The kit contains practice tests for the Preliminary Scholastic Aptitude Test/National Merit Scholarship Qualifying Test (PSAT/NMSQT), twenty-two lesson plans that cover test-taking skills, and a review of selected mathematics and English grammar concepts. The kit was designed to facilitate formal instruction by counselors and teachers at the junior and senior high school levels. It also can be used in college recruitment programs to help disadvantaged students prepare for other college admissions tests like the Scholastic Aptitude Test (SAT). The current version is now titled *TestSkills: For Teachers of Hispanic Students*.

This report is meant to provide some modest information about students' and teachers' reactions to the pilot version of the kit. In addition to describing the kit and how it was used in a number of school districts over

---

*Reprinted with permission. Originally published as College Board Report No. 89-1, *An Evaluation of a Kit to Prepare Hispanic Students for the PSAT/NMSQT* by María Pennock-Román, Donald E. Powers, and Monte Pérez. Copyright (c) 1989 by College Entrance Examination Board, New York.

the past year, we look at two key questions: whether the test-familiarization kit increased students' confidence and lessened their anxiety about test-taking, and whether the kit increased the likelihood that students would take the PSAT/NMSQT.

Most targeted school districts were in California, where recent legislation (Assembly Bill 2321, Chapter 1210, authored by Assemblywoman Sally Tanner in 1985) provided funding for demonstration sites to help disadvantaged students become more familiar with college admissions tests. Projects at various schools that were designed in coordination with the tenth grade counseling programs to improve the academic preparation of targeted students received the highest priority for funding by the California Legislature (see George, 1988, for a description and evaluation of the projects).

The Tanner Act arose out of the growing realization (Boyer, 1983; Cicourel & Kitsuse, 1963; Commission on Precollege Guidance and Counseling, 1986; Erickson & Shultz, 1982; Ginsburg & Giles, 1984; Holmes, Dalton, Erdmann, Hayden, & Roberts, 1986; Lee & Ekstrom, 1987; National Coalition of Advocates for Children, 1985) that the availability and quality of guidance counseling in junior and senior high schools are key factors that mediate access to higher education for minority and economically disadvantaged youth. Such students have little access to individuals who have attended college and who have the necessary experience with which to aid them in making sound educational decisions for college preparation and in applying to universities. Thus they have a greater necessity than others for adequate school-based counseling in order to ensure appropriate choices in college-preparatory curriculum, admissions test readiness, and college application requirements. In particular, Lee and Ekstrom (1987) found that educational decisions concerning curriculum tracks were related to access to guidance counselling, and that such services were less likely to be received by students who needed it most. Thus, the Tanner Act was designed to address the counseling needs of disadvantaged students as a means to increase their access to higher education.

The project outlined here was not intended to be a rigorous experimental evaluation of how the kit affected student attitudes or posttreatment test scores. An evaluation of this nature would require control groups and standardized instruction across sites. In the present project, it was not possible to control the design of the programs or how the kit was used. Most school districts developed their own programs and incorporated other activities related to test preparation, in addition to using the kit. Thus, it was not possible to separate the effects of the kit from the effects of the other activities. Therefore, the emphasis of this evaluation is on perceptions of the extent to which the kit was helpful. This information may have some value for refining the kit as new editions are produced and for helping to inform potential users of ways the kit may be used most effectively.

Description of the Kit

The kit is based largely on material already available to most schools and test-takers. However, in some respects, the kit goes beyond the materials available to date. Lesson plans in the kit facilitate classroom instruction, involve multiple practice tests, and include units on reducing test anxiety and using knowledge of Spanish cognates.

It takes about forty-five minutes to present each of the twenty-two lesson plans. Each plan describes the lesson objectives and lists the handouts, other materials, and steps required to prepare and present the lesson. A content summary and a list of procedures for working through the materials also are provided for each lesson. The lessons cover such topics as PSAT/NMSQT format, general information about test-taking, answer-sheet familiarization, and cognates. Four lessons involve answering several kinds of questions based on reading passages, two concern verbal analogy problems, and one deals with sentence completion items. The six lessons devoted to mathematics involve reviewing math concepts, discussing strategies for the regular mathematics and quantitative comparison items, and through "Quick Tests," evaluating the need for additional review. Students apply what they have learned by taking either the verbal or mathematical sections of simulated PSAT/NMSQTs in two other lesson periods. Performance on each of these sections is reviewed in two subsequent lessons. A final supplementary session includes suggestions for dealing with test anxiety.

As described in the kit's statement of objectives, these lessons are designed to help students:

- understand the testing process and how to prepare physically and mentally for a test
- learn general strategies for test-taking, including time management, following directions, guessing, changing answers, and handling test anxiety
- understand and respond efficiently to each of several kinds of PSAT/NMSQT questions, and
- better understand their PSAT/NMSQT test scores.

Method

When the project was initiated, the kit was used in more than a dozen school districts in California and in Hartford, Connecticut, and it seemed likely, in light of the substantial interest in the kit, that more districts would adopt it. For evaluation purposes, we proposed selecting three districts that currently were using the kit, two in California and the other in Hartford. The California districts were selected from those that had received grants under the Tanner Act, which provided funding for projects designed to increase college administrations test-taking and subsequent enrollment of traditionally underrepresented students. The California districts were selected after a perusal of the program descriptions they provided when applying for Tanner funding, and because of the predominance of Mexican-American students. The Hartford, Connecticut, district was chosen because of its large Puerto Rican student population. As data collection proceeded, two additional California districts were included in the study. Districts selected included both urban and rural areas.

Eight staff members who had worked with the kit (at least one at each of the five different sites) responded to our survey on how the kit was used. These educators were asked for their perceptions of the effects of the kit, particularly whether or not it affected the likelihood that participating students would eventually take the PSAT/NMSQT and SAT. The questions were organized around the objectives of the various lesson plans in the kit. (Appendix A contains the questionnaire.)

The kit was intended to be flexible enough to be used in a variety of different contexts. Hence, documenting the characteristics of these programs was an important part of the evaluation because, it was thought, the kit might be perceived as more useful in some contexts than in others.

The first task was to read the proposals that districts had submitted to obtain funding under the Tanner Act. This reading suggested significant variation among test-preparation programs with respect to instructional objectives, characteristics and duration of components, and characteristics of students and schools (e.g., grade level, race/ethnicity, socioeconomic status, and proportion of minority students in the school).

Because there is seldom perfect correspondence between what is proposed and what is implemented, each of the California districts was visited by one of the authors; another author visited the Hartford District. These visits provided information on the actual operation of the programs, particularly with respect to any unique characteristics.

A brief questionnaire, shown in Appendix B, was also developed for administration to participating students. Topics included whether students became more confident and less anxious about test-taking, whether they became more aware of appropriate procedures for test-taking, and whether they were likely to take the PSAT/NMSQT and SAT in the future. Again, to the extent possible, reactions to the various lessons in the kit were solicited.

Results

Site Visits

The site visits helped the authors identify ways the kit was used.

At Hartford, discussions with counselors, program coordinators, and teachers revealed a number of interesting facts about the program and the school district. For example, the district includes three high schools that differ in the degree of their academic orientation. As a rule, relatively few students in the Hartford School District enroll in four-year colleges and, according to school officials, many of these are first-generation college students. A majority of students, even the most academically able, were described as being more job-oriented than academics-oriented. As one counselor put it, "the SAT is foreign to this environment; it's a suburban type thing." Relatively few students in the district take the SAT, and average test scores are relatively low (in the mid 300s on each section of the test).

The district has a high proportion of students whose first language is not English. It was estimated by one principal that 50 to 70% of his students are not native speakers of English. Many of these students are bilingual and most are Hispanic, but there is also a significant number of students from Southeast Asia.

The Hartford school board has made preparation for the SAT a priority. The kit is used in one of several test-preparation programs in the district; that program was described as the most significant one. The program using the kit involves small groups of ten to fifteen students who participate in a one-semester, eighteen-week course. Sessions run for forty-five minutes each day. Nine weeks are devoted to SAT verbal preparation and nine weeks to mathematics preparation. Most students take the course on a pass/fail basis, for which they receive half a credit toward graduation. The course is open to all students who express interest in college. The kit, along with other College Board-provided materials such as *10 SATs*, is the major resource. One teacher described the kit as being so "self-contained" that a teacher isn't necessary. Approximately forty-four students in the three district high schools had taken the course during the first semester of the 1986–87 academic year. School staff administered a questionnaire to students who had participated in the program. According to the program coordinators, students said that the course was valuable in helping them gain familiarity with test procedures. As one staff member commented, "The kids are firm believers that it's helping."

The California districts selected represent quite different contexts with respect to distinguishing characteristics of the school and the community, structure and focus of the programs in which the kit was used, and ways the kit was used. The Long Beach Unified School District program, for instance, was conducted at a high school in a predominantly blue-collar section of the city. According to the proposal for Tanner funding, students at this high school are generally from low-income families. Parents typically have no more than a high school education and "single-parent households are a way of life." A plurality of students are white (41%), but there are significant percentages of black (28%), Hispanic (16%), and Asian/Filipino (14%) students. Few students (5 to 6%, with an even lower percentage minorities) go on to four-year colleges, and very few students take the SAT.

The Long Beach program concentrated primarily on 9th and 10th graders, but other college preparatory activities were planned at the 11th- and 12th-grade levels. Some 260 9th and 10th graders participated in a wide variety of college preparatory activities during the 1986–87 academic year, including a workshop on study skills, advice on the selection of college preparatory courses, discussions of career aspirations and career choices, visits to a college campus, and review of topics covered on the PSAT/NMSQT.

Gilroy High School is located in a rural area south of San Jose. As described in its Tanner proposal, the community has two distinct populations with quite different needs: One is composed of the newly arrived, high-tech families supported by the Silicon Valley. The other is made up of the families employed in agriculture. Hispanic students represent about 40% of the 2,000-plus student population.

A major component of Gilroy's effort to increase the number of college-bound students is a greater emphasis on counseling. This has entailed creation of a counseling position to enable identification of academically promising Hispanic students. In an effort to encourage SAT test-taking, the high school has been made a testing center; students no longer need to travel twenty-five to thirty miles to take the test. Previously, only about 20% of Gilroy students took the SAT.

At Gilroy proposed project activities for the first year involved identifying promising 9th- and 10th-grade Hispanic students on the basis of scores on the Comprehensive Test of Basic Skills. Field trips were scheduled to campuses so students could learn about college systems and admissions requirements. Students were encouraged to take the PSAT/NMSQT, and the SAT preparation course was offered to all students. Parents were offered courses about various aspects of college admissions, and teachers were trained in understanding the SAT.

The San Diego County District operated its college preparatory program at Clairemont High School, which has a minority student enrollment of 52%. According to the district's Tanner's proposal, 43% of students are enrolled in English as a second language, bilingual, or special education programs. Nonetheless, 55% of students enroll in college (25% in four-year institutions).

The program at Clairemont has been in operation for five years, and has been cited by the National Council of Teachers of English for its effectiveness. One emphasis is frequent, repeated taking of the SAT. About a third of the full-year course is devoted to test preparation, which includes familiarizing students with the test as well as instruction directed at increasing reading speed and comprehension, among other aspects. By the time students complete their senior year, they have received the equivalent of a full year of preparation, having been in the program for a total of four years.

The San Diego project is very comprehensive in that it includes aspects for teachers, students, and parents. For example, students receive instruction in college-entry-level reading, writing, mathematics, and science in programs developed by area college professors; regular sessions for teachers are conducted to develop learning environments appropriate for culturally diverse students; college tutors are available; and the role of parents is specified in formal "contracts" with the program. Thus, the kit plays a somewhat less important role here than in other settings.

The project in Fresno is an effort by a consortium of four rural school districts in Fresno County, headed by one of the districts—the Central Unified School District. Two of the high schools in this district provided data for the study. In one school, the majority of students are White, but about a third are Hispanic and small percentages are Black (3%) or Asian (3%). Typically, fewer than 25% of students take the SAT. In a recent senior class of 175, only six students enrolled at four-year postsecondary schools. The other district school that provided data has had its college-bound population quadruple over the past four years. Still, only about 16% of its students pursue postsecondary study. The percentage of students who take college admission tests is proportionately low.

The program at these schools employs one full-time staff member, who rotates among the five participating schools. Ninth- and 10th-grade students meet for fifty minutes once a week to discuss various test-taking strategies. English and mathematics teachers are provided with test-preparation materials for use during their classes. In addition to the kit, *10 SATs, TestSense,* and materials developed by a test preparation consultant are used, among others. Most of the students in the two schools that participated in our study are Hispanic, 89% in one and 82% in the other.

Evaluations by Counselors and Teachers

As explained earlier, eight staff members who used the kit in test-preparation programs responded to our request for information. Five of the respondents perceived the kit to be "the single most important component" in their school's test-preparation program; two others viewed it as "one of several important components"; and one saw it as only "a minor component." Seven of eight found it "very easy" to use and the other found it "somewhat easy" to use. For six of the eight respondents, the kit fit "very well" into the program, and the other two rated it as fitting in "somewhat well." All eight found that the kit was flexible.

Counselors and teachers agreed nearly unanimously that the kit was very helpful in teaching students to follow test directions, gain an overview of test content and format, and guess wisely. All who used it rated the components dealing with the verbal items as "very helpful." Three of four instructors who taught the mathematics components rated those sections as "very helpful," and one teacher rated them as "somewhat helpful." Other areas were rated slightly less positively, although each was considered, on average, to be between "very helpful" and "somewhat helpful." These components covered how to prepare physically and mentally for a test, budgeting time, handling test anxiety, and understanding areas of strength and weakness.

Almost all staff members seemed to perceive the practice tests as the most useful component of the kit, followed by the review of math concepts. The material on cognates and test anxiety and the filmstrip/cassette frequently were not used and received mixed ratings. Instruction on filling in the answer sheet was found to be "very useful" by some but "not useful" by others, probably because many students knew this material already. In terms of increasing students' confidence to try the test, five of the seven staff members who responded to this question believed that the kit led to "a moderate increase in the number of students" who would take the test, and two believed that the increase was "substantial."

Three staff members responded to the open-ended section on how to improve the kit. Their suggestions included: expanding the guessing strategy section; adding more practice handouts for each section (which would facilitate measuring student gains); grouping mathematics items according to the kind and level of mathematics involved (e.g., arithmetic, algebra 1, geometry 2); and possibly incorporating additional items in supplementary material so the basic kit would not be bulky. Most indicated that nothing should be deleted; rather, kit users should be free to decide what to use.

One individual explained that "the problem with the cognate section is that most of our Hispanics can't *read* Spanish. I wouldn't take it out, but it is of limited use." Another commented: "For most of our students taking this course, I could spend the *entire* time just reviewing [math concepts]. But then they get bored because they say they've 'had' this already . . . I've found that most students want to get right to the test as soon as the course begins. I've tried that and, *after* the test, have gone back to the kit." One mentioned that: "It was a good program. It was easy for the students to use and gave them a good view of the test." Another said: "I feel the kit is useful for all students—not just the Hispanic youngster. The kit is nicely put together. It has been a lifesaver."

Evaluations by Students

Description of Student Sample. Tables 1 and 2 list the grade level, sex, race/ethnicity, and language background of the 127 students responding to the questionnaire. The greatest number of respondents were from California. Unfortunately, only four participants from Hartford responded to the questionnaire. These students were retained in the sample, despite their small number, because they were the only Puerto Rican students in the study.

The respondents were mostly 9th and 10th graders. Two-thirds of them were female. Hispanic students, predominantly Mexican-American, constituted more than half the sample. The non-Hispanic White and Asian subsamples were the second and third largest groups. There were also nine Black and three Native American students. The 127 respondents represented about 15% of the approximately 800 students who participated in the programs.

Sixty-three percent of the respondents indicated that they had a background in Spanish, but only one student said that a language other than English was his or her best language. Cross-tabulation of the two language questions for Spanish-background students revealed that 72% said English was their best language, 28% answered that they could communicate well in both languages, and none responded that Spanish was their best language. (The individual whose best language was not English was therefore most likely Asian American.)

Increase in the Number of Students Planning to Take the PSAT/NMSQT. The main purposes of the evaluation were to determine whether students became more confident and less anxious about test-taking after experience with the test-familiarization kit, and whether this encouraged them to go on to take the PSAT/NMSQT or SAT. Three questions in the student questionnaire addressed these issues.

Table 1
Breakdown of Sample by Grade and Gender

		School*						
	(N)	1 (9)	2 (11)	3 (28)	4 (35)	5 (40)	6 (4)	Total (127)
Grade
Ninth	N	4	9	—	3	1	—	17
	%	44	82	—	9	2	—	13
Tenth	N	5	2	15	18	39	—	79
	%	56	18	56	51	98	—	63
Eleventh	N	—	—	12	12	—	4	28
	%	—	—	44	34	—	100	22
Twelfth	N	—	—	—	2	—	—	2
	%	—	—	—	6	—	—	2
No Response	—	—	—	1	—	—	—	1
Sex
Male	N	3	6	9	12	12	—	42
	%	33	55	32	34	30	—	33
Female	N	6	5	19	23	28	4	85
	%	67	45	68	66	70	100	67

Note: Percentages may not total 100 percent because of rounding.

*School Key:
1—Central High School, Fresno, California
2—Kerman High School, Fresno, California
3—Gilroy High School, Gilroy, California
4—Clairemont High School, San Diego, California
5—Jordan High School, Long Beach, California
6—Hartford High School, Hartford, Connecticut

Questionnaire Item 6 asked how helpful the program was in helping students learn how to handle their nervousness. The average rating for this item ranged from 1.50 (Jordan High School, Long Beach) to 2.09 (for Kerman High School, Fresno) with an overall mean of 1.80, which places this item between "very helpful" (value of one) and "somewhat helpful" (value of two). Thus, most students believed that they were better able to cope with their anxieties about test-taking after the course. The rating might have been even more favorable if the unit on test anxiety had been used more frequently by instructors.

Students also were asked the following questions: "Do you think you will take the PSAT/NMSQT next year?" and "If you had *not* participated in the test preparation program at your school this year, do you think you would have taken the PSAT/NMSQT?" The cross-tabulated responses to these two questions are shown in Table 3.

Table 2
Breakdown of Sample by Race/Ethnicity and Language Background

		School*						
		1	2	3	4	5	6	Total
	(N)	(9)	(11)	(28)	(35)	(40)	(4)	(127)
Race/Ethnicity								
Mexican American	N	3	9	22	15	1	—	50
	%	33	82	81	43	3	—	39
Puerto Rican	N	—	—	—	—	—	4	4
	T	—	—	—	—	—	100	3
Other Hispanic	N	2	1	4	4	1	—	12
	%	22	9	15	11	3	—	9
Subtotal Hispanic	N	5	10	26	19	2	4	66
	%	56	91	96	54	5	100	52
Non-Hispanic White	N	4	1	1	7	20	—	33
	%	44	9	4	20	50	—	26
Black	N	—	—	—	3	6	—	9
	%	—	—	—	9	15	—	7
Asian American	N	—	—	—	6	9	—	15
	%	—	—	—	17	23	—	12
Native American	N	—	—	—	—	3	—	3
	%	—	—	—	—	8	—	2

We found that of 118 students who answered both questions, 101 students (86%) indicated that they would "probably" or "definitely" take the PSAT/NMSQT, as compared to sixty-eight (58%) who said they would have taken it even if they had not participated. Thus, there was a net increase of thirty-three (28%) in the number of students planning to take the PSAT/NMSQT after exposure to the kit and to other test-preparation activities.

Naturally, these increases came mostly from students who were uncertain initially about taking the test, or from those previously unlikely to take the test. The cross-tabulated responses to the two questions show that, of the twenty-three who were uncertain about taking the test before having experience with the kit, twenty (87%) answered that they would definitely or probably take the test, whereas only two (9%) remained uncertain, and one (4%) would definitely not take the test. Of the twenty-seven who indicated that they would "probably not" or "definitely not" have taken the test before experience with the kit, eighteen (67%) answered that they would "probably" or "definitely" take the test, five (19%) were "uncertain," and four (15%) indicated that they would "definitely not" take the test. Overall, exactly half of the 118 students changed to a more confident, positive outlook toward taking the test (i.e., their responses are in the cells above the diagonal of the table) whereas only ten (8%) changed to a more

Table 2 Continued
Breakdown of Sample by Race/Ethnicity and Language Background

		School*						Total
		1	2	3	4	5	6	
	(N)	(9)	(11)	(28)	(35)	(40)	(4)	(127)
Language Spoken Other than English								
None	N	4	2	3	4	22	—	35
	%	44	18	11	11	55	—	28
Spanish	N	5	9	23	25	14	4	80
	%	56	82	85	71	35	100	63
Other	N	—	—	1	6	4	—	11
	%	—	—	4	17	10	—	9
No Response	N	—	—	1	—	—	—	1
Language Dominance								
Communicate well only in English	N	6	3	7	3	25	—	44
	%	67	27	26	9	64	—	35
English best but can communicate in other language	N	3	8	15	17	9	3	55
	%	33	73	56	49	23	75	44
Both languages equal	N	—	—	5	14	5	1	25
	%	—	—	19	40	13	25	20
Other language best	N	—	—	—	1	—	—	1
	%	—	—	—	3	—	—	1
No Response	N	—	—	1	—	1	—	2

Note: Percentages may not total 100 percent because of rounding.

*School Key:
1—Central High School, Fresno, California
2—Kerman High School, Fresno, California
3—Gilroy High School, Gilroy, California
4—Clairemont High School, San Diego, California
5—Jordan High School, Long Beach, California
6—Hartford High School, Hartford, Connecticut

tentative approach to taking the test (cells below the diagonal of the table), and 42% remained the same (diagonal cells). Thus, these results imply that the test-taking kit and other program activities were very successful in increasing students' confidence about taking the PSAT/NMSQT.

How New Was the Information in the Kit? One of our concerns was whether the kit covered new ground for students, or simply repeated material they already knew, particularly in components dealing with general

Table 3
Cross-Tabulation of Likelihood of Taking PSAT/NMSQT before and after Exposure to Test-Preparation Kit

	\multicolumn{6}{c}{Do you think you would have taken the test next year without preparation?}	
Do you think you will take the test next year?	Definitely yes	Probably yes	Uncertain	Probably not	Definitely not	Total	No Response "before"
Definitely yes	35	16	13	8	5	77	5
Probably yes	3	9	7	5	—	24	—
Uncertain	1	—	2	4	1	8	—
Probably not	1	1	—	—	—	2	—
Definitely not	1	1	1	1	3	7	—
Total	41	27	23	18	9	118	
No Response "after"	—	—	—	—	—		4

Note: Table entries indicate the number of students making each pair of responses when asked whether they thought they (a) would take the test next year and (b) *would have* taken the test next year if they had *not* participated in the test-preparation program.

test-taking skills. Chart 1 shows the percentage of students who responded that they already knew the material in the first eleven items of the evaluation instrument. The items are classified into three groups in the chart: general test-taking (Q1–Q9), Spanish cognates (Q10), and mathematics instruction (Q11). (The coding corresponds to the questions in the student questionnaire, Appendix B.) The chart is an inside-out display in which the possible values for ratings (1–3) are shown on the left in intervals of 0.1. The item-identification number (Q1–Q17) is placed in the interval representing the percentage of those who already knew the material corresponding to that item. Like a graph, this chart shows the differences in the percentage of students who were not familiar with the content of the questionnaire items.

Chart 1 shows that, in general, most of the content was new to the great majority of students. Only one item—Q4, evaluating instruction on "how to mark the answer sheet properly"—was familiar to more than 50% of the students before experience with the kit. The percentages of students who already knew the content mentioned in the other items ranged from 2% to 19.5%. These figures indicate that most material was new to most of the group. Some components presented information that was new to more than 95% of the students. These were units covering the purpose of each kind of

Chart 1
Percentage of Total Sample Who Knew Content Areas before Exposure to Kit (Inside-Out Display)

Intervals of % Who Knew Already	General Test-Taking	Math Concepts	Use of Spanish Cognates
0–4.5	Q5, Q8, Q9		
4.6–9.5	Q1, Q2, Q3	Q11	
9.6–14.5	Q7		Q10*
14.6–19.5	Q6		Q10†
19.6–24.5			
24.6–29.5			
29.6–34.5			
34.6–39.5			
39.6–44.5			
44.6–49.5			
49.6–54.5	Q4		
54.6–59.5			
59.6–100.0			

*Total sample.
†Spanish-speaking subsample.

question (Q5), the meaning of test scores (Q8), and ways to approach different questions (Q9). Instruction on the best use of time (Q1), knowing when to guess (Q2), test directions (Q3), and math concepts and symbols (Q11) also was relatively new to more than 90% of the students. Although somewhat more familiar to students, the units on strengths and weaknesses (Q7), how to handle nervousness (Q6), and how to understand Spanish cognates (Q10) also provided information that was new to more than 80% of the students. The content in these units was more familiar to those students who said that they could communicate fairly well in Spanish.

Mean Student Ratings for Content Items. The ratings for each content item were averaged twice, once for the full sample (i.e., including those who already knew the material covered in that item), and again for only those for whom the material was new. These means are presented in Charts 2 and 3 as an inside-out display in which questionnaire identification numbers (Q1–Q17) are placed in intervals corresponding to their mean ratings.

For the complete sample, the responses of students who said that they already knew the item material before exposure to the kit (value of 4) were recoded to a value of 3 ("not helpful"). Chart 2 shows that all items received mean ratings between 1.3 and 2.2 in the total sample, indicating that

Chart 2
Means Ratings by Item for Total Sample (Inside-Out Display)

	Intervals of Mean Ratings	General Test-Taking Skills	Verbal Section	Mathematical Section	Use of Spanish Cognates
Very Helpful	1.0–1.09				
	1.1–1.19				
	1.2–1.29				
	1.3–1.39	Q8, Q9	Q13		
	1.4–1.49	Q2, Q3	Q12		
	1.5–1.59	Q5	Q15	Q16	
	1.6–1.69	Q1, Q7	Q14	Q11, Q17	
	1.7–1.79				
	1.8–1.89				
	1.9–1.99				
Somewhat Helpful	2.0–2.09	Q6			Q10*, Q10†
	2.1–2.19	Q4			
	2.2–2.29				
	2.3–2.39				
	2.4–2.49				
	2.5–2.59				
Not Helpful	3.0				

*Spanish-speaking subsample.
†Total sample

the content covered in the course was either "very helpful" (value of 1) or "somewhat helpful" (value of 2) for most students. The most favorable ratings were found for content covering guessing strategies (Q2), test directions (Q3), meaning of scores (Q8), approaching different kinds of questions (Q9), and how to answer questions on analogies and antonyms (Q12 and Q13). Slightly less favorable ratings were found for instruction on the purpose of test questions (Q5), budgeting time (Q1), knowing one's strengths and weaknesses (Q7), sentence completion (Q14), reading-passage questions (Q15) mathematics questions (Q16, Q17), and mathematics concepts (Q11).

The least favorable mean ratings were found for instruction on handling nervousness (Q6), marking the answer sheet (Q4), and using Spanish cognates (Q10). These content units were more familiar, as shown in the previous chart. When we restricted the evaluation of the Spanish cognates unit to those students with a background in Spanish, we found a nearly identical mean for this group and the total sample (2.168 for the total sample and 2.175 for those who could communicate in Spanish). While the

Chart 3
Mean Ratings of Each Item by Students for Whom the Material Was New (Inside-Out Display)

	Intervals of Mean Ratings	General Test-Taking Skills	Verbal Section	Mathematical Section	Use of Spanish Cognates
Very Helpful	1.0–1.09				
	1.1–1.19				
	1.2–1.29	Q4			
	1.3–1.39	Q2, Q3, Q8, Q9	Q13		
	1.4–1.49	Q1	Q12		
	1.5–1.59	Q5, Q7	Q15	Q11, Q16	
	1.6–1.69		Q14	Q17	
	1.7–1.79				
	1.8–1.89	Q6			
	1.9–1.99				
Somewhat Helpful	2.0–2.09				Q10*, Q10†
	2.1–2.19				
	2.2–2.29				
	2.3–2.39				
	2.4–2.49				
	2.5–2.59				
	2.6–2.69				
	2.7–2.79				
	2.8–2.89				
	2.90–2.99				
Not Helpful	3.0				

*Spanish-speaking subsample.
†Total subsample.

mean ratings for these three areas (nervousness, marking answer sheets, Spanish cognates) were somewhat less favorable than ratings for the other areas, the units nevertheless received a positive endorsement. The mean rating indicated that, on average, these areas were "somewhat helpful" to the students.

When we excluded those who already knew the item material before the course, the mean ratings (Chart 3) became more favorable by 0.1 or 0.2 for most items. Also, the ordering of items was somewhat different. The most notable change was for Q4 (marking the answer sheet). Among the 49% of students who did not know the material beforehand, the average rating for this unit was 1.27 (closest to "very helpful") in contrast to a rating of 2.14 for all students.

Means of Student Ratings by Content Areas. To examine whether there were overall differences in the usefulness of specific content areas, the items in the evaluation questionnaire were grouped into four scales: General Test-Taking Skills (Q1–Q9), Verbal Content (Q12–Q15), Math Content (Q16–Q17, Q11), and total (Q1–Q9, Q11–Q17). Because the scales included different numbers of items, the score on each was divided by the number of items in that scale. To test whether any portion of the kit was rated as more useful than others, a repeated-measures analysis of variance was run on the scale means. This analysis revealed a significant difference among scales. The means for the three scales and the total sample are presented at the bottom of Chart 4. It can be seen that, overall, the most favorable ratings were found for the verbal-content units, with no differences between the mathematics-content and the general test-taking units.

Group Differences in Student Means for Content Areas. We also examined whether there were any statistically significant differences in the evaluation of the kit by various groups. For each of the three scale scores discussed above, analyses of the variance were run to test the differences between males and females, among race/ethnic groups, among different language groups, and among grades. Because of the large number of comparisons that were made, we set the significance level at .01.

We found no significant differences between males and females on any of the scales, but there were three marginally significant differences ($p \leq$ .04) on the General Test-Taking Scale among students of different language backgrounds and grades, and on the mathematics scale among race/ethnic groups and language groups. The means for these scales are also shown in Chart 4.

It appears that students who could communicate equally well in two languages (balanced bilinguals) found the material on general test-taking skills more useful than did the others. Not surprisingly, the 9th graders, who can be expected to have the least experience taking tests, perceived the information on general test-taking skills to be more helpful than did the older students.

As for the mathematics-content units, Asian American students evaluated them as more helpful than did the other students, but the balanced bilinguals found the mathematics units slightly less helpful than did other students.

Free-Response Evaluations. In addition to the structured questions, the questionnaire included a free-response section to allow students to express their opinions about the program and to make suggestions for improvements. Many students indicated that they liked the whole program and saw no need for improvement. Several themes emerged from the specific feedback in reference to the kit itself.

Chart 4
Means (M) and Standard Deviations (SD) of Scales Corresponding to Different Content Areas by Grade Level, Language Background, and Race/Ethnicity

	N	General Test-Taking Scale M	General Test-Taking Scale SD	Verbal Section M	Verbal Section SD	Mathematical Section M	Mathematical Section SD	Total* M	Total* SD
Grade									
Ninth	9–16	1.48	.17	1.48	.31	1.72	.38	1.50	.16
Tenth	75–78	1.63	.38	1.48	.37	1.57	.48	1.58	.33
Eleventh	27–28	1.55	.32	1.45	.41	1.62	.55	1.53	.27
Language Background									
Can communicate well in:									
English only	41–44	1.59	.38	1.42	.38	1.55	.47	1.53	.34
Both, but English better	47–53	1.65	.36	1.48	.38	1.58	.53	1.59	.31
Both languages equally	23–25	1.53	.29	1.56	.33	1.74	.40	1.57	.24
Race/Ethnicity									
Asian American	14–15	1.63	.42	1.40	.31	1.53	.50	1.54	.37
Mexican-American	42–49	1.58	.34	1.55	.38	1.62	.46	1.58	.29
Other Hispanic	12	1.51	.23	1.50	.35	1.58	.36	1.52	.22
Non-Hispanic White	30–33	1.65	.40	1.42	.38	1.58	.53	1.57	.35
Total Sample	114–125	1.61	.37	1.48	.37	1.61	.49	1.57	.32

Note: Only groups having at least ten members are reported separately. All groups are included in the total sample means. N is given as a range since not all respondents answered each question. The scale units are in the same units as the original item ratings. That is, the mean scale score is the average rating for items in that content area. A rating of "1" = "very helpful," "2" = "somewhat helpful," and "3" = "not helpful."

*Excludes ratings for Spanish-language cognates.

The Test Preparation Kit. The most common theme (about sixty-five comments) concerned the advantage students had gained in general test-taking. Most respondents (thirty-nine) commented on the value of exposure to and practice with the test. Others praised units on strategies and approaches to questions (sixteen), eliminating wrong choices and guessing (five), budgeting time (three), and dealing with nervousness (two).

The second most common category of comments concerned preparation for the verbal test (eighteen remarks), which many found useful and interesting. For example, one student at Hartford said, "I really enjoyed the English and grammar that I learned." Many referred to analogies (seven); other comments were fairly evenly distributed among reading passages (three), the general English section and grammar (three), and antonyms and synonyms (two). One student at Clairemont High in San Diego revealed, "before [the program] I didn't know how to tell the difference between [antonyms and synonyms]."

The third most common group of remarks (twelve) referred to the support that the program provided through workshops, the camaraderie of group meetings, and individual attention from instructors. Students at Gilroy High said, "Our adviser was constantly making sure we were on track," and the best part was the "encouragement of taking classes for college."

Eight comments mentioned the self-knowledge students gained with regard to gaps in their background and how to plan their studies for college preparation. For example, one student at Clairemont High said the program was valuable in "reevaluating basic skills and learning what I missed in elementary school." A few students (six) also commented on how valuable the mathematics review had been, especially for geometry and algebra.

In terms of improving the kit, students generally wanted more: more classes over a longer period of time (seventeen comments), more practice tests (four comments), more exercises, more detail on math, more vocabulary and reading, etc. Several thought that the mathematics section could be more varied and entertaining. One suggested having more reading passages but shorter and simpler practice sheets.

Other Program Characteristics. Students also commented on aspects of the programs that went beyond the kit, for example, material on college applications or visits to college campuses. These components were very enthusiastically received. At least eight students mentioned how much they have profited from the information on the application process. One student at Central High in Fresno pointed out that before the program she "didn't even know there [were] college entrance exams." Nine students from Long Beach and nine from Gilroy thought that the best part was the college visits, and seven wanted more college visits incorporated into the program.

Discussion

In general, staff and students agreed that the test-preparation programs had high-quality materials and provided much new information. Students and staff also agreed that the practice tests were particularly valuable and that more of them should be included in the kit. Staff members predicted a modest to substantial increase in the number of students taking PSAT/NMSQT. This prediction was corroborated by students' responses. Those who were uncertain beforehand about taking the test became substantially more likely to attempt the test. For the total sample, the net increase in the likelihood of taking the test was modest (28%) only because the majority of students (58%) were already planning to take it.

Teachers and counselors placed more emphasis on the helpfulness of the mathematics section than did students; the latter seemed to be more enthusiastic about the verbal content. All content units were rated favorably, but those with means closest to "somewhat helpful" (2) rather than "very helpful" (1) were often those components that instructors reported were used least, such as the material on handling nervousness. It is not clear whether these materials were sometimes omitted because they were not as good as other units, or whether they were rated less favorably simply because they weren't covered.

One teacher's comments shed light on why instruction on Spanish cognates was not received more favorably. Apparently, when students reported that they communicated well in Spanish, they were often referring to oral, not written, communication. According to the teacher, many students could not read Spanish well. Perhaps the cognates unit will be most helpful for recent immigrants and for students residing in Puerto Rico who have had more formal schooling in Spanish.

The most salient recommendation from students was to extend the program, both in terms of length and materials. It is apparent from their comments that many students viewed the course as an opportunity to improve their problem-solving strategies and other skills, and not just as a chance to gain test experience. Apparently, for the first time, many students became aware of gaps in their schooling; they frequently remarked on the need for more time for remediation. Hence, instituting programs such a these as early as possible in high school might be a practical way of demonstrating to students their need for more college preparatory courses. Furthermore, the students' enthusiasm for both group and tutorial support suggests that many would probably have had difficulty with independent study.

Finally, it is necessary to repeat what this study could not, and was not intended to, accomplish. This study was not a rigorous formal evaluation of the kit. The kit was already being used when the evaluation commenced, and targeted districts offered a wide variety of other activities designed to improve students' facility with test-taking and interest in college admission. Thus, it is not possible to attribute any effects directly to the introduction of the kit. Results, however, do suggest a positive effect.

Summary and Conclusions

A kit containing materials intended to familiarize Hispanic students with the PSAT/NMSQT was developed by the College Board, the ETS, and the Hispanic Higher Education Coalition.* This report provides some data on the extent to which the kit's objectives were achieved at some of the sites in which it has been used. Reactions to the kit were obtained from both staff and students. A number of these comments should have value in planning the final revision and distribution of the kit.

The schools chosen for study were diverse, as were their approaches to test preparation. This diversity was useful in assessing one of the kit's objectives—sufficient flexibility for use in various instructional settings, with many different approaches, schedules, and instructors. There was every indication that the kit is indeed usable in diverse settings.

The material in the kit was regarded as "new" by a large majority of responding students. This finding would seem to reinforce the original concept and purpose of the kit, which was based on the assumption that Hispanic students may not be as familiar as other students with standardized tests. This lack was thought to negatively affect Hispanic students' decisions to take college admissions tests.

The results of this evaluation show that, in conjunction with other test-preparation activities, the test-familiarization kit elicited an extremely positive response from students and staff members. Average student ratings for seventeen content objectives fell closest to "very helpful" for six items, about halfway between "very helpful" and "somewhat helpful" for eight items, and closest to "somewhat helpful" for three items. The material covered, with the exception of instruction on how to mark the answer sheet, was novel to most students. (About half the students reported that they already knew how to mark the answers.) However, those students who did not know how to mark the answer sheet beforehand rated the instruction on answer sheets very favorably.

Overall, the instruction on the verbal section of the test, particularly the analogies and antonym questions, was rated as the most helpful by students. Some of the units on general test-taking skills—the topics covering guessing strategies, meaning of test scores, and approaches to different question types—were also very favorably received. Although all units on average were perceived as at least "somewhat helpful," instruction on coping with nervousness and using Spanish cognates was rated less favorably than was the other instruction. This was probably because the former was

---

*The kit is currently titled *TestSkills: For Teachers of Hispanic Students* and is available from ETS, Box 6721, Princeton, N.J. 08541-6721.

omitted by some instructors and, in the latter case, few students were proficient in reading Spanish.

Although the evidence is limited to open-ended remarks made by some students, certain responses support the appropriateness of the instructional methodology on which the kit is based. There were indications that students often were able to evaluate their own skills and, as a result, to seek help in areas in which they were deficient. The students found the instructional methodology, i.e., group instruction and peer support, effective.

Finally, there is very clear evidence that the kit seems to meet its most important objective, i.e., increasing the likelihood of students taking the PSAT/NMSQT. Eighty-seven percent of students who were previously uncertain about taking the test indicated that they would "probably" or "definitely" take the PSAT/NMSQT after the course. Overall, there was a net increase of 28% (from 58 to 86%) in the number of students who were "probably" or "definitely" planning to take the PSAT/NMSQT. Of the 118 responding students, 50% had a more positive outlook, 42% remained the same, and only 10% became more tentative about taking the PSAT/NMSQT after using the kit material.

There is relatively strong evidence that programs involving the use of the test-familiarization kit can successfully encourage disadvantaged students to take the PSAT/NMSQT. In turn, more of these students may enter the higher-education pipeline. Students' comments suggested that not only their test-taking but also their problem-solving and language skills improved after use of the kit materials, which may lead to real improvement in their college preparedness. Often, after exposure to the kit, students were encouraged to pursue further study and get help in areas where they were academically weak. Hence, the kit can serve as a catalyst in college-preparation courses to expand the pool of college applicants drawn from groups that have traditionally been underrepresented in higher education. College administrators and secondary school counselors seem to have another tool to use (e.g., in high school courses or precollege programs) in recruiting and preparing students for higher education. Based on this evaluation, the test-preparation kit may be useful not just for Hispanic students, but for all students.

Notes

Introduction. Advances in Assessment and the Potential for Increasing the Number of Hispanics in Higher Education

1. The early history of the College Entrance Examination Board is intertwined with the development of mental tests. In fact, the first SAT, 1926, was developed by a commission headed by Carl Campbell Brigham who had published *A Study of American Intelligence* two years earlier and who helped develop the Army Alpha test that was administered to World War I recruits. The founding commission explicitly related the SAT to intelligence tests. For a review of the early history of the College Board, the ETS, and the development of the SAT, see Crouse and Trusheim (1988, chapter 2), Fuess (1950), Valentine (1987), College Entrance Examination Board (1926), and Schudson (1972). For an overview of the history of intelligence tests and their impact, mostly negative, on U.S. Hispanics see A. Padilla (1979) and Garciá, (1977).

The early history of mental and educational testing, including the establishment of the College Entrance Examination Board also is associated with the eugenics movement and with Social Darwinism, particularly from the turn of the century through the post World War I period, but probably not more so than institutions such as Columbia, Harvard, Princeton, Yale, and other colleges or founding members of the College Board including Nicholas Murray Butler, president of Columbia; and Charles Eliot, president of Harvard. Both the College Board and the ETS, and most everybody else related to education, have long since overcome and overturned those earlier influences. For a review of this period, which generates considerable controversy among researchers, see Gould (1981), Karier (1975), Kamin (1974), Davis (1983), Jensen (1982), Samelson (1982), and Snyderman and Herrnstein, (1983).

2. For a review of the college admission situation from the turn of the century through the post-World War II period see Levine (1986, chapter 7), Synnott (1979), Wechsler (1977), McKown (1925), and Horowitz (1987). The history of standardized testing shows strange turns of events. For example, Columbia president Nicholas Murray Butler, one of the people who helped found the College Board, favored using and in fact arranged for the administration of intelligence tests such as the Thorndike Test for Mental Alertnness as an admissions test because he was alarmed

at the changes in the Columbia student body that he perceived. Butler found the 1917–18 freshmen class "depressing in the extreme" because it was made up of too few "boys of old American stock" and too many of the foreign born and children of immigrants. The tests were supposed to address this problem because he and some of the Social Darwinists believed that their tests would show that people of Nordic stock would outperform stock from the Alpine (e.g., Slavic) or Mediterranean races. For Butler's purposes the tests countered what his institution could have achieved by quotas; but these were politically unacceptable in a university set in the the great immigrant metropolis of New York City and which had in 1908 permitted part of Columbia's entrance requirements to be met by New York State Board of Regents' certified work in secondary school.

3. I need to note that some of what I have witnessed with respect to the negative impact of subjective appraisals can and does happen as a result of taking tests. James Crouse has summarized how aspirations may be shaped by testing that begins early in the school career, particularly with mental tests.

> High-scoring individuals are treated differently than lower-scoring individuals especially in school. Adolescents with high scores are more likely to be in a college curriculum, more likely to receive high grades, more likely to report that their parents want them to attend college, more likely to say that their friends plan to attend college, more likely to discuss college with teachers, and more likely to have ambitious educational and occupational plans. (Crouse, 1979, 106)

During the truth-in-testing movement, consumer forces, particularly Ralph Nader and his associates, presented a number of poignant examples of the test gone awry in one way or another and of the consequent debilitating effect on self-image and academic and career aspirations of test-takers who had earned unacceptable test scores in their minds and in the minds of admissions decision makers. The HHEC thoroughly supported the test reform movement at the time which led to some correction in what testmakers were claiming for their products. However, there is no substitute for vigilance; precisely because the effects of evaluation can be so profound, we constantly need to be on guard against extravagant, overblown, or pseudo-scientific claims for what test results document. Currently, the claims for the SAT appear to be comfortably modest; the measurement of developed, learned academic abilities that help predict first-year college freshman grades, particularly when used in tandem with other predictors and information such as high school grade point average, class rank, references, and relevant information about personal qualities, skills, and talents. Nevertheless, institutions continue to misuse tests, for example using cutoff scores and setting minimum scores for athletic eligibility.

4. The written acknowledgment that George Hanford made for this important event is worth highlighting:

> The question of whether the College Board should publish aggregated data according to the racial/ethnic characteristics of the students who participate in its programs has been a controversial one since we began collecting such data. Briefly,

the honest difference of opinion has been between those who fear that publication of these data will serve to convey a misperception of minority students' ability, and those who believe that exposure of the data to public scrutiny will better minority interests by demonstrating the need for (and thus lead to) more affirmative action with respect to access to higher education. We have been encouraged toward the latter position in recent years, first, by requests for the data by minority researchers in the aftermath of the *Bakke* decision and, second, by the charge of secrecy leveled against test sponsors by proponents of legislation to regulate testing.

We concluded that in such circumstances the College Board, as a matter of principle, should not impose restraints on access to generalized program data because of our own concept of public interest. We did so knowing that the question continues to be controversial, and we did so knowing that it is possible for any data to be irresponsibly or incorrectly used and that such misuse is an inevitable risk. Nevertheless, we are convinced that the data, to the clear advantage of minority youth, will serve to illuminate the extent and nature of the educational deficit this nation must overcome. (Hanford, 1982, iii)

5. Crouse and Trusheim (1988, chapter 1) argue that the ETS and the College Board continue to be unresponsive and secretive. Their book, which has emerged in part from the consumer movement (especially Nairn, 1980), is substantive and not to be taken lightly. However, I don't view its judgment that ETS functions in a monolithic way—it uses a 1973 quote about the 'bunker mentality (p.13)—is particularly accurate for the current corporate posture and it is absurdly untrue for the researchers at the ETS, who, in my experience, have considerable latitude and discretion in conceptualizing and pursuing their work, similar to professors at a university. ETS researchers also seem to have no more loyalty—expected, imposed or self-imposed—to their institution that would be the case of a professor.

Crouse and Trusheim's *The Case Against the SAT* is a curious book. Every few years over the past twenty someone comes along and takes a muckraking swipe at the testmaking industry, usually with special focus on the ETS; and that is probably to be expected given the importance and gravity of nationally administered admissions tests. Much more scholarly and objective than Nairn (1980) or Owen (1985), Crouse and Trusheim nevertheless share the penchant for the wide brush. It does much more that make a case against the SAT; it indicts the ETS and the College Board rather severely. In one interesting chapter, the book also takes a concerted stand against the SAT in part because it claims it has an adverse impact on Black applicants. Unfortunately, except one for one quaint footnote (196, n. 6) which acknowledges its lack of coverage, the book virtually is devoid of any attention to U.S. Hispanic issues. Therefore it misses a lot: the HHEC's suggestion of utilizing the within ethnic score, the current work in differential item functioning, the research of Mestre and the work of Durań (1983), and the relevant papers in Olivas (1986). This is doubly unfortunate because the chapter on Black applicants describes as one option with respect to using the SAT for Blacks, that colleges would have to reduce admissions standards to permit Blacks to attend. The point that the Hispanic community makes, contrary to reducing standards, is that test inaccuracy as documented by Durań and Mestre among others, can be reduced for minorities through a variety of ways including college admission use of the within ethnic score, special cautions about less predictive accuracy of high school grade point averages and test scores for Hispanics and others, and the use of a fuller arsenal of important supplemental information. These kinds of issues are not substantively engaged in by Crouse and Trusheim although they do get close at one point early on: "With blacks . . . colleges must decide whether to develop a single prediction equation (based on the high school record and the SAT) for blacks and whites combined, or whether to treat blacks and whites as separate groups and develop separate prediction equations for each group. . . . This is a critical decision because the choice of a combined or separate equation can lead to different predicted grades for a black student." (8).

Crouse and Trusheim go on to say that when they wrote to the ETS about whether colleges should treat Blacks differently from Whites when predicting freshman grades, and, if so, how they should do it, the response from the ETS was that it had no established position on the issue. I am confident that the ETS's response was not because, as Crouse and Trusheim would have it, that it has failed to expand the public's understanding of SAT use and equal opportunity. Contrary to their view that ETS is monolithic in its approach, there is a variety of viewpoints about these issues at the ETS and especially among ETS researchers. And here I need to press my point: Crouse and Trusheim point specifically to an article by Winton Manning and Rex Jackson (1984, former vice president and vice president at ETS, respectively) as an example of how "ETS dismisses its critics." (p. 11) This is a remarkably poor example inasmuch as the material they cite did not appear in an ETS publication; the claim that it somehow represents an official ETS position is singularly far-fetched. Even more unfair, however is the singling out of Winton Manning as one who dismissed critics. The Hispanic community has greatly appreciated the work of this senior research scientist and former senior vice president (in fact, Duran's 1983 study is dedicated to him). Manning may be a consumate ETSer but it is well known that he is a person of highly independent options who has made important suggestions for establishing the kinds of admissions procedures that would lead to greater access by minorities (Manning, 1977, 1979, 1984, 1989; Manning and Jackson, 1984). In fact, Manning currently has underway a project with Michael S. Hendryx and Julie Noble of the American College Testing Program (a competitor of ETS!) and Wanda E. Ward at the University of Oklahoma which investigates the validity of a newly developed measurement for identifying talented minority college students called the "Measure of Academic Talent" (MAT). The MAT takes into consideration the effect that low socioeconomic status (SES) and minority group status might have on the SAT by calculating the difference between students' actual SAT (composite) score and the SAT score predicted on the basis their of SES and minority status. However, Durań (1983) is a good refuting example since his research was conducted at the ETS and published by the College Board. If Crouse and Trusheim had reviewed Durań's 1983 study they would have seen Durań's conclusions and Olivas' vigorous remarks in the foreword as examples of what both the ETS and the College Board, in support of both scientific inquiry and criticism of uncritical use of admissions tests, are willing to underwrite and publish.

6. Durań's conclusions were prefigured by ETS research scientist Breland (1979), but the latter's results did not get nearly the play that Durań's did: a good example of what can be achieved by Hispanic researchers in positions of influence. It must also be noted that Durań's study goes much deeper into the Hispanic circumstances. Breland's conclusions about the predictability of the high school record and standardized tests were that for Black populations the data did not suggest any consistent superiority of high school record over standardized tests as a predictor of college performance. Also, while in his judgment the amount of data available for Mexican American/Chicano samples was not sufficient for any generalizations about predictive correlations, on the average the magnitude of those correlations were lower and the correlations for Black samples tended to be slightly lower than those for Anglo samples.

7. See Mathews (1988, 299ff.) for details on additional schools, school districts, and entire states including Utah, Alabama, Florida, Kentucky, Louisiana, and South Carolina, that have been inspired to provide special support for the AP programs.

Chapter 5. "Factors Related" to Differential Item Functioning.

1. The term "casual" false cognate was suggested by Dr. Gary Keller in review of an earlier draft of the chapter.

Chapter 6. Equating the Scores.

1. The delta index is a transformation of the proportion of the group who answer an item correctly (p+) to a normal deviate (z) and from z to scale with a mean of thirteen and a standard deviation of four by means of the equation, $\Delta - 4z + 13$.

Chapter 7. Competency Testing and Latino Student Access to the Teaching Profession. An Overview of Issues.

1. The term Latino (also popularly referred to as Hispanic) refers to a diverse group of Americans, including people of Mexican, Puerto Rican, Cuban, Spanish, other Central and South American, and other Latino descent. The target Latinos of this chapter are the two principal subgroups who comprise the largest percentages of the total U.S. Latino population—Chicanos (62%) and Puerto Ricans (12%) (Bureau of the Census, 1987).

2. The term teacher tests is a rubric for three types of paper-and pencil teacher competency tests: (a) an admissions test—a basic skills test required as an entry criterion to a teacher education program; (b) a certification test—a basic skills test

and/or professional knowledge test and/or a subject matter test required as a condition for obtaining an initial teaching credential by the state; (c) a recertification test—a basic skills test required of current teachers. For a case in point, refer to Nava (1985) to see how these three types of teacher tests are expressed in Texas. In the present chapter, our focus will be on admissions and certification tests.

3. Jackson also refers to these dimensions of teacher-student dissimilarity: age, sex, and handicap.

4. The empirical evidence on whether the academic performance of Latino elementary or secondary students is enhanced by having Latino teachers, compared to White teachers, is basically nonexistent. The closest (and only investigation) we found was a study by Vierra (1984). This investigation sought to compare the relationship between third- and fourth-grade Chicano children's reading gain scores. At each grade level, the children were taught either by an Anglo or Hispanic teacher. The results supported the null hypothesis, indicating that there was neither an academic advantage nor disadvantage to matching Chicano students with Chicano teachers. Methodologically, there were problems in this study: a high subject attrition, a blanket definition of Chicano ethnicity (i.e., likelihood that the heterogeneity of the Chicano subjects was masked), and lack of control of the Chicano teachers' backgrounds (e.g., teaching experience). The author, after acknowledging she had glossed over a number of potentially important variables, concludes: "Matching student and teacher ethnicity seems to be ineffective when ethnicity is broadly defined, but it is *still plausible* [italics added] that Hispanic children's achievement is enhanced when their teachers in fact have *backgrounds similar* [italics added] to those of the students and/or self-identity with their students' ethnicity, for example" (p. 288–89).

5. This conclusion, though reasonable, needs to be tempered with caution. There indeed appears to be a growing interest in multicultural education among teachers, textbook publishers, and researchers, but it is not known to what degree this is occurring. Furthermore, there is some evidence to the contrary. For example, King and Ladson-Billings (1988) report that meeting the curricula needs of students from culturally diverse backgrounds is not a priority in most schools in some areas of California. Mahan and Boyle (1981) report in their twenty-five-state survey that a very large percentage of preservice teachers did not desire multicultural education training (as deemed by student teacher directors).

6. Gonzalez' target population is Chicano. Yet, generalizations to Puerto Rican students appear tenable.

7. Olsen's study involved structured in-depth interviews of 360 immigrant students from thirty-three California communities. The major immigrant groups were Mexican (45%), Southeast Asian (29%), Central American (10%), Filipino (10%), and other Asian (15%).

8. Olsen (1986) reports that from two-thirds to three-fourths of students in bilingual education programs in the country are Latino. Bilingual education (in 1983) had the largest proportion of teacher shortages of any field in education. Further-

more, because of the severe shortage, 12% of all teachers in bilingual programs were uncertified. From these several points, one could argue, as does Olsen, that the quality of education to Latinos suffers.

On a related point, there has been a longstanding debate over the question, "Does bilingual education work?" The controversy races onward, ranging from those who claim the case for bilingual education is very weak (e.g., Baker, 1987; Baker and deKanter, 1981, 1983) to those who contend that the available research evidence, as a whole, shows positive effects for bilingual education (e.g., Willig, 1985, 1987). Although the debate continues over the effectiveness of bilingual education, the strong consensus is that existing research on bilingual education favors the conclusion that student achievement is enhanced (Secada, 1987). Furthermore, it has been demonstrated that in the research paradigm of "school effectiveness," accomplished bilingual education programs within effective schools can be identified, described, and analyzed (Carter and Chatfield, 1986). The major consequence for Latino students is that such programs can and do produce high levels of academic performance.

9. Smith (1985) also refers to a reduction in the numbers of minority curriculum supervisors and counselors. Our concern here, however, is with the reduced numbers of principals and superintendents, leaders that are in key administrative positions who can improve the educational lot for Latino and other minority students.

10. Mingle (1987), drawing from the 1985 U.S. Bureau of Labor Statistics data base, reports that nationally Latinos comprised 2.6% of "educational administrators." This information is not particularly useful in the present discussion because of the aggregated nature of such category.

11. Although the available literature does not identify ethnicity of the principals, we assume that in most cases minority principals are assigned to high-density minority schools. Our argument is that given the importance of the principalship coupled with the shared identity notion, minority principals can be very influential in promoting school effectiveness in minority schools.

12. For this section, the term "Hispanic" is used at times to be consistent with terminology described in the various demographic reports.

13. The year 2080 will also bring forth another major demographic shift: It is projected that the White population will become the *minority* (less than 50%) population, *nationally* (Cannon, 1986).

14. Refers to 18–24 year-old high school graduates in the civilian population enrolled in colleges.

15. Eissenberg and Rudner (1988) advise readers to interpret these numbers with caution, as the testing programs and statistical reporting systems vary widely from state to state. Yet, while pass rates vary as a function of definition, the numbers are closely related, usually within 10% of each other, thus allowing the use of the mean as a rough indicator.

Chapter 8. Research Directions and Practical Strategies in Teacher Testing and Assessment: Implications for Improving Latino Access to Teaching.

1. *Standards* refers to *Standards for Educational and Psychological Testing*. a joint 1985 publication by the American Educational Research Association, the American Psychological Association, and the National Council on Measurement in Education. For reference, see reference list under "American Educational Research Association."

2. For the reader who merely wishes a general, clearly written overview that offers assistance in helping select and apply a method for choosing the cut score on tests in general, we recommend the manual by Livingston and Zieky (1982). For readers interested more in theory of standard setting methods as well as research findings, consult the bibliography listed in Livingston and Zieky. Other pertinent references along the lines of theory, issues, and research findings are: Berk (1986), Cross (1985), Cross, Impara, Frary, and Jaeger (1984), Glass (1978), Roth (1983, 1986), Shepard (1984), and van der Linden (1984).

3. In our discussion of teacher tests, a false positive and false negative error are defined as: "A false positive occurs when an examinee with insufficient skill to perform adequately in the classroom earns a passing score, and a false negative occurs when an adequately skilled examinee fails the examination" (Haertel, 1988b, 9).

4. Suffice it to say that Haertel does believe there are more defensible ways to develop standard-setting methods. In brief, his ideas center around mounting empirical investigations examining the relation between test performance and instructional activities. Also, see Haertel (1985) for further discussion of more defensible standard setting methods.

5. A case in point as to how political considerations play powerful roles in the determination of cut scores on teacher tests is illustrated by Peterson (1984) of the Educational Testing Service (ETS). Presenting a prepared talk to the California Council on the Education of teachers, Peterson shared this:

> The experience with cut scores for CBEST has also been interesting, and rather lucky. Working together, the State Department of Education and ETS first assembled data to permit determination of passing scores for the three parts of the test, following a procedure that we (ETS) have found to be legally defensible. State Department staff then forwarded recommended cut scores to Superintendent Honig, who had the responsibility for final determination of the passing scores. Also available were data (from earlier field tests) on the proportions of people who would pass at *any* set of cut scores he has chosen. As you know, the Superintendent set the passing score several points higher than were recommended (p. 8).

6. The Bruno and Marcoulides (1985) study is particularly relevant to the present topic because the sample was drawn from an urban state university (in Los Angeles) serving a large ethnic minority student population. The sample of 188 CBEST examinees included 42.6% Black, 11.2% Mexican-American, and 4.8% other Hispanic.

7. The distinction between the "dominant" and "minority" group is not necessarily made on differences between numerical status, but rather on the nature of power relations between the groups. That is, the dominant group is superordinate, and the minority group is the subordinate group (e.g., in the United States, Chicanos and Puerto Ricans are minority groups as compared with the dominant White group). For further discussion, Ogbu (1983).

8. Although linguistic bias is our primary area of concern, we also propose that racial/ethnic prejudice and discrimination may operate during performance assessment. We briefly touch upon this potential problem area in pages 00–00. Although our coverage of ethnic/racial bias is not close in size compared to the proportion of space given to linguistic bias, this should not be construed that the former has less importance as a potential issue in performance assessment.

9. The major reason for lack of evidence is that research on this topic has not been undertaken. That is, performance assessment as an institutionalized alternative assessment has not yet been implemented in any wide fashion. This is not to suggest, however, that "observational assessment" of teacher candidates does not exist in any form at all. On the contrary, observational assessment does occur quite often in teacher preparation programs (e.g., admissions interview, academic performance in coursework, and student teaching assignment). Our concerns, however, are with potential biases that may surface during "performance assessment," an alternative assessment procedure previously described.

10. A "language attitude" can be broadly and flexibly seen "as any affective, cognitive or behavioral index of evaluative reactions toward different language varieties or their speakers" (Ryans, Giles, and Sebastian, 1982, 7).

11. There is evidence, however, that low-prestige language varieties do persist, and in some cases, become regional standards over a higher status variety. See, Ryan (1979).

12. For examples of theoretical writing on differential evaluation of high-prestige language varieties over low-prestige language varieties see Giles, Bourhis, and Taylor (1976); and Trudgil and Giles (1976).

13. For the purposes of our discussion, we follow Ryan (1973) who operationally defines accentedness "in terms of the degree to which only the phonological structures of Spanish influence speech produced in English" (p. 62) by bilingual Latinos. Placed in a larger context of dialect vs. accent distinctions, "dialect . . . involves variation from the standard pronounciation" (Ryan et al., 1977, p. 268).

14. In some cases, Chicano-accented English is influenced by Spanish phonological interference during the formative stages when a Spanish monolingual is becoming bilingual (i.e., learning English). Some scholars, however, argue that for many Chicanos, "Chicano English" (accented English, in this case) is a native, first language. As Arthur et at. contend: "many speakers of Mexican-American English are not fluent speakers of Spanish. . . . The dialect of English spoken by Mexican-Americans raised in bario [sic] areas is not an attempt of native speakers of Spanish

to produce English; it is a succesful attempt of native speakers of English to produce the dialect of English which they grew up hearing" (p. 256–57).

15. For reviews of this body of literature see Brennan (1977), Carranza (1982), Mendoza-Hall (1980), and Ryan and Carranza (1976).

16. The matched guise technique is a common, well-known, and widely used method in language attitude research. In brief, the technique uses the same individual or individuals speaking the two dialects. The evaluators react to the two guises of the sole speaker as though they were reacting to two different individuals speaking (Arthur et al., 1974).

17. In McConahay et al. (1981), the order of Black and White resumes was manipulated. See the study for discussion of how order was manipulated and why racial prejudice was expected in one condition and not the other.

18. The Partnership Program began in 1975. It is typically housed as part of the outreach programs of the Educational Opportunity Program/Student Affirmative Action. The Partnership Program identifies students as early as 7th grade and provides, for example, academic advising, campus visits, printed material, and parental meetings.

References

Introduction. Advances in Assessment and the Potential for Increasing the Number of Hispanics in Higher Education.

Adelman, C. (1985). *The standardized test scores of college graduates: 1964–1982.* Washington, DC: National Institute of Education and American Association for Higher Education.

Adolphus, S. H., ed. (1984). *Equality postponed: Continuing barriers to higher education.* NY: College Entrance Examination Board.

Airaisan, P. W. (1987). State mandated testing and educational reform: Context and consequences. *American Journal of Education,* 95, 392–412.

Alderman, D. L. (1982). Language proficiency as a moderator variable in testing academic aptitude. *Journal of Educational Psychology,* 74(4), 580–87.

Alderman, D. L., and Holland, P. W. (1981). *Item performance across native language groups on the Test of English as a Foreign Language* (TOEFL RR-9). Princeton, NJ: Educational Testing Service.

Allan, R. G., Nassif, P. M., and Elliot, S. M., eds. (1988). *Bias issues in teacher certification testing.* Hillsdale, NJ: Erlbaum.

American Association of Collegiate Registrars and Admission Officers and The College Board (1980). *Undergraduate admissions: The realities of institutional policies, practices, and procedures.* NY: College Entrance Examination Board.

American Educational Research Association, American Psychological Association, and National Council on Measurement in Education (1985). *Standards for educational and psychological testing.* Washington, DC: American Psychological Association.

Angoff, W. H. (1982). Use of difficulty and discrimination indices for detecting item bias. In Berk, R. A., ed., *Handbook of methods for detecting bias,* 96–116.

Anrig, G. R. (1985). A challenge for the states: Protecting minority access within systemwide admissions standards. *AAHE Bulletin,* May 1985, 3–7.

Anrig, G. R. (1986). Teacher education and teacher testing: The rush to mandate. *Phi Delta Kappan, 67,* 447–51.

Anrig, G. R. (1981). Testimony before the joint hearing of the Subcommittee on Elementary, Secondary and Vocational Education and the Subcommittee on Postsecondary Education of the Committee on Education and Labor, U.S. House of Representatives. November 4, 1981. Photocopy.

Arce, C. H. (1982). Language shift among Chicanos: Strategies for measuring direction and rate. *The Social Science Journal, 19,* 121–32.

Astin, A. W., King, M. R., and Richardson, G. T. (1978). *The American freshman: National norms for fall 1978.* Los Angeles: University of California, Los Angeles and the American Council on Education.

Baird, L. L. (1984). Relationships between ability, college attendance, and family income. *Research in Higher Education, 21,* 373–95.

Bejar, I., and Blew, E. (1981). Grade inflation and the validity of the Scholastic Aptitude Test. *American Educational Research Journal, 18,* 143–56.

Berendzen, R. (1979). Testimony to the Subcommittee on Elementary, Secondary, and Vocational Education Committee on Education and Labor, U.S. House of Representatives by American Association of State Colleges and Universities, American Council on Education, Association of American Universities, Association of Catholic Colleges and Universities, Council of Graduate Schools of the United States, National Association for Equal Opportunity in Higher Education, National Association of Independent Colleges and Universities, and National Association of State Universities and Land-Grant Colleges. September 24, 1979. Photocopy.

Berk, R. A. (1986). A consumer's guide to setting performance standards on criterion-referenced tests. *Review of Educational Research, 56,* 137–72.

Berk, R. A. (1982). *Handbook of methods for detecting test bias.* Baltimore, MD: Johns Hopkins University Press.

Boldt, R. F. (1969). *Concurrent validity of the PAA and SAT for bilingual Dade County high school volunteers.* Statistical Report 69-31. Princeton, NJ: Educational Testing Service.

Bracey, G. W. (1985). ETS as big brother: An essay review of *None of the above. Phi Delta Kappan, 67,* 75–79.

Breland, H. (1985). *An examination of state university and college admissions policies.* Research Report. Princeton, NJ: Educational Testing Service.

Breland, H. (1981). *Assessing student characteristics in admissions to higher education.* NY: College Entrance Examination Board.

Breland, H. (1979). *Population validity and college entrance measures.* Research Monograph No. 8. NY: College Entrance Examination Board.

Breland, H., and Durán, R. P. (1985). Assessing English composition skills in Spanish-speaking populations. *Educational and Psychological Measurement*, 45, 309–18.

Breland, H., Wilder, G., and Robertson, N. (1986). *Demographics, standards and equity: Challenges in College Admissions.* Report of a Survey of Undergraduate Admissions Policies, Practices and Procedures. NY: American Association of Collegiate Registrars and Admissions Officers, The American College Testing Program, The College Board, Educational Testing Service, and the National Association of College Admissions Counselors.

Brigham, C. C. (1923). *A study of American intelligence.* Princeton, NJ: Princeton University Press, 1923.

Brill, S. (1973). The secrecy behind the College Boards. *New York*, October 7, 1973, 67–75.

Brown, G., Rosen, N., and Olivas, M. (1980). *The condition of education for Hispanic Americans.* Washington, DC: National Center for Education Statistics.

Brown, R. (1980). *Searching for the truth about "Truth in Testing" legislation: A background report.* Report No. 132. Denver, CO: Education Commission of the States.

Burill, L. E. (1982). Comparative studies of item bias methods. In Berk, R. A., ed., *Handbook for methods of detecting test bias*, 161–179.

Burton, N., Lewis, C., and Robertson, N. (1988). *Sex differences in SAT scores.* College Board Report 88-9. NY: College Entrance Examination Board.

Bush, G. (1989). *Memorandum on Education of Hispanic Americans.* Washington, DC: The White House, Office of the Press Secretary, December 6, 1989. Photocopy.

Cameron, R. G. (1989). *The common yardstick: A case for the SAT.* NY: College Entrance Examination Board.

Carlton, S. T., and Marco, G. L. (1982). Methods used by test publishers to "debias" standardized tests: Educational Testing Service. In Berk, R. A., ed., *Handbook of methods for detecting test bias*, 278–313.

Center for Education Statistics (1988). *Trends in minority enrollment in higher education. Fall 1976–Fall 1986.* Washington, DC: U.S. Department of Education.

Change: The Magazine of Higher Learning (1988). Special Report. Hispanics and the Academy. *Change*, 20, May/June 1988.

Chauncey, H., and Dobbins, J. E. (1963). *Testing: Its place in education today.* NY: Harper and Row.

Chen, Z., and Henning, G. (1985). Linguistic and cultural bias in language proficiency tests. *Language Testing*, 2, 155–63.

Clark, K. B. (1979). This so-called Truth-in-Testing law is a placebo. *The New York Times*, August 18, 1979.

Clewell, B. C., and Joy, M. F. (1988). *The national Hispanic scholar awards program: A descriptive analysis of high-achieving Hispanic students.* College Board Report No. 88-10. NY: College Entrance Examination Board.

Cocking, R. R., and Mestre, J. P., eds. (1988). *Linguistic and cultural influences on learning mathematics.* Hillsdale, NJ: Lawrence Erlbaum Associates.

Coffman, W. E. (1982). Methods used by test publishers to "debias" standardized tests: Riverside Publishing Company/Houghton Mifflin. In Berk, R. A., ed., *Handbook of methods for selecting bias*, 240–55.

College Board (1986). *ATP guide for high schools and colleges.* NY: College Entrance Examination Board.

College Board (1988). *Guidelines on the uses of College Board tests scores and related data.* NY: College Entrance Examination Board.

College Board (1986). *Measures in the college admissions process.* NY: College Entrance Examination Board.

The College Board and Educational Testing Service (1989). *Test Skills: A kit for teachers of Hispanic students.* NY and Princeton, NJ: The College Board and Educational Testing Service.

College Entrance Examination Board (1977). *On further examination: Report of the advisory panel on the Scholastic Aptitude Test score decline.* NY: College Entrance Examination Board.

College Entrance Examination Board (1982). *Options for excellence: Annual report, 1981–82.* San Antonio, TX: The College Board.

College Entrance Examination Board (1982). *Profiles, college-bound seniors, 1981.* NY: College Entrance Examination Board.

College Entrance Examination Board (1980). *Undergraduate admissions: The realities of institutional policies, practices, and procedures.* NY: College Entrance Examination Board.

College Entrance Examination Board (1926). *The work of the College Entrance Examination Board: 1900–1925.* Boston: Ginn and Co.

Crouse, J., and Trusheim, D. (1988). *The case against the SAT.* Chicago: University of Chicago Press.

Crouse, J. (1979). The effects of academic ability. In Jencks, C. *Who gets ahead?* NY: Basic Books.

Cruise, P. I., and Kimmel, E. W. (1990). *Changes in the SAT-Verbal: A study of trends in content and gender references, 1961–1987.* College Board Report No. 90-1. NY: College Entrance Examination Board.

Davis, B. D. (1983). Neo-Lysenkoism, IQ and the press. *Public Interest*, 73, 41–59.

Donlon, F. (1984). *The College Board technical handbook for the Scholastic Aptitude Test and achievement tests.* NY: College Entrance Examination Board.

Dorans, N. J., and Kulick, E. (1986). Demonstrating the utility of the standardization approach to assessing differential item functioning on the Scholastic Aptitude Test. *Journal of Educational Measurement*, 23, 355–68.

Dorans, N. J., Schmitt, A. P., and Leistein, C. A. (1988). *The standardization approach to assessing differential speededness* (RR-88-31). Princeton, NJ: Educational Testing Service.

Durán, R. P. (1984). An information-processing approach to the study of Hispanic bilinguals' cognition. In Martínez, J., and Mendoza, R., eds. *Chicano psychology.* 2nd edition.

Durán, R. P. (1988). Bilinguals' logical reasoning aptitude: A construct validity study. In Cocking, R. R., and Mestre, J. P., eds., *Linguistic and cultural influences on learning mathematics.*

Durán, R. P. (1983). *Hispanics' Education and Background: Predictors of College Achievement.* NY: College Entrance Examination Board.

Durán, R. P., Enright, M. K., and Rock, D. A. (1985). *Language factors and Hispanic freshmen's student profile.* College Board Report No. 85-3. NY: College Entrance Examination Board.

Educational Testing Service (1980). *Accountability, fairness, and quality in testing.* Princeton, NJ: Educational Testing Service.

Educational Testing Service (1983). *ETS standards for quality and fairness.* Princeton, NJ: Educational Testing Service.

Educational Testing Service (1988, October). New teacher assessment tests to offer an alternative to the NTE. *Examiner*, 18, 1, 7.

Educational Testing Service (1981). *Public interest principles for the design and use of admissions testing programs.* Princeton, NJ: Educational Testing Service.

Educational Testing Service (1979). Statement submitted by Educational Testing Service, Princeton, N.J. in a Hearing of May 15, 1979, of the U.S. House of Representatives Subcommittee on Civil Service. (An abbreviated oral version was presented by Winton H. Manning, Senior Vice-President, ETS). Photocopy.

Educational Testing Service (1988). *A summary of data collected from Graduate Record Examinations test takers during 1986–87.* Data Summary Report Number 12. Princeton, NJ: Educational Testing Service.

Educational Testing Service (1980). *Test scores and family income: A response to charges in the Nader/Nairn report on ETS.* Princeton, NJ: Educational Testing Service.

Educational Testing Service (1980). *Test use and validity: A response to charges in the Nader/Nairn report on ETS*. Princeton, NJ: Educational Testing Service.

Espinoza, R. W., Fernández, C. and Dornbush, S. M. (1977). Chicano perceptions of high school and Chicano performance. *Aztlán*, 8, 133–55.

Evans, F. R. (1980). *A study of the relationship among speed and power, aptitude test scores, and ethnic identity*. College Board Research and Development Report RDR 80-81, No. 2. Princeton, NJ: Educational Testing Service.

Evans, F. R., and Reilly, R. R. (1973). A study of test speededness as a potential source of bias in the quantitative score of the Admissions Test for Graduate Study in Business. *Research in Higher Education*, 1, 173–83.

Flaugher, R. L. (1970). *Testing practices, minority groups, and higher education: A review and discussion of the research*. Research Bulletin 70-41. Princeton, NJ: Educational Testing Service.

Fleming, J. (1986). *Standardized test scores and the Black college environment*. Research report volume 10 (Number 1). NY: United Negro College Fund.

Fredericksen, N. (1984). The real test bias: Influences of testing on teaching and learning. *American Psychologist*, 39, 193–202.

Fuess, C. M. (1950). *The College Board: Its first fifty years*. NY: Columbia University Press.

García, J. (1977). Intelligence testing: Quotients, quotas, and quackery. In Martínez, J., ed., *Chicano psychology*. NY: Academic Press.

Goetz, M. E., and Johnson, L. M. (1985). *State policies for admission to higher education*. College Board Report No. 85-1. NY: College Entrance Examination Board.

Goldsmith, R. P. (1979). *The effect of training in test taking skills and test anxiety on Mexican American student's aptitude test performance*. Doctoral dissertation. University of Texas, Austin.

Gould, S. J. (1981). *The mismeasure of man*. NY: Norton.

Hanford, G. H. (1982). Preface. In Admissions Testing Program of the College Board, *Profiles, College-Bound Seniors, 1981*. NY: College Entrance Examination Board.

Hanford, G. H. (1985). Yes, the SAT does help colleges. *Harvard Educational Review*, 55, 324–31.

Hargadon, F. A. (1979). Testimony for the Subcommittee on Elementary, Secondary, and Vocational Education Committee on Education and Labor. July 31, 1979. Photocopy.

Hartnett, R., and Feldmesser, D. (1980). College admissions testing and the myth of selectivity: Unresolved questions and needed research. *AAHE Bulletin*, 32, 3–6.

Hedges, L. V., and Majer, K. (1976). An attempt to improve prediction of college success of minority students by adjusting for high school characteristics. *Educational and Psychological Measurement*, 36, 953–57.

Hendrick, F. A., and Loyd, B. H. (1982). Methods used by publishers to "debias: standardized tests: The American College Testing Program. In Berk, R. A., ed., *Handbook of methods for detecting test bias*, 272–78.

Hilton, T. L., and Rhett, H. (1973). *Final report: The base-year survey of the national longitudinal study of the high school class of 1972. Appendiz B, Part II*. Washington, DC: National Center for Educational Statistics.

Hoffman, B. (1967). Multiple-choice tests. *Physics Education*, 2, 247–51.

Hoffman, B. (1962). *The tyranny of testing*. NY: Crowell-Collier.

Horowitz, H. (1987). *Campus life: Undergraduate cultures from the end of the eighteenth century to the present*. NY: Knopf.

Hunter, R. V., and Slaughter, C. D. (1980). *ETS test sensitivity review process*. Princeton, NJ: Educational Testing Service.

Ironson, G. H., and Subkoviak, M. (1979). A comparison of several methods of assessing item bias. *Journal of Educational Measurement*, 16, 209–25.

Jensen, A. (1980). *Bias in mental testing*. NY: Basic Books.

Jensen, A. (1982). The debunking of scientific fossils and straw persons. *Contemporary Education Review*, 1, 121–35.

Jensen, A. (1981). *Straight talk about mental tests*. NY: Free Press.

Jones, J. Quentin (1985). *Options for excellence*. NY: College Entrance Examination Board.

Kamin, L. J. (1974). *The science and politics of IQ*. Potomac, MD: Lawrence Erlbaum.

Karier, C., ed. (1975). *Shaping the American educational state: 1900 to the present*. NY: Free Press.

Keller, G. D. (1990). Creating Candidates for success: The story of Project PRIME. *The College Board Review*, No. 156, 1990, 10–15 and 28–29.

Keller, G. D. (1984). Increasing the admissability of Hispanics who take the GRE. In Council of Graduate Schools, *Graduate Education: A national investment of knowledge*. Washington, DC: Council of Graduate Schools in the United States.

Keller, G. D. (1975). Psychological stress among speakers of United States vernacular Spanish. In Ortega, L., ed. *Introduction to bilingual education*. NY: Las Américas-Anaya.

Keller, G. D. (1986). Review of Adolphus, S. H., ed. *Equality Postponed: Continuing Barriers to Higher Education*. In *The Journal of Higher Education*, 57, 333–34.

Keller, G. D. (1990). *Sí Se Puede. Information on Academic Planning and Obtaining Financial Aid*. New York and Princeton, NJ: College Board and Educational Testing Service.

Keller, G. D. (1979). Testimony. *Hearings before the subcommittee on elementary, secondary and vocational education of the committee on education and labor, House of Representatives*. Ninety-Sixth Congress, First Session on H.R. 3564 and H.R. 4949 (Truth in Testing Act of 1979; The Educational Testing Act of 1979), 828–52.

Keller, G. D. (1982). The Ultimate Goal of Bilingual Education with Respect to Language Skills. In Fishman, J. A. and Keller, G. D. eds. *Bilingual Education for Hispanic Students in the United States*. New York: Teachers College Press.

Keller, G. D., and Magallán, R. (1989). Preface. In The College Board and the Educational Testing Service, *TestSkills: A Kit for Teachers of Hispanic Students*.

Keller, G. D., and Sullivan, M. J. (1988). *Project 1000: Recruiting, Admitting, and Graduating an Additional 1000 U.S. Hispanic Students*. Student Information Booklet. Tempe, AZ: Project 1000, Graduate College, Arizona State University.

Keller, G. D., and Sullivan, M. J. (1990). *Project 1000: Recruiting, Admitting, and Graduating an Additional 1000 U.S. Hispanic Students*. Student Information Booklet. 2nd edition. Tempe, AZ: Project 1000, Graduate College, Arizona State University.

Lerner, B. (1980). The war on testing: David, Goliath, and Gallup. *Public Interest*, 60, 119–47.

Levine, D. O. (1986). *The American college and the culture of aspiration, 1915–1940*. Ithaca, NY: Cornell University Press.

Linn, R. L. (1982). Admissions testing on trial. *American Psychologist*, 37, 279–91.

Linn, R. L. (1984). Range restriction problems in the use of self-selected groups for test validation. *Psychological Bulletin*, 69, 69–73.

Linn, R. L., and Harnisch, D. L. (1981). Interactions between item content and group membership on achievement test items. *Journal of Educational Measurement*, 18, 109–18.

Llabre, M. M., and Froman, T. W. (1987). Allocation of time to test items: A study of ethnic differences. *Journal of Experimental Education*, 55, 137–40.

Lunneborg, C. E., and Lunneborg, P. W. (1986). Beyond prediction: The challenge of minority achievement in higher education. *Journal of Multicultural Counseling and Development*, 14, 77–84.

McKown, H. (1925). *The trend in college entrance requirements, 1913-1922.* Department of Interior Bureau of Education Bulletin No. 35. Washington, DC: Government Printing Office.

Madus, G. (1985). Public policy and the testing profession—you never had it so good? *Educational Measurement: Issues and Practice,* 4, 5–11.

Manning, W. H. (1989). Broadening the basis for admissions decisions: The role of standardized testing in the admission of minority students. In Ward, W. E., and Cross, M. M., eds. *Key issues in minority education: Research directions and practical implications.* Center for Research on Minority Education, University of Oklahoma, Norman, OK, 155–69.

Manning, W. H. (1979). Diversity and due process in admissions. *Howard Law Journal,* 1979, 22(3), 317–26.

Manning, W. H. (1977). The Pursuit of Fairness in Admission. In *Selective admissions in higher education,* a report of the Carnegie Council on Policy Studies in Higher Education. San Francisco: Jossey-Bass.

Manning, W. H. (1984). Revisiting the case for affirmative action in admissions. *Selections,* Spring, 25–30.

Manning, W. H., and Jackson, R. (1984). College entrance examinations: Objective selection or gatekeeper for the economically privileged? In Reynolds, C. R., and Brown, R. T., eds., *Perspectives on bias in mental testing.*

Martínez, J., ed. (1977). *Chicano psychology.* NY: Academic Press.

Martínez, J., and Mendoza, R., eds. (1984). *Chicano psychology.* 2nd edition. NY: Academic Press.

Maspone, M. M., and Llabre, M. M. (1985). The influence of training Hispanics in test-taking on the psychometric properties of a test. *Journal for Research in Mathematics Education,* 16, 177–83.

Mathews, J. (1988). *Escalante, the best teacher in America.* NY: Henry Holt and Co.

Mayo, G. D., and Manning, W. H. (1961). Motivation measurement. *Educational and Psychological Measurement,* 21, 73-83.

Mestre, J. P. (1981). Predicting academic achievement among bilingual Hispanic college technical students. *Educational and Psychological Measurement,* 41, 1255–64.

Mestre, J. P. (1988). The role of language comprehension in mathematics and problem solving. In Cocking, R. R. and Mestre, J. P. *Linguistic and cultural influences on learning mathematics.*

Mestre, J. P. (1986). Teaching problem-solving strategies to bilingual students: What do research results tell us? *International Journal of Mathematical Education in Science and Technology,* 17, 393–401.

Mestre, J. P., Gerace, W. J., and Lochhead, J. (1982). The interdependence of language and translational math skills among bilingual Hispanic engineering students. *Journal of Research in Science Teaching*, 19, 399–410.

Mroscak, D. (1990). Letter to G. D. Keller, July 24, 1990.

Nader accuses ETS of "Fraud," plans drive for testing reform. *The Chronicle of Higher Education*, January 21, 1980, 5–6.

Nader, R., and Nairn, A. (1980). Startling Admissions. *Student Lawyer*, 8 (March 1980), 28–31 and 52–54.

Nairn, A., and associates. (1980). *The reign of ETS: The corporation that makes up minds.* Washington, DC: Ralph Nader.

National Commission on Excellence in Education (1983). *A nation at risk: The imperatives for educational reform.* Washington, DC: U.S. Government Printing Office.

Ogbu, J. (1978). *Minority education and caste: The American system in cross-cultural perspective.* NY: Academic Press.

Olivas, M. A. (1979). *The Dilemma of Access.* Washington, DC: Howard University Press.

Olivas, M. A. (1982). Hispanics in higher education: status and issues. *Educational Evaluation and Policy Analysis*, 4, 301–10.

Olivas, M. A. (ed.). (1986). *Latino college students.* New York: Teachers College Press.

Olmedo, E. (1977). Psychological testing and the Chicano: A reassessment. In Martínez, J., Jr., ed., *Chicano Psychology*, 175–95.

Olson, D. (1977). From utterance to text: The bias of language in speech and writing. *Harvard Educational Review*, 47, 257–81.

Orfield, G. (1988, July). *The growth and concentration of Hispanic enrollment and the future of American education.* Paper presented at the National Council of La Raza Conference, Albuquerque, New Mexico.

Orum, L. S. (1986). *The education of Hispanics: Status and implications.* Washington, DC: National Council of La Raza.

Owen, D. (1983). The last days of ETS. *Harper's*, May 1983.

Owen, D. (1985). *None of the above: Behind the myth of scholastic aptitude.* Boston: Houghton Mifflin.

Padilla, A. (1979). Critical factors in the testing of Hispanic Americans: A review and some suggestions for the future. In Tyler, R. W., and White, S. H. *Testing, Teaching, and Learning.* Washington, DC: U.S. Department of Health, Education, and Welfare.

Payan, R. M., Peterson, R. E., and Castille, N. A. (1984). *Access to college for Mexican Americans in the Southwest: Replication after 10 years.* College Board Report No. 84-3. NY: College Entrance Examination Board.

Pike, L. (1980). *Implicit guessing strategies of GRE-Aptitude examinees classified by ethnic group and sex.* GRE Board Professional Report (GREB No. 75-10P). Princeton, NJ.

Raju, N. S. (1982). Methods used by test publishers to "debias" standardized tests: Science Research Associates. In Berk, R. A., ed., *Handbook of methods for selecting bias,* 261–72.

Ramos, R. (1981). Employment battery performance of Hispanic applicants as a function of English or Spanish test instructions. *Journal of Applied Psychology,* 66, 191–95.

Rebell, M. A. (1988). Disparate impact of teacher competency testing on minorities: Don't blame the test-takers—or the test. *Yale Law and Policy Review,* 4, 375–403.

Reynolds, C. R., and Brown, R. T. (1984). *Perspectives on Bias in Mental Testing.* NY: Plenum Press, 1984.

Rincón, E. (1979). *Test speededness, test anxiety, and test performance: A comparison of Mexican American and Anglo American high school juniors.* Unpublished dissertation. University of Texas at Austin.

Rivera, C., and Schmitt, A. P. (1988). *A comparison of Hispanic and White Non-Hispanic students' omit patterns on the Scholastic Aptitude Test* (RR-88-44). Princeton, NJ: Educational Testing Service.

Robertson, J. D. (1980). Examining the examiners: The trend toward truth in testing. *Journal of Law and Education,* 9(2), 167–99.

Rock, D., and Werts, C. (1979). *Construct validity of the SAT across populations: An empirical confirmatory study.* College Entrance Examination Board, RDR 78-79, No. 5, Princeton, NJ: Educational Testing Service.

Rudner, L. M., Getson, P. R., and Knight, D. L. (1980). A Monte Carlo comparison of seven biased item detection techniques. *Journal of Educational Measurement,* 17.

Samelson, F. (1982). H. H. Goddard and the immigrants. *American Psychologist,* 37, 1291–92.

Samuda, R. (1975). *Psychological testing of American minorities: Issues and consequences.* NY: Harper and Row.

Santiago, I. (1978). *A community struggle for equal educational opportunity: Aspira vs. Board of Education.* OME Monograph No. 2. Princeton, NJ: Educational Testing Service, Office for Minority Education.

Schaffner, P. (1985). Competitive admissions practices when the SAT is optional. *Journal of Higher Education*, 56, 55–72.

Scheuneman, J. D. (1982). A posteriori analyses of biased items. In Berk, R. A., ed., *Handbook of methods for detecting test bias*, 181–98.

Schmitt, A. P. (1985). *Assessing unexpected differential item performance of Hispanic candidates on SAT form 3FSA08 and TSWE form E47* (SR-85-169). Princeton, NJ: Educational Testing Service.

Schmitt, A. P. (1988). Language and cultural characteristics that explain differential item functioning for Hispanic examinees on the Scholastic Aptitude Test. *Journal of Educational Measurement*, 25, 1–13.

Schmitt, A. P., and Bleistein, C. A. (1987). *Factors affecting differential item functioning for Black examinees on Scholastic Aptitude Test anology items* (RR-87-23). Princeton, NJ: Educational Testing Service.

Schmitt, A. P., and Dorans, N. J., eds. (1987). *Differential item functioning on the Scholastic Aptitude Test*. Princeton, NJ: Educational Testing Service.

Schudson, M. S. (1972). Organizing the 'meritocracy': A history of the College Entrance Examination Board. *Harvard Educational Review*, 42, 34–69.

Shannon, L. (1975). Development of time perspective in three cultural groups. *Developmental Psychology*, 11, 114–15.

Silverman, B., Barton, F., and Lyon, M. (1976). Minority group status and bias in college admissions criteria. *Educational and Psychological Measurement*, 36, 401–7.

Sinnott, L. (1980). *Differences in item performance across groups*. ETS RR-80-3. Princeton, NJ: Educational Testing Service.

Slack, W., and Porter, D. (1980). The Scholastic Aptitude Test: A critical appraisal. *Harvard Educational Review*, 50, 154–75.

Smith, G. P. (1987). *The effects of competency testing on the supply of minority teachers*. A report prepared for the National Education Association and the Council of Chief State School Officers.

Snyderman, M., and Herrnstein, R. (1983). Intelligence tests and the Immigration Act of 1924. *American Psychologist*, 38.

Solomon, R. J. (1979). Statement before the Subcommittee on Elementary, Secondary and Vocational Education of the Committee on Education and Labor of the U.S. House of Representatives. July 31, 1979. Photocopy.

Synnott, M. G. (1979). *The half opened door: Discrimination and admissions at Harvard, Yale, and Princeton, 1900–1970*. Westport, CT: Greenwood Press.

Thurgood, D. H., and Weinman, J. M. (1989). *Summary report 1988: Doctorate recipients from United States universities*. Washington, DC: National Academy Press.

Truth in Testing (1980). *The Washington Post,* June 21, 1980, A14.

Tyler, R. W., and White, S. H. (1979). *Testing, teaching and learning.* Report of a conference on research on testing. Washington, DC: U.S. Department of Health, Education, and Welfare.

Turnbull, W. W. (1968). Relevance in Testing. *Science,* 160, June 28, 1968.

Turnbull, W. W. (1985). *Student change, program change: Why SAT scores kept falling.* College Board Report No. 85-2. NY: College Entrance Examination Board.

Valentine, J. A. (1987). *The College Board and the school curriculum.* NY: College Entrance Examination Board.

Venti, S., and Wise, D. (1982). Test scores, educational opportunities, and individual choice. *Journal of Public Economics,* 18, 35–63.

Wechsler, H. S. (1977). *The qualified student.* NY: John Wiley and Sons.

Weitzman, R. A. (1982). The prediction of college achievement of the Scholastic Aptitude Test and the high school record. *Journal of Educational Measurement,* 19, 179–91.

Western Interstate Commission for Higher Education (1982). *Getting into college: A survey of changing admission requirements in western public higher education.* Boulder, CO: WICHE.

"White students score highest on SAT exams." (October 13, 1982). *The Chronicle of Higher Education.* 1 and 14.

Whitla, D. K. (1984). The admissions equation. *Change* (November/December 1984), 21–30.

Wigdor, A. K., and Garner, W. R., eds. (1982). *Ability testing: Uses, consequences, and controversies. Part I: Report of the Committee. Part II: Documentation section.* Washington, DC: National Academy Press.

Willingham, W. W. (1985). *Success in college: The role of personal qualities and academic ability.* NY: College Entrance Examination Board.

Willingham, W. W., and Breland, H. M. (1982). *Personal Qualities and College Admissions.* NY: College Entrance Examination Board.

Willingham, W. W., and Ramist, L. (1982). The SAT debate: Do Trusheim and Crouse add useful information? *Phi Delta Kappan,* 64, 207–8.

Younkin, W. (1986). *Speededness as a source of test bias on the College Level Academic Skills Test.* Doctoral dissertation, University of Miami.

Chapter 1. Cultural and Linguistic Influences on Latino Testing.

Aiken, L. R. (1979). Educational values of Anglo-American and Mexican-American college students. *The Journal of Psychology,* 102, 317–21.

Anderson, R. C., and Shifrin, Z. (1980). The meaning of words in context. In Spiro, R. J., Bruce, B. C., and Brewer, W. F., eds., *Theoretical Issues in Reading Comprehension*. Hillsdale, NJ: Lawrence Erlbaum Associates.

Brown, A. L., Bransford, J. D., Ferrara, R. A., and Campione, J. C. (1983). Learning, remembering, and understanding. In Flavell, J. H., and Markman, E. M., eds., *Carmichaels Manual of Child Psychology* (vol. 1). New York: John Wiley.

Cabello, B. (1984). Cultural interference in reading comprehension: An alternative explanation. *Bilingual Review*, 11, 12–20.

Carlisle, J. F. (1989). The use of the Sentence Verification Technique in diagnostic assessment of listening and reading comprehension. *Learning Disability Research*, 5, 33–34.

Carroll, J. B. (1972). Defining language comprehension: Some speculations. In Carroll, J. B., and Freedle, R. O., eds., *Language comprehension and the acquisition of knowledge*. Washington, DC: Winston and Sons.

Cummins, J. (1980). Psychological assessment of immigrant children: Logic or intuition? *Journal of Multilingual and Multicultural Development*, 1, 97–111.

Cummins, J. (1981). The role of primary language development in promoting educational success for language minority students. In *Schooling and Language Minority Students: A Theoretical Framework*, compiled by the California State Department of Education, Los Angeles: National Dissemination and Assessment Center.

Cummins, J. (1982, February). Tests, achievement, and bilingual students. *Focus*, 1–8. Rosslyn, VA: National Clearinghouse for Bilingual Education.

Dalton, S. (1974). Predictive validity of high-school rank and SAT scores for minority students. *Educational and Psychological Measurement*, 34, 367–70.

Dawe, L. (1984, August). A theoretical framework for the study of the effects of bilingualism on mathematics teaching and learning. *Paper presented at the Fifth International Congress on Mathematical Education*, Adelaide, Australia.

De Avila, E. A. (1988). Bilingualism, cognitive function, and language minority group membership. In Cocking, R., and Mestre, J., eds., *Linguistic and Cultural Influences on Learning Mathematics* (pp. 101–21). Hillsdale, NJ: Lawrence Erlbaum Associates.

diSibio, M. (1982). Memory for connected discourse: A constructivist view. *Review of Educational Research*, 52, 149–74.

Espinoza, R. W., Fernandez, C., and Dornbush, S. M. (1977). Chicano perceptions of high school and Chicano performance. *Atzlan*, 8, 133–55.

Grebler, L., Moore, J. W., and Guzman, R. C. (1973). The family: Variations in time and space. In Duran, I. L., and Bernard, H. R., eds., *Introduction to Chicano Studies* (pp. 309–31). New York, NY: Macmillan. (Originally published in 1970).

Greene, B. A., Royer, J. M., and Anzalone, S. J. (1990). A new technique for measuring listening and reading literacy in developing countries. *International Review of Education*, 36, 57–68.

Hakuta, K. (1986). *Mirror of Language: The Debate on Bilingualism.* New York: Basic Books, Inc.

Halliday, M. A. K. (1975). Some aspects of sociolinguistics. In Jacobson, E., ed., *Interactions Between Linguistics and Mathematics Education* (pp. 64–73). Final Report on the Symposium Sponsored by UNESCO, CEDO, and ICMI, Nairobi, Kenya, September 1–11, 1974. (UNESCO Report No. ED-74/CONF. 808. Paris: UNESCO)

Hedges, L. V., and Majer, K. (1976). An attempt to improve prediction of college success of minority students by adjusting for high school characteristics. *Educational and Psychological Measurement*, 36, 953–57.

Houston, L. N. (1980). Predicting academic achievement among specially-admitted Black female college students. *Educational and Psychological Measurement*, 40, 1189–95.

Jenkins, J. J. (1974). Remember that old theory of memory? Well, forget it! *American Psychologist*, 29, 785–95.

Jenkins, J. J. (1979). Four points to remember. A tetrahedral model of memory experiments. In Cernak, L. S., and Craik, I. M., eds., *Levels of processing in human memory.* Hillsdale, NJ: Erlbaum.

Juarez, R. Z., and Kuvlesly, W. P. (1969). Ethnic group identity and orientations toward educational attainment: A comparison of Mexican-American and Anglo boys. Washington, DC: National Institute of Education. (ERIC Document Reproduction Service No. ED 023 497).

Kessler, C. (1987). Language minority children's linguistic and cognitive creativity. *Journal of Multilingual and Multicultural Development*, 8, 173–86.

Kintsch, W., and Greeno, J. G. (1985). Understanding and solving word arithmetic problems. *Psychological Review*, 92, 109–29.

Kintsch, W., and van Dijk, T. (1978). Toward a model of text comprehension and production. *Psychological Review*, 85, 363–94.

Leap, W. L. (1988). Assumptions and strategies guiding mathematics problem solving by Ute Indian students. In Cocking, R., and Mestre, J., eds., *Linguistic* and cultural influences on learning mathematics (pp. 161–86). Hillsdale, NJ: Lawrence Erlbaum Associates.

Lopez-Lee, D. (1972). The academic performance and attitudes among Chicanos and Anglos in college. *The Journal of Mexican-American Studies,* 1, 201–22.

Lynch, D. J. (1986). Reading comprehension performance as a function of individual differences in working memory for texts of varying reading difficulty. *Paper presented at the Annual Meeting of the American Educational Research Association,* San Francisco.

Lynch, D. J. (1987). Reading comprehension under listening, silent, and round robin reading conditions as a function of text difficulty and working memory. *Paper presented at the Annual Meeting of the American Educational Research Association,* Washington, D.C.

MacCorquodale, P. (1988). Mexican-American women and mathematics: Participation, aspirations, and achievement. In Cocking, R., and Mestre, J., eds., *Linguistic and cultural influences on learning mathematics* (pp. 137–60). Hillsdale, NJ: Lawrence Erlbaum Associates.

MacCorquodale, P. (1984). Social influences on the participation of Mexican-American women in science (Final report). Washington, DC: National Institute of Education. (ERIC Document Reproduction Service No. ED 234 991).

Marchant, H. G., Royer, J. M., and Greene, B. A. (1988). Superior reliability and validity for a new form of the Sentence Verification Technique. *Educational and Psychological Measurement,* 48, 827–34.

Messick, S. (1980). Test validity and the ethics of assessment. *American Psychologist,* 35, 1012–27.

Mestre, J. P. (1981). Predicting academic achievement among bilingual Hispanic college technical students. *Educational and Psychological Measurement,* 41, 1255–64.

Mestre, J. P. (1986a). Teaching problem solving strategies to bilingual students: What do research results tell us? *International Journal of Mathematics Education in Science and Technology,* 17, 393–401.

Mestre, J. P. (1986b). The Latino science and engineering student: Recent research findings. In Olivas, M., ed., *Latino College Students* (pp. 157–92). New York, NY: Teachers College Press.

Mestre, J. P. (1988). The role of language comprehension in mathematics and problem solving mathematics and problem solving. In Cocking, R., and Mestre, J., eds., *Linguistic and cultural influences on learning mathematics* (pp. 201–20). Hillsdale, NJ: Lawrence Erlbaum Associates.

Montez, P. (1960). *Some difference in factors related to educational achievement of two Mexican-American groups.* San Francisco, CA: R and E Research Associates.

Rasool, J. M., and Royer, J. M. (1986). Assessment of reading comprehension using the Sentence Verification Technique: Evidence from narrative and descriptive texts. *Journal of Educational Research*, 79, 180–84.

Royer, J. M. (1990). The Sentence Verification Technique: A new direction in the assessment of reading comprehension. In S. Legg and J. Algina, eds., *Cognitive assessment of language and math outcomes*. Norwood, N.J.: Ablex. (pp. 144–191).

Royer, J. M. (1985). Reading from the perspective of a biological metaphor. *Contemporary Educational Psychology*, 10, 150–200.

Royer, J. M. (1986). *The Sentence Verification Technique as a measure of comprehension: Validity, reliability, and practicality*. Unpublished manuscript.

Royer, J. M., and Carlo, M. S. (in press). Assessing the language acquisition progress of limited-English-proficient students: Problems and a new alternative. *Applied Measurement in Education*.

Royer, J. M., and Cunningham, D. J. (1981). On the theory and measurement of reading comprehension. *Contemporary Educational Psychology*, 6, 187–216.

Royer, J. M., and Hambleton, R. K. (1983). *Normative study of 50 reading comprehension passages that use the Sentence Verification Technique*. Unpublished study.

Royer, J. M., Abranovic, W. A., and Sinatra, G. M. (1987). Using entering reading performance as a predictor of course performance in college classes. *Journal of Educational Psychology*, 79, 19–26.

Royer, J. M., Greene, B. A., and Sinatra, G. M. (1987). The Sentence Verification Technique: A practical procedure teachers can use to develop their own reading and listening comprehension tests. *Journal of Reading*, 30, 414–23.

Royer, J. M., Hastings, C. N., and Hook, C. (1979). A sentence verification technique for measuring reading comprehension. *Journal of Reading Behavior*, 11, 355–63.

Royer, J. M., Sinatra, G. M., and Schumer, H. (1990). Individual patterns in the development of listening and reading comprehension. *Contemporary Educational Psychology*, 15, 183–96.

Royer, J. M., Carlo, M. S., Carlisle, J. F., and Furmon, G. A. (in press). A new procedure for assessing progress in transitional bilingual education programs. *The Bilingual Review/La Revista Bilingue*.

Royer, J. M., Kulhavy, R. W., Lee, J. B., and Peterson, S. E. (1986). The Sentence Verification Technique as a measure of listening and reading comprehension. *Educational and Psychological Research*, 6, 299–314.

Royer, J. M., Lynch, D. J., Hambleton, R. K. and Bulgarelli, C. (1984). Using the Sentence Verification Technique to assess the comprehension of technical text as a function of subject matter expertise. *American Educational Research Journal*, 21, 839–69.

Royer, J. M., Marchant, H., Sinatra, G., and Lovejoy, D. (1990). The prediction of college course performance from reading comprehension performance: Evidence for general and specific factors. *American Educational Research Journal, 27,* 158–79.

Royer, J. M., Tirre, W. C., Sinatra, G. M., and Greene, B. A. (1989). The assessment of on-line computer-presented text. *Journal of Educational Research, 82,* 348–55.

Saxe, G. B. (1985). Effects of schooling on arithmetical understanding: Studies with Oksapmin children in Papua New Guinea. *Journal of Educational Psychology, 77,* 503–13.

Schwartz, A. J. (1971). A comparative study of values and achievement: Mexican-American and Anglo youth. *Sociology of Education, 44,* 438–62.

Spanos, G., Rhodes, N. C., Dale, T. C., and Crandall, J. (1988). Linguistic features of mathematical problem solving: Insights and applications. In Cocking, R., and Mestre, J., eds., *Linguistic and cultural influences on learning mathematics* (pp. 221–40). Hillsdale, NJ: Lawrence Erlbaum Associates.

Steffensen, M. S., Joag-Dev, C., and Anderson, R. C. (1979). A cross-cultural perspective on reading comprehension. *Reading Research Quarterly, 15,* 10–29.

Swets, J. A., Tanner, W. P., and Birdsall, T. G. (1961). Decision processes in perception. *Psychological Review, 68,* 301–40.

Taylor, O. L. (1978). Language issues and testing. *Journal of Non White Concerns, 6,* 125–32.

van Dijk, T. A., and Kintsch, W. (1983). *Strategies of discourse comprehension.* New York: Academic Press.

Voss, J. F., Vesonder, G. T., and Spilich, G. J. (1980). Text generation and recall by high knowledge and low knowledge individuals. *Journal of Verbal Learning and Verbal Behavior, 19,* 651–67.

Walczyk, J. J., and Royer, J. M. (1989). A program for constructing SVT tests: An alternative way of assessing text comprehension. *Behavioral Research Methods and Instrumentation, 21,* 369–70.

Wilen, D. K., and Sweeting, C. V. M. (1986). Assessment of limited English proficient students. *School Psychology Review, 15,* 59–75.

Chapter 2. Diagnostic Testing of Reasoning Skills.

Durán, R. P. (1983). *Hispanics' education and background. Predictors of college achievement.* New York, NY: College Entrance Examination Board.

Goldman, S., and Durán, R. (1988). Answering questions from oceanography texts: Learner, task, and text characteristics. *Discourse Processes,* 11, 373–412.

Linn, R. and Dunbar, S. (1990, unpublished). Complex, performance-based assessment: Expectations and validation criteria. Boulder Colorado: Center for Research on Evaluation Standards and Student Testing.

Resnick, L. B. (1987). *Education and learning to think.* Washington, D.C.: National Academy Press.

Snow, R. E. (1988). Progress in measurement, cognitive science, and technology that can change the relation between instruction and assessment. In *Assessment in the service of learning. Proceedings of the 1987 ETS Invitational Conference.* Princeton, NJ: Education Testing Service.

Chapter 3. Assessing Heuristic Knowledge to Enhance College Students' Success.

Durán, Richard P. (1983). *Hispanics' education and background.* New York: College Entrance Examination Board.

Freire, Paulo (1982). *Pedagogy of the oppressed.* New York: Continuum.

Harmon, Paul, and King, David, (1985). *Expert systems.* New York: John Wiley and Sons.

Miles, Mathew, and Huberman, A. Michael (1984). *Qualitative data analysis. A sourcebook of new methods.* Beverly Hills, CA: Sage.

Morgan, David L. (1988). *Focus groups as qualitative research.* Beverly Hills: Sage Publications.

Padilla, Raymond V. (1987). *HyperQual.* Software and User's Guide. Tempe, AZ: Hispanic Research Center, Arizona State University.

Padilla, Raymond V., and Pavel, Michael (April 5–9, 1988). Successful Hispanic Community College Students: An Exploratory Qualitative Study. *Paper presented at the Annual Meeting of the American Educational Research Association,* New Orleans.

Reason, Peter, and Rowan, John, eds. (1981). *Human inquiry. A sourcebook of new paradigm research.* New York: John Wiley and Sons.

Spradley, James P. (1979). *The ethnographic interview.* New York: Holt, Rinehart, and Winston.

Tinto, Vincent (1987). *Leaving college. Rethinking the causes and cures of student attrition.* Chicago: University of Chicago Press.

Chapter 4. Time as a Factor in the Cognitive Test Performance of Latino College Students.

Benson, J., Urman, H., and Hocevar, D. (1986). Effects of testwiseness training and ethnicity on achievement of third and fifth-grade students. *Measurement and Evaluation in Counseling and Development,* 18, 154–62.

CTB/McGraw-Hill (1982). *Test of Cognitive Skills.* Monterey, CA. Author.

Deregowski, J. B. (1979). Effect of cultural value of time upon recall. *British Journal of Social and Clinical Psychology,* 9, 37–41.

Dornic, S. (1980). Information processing and language dominance. *International Review of Applied Psychology,* 29, 119–40.

Dreisbach, M., and Keogh, B. K. (1982). Testwiseness as a factor in readiness test performance of young Mexican-American children. *Journal of Educational Psychology,* 74, 224–29.

Evans, F. R., and Reilly, R. R. (1972). A study of speededness as a source of test bias. *Journal of Educational Measurement,* 9, 123–31.

Evans, F. R., and Reilly, R. R. (1973). A study of test speededness as a potential source of bias in the quantitative score of the Admissions Test for Graduate Study in Business. *Research in Higher Education,* 1, 173–83.

Frank, L. K. (1939). Time perspectives. *Journal of Social Philosophy,* 4, 293–312.

Goldsmith, R. P. (1979). *The effect of training in test taking skills and test anxiety management on Mexican American student's aptitude test performance.* Doctoral dissertation. University of Texas at Austin.

Immerman, M. A. (1980). The effect of eliminating time restraints on a standardized test with American Indian adults. Southwestern Indian Polytechnic Institute.

Knapp, R. R. (1960). The effects of time limits on the intelligence test performance of Mexican and American subjects. *Journal of Educational Psychology,* 51, 14–20.

Levine, R. V., West, L. J., and Reis, H. T. (1980). Perceptions of time and punctuality in the United States and Brazil. *Journal of Personality and Social Psychology,* 38, 541–50.

Llabre, M. M., and Froman, T. W. (1987). Allocation of time to test items: A study of ethnic differences. *Journal of Experimental Education,* 55, 137–40.

Llabre, M. M., and Froman, T. W. (1988). *Allocation of time and item performance in hispanic and anglo examinees.* Final Report. Institute for Student Assessment and Evaluation, University of Florida.

References

Maspons, M. M., and Llabre, M. M. (1985). The influence of training Hispanics in test-taking on the psychometric properties of a test. *Journal of Research in Mathematics Education,* 16, 177–83.

Millman, J., Bishop, C. H., and Ebel, R. (1965). An analysis of testwiseness. *Educational and Psychological Measurement,* 25, 707–26.

Oakland, T. (1972). The effects of test-wiseness materials on standardized test performance of preschool disadvantaged children. *Journal of School Psychology,* 10, 355–60.

Pronovost, G. (1985). Introduction: Time in a sociological and historical perspective. *International Social Science Journal,* 5–17.

Raven, J., and Court, D. (1978). *Manual for the Standard Progressive Matrices.* Psychological Corporation.

Rincon, E. T. (1979). *Test speededness, test anxiety, and test performance: A comparison of Mexican American and Anglo American high school juniors.* Unpublished doctoral dissertation, University of Texas at Austin.

Roberts, A. H., and Greene, J. E. (1971). Cross-cultural study of relationships among four dimensions of time perspective. *Perceptual and Motor Skills,* 33, 163–73.

Sanders, J. L., and Brizzolara, M. S. (1985). Connotative meaning of time among Egyptian and American students. *The Journal of Social Psychology,* 125, 587–90.

Schmitt, A. P., Bleistein, C. A., and Scheuneman, J. D. (1987, April). *Determinants of differential item functioning for black examinees on Scholastic Aptitude Test analogy items.* Paper presented at the annual meeting of the National Council on Measurement in Education, Washington, DC.

Schmitt, A. P., and Dorans, N. J. (1987, August). *Differential item functioning for minority examinees on the SAT.* Paper presented at the annual meeting of the American Psychological Association, New York.

Shannon, L. (1975). Development of time perspective in three cultural groups. *Developmental Psychology,* 11, 114–15.

Sullivan, E. T., Clark, W. W., and Tiegs, E. W. (1957). *California Test of Mental Maturity.* California Test Bureau.

Wild, C. L., Durso, R., and Rubin, D. R. (1982). Effects of increased test taking time on test scores by ethnic group, years out of school, and sex. *Journal of Educational Measurement,* 19, 19–28.

Wright, T. (1984). *The effects of increased time-limits on a college-level achievement test.* (Research Report No. 84-12). Miami-Dade Community College, Miami, FL.

Younkin, W. (1986). *Speededness as a source of test bias on the College Level Academic Skills Test.* Doctoral dissertation, University of Miami.

Chapter 5. Factors Related to Differential Item Functioning for Hispanic Examinees on the Scholastic Aptitude Test.

Alderman, D. L., and Holland, P. W. (1981). *Item performance across native language groups on the Test of English as a Foreign Language* (RR-81-16). Princeton, NJ: Educational Testing Service.

Arce, C. H. (1982). Language shift among Chicanos: Strategies for measuring direction and rate. *The Social Science Journal,* 19, 121–32.

Bleistein, C. A., and Wright, D. (1987). Assessment of unexpected differential item difficulty for Asian-American candidates on the Scholastic Aptitude Test. In A. P. Schmitt and N. J. Dorans, eds., *Differential item functioning on the Scholastic Aptitude Test* (RM-87-1). Princeton, NJ: Educational Testing Service.

Breland, H. M., Stocking, M., Pinchak, B. M., and Abrams, N. (1974). *The cross-cultural stability of mental test items: An investigation of response patterns for ten sociocultural groups* (PR-74-2). Princeton, NJ: Educational Testing Service.

Chen, Z., and Henning, G. (1985). Linguistic and cultural bias in language proficiency tests. *Language Testing,* 2, 155–63.

College Entrance Examination Board and Educational Testing Service (1989). *Test skills: A kit for teachers of Hispanic students.* New York, NY: Princeton, NJ: Educational Testing Service.

Dorans, N. J. (1989). Two new approaches to assessing differential item functioning: Standardization and the Mantel-Haenszel method. *Applied Measurement in Education,* 2, 217–33.

Dorans, N. J., and Kulick, E. (1986). Demonstrating the utility of the standardization approach to assessing differential item functioning on the Scholastic Aptitude Test. *Journal of Educational Measurement,* 23, 355–68.

Dorans, N. J., Schmitt, A. P., and Curley, W. E. (1988, April). *Differential speededness: Some items have DIF because of where they are, not what they are.* Paper presented at the annual meeting of the National Council on Measurement in Education, New Orleans, LA.

Dorans, N. J., Schmitt, A. P., and Bleistein, C. A. (1988). *The standardization approach to assessing differential speededness* (RR-88-31). Princeton, NJ: Educational Testing Service.

Holland, P. W., and Thayer, D. T. (1988). Differential item functioning and the Mantel-Haenszel procedure. In H. Wainer & H. I. Braun, eds., *Test Validity.* Hillsdale, NJ: Erlbaum.

Hunter, R. V., and Slaughter, C. D. (1980). *ETS test sensitivity review process.* Princeton, NJ: Educational Testing Service.

Kulick, E., and Hu, P. G. (1989). *Examining the relationship between differential item functioning and item difficulty* (CBR-89-5). New York, NY: College Entrance Examination Board.

Linn, R. L., and Harnisch, D. L. (1981). Interactions between item content and group membership on achievement test items. *Journal of Educational Measurement*, 18, 109–18.

Ortiz, V., and Gurak, D. T. (1982). *School-to-work transition: A comparative analysis of Hispanic and white youth*. Washington, DC: Hispanic Youth Employment Research Center, National Council of La Raza.

Rivera, C., and Schmitt, A. P. (1988). *A comparison of Hispanic and White Non-Hispanic students' omit patterns on the Scholastic Aptitude Test* (RR-88-44). Princeton, NJ: Educational Testing Service.

Scheuneman, J. D. (1982). A posteriori analyses of biased items. In R. A. Berk, ed., *Handbook of methods for detecting test bias* (pp. 181–98). Baltimore, MD: Johns Hopkins University Press.

Schmitt, A. P. (1985). *Assessing unexpected differential item performance of Hispanic candidates on SAT form 3FSA08 and TSWE form E47* (SR-85-169). Princeton, NJ: Educational Testing Service.

Schmitt, A. P. (1988). Language and cultural characteristics that explain differential item functioning for Hispanic examinees on the Scholastic Aptitude Test. *Journal of Educational Measurement*, 25, 1–13.

Schmitt, A. P., and Bleistein, C. A. (1987). *Factors affecting differential item functioning for Black examinees on Scholastic Aptitude Test analogy Items* (RR-87-23). Princeton, NJ: Educational Testing Service.

Schmitt, A. P., Curley, W. E., Bleistein, C. A., and Dorans, N. J. (1988, April). *Experimental evaluation of language and interest factors related to differential item functioning for Hispanic examinees on the SAT-Verbal*. Paper presented at the annual meeting of the National Council on Measurement in Education, New Orleans, LA.

Schmitt, A. P., and Dorans, N. J. (1990). Differential item functioning for minority examinees on the SAT. *Journal of Educational Measurement*, 27, 67–81.

Shepard, L. A. (1987). Discussant comments on the NCME Symposium: Unexpected differential item performance and its assessment among Black, Asian-American, and Hispanic students. In A. P. Schmitt and N. J. Dorans, eds., *Differential item functioning on the Scholastic Aptitude Test* (RR-87-1). Princeton, NJ: Educational Testing Service.

Wright, D. (1987). An empirical comparison of the Mantel-Haenszel and standardization methods of detecting differential item performance. In A. P. Schmitt and N. J. Dorans, eds., *Differential item functioning on the Scholastic Aptitude Test* (RM-87-1). Princeton, NJ: Educational Testing Service.

Chapter 6. Equating the Scores of the College Board Prueba de Aptitud Académica and the College Board Scholastic Aptitude Test.

Angoff, W. H. (1966). Can useful general-purpose equivalency tables be prepared for different college admissions tests? In *Testing problems in perspective.* Anastasi, A., ed. Washington, DC: American Council on Education, 251–64.

Angoff, W. H. (1984). *Scales, norms and equivalent scores.* Princeton, NJ: Educational Testing Service. Reprint of chapter in *Educational Measurement* 2d ed. Thorndike, R. L., ed. Washington, DC: American Council on Education, (1971).

Angoff, W. H., and Ford, S. F. (1973). Item-rate interaction on a test of scholastic ability. *Journal of Educational Measurement* 10, 95–106.

Angoff, W. H., and Modu, C. C. (1973). Equating the scales of the Prueba de Académica and the Scholastic Aptitude Test. Research Report 3. New York: College Entrance Examination Board.

Boldt, R. F. (1969). Concurrent validity of the PAA and SAT for bilingual Dade County high school volunteers. College Entrance Examination Board Research and Development Report 68-69, Number 3. Princeton, NJ: Educational Testing Service.

Cook, L. L., and Eignor, D. R. (1983). Practical considerations regarding the use of item response theory to equate tests. In *Applications of item response theory.* Hambleton, R. K., ed. Vancouver: Educational Research Institute of British Columbia.

Cook, L. L., Eignor, D. R., and Petersen, N. S. (1985). A study of the temporal stability of item parameter estimates. ETS Research Report 85-45. Princeton, NJ: Educational Testing Service.

Levine, R. S. (1955). Equating the score scales of alternate forms administered to samples of different ability. Research Bulletin 23. Princeton, NJ: Educational Testing Service.

Lord, F. M. (1977). A study of item bias using item response curve theory. In *Basic problems in cross-cultural psychology.* Poortinga, N. H., ed. Amsterdam: Swits and Vitlinger.

Lord, F. M. (1980). *Applications of item response theory to practical testing problems.* Hillsdale, NJ: Erlbaum.

Petersen, N. S. (1977). Bias in the selection rule: Bias in the test. Paper presented at Third International Symposium on Educational Testing, University of Leyden, The Netherlands.

Petersen, N. S., Cook, L. L, and Stocking, M. L. (1983). IRT versus conventional equating methods: A comparative study of scale stability. *Journal of Educational Statistics* 8, 137–56.

Shepard, L. A., Camilli, G., and Williams, D. M. (1984). Validity of approximation techniques for detecting item bias. *Paper presented at annual meeting of the American Educational Research Association*, New Orleans.

Stocking, M. L., and Lord, F. M. (1983). Developing a common metric in item response theory. *Applied Psychological Measurement* 1, 201–10.

Wingersky, M. S. (1983). LOGIST: A program for computing maximum likelihood procedures for logistic test models. In *Applications of item response theory*. Hambleton, R. K., ed. Vancouver: Educational Research Institute of British Columbia.

Wingersky, M. S., Barton, M. A., and Lord, F. M. (1982). LOGIST V user's guide. Princeton, NJ: Educational Testing Service.

Chapter 7. Competency Testing and Latino Student Access to the Teaching Profession: An Overview of Issues.

American Council on Education (1987). *Minorities in higher education: Sixth annual status report 1987*. Office of Minority Concerns. Washington, DC: Author.

Andrews, T. E. (1983). Minority children increasing: Majority teachers decreasing. *Teacher Education Reports*, 5, 2–4.

Andrews, T. E., Lyle, E. L., and Langland, A. (1984). *Teacher competency testing*. Olympia, WA: Superintendent of Public Instruction, Division of Special Services and Professional Programs.

Bandura, A. (1969). *Principles of behavior modification*. New York: Holt, Rinehart, and Winston.

Bandura, A. (1977). *Social learning theory*. Englewood Cliffs, NJ: Prentice-Hall.

Baker, K. (1987). Comment on Willig's "A meta-analysis of selected studies in the effectiveness of bilingual education." *Review of Educational Research*, 57, 351–62.

Baker, K., and de Kanter, A. (1983). Effectiveness of bilingual education. In Baker, K., and de Kanter, A., eds., *Bilingual education: A reappraisal of federal policy* (pp. 33–86). Lexington, MA: Lexington Books.

Baker, K., and de Kanter, A. (1981). *Effectiveness of bilingual education: A review of the literature*. Final draft report. Washington, DC: Office of Technical and Analytic Systems, U.S. Department of Education.

Banks, J. A. (1984). *Teaching strategies for ethnic studies* (3rd ed.). Boston: Allyn and Bacon.

Barton, E. J., and Osborne, J. G. (1978). The development of classroom sharing by a teacher using positive practice. *Behavior Modification*, 2, 231–49.

Bass de Martinez, B. (1988). Political and reform agendas' impact on the supply of Black teachers. *Journal of Teacher Education, 39*, 10–13.

Brophy, J. E., and Puttham, J. G. (1979). Classroom management in the elementary grades. In Duke, D., ed., *Classroom management: The seventy-eighth yearbook of the National Society for the Study of Education* (pp. 182–216). Chicago: The National Society for the Study of Education.

Bureau of the Census (1987). *The Hispanic population in the United States: March 1986 and 1987.* Washington, DC: U.S. Department of Education.

Cannon, C. M. (1986, November 13). How immigration is tipping nation's ethnic balance. *San Jose Mercury,* p. 1A.

Carter, T. P., and Chatfield, M. L. (1986). Effective bilingual schools: Implications for policy and practice. *American Journal of Education, 95,* 200–34.

Center for Education Statistics (1987). *Digest of education statistics, 1987.* Washington, DC: U.S. Government Printing Office.

Center for Education Statistics (1988). *Trends in minority enrollment in higher education, Fall 1976–Fall 1986.* Washington, DC: U.S. Department of Education.

Crawford, J. (1987). Bilingual education: Language, learning, and politics. *Education Week, 6,* 19–50.

Duran, R. P. (1983). *Hispanics' education and background: Predictors of college achievement.* New York: College Entrance Examination Board.

Edmonds, R. (1979). Effective schools for the urban poor. *Educational Leadership, 37,* 57–62.

Edmonds, R. (1986). Characteristics of effective schools. In Neiser, U., ed., *The school achievement of minority children: New perspectives* (pp. 93–104). Hillsdale, NJ: Lawrence Erlbaum.

Eissenberg, T. E., and Rudner, L. M. (1988). State testing of teachers: A summary. *Journal of Teacher Education, 39,* 21–22.

Garcia, E. (1988). Attributes of effective schools for language minority students. *Education and Urban Society, 20,* 387–98.

Garcia, G. X. (1989, November 25). 74% of graduates pass TASP tests: Failure rate among Black students 52%. *Austin American Statesman,* pp. A1, A8.

Garcia, E., Flores, B., Moll, L., and Prieto, A. (1988). *Effective schooling for Hispanics: A final report.* Tempe: Arizona State University, Bilingual/Bicultural Education Center.

Gay, G. (1988). Designing relevant curricula for diverse learners. *Education and Urban Society, 20,* 327–40.

References

Gonzalez, J. M. (1974). *A developmental and sociological rationale for culture-based curricula and cultural context teaching in the early instruction of Mexican-American children.* Unpublished doctoral dissertation, University of Massachusetts.

Graham, P. A. (1987). Black teachers: A drastically scarce resource. *Phi Delta Kappan,* 68, 598–605.

Haertel, E. H. (1988). *Validity of teacher licensure and teacher education admissions tests.* Paper prepared for the National Education Association and Council of Chief State School Officers.

Jackson, P. W. (1986). *The practice of teaching.* New York: Teachers College Press.

King, J. E., and Ladson-Billings, G. (1988, February). *The teacher education challenge in elite university settings: Developing crucial perspectives for teaching in a democratic and multicultural society.* Paper presented at the meeting of the American Association of Colleges of Teacher Education, New Orleans, LA.

Mahan, J., and Boyle, V. (1981). Multicultural teacher preparation: An attitudinal survey. *Educational Research Quarterly,* 6, 97–112.

Mercer, W. (1983). The gathering storm: Teacher testing and Black teachers. *Educational Leadership,* 41, 70–71.

Mercer, W., and Mercer, M. M. (1986). The emerging minority teacher shortage: Implications for the middle school. *American Middle School Education,* 9, 14–18.

Middleton, E. J., Mason, E. J., Stillwell, W. E., and Parker, W. C. (1988). A model for recruitment and retention of minority students in teacher preparation programs. *Journal of Teacher Education,* 39, 14–18.

Mingle, J. R. (1987). *Focus on minorities: Trends in higher education participation and success.* Denver, CO: A joint publication of the Education Commission of the States and State Higher Education Executive Officers.

Muñoz, D. G. (1986). Identifying areas of stress for Chicano undergraduates. In Olivas, M. A., ed., *Latino college students* (pp. 131–56). New York: Teachers College Press.

National Commission on Excellence in Education (1983). *A nation at risk: The imperatives for educational reform.* Washington, DC: U.S. Government Printing Office.

Nava, R. (1985). Caveat: Teacher competency tests may be hazardous to the employment of minority teachers and the education of language minority students. *Thrust,* 14, 33–34.

Olivas, M. A. (ed.). (1986a). *Latino college students.* New York: Teachers College Press.

Olivas, M. A. (1986b). Research on Latino college students: A theoretical framework and inquiry. In Olivas, M. A., ed., *Latino college students* (pp. 1–25). New York: Teachers College Press.

Olsen, L. (1988). *Crossing the schoolhouse border: Immigrant students and the California public schools.* Boston, MA: California Tomorrow.

Orfield, G. (1988, July). *The growth and concentration of Hispanic enrollment and the future of American education.* Paper presented at the National Council of La Raza Conference, Albuquerque, NM.

Orum, L. S. (1986). *The education of Hispanics: Status and implications.* Washington, DC: National Council of La Raza.

Ottinger, C. A. (1987). (Ed.). *Higher education today: Facts in brief.* American Council on Education, Division of Policy Analysis and Research.

Payan, R. M., Peterson, R. E., and Castille, N. A. (1984). *Access to college for Mexican Americans in the Southwest: Replication after 10 years* (College Board Report No. 84-3). New York: College Entrance Examination Board.

Pressman, H., and Gartner, A. (1986). The new racism in education. *Social Policy*, 16, 11–15.

Rosenthal, T. L., and Bandura, A. (1978). Psychological modeling: Theory and practice. In Garfield, S. L., and Bergin, A. E., eds., *Handbook of psychotherapy and behavior change: An empirical analysis* (2nd ed.) (pp. 621–58). New York: Wiley.

Secada, W. (1987). This is 1987, not 1980: A comment on a comment. *Review of Educational Research*, 57, 377–84.

Shepard, L. A., and Kreitzer, A. E. (1987). The Texas teacher test. *Educational Researcher*, 16, 22–31.

Shulman, L. S. (1986). Those who understand: A conception of teacher knowledge. *American Educator*, 10, 8–15, 42–44.

Slavin, R. E. (1986). *Educational psychology: Theory into practice.* Englewood Cliffs, NJ: Prentice-Hall.

Sleeter, C. E., and Grant, C. A. (1987). An analysis of multicultural education in the United States. *Harvard Educational Review*, 57, 421–43.

Smith, G. P. (1985). Competence testing: Excellence without equity. *Texas Technological Journal of Education*, 12, 125–29.

Smith, G. P. (1987). *The effects of competency testing on the supply of minority teachers.* A report prepared for the National Education Association and the Council of Chief State School Officers.

Suzuki, B. H. (1984). Curriculum transformation for multicultural education. *Education and Urban Society*, 16, 294–322.

United States v. South Carolina, 445 F. Supp. 1094 (D. South Carolina, 1977), aff'd 434 U.S. 1026 (1978).

Valencia, R. R. (1991). The plight of Chicano students: An overview of schooling conditions and outcomes. In Valencia, R. R., ed., *Chicano school failure and success: Research and policy agendas for the 1990s*. The Stanford Series on Education and Public Policy. Basingstoke: Falmer Press. (pp. 3–26).

Vierra, A. (1984). The relationship between Chicano children's achievement and their teacher's ethnicity. *Hispanic Journal of Behavioral Sciences*, 6, 285–90.

Watson, A. (1988, December 31). Minority teachers sought. *San Jose Mercury News*, pp. 1A, 16A.

Willing, A. (1985). A meta-analysis of selected studies on the effectiveness of bilingual education. *Review of Educational Research*, 55, 269–317.

Willig, A. C. (1987). Examining bilingual education research through meta-analysis and narrative review: A response to Baker. *Review of Educational Research*, 57, 363–76.

Zapata, J. T. (1988). Early identification and recruitment of Hispanic teacher candidates. *Journal of Teacher Education*, 39, 19–23.

Chapter 8. Research Directions and Practical Strategies in Teacher Testing and Assessment: Implications for Improving Latino Access to Teaching.

Aburto, S., and Haertel, E. (1986). *Study group on alternative assessment methods: Executive summary*. Palo Alto: Stanford University, Teacher Assessment Project.

Acuña, R. (1981). *Occupied America: A history of Chicanos* (2nd ed.). New York: Haynes and Ross.

Airasian, P. W. (1987). State mandated testing and educational reform: Context and consequences. *American Journal of Education*, 95, 392–412.

Aksamit, D., Mitchell, J. V., and Pozehl, B. (1987). Relationships between PPST and ACT scores and their implications for the basic skills testing of prospective teachers. *Journal of Teacher Education*, 38, 48–52.

Allan, R. G., Nassif, P. M. and Elliot, S. M., eds. (1988). *Bias issues in teacher certification testing*. Hillsdale, NJ: Erlbaum.

American Educational Research Association (AERA), American Psychological Association (APA), National Council on Measurement in Education (NCME) Joint Committee (1985). *Standards for educational and psychological testing*. Washington, DC: American Psychological Association.

Anastasi, A. (1986). Evolving concepts of test validation. *Annual Review of Psychology,* 37, 1–15.

Andrews, J. W., Blackmon, C. R., and Mackey, J. A. (1980). Preservice performance and the National Teacher Examinations. *Phi Delta Kappan,* 61, 358–59.

Andrews, T. E., Lyle, E. L., and Langland, A. (1984). *Teacher competency testing.* Olympia, WA: Superintendent of Public Instruction, Division of Special Services and Professional Programs.

Anrig, G. R. (1986). Teacher education and teacher testing: The rush to mandate. *Phi Delta Kappan,* 67, 447–51.

Arthur, B., Farrar, D., and Bradford, G. (1974). Evaluation reactions of college students to dialect differences in the English of Mexican-Americans. *Language and Speech,* 17, 255–70.

Arvey, R. D. (1979). Unfair discrimination in the employment interview: Legal and psychological aspects. *Psychological Bulletin,* 86, 736–65.

Baratz, J. C. (1986, January). *Black participation in the teaching pool.* Paper presented to the Carnegie Forum Task Force on Teaching as a Profession, New York.

Barrera, M. (1979). *Race and class in the Southwest: A theory of racial inequality.* South Bend, IN: University of Notre Dame Press.

Berk, R. A., ed. (1982). *Handbook of methods for detecting test bias.* Baltimore, MD: Johns Hopkins University Press.

Berk, R. A. (1986). A consumer's guide to setting performance standards on criterion-referenced tests. *Review of Educational Research,* 56, 137–72.

Brekke, A. M. (1973). *Evaluational reactions of adolescent and pre-adolescent Mexican American and Anglo American students to selected samples of spoken English.* Unpublished doctoral dissertation, University of Minnesota.

Brennan, E. M. (1977). *Mexican American accented English: Phonological analysis, accent scaling, and evaluative reactions.* Unpublished doctoral dissertation, University of Notre Dame, IN.

Brennan, E. M., and Brennan, J. S. (1981a). Accent scaling and language attitudes: Reactions to Mexican-American English speech. *Language and Speech,* 24, 207–21.

Brennan, E. M., and Brennan, J. S. (1981b). Measurements of accent and attitude toward Mexican-American speech. *Journal of Psycholinguistic Research,* 10, 487–501.

Brennan, E. M., Ryan, E. B., and Dawson, W. E. (1975). Scaling of apparent accentedness by magnitude estimation and sensory modality matching. *Journal of Psycholinguistic Research,* 4, 27–36.

Browne, B. A., and Rankin, R. J. (1986). Predicting employment in education: The relative efficiency of the National Teacher Examinations scores and student teaching ratings. *Educational and Psychological measurement, 46,* 191–97.

Bruno, J. E., and Marcoulides, G. A. (1985). Equality of educational opportunity at racially isolated schools: Balancing the need for teacher certification with teacher shortage. *Urban Review, 17,* 155–65.

Burns, R. (1983). *The Pre-Basic Skills Mathematics Test, Form A.* El Paso: The University of Texas at El Paso.

Burns, R. (1985). *Basic Mathematics Skills Test, Form B.* El Paso: El Paso Education Services.

Carlton, S. T., and Marco, G. L. (1982). Methods used by test publishers to "debias" standardized tests: Educational Testing Service. In Berk, R. A., ed., *Handbook of methods for detecting test bias.* Baltimore: The Johns Hopkins University Press, 278–313.

Carnegie Forum on Education and the Economy (1986). *A nation prepared: Teachers for the 21st century.* New York: Carnegie Foundation.

Carranza, M. A. (1982). Attitudinal research on Hispanic language varieties. In Ryan, E. R., and Giles, H., eds., *Attitudes toward language variation: Social and applied contexts.* London: Edward Arnold, 63–83.

Case, C. W., Shive, R. J., Ingelbretson, K., and Spiegel, V. M. (1988). Minority teacher education: Recruitment and retention methods. *Journal of Teacher Education, 39,* 54–57.

Center for Policy Research (1987, September). *Testing to improve the quality of our school teachers.* Washington, DC: Author.

Cronbach, L. J. (1984). *Essentials of psychological testing* (4th ed.). New York: Harper and Row.

Cross, L. H. (1985). Validation of the NTE tests for certification decisions. *Educational Measurement: Issues and Practices, 4,* 7–10.

Cross, L. H., Impara, J. C., Frary, R. B., and Jaeger, R. M. (1984). A comparison of three methods for establishing minimum standards on the National Teachers Examinations. *Journal of Educational Measurement, 21,* 113–29.

DeLeon, A. (1983). *They call them greasers: Anglo attitudes toward Mexicans in Texas, 1821–1900.* Austin, TX: University of Texas Press.

Educational Testing Service (1987). *Test Analysis: Pre-Professional Skills Tests Spring 1987 Administrations* (Unpublished statistical report No. SR 87-117). Princeton, NJ: Author.

Educational Testing Service (1988, October). New teacher assessment tests to offer an alternative to the NTE. *Examiner, 18,* 1, 7.

Flores, N. De La Zerda, and Hopper, R. (1975). Mexican American's evaluation of spoken Spanish and English. *Speech Monographs*, 42, 91–98.

Galván, J. L., Pierce, J. A., and Underwood, G. N. (1975). *Relationships between teacher attitudes and differences in the English of bilinguals.* Paper presented at Southwest Area Linguistics Workshops, San Diego, CA.

Giles, H., Bourhis, R. Y., and Taylor, D. M. (1976). Towards a theory of language in group relations. In Giles, H., ed., *Language, ethnicity, and intergroup relations.* London: Academic Press, 307–48.

Glass, G. V. (1978). Standards and criteria. *Journal of Educational Measurement*, 15, 237–61.

Haberman, M. (1988). Proposals for recruiting minority teachers. Promising practices and attractive detours. *Journal of Teacher Education*, 39, 38–44.

Hackley, L. V. (1985). The decline in the number of black teachers can be reversed. *Educational Measurement: Issues and Practice*, 4, 17–19.

Haertel, E. H. (1985). Construct validity and criterion-referenced testing. *Review of Educational Research*, 55, 23–46.

Haertel, E. H. (1988a). Assessing the teaching function. *Applied Measurement in Education*, 1, 99–107.

Haertel, E. H. (1988b). *Validity of teacher licensure and teacher education admissions tests.* Paper prepared for the National Association and Council of Chief State School Officers.

Haney, W., and Maduas, G. (1978). Making sense of the competency test movement. *Harvard Educational Review*, 48, 462–84.

Holmes Group (1986). *Tomorrow's teachers: A report of the Holmes Group.* East Lansing, MI: Author.

Jensen, A. R. (1980). *Bias in mental testing.* New York: Fress Press.

Johnson, S. (1988). Validity and bias in teacher certification testing. In Allan, R. G., Nassif, P. M., and Elliot, S. M., eds., *Bias issues in teacher certification testing.* Hillsdale, NJ: Lawrence Erlbaum, 35–49.

Jones, C. (1986). Evaluation shows Black and White teachers equal. *Black Issues in Higher Education*, 3, 1, 5.

Kortokrax-Clark, D. (1986–87). The minority teacher shortage: An overview and a solution. *Action in Teacher Education*, 8, 7–13.

Leach, W. J., and Solomon, L. (1986). Performance-based certification in Georgia: Present and future. In Lasley, T. J., ed., *Issues in teacher education.* Washington, DC: American Association of Colleges for Teacher Education, 163–75.

Livingston, S. A., and Zieky, M. J. (1982). *Passing scores: A manual for setting standards of performance on educational and occupational tests.* Princeton, NJ: Educational Testing Service.

Longres, J. F. (1974). Racism and its effects on Puerto Rican continentals. *Social Casework*, 55, 67–75.

Marcoulides, G. A., and Bruno, J. (1986). Analysis of policy issues in teacher certification. *Teacher Education Quarterly*, 13, 68–81.

McConahay, J. B. (1983). Modern racism and modern discrimination: The effects of race, racial attitudes, and context on simulated hiring decisions. *Personality and Social Psychology Bulletin*, 9, 551–58.

McConahay, J. B., Hardee, B. B., and Batts, V. (1981). Has racism declined in America? It depends on who is asking and what is asked. *Journal of Conflict Resolution*, 25, 563–79.

Mendoza-Hall, M. M. (1980). *The effect of sociocultural environment on Chicano language attitudes, language use patterns and ethnic identity.* Unpublished doctoral dissertation, University of Colorado at Boulder.

Mercer, W., and Mercer, M. M. (1986). The emerging minority teacher shortage: Implications for the middle school. *American Middle School Education*, 9, 14–18.

Messick, S. (1989). Validity. In Linn, R. L., ed., *Educational measurement.* New York: MacMillan, 13–104.

Montalvo, F. F. (1987). *Skin color and Latinos: The origins and contemporary patterns of ethnoracial ambiguity among Mexican Americans and Puerto Ricans.* San Antonio, TX: Institute for Intercultural Studies and Worden School of Social Service, Our Lady of the Lake University of San Antonio.

Morehead, M. A. (1986). Minorities and admission to teacher education. *Action in Teacher Education*, 8, 61–64.

Nakanishi, D. T. (1986). The untapped recruiters: Minority alumni and undergraduate admissions. *Journal of College Admissions*, 112, 15–19.

Nava, R. (1985). Caveat: Teacher competency tests may be hazardous to the employment of minority teachers and the education of language minority students. *Thrust*, 14, 33–34.

Nieto, C. (1986). The California challenge: Preparing teachers for a growing Hispanic population. *Action in Teacher Education*, 8, 1–8.

Ogbu, J. R. (1983). Minority status and schooling in plural societies. *Contemporary Education in Review*, 27, 168–90.

Parsons, C. K., and Liden, R. C. (1984). Interviewer perceptions of applicant qualifications: A multivariate field study of demographic characteristics and nonverbal cues. *Journal of Applied Psychology*, 69, 557–68.

Petersen, R. E. (1984, April). *CBEST, NTE and other mensurations: Notes on testing would-be teachers in California, and elsewhere.* Paper presented at the Conference of the California Council on the Education of Teachers, San Diego.

Politzer, R. L., and Ramirez, A. (1973a). *Judging personality from speech: A pilot study of the effects of bilingual education on attitudes toward ethnic groups* (Research and Development Memorandum No. 16). Stanford, CA: Stanford University, Stanford Center for Research and Development in Teaching.

Politzer, R. L., and Ramirez, A. (1973b). *Judging personality from speech: A pilot study of the attitudes toward ethnic groups of students in monolingual schools* (Research and Development Memorandum No. 107). Stanford, CA: Stanford University, Stanford Center for Research and Development in Teaching.

Pressman, H., and Gartner, A. (1986). The new racism in education. *Social Policy,* 16, 11–15.

Quirk, T. J., Witten, B. J., and Weinberg, S. F. (1973). Reviews of studies of the concurrent and predictive validity of the National Teacher Examinations. *Review of Educational Research,* 43, 89–113.

Rebell, M. A. (1986). Disparate impact of teacher competency testing on minorities: Don't blame the test-takers—or the tests. *Yale Law and Policy Review,* 4, 375–403.

Rebell, M. A. (1988). Legal issues concerning bias in testing. In Allan, R. G., Nassif, P. M., and Elliot, S. M., eds., *Bias issues in teacher certification testing.* Hillsdale, NJ: Erlbaum, 1–18.

Reynolds, C. R. (1982). The problem of bias in psychological assessment. In Reynolds, C. R., and Gutkin, T. B., eds., *The handbook of school psychology.* New York: Wiley, 178–208.

Rodriguez, I. V. (1984). *Hispanics in math and sciences: Attracting student teachers and retraining experienced teachers.* Las Cruces, NM: ERIC Clearinghouse on Rural Education and Small Schools. (ERIC Document Reproduction Services No. ED 260 870).

Rosner, F. C., and Howey, K. (1982). Construct validity in assessing teacher knowledge: New NTE interpretations. *Journal of Teacher Education,* 33, 7–12.

Roth, R. (1983, November). *Relationships among NTE cut-scores, not valid items, NTE tests and curriculum match and minimally competent examinees.* Paper presented at the meeting of the Mid-South Educational Research Association, Nashville, TN.

Roth, R. (1986, November). *The difference between teachers and teacher educators when judging the NTE professional knowledge test to determine a cut score.* Paper presented at the Mid-South Educational Research Association, Mobile, AL.

References

Rothwell, J. G. (1987). *Racial discrimination in the personnel setting: Strategies for change.* Unpublished doctoral dissertation, University of California at Santa Cruz.

Ryan, E. B. (1973). Subjective reactions toward accented speech. In Shuy, R. W., and Fasold, R. W., eds., *Language attitudes: Current trends and prospects.* Washington, DC: Georgetown University Press, 60–73.

Ryan, E. B. (1979). Why do low-prestige language varieties exist. In Giles, H., and St Clair, R. N., eds., *Language and social psychology.* Oxford, England: Basil Blackwell, 145–57.

Ryan, E. B., and Carranza, M. A. (1975). Evaluative reactions of adolescents towards speakers of standard English and Mexican American accented English. *Journal of Personality and Social Psychology,* 31, 855–63.

Ryan, E. B., Carranza, M. A., and Moffie, R. W. (1977). Reactions toward varying degrees of accentedness in the speech of Spanish-English bilinguals. *Language and Speech,* 20, 267–73.

Ryan, E. B., Giles, H., and Sebastian, R. J. (1982). An integrative perspective for the study of attitudes toward language variation. In Ryan, E. B., and Giles, H., eds., *Attitudes towards language variation: Social and applied contexts.* London: Edward Arnold, 1–19.

Salinger, T. (1983). *The Pre-Basic Skills Reading Test, Form A.* El Paso: The University of Texas at El Paso.

Salinger, T. (1985). *Basic Reading Skills Test, Form B.* El Paso: El Paso Education Services.

Salinger, T. S., and Heger, H. K. (1986). Screening and advising for the P-PST: Positive action. *Urban Educator,* 8, 119–25.

Sandefur, J. T. (1986). State assessment trends. *AACTE Briefs,* 7, 12–14.

Schmitt, N. (1976). Social and situational determinants of interview decisions: Implications for the employment interview. *Personnel Psychology,* 29, 79–102.

Sebastian, R. J., Ryan, E. B., Keogh, T. F., and Schmidt, A. C. (1980). The effects of negative affect arousal on reactions to speakers. In Giles, H., Robinson, W. P., and Smith, P. M., eds., *Language: Social psychological perspectives.* Oxford, England: Permagon Press, 203–208.

Shepard, L. A. (1980). Standard setting issues and methods. *Applied Psychological Measurement,* 4, 447–67.

Shepard, L. A. (1982). Setting performance standards. In Berk, R. A., ed., *A guide to criterion-referenced test construction.* Baltimore, MD: Johns Hopkins University Press, 169–98.

Shulman, L. S. (1987). Assessment for teaching: An initiative for the profession. *Phi Delta Kappan,* 69, 38–44.

Shulman, L. S., Haertel, E., and Bird, T. (1988). *Toward alternative assessments of teaching: A report of work in progress* (Technical Report No. 10). Stanford, CA: Stanford University, Teacher Assessment Project.

Smith, G. P. (1988). *The effects of competency testing on the supply of minority teachers.* A report prepared for the National Education Association and the Council of Chief State School Officers.

Spellman, S. O. (1988). Recruitment of minority teachers: Issues, problems, facts, possible solutions. *Journal of Teacher Education, 39,* 58–63.

Spencer, T. L. (1986). Teacher education at Grambling State University: A move toward excellence. *Journal of Negro Education, 55,* 293–303.

Stewart, D. K. (1988). Materials on recruitment and retention of minority teachers and teacher education students in the ERIC database. *Journal of Teacher Education, 39,* 24–26.

Stoker, W. M., and Tarrab, M. (1985). The relationship between Pre-Professional Skills Tests and American College Tests. *Teacher Education and Practice, 2,* 43–45.

Trudgill, P., and Giles, H. (1976). *Sociolinguistics and linguistic value judgements: Correctness, adequacy and aesthetics* (Series B, Paper No. 10). Trier: University of Trier.

van der Linden, W. J. (1984). Some thoughts on the use of decision theory to set cutoff scores: Comment on de Gruijter and Hambleton. *Applied Psychological Measurement, 8,* 9–17.

Warren, S. (1985). *Minorities in teacher education.* Washington, DC: ERIC Clearinghouse on Teacher Education. (ERIC Document Reproduction Service No. ED 272 504).

Williams, F. (1970). Language, attitude, and social change. In Williams, F., ed., *Language and poverty: Perspectives on a theme.* Chicago: Markham, 380–99.

Witty, E. P. (1986). Testing teacher performance. *Journal of Negro Education, 55,* 358–67.

Zapata, J. T. (1988). Early identification and recruitment of Hispanic teacher candidates. *Journal of Teacher Education, 39,* 19–23.

Chapter 9: The Development of *TestSkills;* A Test Familiarization Kit on the Preliminary Scholastic Aptitude Test/National Merit Scholarship Qualifying Test.

Benjamin, L. T., Jr., Cavell, T. A., and Shallenberger, W. R., III (1984). Staying with initial answers on objective tests: Is It a Myth? *Teaching of Psychology, 11,* 133–41.

Clewell, B. C., and Joy, M. F. (1988). *The National Hispanic Scholar Awards Program: A descriptive analysis of high-achieving Hispanic students.* College Board Report No. 88-10. New York: College Entrance Examination Board.

Liebert, R. M., and Morris, L. W. (1967). Cognitive and emotional components of test anxiety: A distinction and some initial data. *Psychological Reports,* 20, 975–78.

Mandler, G., and Sarason, S. B. (1952). A study of anxiety and learning. *Journal of Abnormal and Social Psychology,* 47, 166–73.

Millman, J., Bishop, C. H., and Ebel, R. (1965). An analysis of test-wiseness. *Educational and Psychological Measurement,* 25, 707–26.

Morris, L. W., and Liebert, R. M. (1969). Effects of anxiety on timed and untimed intelligence tests: Another look. *Journal of Consulting and Clinical Psychology,* 33, 240–44.

Morris, L. W., and Liebert, R. M. (1970). Relationship of cognitive and emotional components of test anxiety to physiological arousal and academic performance. *Journal of Consulting and Clinical Psychology,* 35, 332–37.

Pennock-Roman, M., Powers, D. E., and Perez, M. (1989). *An evaluation of a kit to prepare Hispanic students for the PSAT/NMSQT.* College Board Report No. 89-1. New York: College Entrance Examination Board.

Richardson, F. C., O'Neil, H. F., Whitmore, S., and Judd, W. A. (1977). Factor analysis of the test anxiety scale and evidence concerning the components of test anxiety. *Journal of Consulting and Clinical Psychology,* 45, 704–705.

Rincon, Edward T. *Improving standardized test scores through short-term instructional activities: Implications for Hispanic test-takers.* Paper presented to the Sixth Annual RACHE Conference on "The Chicano Reality in Higher Education: Policy Development in the 80s for the 90s."

Rivera, C., and Schmitt, A. P. (1988). *A comparison of Hispanic and White non-Hispanic students' omit patterns on the Scholastic Aptitude Test,* (RR-88-44), Princeton, NJ: Educational Testing Service.

Sarason, I. G. (1972). Experimental Approaches to Test Anxiety: Attention and the Uses of Information. In Spielberger, C. D., ed., *Anxiety: Current Trends in Theory and Research,* Vol. 2, 381–403. New York: Academic Press.

Whimbey, A., and Lochhead, J., (1986). *Problem Solving and Comprehension,* Lawrence Erlbaum Associates, Hillsdale, New Jersey.

Wine, J. (1971). Test anxiety and direction of attention. *Psychological Bulletin,* 76, 92–104.

Chapter 10. A Preliminary Evaluation of *TestSkills*.

Boyer, E. L. (1983). *High school: A report on secondary education in America.* New York: Harper & Row.

Cicourel, A. V., and Kitsuse, J. I. (1963). *The educational decision-makers.* Indianapolis, IN: Bobbs-Merrill.

Commission on Precollege Guidance and Counseling (1986). *Keeping the options open: An overview* (Interim Report). New York: College Entrance Examination Board.

Erickson, F., and Schultz, J. (1982). *The counselor as gatekeeper: Social interaction in interviews.* New York: Academic Press.

George, C. A. (1988). *Increasing the number of minority students taking the SAT and ACT: Evaluation Report on Pilot Projects Funded by AB 2321. (Chapter 1210, Statutes of 1985).* Department of Special Studies and Evaluation Reports Unit, Program Evaluation and Research Division, California State Department of Education. (Available from the aforementioned Department, P.O. Box 944272, Sacramento, California 94244–2720.)

Ginsburg, M. B., and Giles, J. R. (1984). Sponsored and contest modes of social reproduction in selective community college programs. *Research in Higher Education,* 21(3), 281–299.

Holmes, D. R., Dalton, H. F., Erdmann, D. G., Hayden, T. C., and Roberts, A. O. (1986). *Frontiers of possibility: Report of the National College Counseling Project.* Burlington: University of Vermont, Instructional Development Center.

Lee, V. E., and Ekstrom, R. B. (1987). Student access to guidance counseling in high school. *American Educational Research Journal,* 24, 287–310.

National Coalition of Advocates for Children (1985). *Barriers to excellence: Our children at risk.* Boston: Author.

Appendix A. The Teacher/Counselor Questionnaire

May 1987

Dear Teacher/Counselor:

On behalf of the College Board we are conducting an evaluation of the pilot version of the kit "Preparing for the PSAT/NMSQT for Hispanic High School Students," which you used in conjunction with the test preparation program offered at your school during the past year. We'd like to find out about the ways the kit was used, in what ways it was helpful, and how it might be made even more useful. Could you please give us your reactions by completing this brief questionnaire?

Thanks for your help.

Sincerely,

Donald E. Powers

Maria Pennock-Román
Study Directors

DEP:MPR/lc

Appendix A

1. How large a part in your school's test preparation program did the kit "Preparing for the PSAT/NMSQT" play?

   The single most important component 1
   One of several important components 2
   A minor component 3

2. How easy was it to use the kit?

   Very easy 1
   Somewhat easy 2
   Somewhat difficult 3
   Very difficult 4

3. How well did the kit fit in with other components of your test preparation program?

   Very well 1
   Somewhat well 2
   Somewhat poorly 3
   Very poorly 4
   It was the only component 5

4. Were you able to use the kit in a flexible manner, i.e., by adding or subtracting material or by using "bits and pieces" as needed? The kit was:

   Very flexible 1
   Somewhat flexible 2
   Somewhat *in*flexible 3
   Very *in*flexible 4

5. How helpful was the kit "Preparing for the PSAT/NMSQT" in achieving each of the following objectives of your test preparation program? Helping students to:

	Very helpful	Somewhat helpful	Not helpful	Not an objective
Gain an overview of test content and format	1	2	3	4
Learn how to prepare physically and mentally for a test	1	2	3	4
Learn the following strategies for test taking:				
Budgeting time	1	2	3	4
Following directions	1	2	3	4
Guessing wisely	1	2	3	4
Handling test anxiety	1	2	3	4

Appendix A

Understand and respond efficiently to each of the types of PSAT/NMSQT questions:

Antonyms	1	2	3	4
Sentence completion	1	2	3	4
Analogies	1	2	3	4
Reading comprehension . . .	1	2	3	4
Regular math	1	2	3	4
Quantitative comparisons . .	1	2	3	4

Understand the meaning of PSAT/NMSQT scores	1	2	3	4
Understand areas of strength and weakness	1	2	3	4

6. How useful was each of the following components of the kit?

	Very useful	Somewhat useful	Not useful	Did not use
Filmstrip/cassette program . . .	1	2	3	4
Material on dealing with test anxiety.	1	2	3	4
Practice tests	1	2	3	4
Material on cognates	1	2	3	4
Section on marking answer sheets	1	2	3	4
Review of math concepts	1	2	3	4

7. Do you feel that, as a result of your test preparation program, some students who would not have taken the PSAT/NMSQT (or SAT) may now feel confident enough to try it?

   Yes, a substantial increase in the number of students. 1
     Yes, a moderate increase in the number of students. 2
       Yes, a slight increase in the number of students. 3
         Probably no increase. 4

8. Was there anything that you would add to, delete from, or change about the kit?

_____
_____
_____
_____
_____

9. Do you have any other comments about the kit?

   _____
   _____
   _____
   _____
   _____

10. What is your position at your school?

    Counselor 1
    Math teacher 2
    English teacher 3
    Other 4
    (please specify) _____

11. Name of your school: _____

12. What was your role in the program (for example, taught the math component, etc.)?

    _____
    _____

Thanks for your help.

Appendix B. The Student Questionnaire

May 1987

Dear Student:

During the current school year you participated in a program at your school to help you prepare for the Preliminary Scholastic Aptitude Test/National Merit Scholarship Qualifying Test (PSAT/NMSQT), the test that is usually taken by high school juniors or sophomores prior to the Scholastic Aptitude Test (SAT). We at Educational Testing Service would like to get your reactions to the instructional materials that were used in the program in order to make them even better. Will you please help us by completing this questionnaire. Thanks for your help.

Sincerely,

Donald E. Powers

Maria Pennock-Román
Study Directors

DEP:MPR/lc

Appendix B

1. How helpful was the program in helping you learn each of the following. (If you could already do any of these things before the program began, please circle "4".):

	Very helpful	Somewhat helpful	Not helpful	I knew this before the program began
Q1 How to make the best use of time available for test taking. .	1	2	3	4
Q2 When to guess and how to attack questions you don't know	1	2	3	4
Q3 Familiarity with the test directions for the PSAT/NMSQT. .	1	2	3	4
Q4 How to mark the test answer sheet properly	1	2	3	4
Q5 The purpose of each kind of question and the kinds of skills needed to answer them. .	1	2	3	4
Q6 How to handle your nervousness.	1	2	3	4
Q7 What are your strengths and weaknesses	1	2	3	4
Q8 What your test scores mean . .	1	2	3	4
Q9 How to approach the different kinds of questions	1	2	3	4
Q10 How to use your knowledge of Spanish to understand the meaning of words	1	2	3	4
Q11 What mathematical concepts and symbols you should know . .	1	2	3	4

2. How helpful was the program in explaining the following kinds of questions and strategies for answering them?

	Very helpful	Somewhat helpful	Not helpful
Q12 Antonyms, in which you pick the opposite of a word (for example, the opposite of GOOD is BAD)	1	2	3
Q13 Analogies, in which you find the relationships between words (for example, YAWN: BOREDOM :: SMILE: AMUSEMENT)	1	2	3

Appendix B

Q14 Sentence completions, in which you identify missing words (for example, "Unfortunately _____ in one field does not _____ success in another.")   1   2   3

Q15 Reading passages followed by questions about them   1   2   3

Q16 Mathematics questions with 5 choices dealing with algebra, geometry, or arithmetic . . .   1   2   3

Q17 Mathematics questions in which you compare *Column A* with *Column B*   1   2   3

3. Do you think you will take the PSAT/NMSQT next year:

    Definitely yes 1
    Probably yes 2
    Uncertain 3
    Probably not 4
    Definitely not 5

4. If you had *not* participated in the test preparation program at your school this year, do you think you would have taken the PSAT/NMSQT next year:

    Definitely yes 1
    Probably yes 2
    Uncertain 3
    Probably not 4
    Definitely not 5

5. What is your sex?

        Male 1
        Female 2

6. What is your current grade in school?

        9th 1
        10th 2
        11th 3
        12th 4

7. What is your ethnic background?

    American Indian 1
    Asian American 2
    Black or Afro American 3
    Mexican American or Chicano 4

Puerto Rican 5
Other Hispanic/Latino 6
  (e.g., Cuban American, Salvadoran, Venezuelan)
White 7

8. What language other than English can you communicate?

   None 1
   Spanish 2
   Other 3
   (please specify) _____

9. Which statement best describes your language background:

   I communicate well only in English 1
   English is my best language but I can also communicate in
     another language. 2
   I communicate about equally well in English and another language . . 3
   A language other than English is my best language 4

10. What was the best part of the program for you?

    _____
    _____
    _____

11. Is there anything that would have made the program better?

    _____
    _____
    _____

Thanks for your help.

Contributors

Sofía Aburto is a doctoral candidate in education at Stanford University. She is currently working on her dissertation, a validity study examining performance measures of teacher competence. Her major area of interest is the development of teacher performance examinations and equity issues vis-á-vis teacher assessment.

William H. Angoff is Distinguished Research Scientist at Educational Testing Service, where he is engaged in psychological and psychometric research. His publications include: *Scales, Norms, and Equivalent Scores,* in R. L. Thorndike, *Educational Measurement.* American Council in Education, 1971; *The College Board Admissions Testing Program,* College Entrance Examination Board, 1971; and *The Nature-Nurture Debate, Aptitudes, and Group Differences,* published in the *American Psychologist,* 1988.

Gregory Anrig is President of Educational Testing Service.

Linda L. Cook is currently Executive Director of the College Board Admissions and Guidance Area at Educational Testing Service (ETS). At the time of the writing of the report, she was a Principal Measurement Specialist in the College Board Statistical Analysis Unit at ETS. Dr. Cook has published extensively in the areas of item response theory and test equating.

James R. Deneen is a Program Director at Educational Testing Service. He is responsible for planning and managing development projects for the College Board. He directed the development of the General Intellectual Skills Assessment (1989), and the preparation of a software program designed to aid colleges called College Entry: A Counselor Management System.

Neil J. Dorans is Principal Measurement Specialist in the College Board Division of Educational Testing Service, where he is Head of the Aptitude Test Section. He received his Ph.D. in Quantitative Psychology from the University of Illinois. He has done much research in equating and differential item functioning. He has authored several Educational Testing Service Research Reports and published articles in *Applied Measurement in Education, Applied Psychological Measurement, Journal of Applied Psychology, Journal of Educational Measurement, Journal of Educational Statistics, Organizational Behavior and Human Performance,* and *Psychometrika.* He has also co-authored a book, *Computerized Adaptive Testing: A Primer,* and has authored chapters in several books.

Richard P. Durán (Ph.D. University of California, Berkeley) is an Associate Professor in the Graduate School of Education, University of California, Santa Barbara with an affiliated appointment in the Department of Psychology. His publications include *Cognitive and linguistic analyses of test performance* (edited with Roy Freedle), *Hispanics' education and background,* and "Assessment and instruction of at-risk Hispanic students" (*Exceptional Children*).

Lorraine Gaire is Assistant Director of the Middle States Field Service Office of Educational Testing Service. She has experience in planning, delivering, and evaluating workshops in evaluation, testing and measurement, test preparation, test interpretation and use, and critical thinking skills. She also develops instructional texts and media for staff training in educational measurement and evaluation.

María Magdalena Llabre is Associate Professor of Psychology and Education at the University of Miami. She specializes in applied statistics. Her research interests are diverse and include the influence of test factors on minority examinee performance and minority issues in cardiovascular responses to stress.

Gary D. Keller is Regents' Professor at Arizona State University where he specializes in tests and measurements and Chicano Studies. His publications include, *Language Assessment Battery,* New York City Board of Education, 1975, *Ambiguous Word Language Dominance Test,* McGraw-Hill, 1978, and *Bilingual Education for Hispanic Students in the United States,* Teachers College Press, 1981.

Raphael J. Magallán was one of the founding members and is currently chairman of the board of the Hispanic Higher Education Coalition (HHEC). He has been one of the moving forces behind a number of the cooperative projects of HHEC, the College Board, and Educational Testing Service, including Project PRIME (Project to Improve Minority Education), Project 1000, *TestSkills,* and *¡Sí Se Puede!*

José P. Mestre is Associate Professor of Physics at the University of Massachusetts. His research focuses on studying the cognitive processes central to problem solving in mathematics and physics. His publications include *Linguistic and Cultural Influences on Learning Mathematics* (Lawrence Erlbaum Assoc., 1988) and *Academic Preparation in Science* (The College Board, 1990).

Raymond V. Padilla is Director of the Hispanic Research Center and Associate Professor in the Division of Educational Leadership and Policy Studies at Arizona State University. He is a qualitative methodologist and the inventor of HyperQual, a qualitative data analysis program for the Macintosh. He does qualitative research on Hispanics and higher education.

María Pennock-Román is a Research Scientist in the Research Division of Educational Testing Service. Her publications include *Test Validity and Language Background: A Study of Hispanic American Students at Six Universities,* The College Board, 1990, and "New directions for research on Spanish-language tests and test-item bias," in M. A. Olivas (Ed.), *Latino College Students,* Teachers College Press, 1986.

Donald E. Powers is Senior Research Scientist in the Division of Applied Measurement Research at Educational Testing Service. He also serves as Assistant Director for Research for the Graduate Record Examinations. His interests are in applied measurement and validation and recent work has focused on understanding the sources of variation (both relevant and extraneous) in major national admissions tests.

Monte E. Pérez is Director, Community and Organization Relations, Educational Testing Service. He is responsible for community and organization relations leading to the development of partnerships and special projects between ETS and schools, colleges and the legislature.

Currently he is managing the Southwest Network of Exemplary Projects (a coalition of 6 universities demonstrating exemplary models to increase Hispanic access, retention, and professional development in higher education) and Project I-Teach, which encourages 11th grade minority students to pursue higher education and teaching careers.

James M. Royer is Professor of Psychology at the University of Massachusetts, Amherst. His research focuses on the development of language assessment procedures and on evaluating uses for the procedures he has developed. The paper reported in this volume describes using one procedure he has developed to track educational progress in bilingual education programs.

Alicia P. Schmitt is Senior Measurement Statistician in the College Board Division of Educational Testing Service, where she is Statistical Coordinator for the PSAT/NMSQT Program. She received her Ph.D. in Educational Research and Measurement from the University of Florida. She has done extensive research in differential item functioning and has also conducted research on equating, person fit measures, test anxiety, and multiple-choice vs constructed response formats. She has published in the *Journal of Educational Measurement* and in *Applied Measurement in Education* and has authored chapters in several books.

Donald Stewart is President of The College Board.

Richard R. Valencia is an Associate Professor of Educational Psychology and Speech Communication at The University of Texas at Austin. He specializes in educational testing issues and the social/psychological foundations of the minority schooling experience. He has published extensively in his scholarly areas of interest. His most recent major work is an edited volume, *Chicano School Failure and Success: Research and Policy Agendas for the 1990s,* Falmer Press, 1991.

Index

The text contains charts, figures, and tables. Entries that contain a C refer to charts, those that contain an F refer to figures, and those that contain a T refer to tables.

Aburto, Sofía, vii, 29, 33–34, 195
Academic achievement: assessment of, 39; culture and, 30–31, 40–42, 64, 68–80, 103–4; linguistic proficiency and, 30–31, 39–40, 42–45, 58F, 61–62, 62T, 64, 68–80, 103–4. *See also* Assessment; Cultural background; Second language competence; Sentence Verification Technique
Accentedness. *See* Language attitude research
Access. *See* Higher education, access to
Achievement tests, 1, 2, 5, 28–29, 201
ACT, 1, 10, 12, 17, 67, 189, 201
Administrators. *See* Latino administrators; Principal, role of
Admission Test for Graduate Study in Business, 96
Admissions. *See* College admissions. *See also* Higher education, access to; Underrepresentation
Admissions tests: criticism of, 3–4; history of, 5–6. *See also* Test scores, equating of; *TestSkills*
Advanced Placement Program, 20–22
Advanced Placement test. *See* AP
Advisory Committee on Minority Affairs, 242
Airasian, P. W., 205, 208
Aksamit, D., 201
Alfred P. Sloan Foundation, 17
Algebridge, 17, 25, 27–28
Alhambra High School, 21

American College Test. *See* ACT
American College Testing Program, 9, 17
American Council on Education, 6, 179
American Educational Research Association, 14
American Psychological Association, 14
Analysis of variance, 77–80, 79T, 100–101
Anastasi, A., 196
Anchor test, 138–39, 140, 161–62
Andrews, J. W., 198–99
Andrews, T. E., 167, 187, 211
Angoff method, 206–7
Angoff, William H., vii, 5, 29, 33, 133, 135, 140, 160–61
Anrig, Gregory R., 3, 13
Anxiety. *See* Test anxiety
AP, 1, 5, 6, 22–24, 26, 27, 28; effects of, 23–24
Aptitude: nontraditional predictors of, 17
Aptitude test, 1–2, 5, 81–82
Archaic false cognates, 117. *See also* Cognates; False cognate hypothesis; False cognates
Arizona Test of Professional Knowledge, 192
Arriaga, Joe, 20
Arthur, B., 216, 223
Arvey, R. D., 221
ASPIRA consent decree, 8
Assessment: bias in, 11–12, 14–15, 15–16, 45–46, 64, 65, 163, 196, 197, 202–5, 213–14, 218–22; and bilingual subjects, 134–37, 146–49, 148T, 151T; cultural background and, 30–31, 40–42, 50–51, 67, 74–75, 75–80, 95–104, 120–22, 134–37, 145–46, 151T, 160, 162, 163; developments in, vii, 1, 5, 7, 10–11,

27–30, 39, 46–64, 64–66, 86–92, 98–103, 129–31, 136–37, 139–40, 140–56, 161–64, 214–24; differential item functioning and, 129–31; inaccuracy in, 15–16, 29, 30–31, 40; local based, 64–65; open reporting of, 9–10, 11–12, 13–14; predictive power of, 31–32, 66, 81–82, 185; use of, 5; value of, 1–2, 7–9; visual aspect of, 219; work on, 19–20. *See also* Academic achievement; HHEC: testimony of; Performance assessment: bias in; Second language competence; Standardized tests; Test scores, equating of

Assessment centers. *See* Teachers: assessment centers for
Assessment-focused initiatives, 27–28
Assessment instruments: cultural difference and, 135–36, 213–14; problems with, vii, 3, 13, 28, 45–46, 67, 67–68, 195–96, 204–5
Assessment practices: and education of Hispanics, 105, 131–32
Assessment projects, 20–27

Bandura, A., 172
Basic skills tests, 188, 197, 210
Beginning Teacher Assistance Program, 211
Benjamin, L. T., 240
Bias. *See* Assessment: bias in
Bias: elimination of, 202–5, 213–14
Bilingual education, 5, 7–8, 52–63, 176
Bilingual Syntax Measure, 52–53
Bilingual teachers: shortage of, 176–77. *See also* Cultural background: teaching and; Teacher tests; Teaching
Bishop, C. H., 96
Blackmon, C. R., 198–99
Bleistein, C. A., 96, 102, 108, 112, 115–19, 121, 123, 129
Boldt, R. F., 136
Boyle, V., 174–75
Bradford, G., 216, 223
Brekke, A. M., 217, 218
Brennan, E. M., 216, 217
Bronx High School, 21
Browne, B. A., 199
Bruno, J. E., 201–2, 205, 208, 208–9
Bush, George, 25

California Achievement Test. *See* CAT
California Basic Educational Skills Test. *See* CBEST
California Test of Mental Maturity, 98, 99
Carnegie Corporation, 17
Carnegie Forum on Education and the Economy, 212, 224
Carranza, M. A., 214–15, 216, 217, 220
Castille, N. A., 184
Casual false cognates, 117. *See also* Cognates; False cognate hypothesis; False cognates
CAT, 52–53, 189
Cattell Culture Free Intelligence Test, 97
CBEST, 168, 188, 189, 197, 201–2, 208
Center for Educational Statistics, 179, 181
Central High, 261
Central Unified School District, 249–50
Certification. *See* Teacher tests
Certification, performance-based, 210–14. *See also* Teacher certification; Teacher testing
Change: The Magazine of Higher Learning, 19
Chen, Z., 109
Cisneros, Henry G., 20, 22
Clairemont High School, 249, 261
CLAST, 97–98
Clewell, Beatriz Chu, 29, 236
Cocking, R. R., 16, 29
"Code of Fair Testing," 14
Cognates, 245, 250, 255, 256, 262, 263. *See also* False cognate hypothesis; True cognate hypothesis
Cognitive aptitudes: diagnostic testing of, 31, 67–80
Cognitive psychology, 67–68
Cognitive test performance: time and, 95–104
College admissions, 3, 28–29, 81–82, 134, 185, 248. *See also* Admissions tests; College-going rate; Higher education: access to
The College Board, vii, viii, 2, 5, 6, 7, 9, 10, 12, 13, 14, 16, 17, 22, 26, 28, 29, 34, 66, 235, 236, 242, 243, 263. *See also* Advanced Placement Program
College Board Puerto Rico, 133, 141
College-going rate, 3, 183, 184–86, 194
College Level Academic Skills Test. *See* CLAST

Index 327

College Scholarship Service, 6
College success: barriers to, 86–92
Committee on Ability Testing, 3–4
"A Comparison of Hispanic and White non-Hispanic Students' Omit Patterns on the Scholastic Aptitude Test" (Schmitt), 239
Competency testing, 33, 175–78, 187–92, 190T, 193T, 197–98; failure and, 201–2. *See also* Teaching: access to
Compiled knowledge, 82–84, 83F, 84F
Comprehensive Tests of Basic Skills, 189, 248
Computerized tests, 99, 101, 102–3
Concurrent calibration, 155–56
Conference on Latino College Students, 19, 20
Consortium to Identify and Promote Hispanic Professionals, 10, 30
Cook, Linda L., vii, 15, 33
Correlation analyses, 118T, 119–21
Council of Graduate Schools, 17
Credentialing: assessment and, vii, 176–77, 177, 183, 187–92, 190T, 193T, 195–232. *See also* Teacher testing
Cronbach, L. J., 196
"Cultural and Linguistic Influences on Latino Testing" (Mestre and Royer), 30–31
Cultural background: education and, 173–75; sensitivity to in assessment, 30–31, 40–42, 50–51, 67, 74–75, 75–80, 95–104, 120–22, 134–37, 145–46, 151T, 160, 162, 163; teaching and, 170–72, 181–83, 182T, 213–14. *See also* Differential item functioning; Time: cultural difference and; Second language competence
Cummins, J., 43–44, 45
Curley, W. E., 108, 112, 115–19, 121, 129
Curvilinear equating, 155, 160–61. *See also* Test scores: equating of
Cut scores, 195–96, 198; criticism of, 207–8; modification of, 208–10

Dawe, L., 44
Dawson, W. E., 216
De Avila, E. A., 39
Degrees conferred, 185, 186–87, 187T
Delta-plot method, 141
"Diagnostic Testing of Reasoning Skills" (Durán), 31

Dialogic research, 86, 92
Differential criterion validity, 195–204
Differential item difficulty, 142. *See also* Differential item functioning: item easiness and
Differential item functioning, 14, 32–33, 65, 96–98, 105–32, 204, 239; assessment practices and, 129–31; examinee response style and, 122–28, 128–29; false cognate hypothesis and, 114–17, 116T; Hispanics and, 109–29, 110T; homographs and, 117–20; indices of, 126–28, 127T; item easiness and, 123, 126, 127T; not reached items and, 123–26, 127T; special interest and, 120–22, 129; *TestSkills* and, 34, 237; true cognate hypothesis and, 109–14, 113F, 115T
Differential omit effect, 114, 122–23, 126–28, 127T, 131, 239
Differential speededness effect, 103, 108–9, 122, 123–26, 124F, 125F, 126, 129, 131. *See also* Test speededness
Distractors, 116–17, 119, 120, 129, 130
Dorans, Neil J., vii, 14, 29, 32–33, 96, 98, 103, 108, 112, 115–19, 119, 121, 123, 129
Durán, Richard P., vii, 4, 7, 10, 14, 16, 17, 19, 29, 31, 184, 185
Durso, R., 96

Ebel method, 206
Ebel, R., 96
Edmonds, R., 177
Education in the Elementary School Specialty Area Test, 199
Educational Resources Information Center, 224
Educational Testing Act of 1979, 11
Educational Testing Service. *See* ETS
Eissenberg, T. E., 175, 189
Ekstrom, R. B., 244
English as a Second Language Placement Examination, 109
Equal Employment Opportunity Commission, 178–79
ERIC. *See* Educational Resources Information Center
Escalante, Jaime, 6, 8, 20–22
ETS, vii, viii, 1, 2, 6, 7, 9, 10, 11, 12, 13, 14, 16, 17, 18, 19, 21–22, 26, 28, 29, 32,

33, 34, 65, 66, 106, 129, 130–31, 133, 141, 197, 204, 235, 236, 242, 243, 263
"ETS Sensitivity Review Process," 14
ETS Standards for Quality and Fairness, 13
Evans, F. R., 96
Evanston High School, 21
Experiential mode of learning, 85, 85–86

False cognate hypothesis, 114–17, 116T. *See also* Cognates; Differential item functioning; True cognate hypothesis
False cognates, 121, 129, 131
Familism, 41
Farrar, D., 216, 223
Financial aid, 6, 26
Flores, B., 177–78
Florida Performance Measurement System, 192
Focus group research, 87
Formal reasoning, 68–74, 70F, 72T, 76T, 78T, 79T
Frank, L. K., 95
Froman, T. W., 98–102, 102–3, 104

Gaire, Lorraine, vii, 34
Garcia, E., 177–78
García, J., 29
Gay, G., 173
General knowledge, 90–91. *See also* Heuristic knowledge: assessment of
General Test-Taking Scale, 259, 260C
Georgia State Board of Education, 210
Gilroy High School, 248–49, 261
GMAT, 4
Gonzalez, J. M., 173
Gradillas, Henry, 6, 8, 20–22
Graduate and Professional School Financial Aid Service, 17
Graduate Record Exam. *See* GRE
Grambling State University, 226, 229, 231
Grant, C. A., 173
GRE, 1, 4, 11, 15, 17, 17–18, 74, 96
GRE Board, 17
Guessing strategies, 65–66, 237, 239–40, 257, 260, 263. *See also* Test familiarization
Guidance counselors, 244, 248, 264
Gunn High School, 21

Haberman, M., 231
Hackley, L. V., 226
Haertel, E. H., 197, 197–98, 198–99, 200–201, 204, 206–7, 209, 211
Haney, W., 208
Hanford, George H., 20, 22
Harmon, Paul, 82
Hartford School District, 247–48
Hastings, C. N., 46
Heger, H. K., 228
Henning, G., 109
Heuristic knowledge, 31–32, 81–92, 83F, 84F; assessment of, 85–92, 87F, 88F, 89F; localism and, 84–85, 85–86
HHEC/HACU, vii, 2, 7, 10, 11, 11–12, 13, 15–16, 19, 23, 25, 26, 27, 29, 30, 34, 235, 242, 243, 263
HHEC: testimony by, 11–12
Higher education: access to, vii, viii, 1, 18–19, 28–29, 134; barriers to, vii–viii, 3, 184–85; guidance counselors and, 244, 248, 264; historical background, 9–27. *See also* Academic achievement: linguistic proficiency and; Language attitude research; Second language competence; Teaching: access to; Underrepresentation
Hispanic educators: role of, 29
Hispanic Expert Resource Data Base, 30
Hispanic Higher Education Coalition/Hispanic Association of Colleges and Universities. *See* HHEC/HACU
Hispanic Student Success Program. *See* HSSP
Hispanics' Education and Background: Predictors of College Achievement (Durán), 14
Holmes Group, 224
Homographs, 117–19, 118T, 120T, 129, 130; differential item functioning and, 117–20; effects of, 119–20, 129, 131
Hook, C., 46
Hopper, R., 217, 218
HSSP, 2, 6, 10, 19, 20, 24–25, 26, 27–28
Hu, P. G., 122–23, 127
Huberman, A. Michael, 86
Hunter College, 21
Hypothesized cover term, 87

Immerman, M. A., 97
Incremental knowledge, 90–91. *See also* Heuristic knowledge: assessment of
Index of discrepancy, 147, 148T, 162
Inferior schooling, effects of, 231, 232
Informal reasoning, 68–74, 71F, 72T, 76T, 78T, 79T
Institute for Higher Education Law and Governance, 19
Interviews, ethnicity and, 221–22
Item bias methods, 203–4. *See also* Assessment: bias in
Item difficulty index, 146–47, 148T, 150T, 152
Item discrimination index, 146, 148T, 149
Item response curve, 142, 143F, 144, 161
Item response theory, 141–42, 142–44, 143F, 145, 146F, 147F, 155–56, 156, 160–61, 160F
Item-test biserial correlation, 147, 148T, 149, 150T

Jackson, Philip, 170–72
James A. Garfield High School, 2, 6, 8, 10, 20–22
Jiménez, Benjamín, 20
Johnson, S., 198, 200, 211–12
Jones, J. Quentin, 20
Judgment procedures: in test development, 130–31. *See also* Differential item functioning
Judgmental bias procedures, 203. *See also* Assessment: bias in; Test bias research

Keller, Gary D., vii
Keogh, T. F., 219–20
King, David, 82
King, J. E., 174–75
Knapp, R. R., 97
Knowledge estimation, 200
Knowledge vector, 86–90
Kreitzer, A. E., 175
Kulik, E., 122–23, 127

Ladson-Billings, G., 174, 175
Langland, A., 187, 211
Language Assessment Battery, 8

Language Attitude Research, 214–15, 215–18, 219–20
Language proficiency, 5, 43–44. *See also* Academic achievement: linguistic proficiency and; Second language competence
Latino administrators, 177–78, 179
Latino College Students (Olivas), 10, 19, 19–20
Latino teachers: identification and recruitment of, 224–31; value of, 169–75; underrepresentation of, 181–83, 182T, 183–92, 231–32
Law School Admissions Test. *See* LSAT
Lee, V. E., 244
Levine, R. S., 155
Levine, R. V., 95–96
Liden, R. C., 221–22
Liebert, R. M., 238
Limited-English Proficiency Students, 176–77. *See also* Academic achievement: linguistic proficiency and; Second language competence
Linear equating, 155, 160. *See also* Test scores: equating of
Linguistic proficiency. *See* Academic achievement: linguistic proficiency and. *See also* Sentence Verification Technique
Llabre, María Magdalena, vii, 29, 32, 98–102, 102–3, 104
Local based assessment, 64–65
Localism, 84–85, 85–86
LOGIST, 143–44, 155
Long Beach Unified School District, 248
Lord, F. M., 144
Los Angeles City Unified School District, 168
LSAT, 4, 15, 96
Lyle, E. L., 187, 211

Mackey, J. A., 198–99
Madrid, Arturo, 19–20
Magallán, Rafael J., vii, 27
Mahan, J., 174–75
Mandler, G., 237, 237–38
Manning, W. H., 29
Mantel-Haenszel method, 106. *See also* Differential item functioning
Marcoulides, G. A., 201–2, 205, 208, 208–9

Mathematics register, 44
Mathews, Jay, 21–22
McConahay, J. B., 222
Mendoza-Hall, M. M., 217
Mercer, W., 168
Messick, S., 49, 196, 201
Mestre, José P., vii, 16, 17, 19, 29, 30–31
Miami-Dade Community College, 98–99
The Miami Herald, 95
Miles, Mathew, 86
Millman, Jason, 96, 237
Mingle, J. R., 179, 184
Minimally competent examinee, 206, 209
Minnie Stevens Piper Foundation, 22, 23
Mitchell, J. V., 201
Modeling, 172–73
Modern Racism Scale, 222
Modu, C. C., 133, 135, 140, 160–61
Moffie, R. W., 216, 217
Moll, L., 177–78
Montalvo, F. F., 221
Morris, L. W., 238
Motivation, vii, 239–40
Multicultural education, 173–75, 176–77
Multiple regression techniques, 199

Nader, Ralph, 11
A Nation at Risk (National Commission on Excellence in Education), 188
National Commission on Excellence in Education, 188
National Council of La Raza, 26
National Council of Teachers of English, 249
National Council on Measurement in Education, 14
National Education Association, 3
National Hispanic Scholar Awards Program, 19, 235, 236
National Teachers Examination. *See* NTE
Nava, R., 176, 177, 229
Nedelsky method, 206
Negative affect in speech, 219–20. *See also* Language attitude research
Negative differential effect, 117. *See also* Differential item functioning
New York City Board of Education, 8
NTE, 28, 175, 188, 189, 198, 199, 203, 204–5, 212, 226

Oksapmin culture, 40
Olivas, Michael A., 10, 14, 19, 184
Olmedo, E., 29
Olsen, L., 174, 176
Options for Excellence, 2, 6, 10, 19, 20, 22–24, 26, 28
Orfield, G., 179–81
Ortiz, Vilma, 19
Orum, L. S., 178–79, 183, 184, 185

PAA, 11, 15, 133–64
Padilla, A., 29
Padilla, Raymond V., vii, 29, 31–32
PAEG, 11, 15, 17, 29
Pan American University at Edinburg, 229
Parsons, C. K., 221, 222
Payan, R. M., 184
Pearson product-moment correlations, 201
Pennock-Román, María, vii, 19, 29, 34
Pérez, Monte, 34
Performance assessment, 33–34, 189, 196, 210–14; bias in, 34, 214–24
Persistence variability, 185
Peterson, R. E., 184, 197
Pew Charitable Trusts, 17
Politzer, R. L., 217
Powers, Donald E., 29, 34
Pozehl, B., 201
PPST, 168, 188, 189, 197, 201, 208, 227–28, 229
The Practice of Teaching (Jackson), 170–72
Prairie View A & M, 229
Pre-Professional Skills Test. *See* PPST
Preliminary Scholastic Aptitude Test/National Merit Scholarship Qualifying Test. *See* PSAT/NMSQT
"Preparing for the PSAT/NMSQT for Latino High School Students" (Educational Testing Service and the College Board), 66
Presumption of shared identity, 170–72. *See also* Latino teachers: value of
Prieto, A., 177–78
PRIME, viii, 2, 6, 10, 20, 22, 23, 24, 27–28, 30; components of, 25–26
Principal, role of, 177–78
Procedural knowledge, 91. *See also* Heuristic knowledge: assessment of
Professional knowledge tests, 188–89, 197, 199–200, 210

Project: I Teach, 227, 230
Project 1000: Recruiting, Admitting, and Graduating Additional 1,000 U.S. Hispanic Students, 10, 17, 19, 29
Project to Improve Minority Education. *See* PRIME
Pronovost, G., 95
Provisional licensure, 209
Prueba de Aptitud Académica. *See* PAA
Prueba de Aptitud para Estudios Graduatos. *See* PAEG
PSAT/NMSQT, 22–24, 26, 28, 34, 66, 131–32, 235–42, 245, 246, 248, 248–49, 263
Public Interest Principles for the Design and Use of Admissions Testing Programs, 13

Quick Test, 241–42, 245
Quirk, T. J., 198

Ramirez, A., 217
Ramos, R., 29
Rankin, R. J., 199
Reading comprehension, 241; culture and, 41–42, 57–59, 59–61, 60F, 68, 96–98
Rebell, M. A., 230
Reilly, R. R., 96
Reis, H. T., 95–96
Repeated-measures analysis of variance, 259
Revlin, Russell, 68
Richardson, F. C., 237
Rincon, E. T., 97, 236–37, 237
Rivera, Alvin, 11
Rivera, Charlene, 122, 122–23, 236–37, 239
Rock, Donald, 29
Rothwell, J. G., 221
Royer, James M., vii, 29, 30–31, 46
Rubin, D. R., 96
Rudner, L. M., 189
Ryan, E. B., 216, 217, 219–20

Salinger, T. S., 228
Salinger-Burn Tests, 228
San Diego County District, 249
Sandefur, J. T., 189, 210
Sarason, I. G., 237, 237–38
SAT, 1, 4, 10, 11, 15, 17, 28, 32, 45, 65, 67, 96, 98, 103, 129, 133–64, 189, 227, 235, 241, 243, 246, 248–49, 249; differential item function and, 105–32
SAT II, 28–29
SAT Committee, 242
Scaled score conversions, 156, 157T
Scarsdale High School, 21
Scheuneman, J. D., 96, 102
Schmidt, A. C., 219–20
Schmitt, Alicia Pérez, vii, 14, 29, 32–33, 96, 98, 102, 103, 108, 109, 110, 112, 114, 115–19, 119, 120, 121, 122, 122–23, 123, 129, 239
Schmitt, N., 221
Scholastic Aptitude Test. *See* SAT
School and College Ability Tests, 97
School reform, 231–32
Sebastian, R. J., 219–20
Second language competence, 30–31, 39–40, 42–46, 51–52, 53–63, 58F, 64, 68–80, 103–4, 109–14, 146–49, 148T, 163–64, 214–24. *See also* Sentence Verification Technique
Sensitivity Review Process, 130–31, 203, 204
Sentence Verification Technique, 31, 40, 46–64; and educational progress, 52–63; as a measure of language comprehension, 50–52, 59–61, 60F; rationale for, 47–48; reliability and validity of, 49–50; scoring and interpretation of, 48–49; test validity of, 54–55
Shepard, L. A., 131, 175, 202–3, 203
Shulman, Lee, 212, 212–13
Sí Se Puede: Information on Academic Planning and Obtaining Financial Aid, 2, 10, 26–27, 27–28, 30
Sixth Annual RACHE Conference, 236
Sleeter, C. E., 173
Smith, G. P., 175, 182–83, 191–92, 192–94, 231
Smith, Michele, 68
Solomon, Robert J., 15
Southside High School, 24
Specialized content knowledge: testing of, 189, 199–200, 210
Specific knowledge, 90–91. *See also* Heuristic knowledge: assessment of
Spellman, S. O., 224, 225–26
Stand and Deliver, 20, 22
Standard Progressive Matrices test, 99, 100–101

The standardization method, 106, 106–9, 109, 110T, 122, 130. *See also* Differential item functioning
Standardized tests, 2–3, 5–6, 7, 12, 65; criticism of, 3–4; misuse of, 6–7, 8–9; stress and fatigue and, 32; support for, 4–5; time management and, 32, 96–98
Stanford University, 212
Statistical bias procedures, 203. *See also* Assessment: bias in
Statistical screening, 129–30. *See also* Differential item functioning
Stereotyping. *See* Language attitude research
Stewart, D. K., 224
Stocking, M. L., 144
Stoker, W. M., 201
Student outreach programs, 196, 224–31. *See also* Teaching: access to; Teaching force, minorities in: recruitment of; Underrepresentation
Student population: coloring of, 167–69, 179–81, 180T, 181–83, 181T, 182T. *See also* Cultural background
Study Skills and Tutorial Services, 228
Stuyvesant High School, 21
Subcommittee on Elementary, Secondary, and Vocational Education, 11
Subjective evaluation, 7–8
SVT Test Maker, 63–64
SVT Trainer, 64

Tanner Act, 242, 244, 246, 249
Tanner, Sally, 244
Tarrab, M., 201
Taskforce on Hispanic Education, 25
Teacher Association Project, 212, 213
Teacher certification, 28, 33. *See also* Certification, performance-based; Teacher testing
Teacher education programs, 199, 200, 205
Teacher Performance Assessment Instruments, 210–11
Teacher-student relationship: shared identity and, 170–72; ethnicity and, 181–83, 182T
Teacher testing: and classroom experience, 200–201; standard setting and, 195–96, 205–10; and educational opportunity, 205–8; failure rate on, 176–77, 177, 183, 187–92, 193T, 195, 228; negative effects of, 33, 168, 175–78, 189–92, 193T, 195; reform of, 195, 196, 205–10, 222–24; reliability and validity of, 195, 196–98, 204, 211
Teachers: assessment centers for, 212–13
Teaching: access to, 33–34, 167–94, 195, 226–31; cultural background and, 170–72, 181–83, 182T, 213–14; declining preference for, 183, 186–87, 187T; obstacles to, 33, 168–69, 175–78, 183–92, 193T, 197
Teaching force, minorities in, 167–69, 175, 178–83, 182T, 195; effects of, 172–73, 175, 177–78, 192–94; leadership roles in, 177–78; multicultural education and, 173–75; recruitment of, 224–31; teacher testing and, viii, 187–92, 193T
Teaching force: prejudice in, 174–75; as role models, 172–73; whitening of, 33, 167–69
10 SATs, 247, 249
Test anxiety, 5, 241, 246–47, 250, 252, 256, 257–58, 260, 263; interpretation of, 237–38; speededness and, 32; *TestSkills* and, 34, 237–38, 241, 245, 246–47, 250, 252, 256, 257–58, 260, 263. *See also* Test speededness
Test Anxiety Questionnaire, 237–38
Test Anxiety Scale, 237–38
Test bias. *See* Assessment: bias in
Test bias research, 202–5
Test of Cognitive Skills, 99
Test of English as a Foreign Language. *See* TOEFL
Test familiarization, 1, 26, 65; *TestSkills* and, 34, 238–40, 244, 246–47, 263, 264. *See also* Guessing strategies
Test measurement error, 16–17
Test-preparation programs, 247–48, 249–50, 261–62. *See also* TestSkills
Test reform, 12. *See also* Assessment: developments in; Teacher tests: reform of
Test scores, equating of, 33, 133–64, 146F, 147F, 148T, 150T, 151T, 157T; cultural difference and, 5, 134–37, 156–60; difficulties in, 137–40; frequency distributions, 152–55, 153T, 154T; method of, 140–56
TestSense, 249
TestSkills: A Kit for Teachers of Hispanic Students, vii, 2, 10, 26, 26–27, 27–28,

33, 34, 131–32; bilingual test-takers and, 259; and college admission tests, 244, 246, 251–54, 252T, 253T, 254T, 255T, 262, 264; and college recruitment, 264; content areas of, 259, 260C; criticism of, 250–51; development of, 235–37; differential item functioning and, 34, 237; free-response evaluations of, 259–61; organization of, 240–42, 245–46; reaction to, 243–64; and test anxiety, 34, 237–38, 241, 245, 246–47, 250, 252, 256, 257–58, 260, 263

TestSkills, testing of, 246–47; results of, 247–61, 252T, 254T, 255T, 256C, 257C, 258C

Test speededness, 66, 237; ethnicity and, 96–98. *See also* Differential speededness effect; Testing time

Test-taking skills, 65–66, 236–37, 240–41, 243, 246, 254–55, 255C, 259, 260; diagnosis and remediation, 227–31; differential item functioning and, 33, 131–32. *See also* Guessing strategies; Test anxiety; *TestSkills*

Test validity, 66

Testwiseness, 96–98

Test-wiseness taxonomy, 237

Testing: alternatives to, 7–9

Testing time: and Latino college students, 95–104; methodological issues, 102–3

Texas Academic Skills Program test, 168

Texas Education Agency, 229

Theoretical knowledge, 82–84, 83F, 84F, 85, 91

Theory of signal detection, 48–49

Three-parameter logistical model, 155

Time: cultural differences and, 32, 95–104; linguistic differences and, 103–4

Time-using, 96–104

TOEFL, 17, 164

Transitional bilingual education programs: Sentence Verification Technique and, 52–63, 56F

Transparent assessment, 82, 86, 92

True cognate hypothesis, 109–14, 113F, 115F, 118, 128, 130. *See also* Cognates; Differential item functioning; False cognate hypothesis; False cognates

True cognates, 121, 123, 128, 131

Truth in Testing Act of 1979, 11

"Truth-in-Testing" movement, 10

Underrepresentation, vii, viii, 1–2, 2–3, 17–18; causes of, 3, 4

University of Arkansas at Pine Bluff, 226, 229, 231

University of California Partnership Program, 229–30

University of Texas at El Paso, 227–31

University of Texas at San Antonio, 226–27, 229, 231

U.S. v. State of California, 175

Ute tribe, 40–41

Valencia, Richard R., vii, 29, 33–34, 195

Validation: criterion-based, 198–99, 204, 210, 211; content-based, 199–202, 204, 210

Verdugo, Richard R., 19

Vertical relationships. *See* Word associations

Weinberg, S. F., 198

West, L. J., 95–96

Whimbey, Arthur, 238

Wild, C. L., 96

Williams, F., 219

Wine, J., 237

"Within ethnic" score, 15–16, 17, 18–19; access and, 18–19

Witten, B. J., 198

Witty, E. P., 229

Word associations, 118T, 119–20, 120T, 129, 130

Wright, T., 97

Younkin, W., 98

Zapata, J. T., 169